THE FOREIGN POLICY SOCIETY

THE ECONOMIC

WORLD

BALANCE

BY

THORKIL KRISTENSEN

AND ASSOCIATES

MUNKSGAARD
COPENHAGEN · DENMARK

NORTH-HOLLAND PUBLISHING COMPANY
AMSTERDAM · HOLLAND

MUNKSGAARD

INTERNATIONAL BOOKSELLERS AND PUBLISHERS, LTD.

COPENHAGEN K, DENMARK

NORTH-HOLLAND PUBLISHING COMPANY

AMSTERDAM-C, HOLLAND

PRINTED IN DENMARK
VALD. FDDDRGDHG BOGTRYKKERI
KØBENHAVN

THE FOREIGN POLICY SOCIETY was founded in 1946 to advance interest in and understanding of international affairs in Denmark.

The Society arranges lectures for its members, maintains a small library, and issues a number of publications devoted to international problems.

By its laws the Society, as such, is precluded from taking any stand on international problems. The opinions expressed in the publications of the Society are, therefore, only the opinions of the individual authors, not those of the Society.

The present study has been prepared by a study group composed of the following members:

THORKIL KRISTENSEN *Chairman*	Professor, Copenhagen School of Economics and Business Administration, former Minister of Finance, Member of the Folketing	*Economics*
KRISTIAN ANTONSEN	Mag. scient., Cand. polit., Lecturer, University of Copenhagen	*Economics, Geography*
T. BJERGE	Professor, dr. phil., Director of the Danish Atomic Energy Commission's Research Centre at Risø	*Physics*
KJELD H. BJERKE	Cand. polit., Chief of Division, The Statistical Department, Copenhagen, Lecturer, Copenhagen School of Economics and Business Administration	*Statistics, Economics*

ANTON F. BRUUN   Dr. phil. et jur. h. c., Reader,   *Biology*
                          University of Copenhagen

JOHN DANSTRUP   Mag.art., Foreign Editor, "Politiken",   *History*
                          Copenhagen

PETER ILSØE   Cand. polit., Economic Adviser to   *Economics*
                          Chief of Defence, Denmark

S. TOVBORG JENSEN   Professor, Royal Veterinary and   *Agricultural*
                          Agricultural College, Copenhagen   *Chemistry*

ERLING JØRGENSEN   Cand. polit., Assistant Chief of   *Statistics,*
                          Division, The Statistical Department,   *Economics*
                          Copenhagen, Assistant Lecturer,
                          University of Copenhagen

PER KONGSTAD   Mag. scient., H.D., Assistant Lecturer,   *Economics,*
                          Copenhagen School of Economics   *Geography*
                          and Business Administration

LEO MEYER   Cand. polit., Assistant Chief of Divi-   *Statistics,*
                          sion, The Statistical Department,   *Economics*
                          Copenhagen

P. NØRREGAARD RASMUSSEN Dr. polit., Professor, University of   *Economics*
                          Copenhagen

Table of Contents

Symbols employed

The following symbols have been employed throughout:

$\cdots$ = Not available

– = Nil or neglible

Unless the contrary is stated, the standard unit of weight used is the *metric ton*.

The definition of "billion" used is one thousand millions.

Preface

On its tenth anniversary in October, 1956, the DANISH FOREIGN POLICY SOCIETY resolved to initiate a study of the *Economic World Balance*. The study was to attempt an appraisal of the economic status, and the possible economic trends, in the main regions of the world and thus to give an impression of the major changes in this balance that are likely to occur within the foreseeable future. What the Society particularly had in mind was, on the one hand, the relationship between the West and the East, and on the other, that existing between the technically developed, industrial countries and the so-called underdeveloped regions.

It was obvious that in dealing with these matters due regard would have to be paid to the whole cultural background of the economies. The conditions of production, including natural resources, was another factor that had to be considered. The proposed study was therefore entrusted to a Study Group which included not only economists and statisticians, but also historians and representatives of various branches of natural science.

The present book has been written in such a manner that no special knowledge is required by the reader. Parts A and B 2 of Chapter VII do, however, contain some economic arguments of a rather technical nature. These sections may, however, be omitted without detriment to the understanding of the text as a whole.

The writing of this book has been made possible through the financial help of the Rockefeller Foundation and of the following Danish organizations and firms: The Carlsberg Breweries, the Danish Employers' Confederation, Messrs. R. Henriques jr., and the East Asiatic Company Ltd. The Foreign Policy Society owes a great debt of gratitude to the donors for the interest they have taken in this enterprise.

In the course of their studies the Group have received valuable help from

Mr. Erik Kristensen and Mr. H. Juul Madsen. Chapter V B has been read
by Mr. P. G. H. Barter, Director of the Economic Analysis Division of FAO,
who has given much useful advice. It goes without saying, however, that no
person other than the members of the Group can be held responsible for the
contents of this book.

Certain compilations of data and computations have been carried out
with the valuable assistance of the Danish Ministry of Foreign Affairs and
the Statistical Department. Mrs. Karen Bagh has done excellent work in
typing the manuscript. The English translation is by Mr. Henrik Strand-
gaard and Mrs. G. Salto. Mr. D. R. Collard has read through the English
text, and advised on its final form; in so doing he has rendered a service
that cannot be valued too highly. The Group wish to express their sincere
thanks for all the valuable assistance they have received.

Copenhagen, January, 1960

THORKIL KRISTENSEN

Introduction

In the history of mankind, economic strength and political power have influenced, in a fundamental way, the relationship between the nations. With regard to the balance of political power, this has certainly often, to a great extent, been governed by non-economic factors. Nevertheless, we may say that the wealth and productive power of the countries and regions of the earth have, down through the ages, proved to be factors of the greatest significance for the political balance.

Changes in the economic balance between the various parts of the globe have, thus, frequently been accompanied by changes in the general political balance. In certain periods of history some countries have occupied a central position in world economics, other countries forming a periphery under the sway of this centre. Over the centuries, among such dominant powers have been ancient Egypt, the Roman Empire, Spain in the sixteenth century and Great Britain in the nineteenth century.

Now, in some periods the economic world has been governed by more than one such centre. And we do not have to look into the past to realize this for such is the state of things in our own age. The United States and the USSR each hold a central position *vis-a-vis* a circle of other countries and territories, forming two groups of powers that dominate very large areas of the earth. Therefore, whether we discuss the economic or the political balance, what we really have in mind is, first and foremost, the economic or political balance between West and East.

These terms West and East are often understood in a narrow sense; the East being defined as the USSR and Eastern Europe, the West as North America and Western Europe. It is hardly necessary to stress the importance of the relative strength of these two groups of countries.

There are, however, some relationships inside the two blocs that deserve our attention, too. Since World War II Western Europe has been dependent on North American aid for its reconstruction and defence build-up. One of the problems of the foreseeable future is whether this dependence will become less pronounced as Western Europe gains strength or whether, on the contrary, American aid will grow in importance. Correspondingly it is a matter of considerable interest what will be the relative economic strength of Eastern Europe compared with the USSR.

A wider conception of the two power groups would include Mainland China, North Korea, and North Viet-Nam in the Eastern group and some other countries in the Western. From an economic point of view, however, these states differ essentially from the members of the two blocs in the narrow sense, as we shall see later. The Asian members of SEATO, (the South East Asia Treaty Organization), for example, show far more points of similarity with other Asian countries than with the non-Asian members of that organization, and Mainland China, too, has more in common with the rest of Asia than with the USSR. Likewise, it seems reasonable to treat Western Europe as a whole, making no distinction between NATO and other countries. The power blocs as such are not always the most appropriate groups for economic analysis.

Few problems are likely to be more important in the next few decades than those of the countries that are now usually characterized as underdeveloped. What will be their relative strength compared with the industrialized countries? Will they be much dependent on foreign aid, or will at least some of them be able to raise their economic standards by their own efforts and thus attain a stronger position in the world than they have to-day?

These questions are all pertinent to an evaluation of the prospects for international relations. At the same time they are all inter-related, because the various parts of the world are trading with one another, and capital movements, migration, and the spread of ideas are tending to make most countries partially dependent on events in many other parts of the world.

This is the reason why the present study attempts as far as possible to cover all the inhabited parts of the earth. For that purpose the world has been sub-divided into the following nine regions:

1. *North America*
2. *Western Europe*
3. *Oceania*
4. *USSR*

5. *Eastern Europe*
6. *Latin America*
7. *The Middle East*
8. *Asia*
9. *Africa*

A list of the various countries and territories belonging to each region is given on page 14[1].

The regions as defined above correspond fairly closely to those used in the publications of the United Nations and various other institutions. To some extent the regions represent different political systems. The main purpose of defining the regions, however, has been that they should form geographical entities that are fairly relevant to the problems dealt with in this book. Economic development being in the focus of our attention, the fact that the nine regions represent different degrees of development is particularly important. Above they are tentatively listed according to that criterion.

Regions 1–5 may on the whole be described as developed or industrialized, whereas regions 6–9 are, roughly, what we usually term underdeveloped or non-industrialized.

It goes without saying, however, that the extent of industrial development is uneven within most of the regions. Thus, North-West Europe is more highly developed than South-West Europe, Japan is more developed than most other countries in *Asia,* and so on. No method of classifying the countries or regions of the world can obviate such difficulties. To some extent they are even found within individual countries. The difference between Northern and Southern Italy is an example of this.

Our first task must obviously be to make an estimate of the balance of economic power at the time of writing or at least at some fairly recent juncture. This has been attempted in Chapter I, and the year 1955 has been chosen as starting point, because no sufficient statistical material was available for more recent years. For each region the chapter gives an evaluation of population and total production in or about 1955.

Among a variety of terms relating to total production or income the one generally used in this book is *net domestic product,* because this seems to be

---

[1] The geographical positions of the nine regions are shown in the two maps on the inside cover.

1. *North America*

Canada
Greenland
USA

2. *Western Europe*

Austria
Belgium
Denmark
Eire
Finland
France
Greece
Iceland
Italy
Luxembourg
Netherlands
Norway
Portugal
Spain
Sweden
Switzerland
United Kingdom
West Germany

3. *Oceania*

Australia
New Zealand
Pacific Islands

4. *USSR*

5. *Eastern Europe*

Albania
Bulgaria
Czechoslovakia
East Germany
Hungary
Poland
Rumania
Yugoslavia

6. *Latin America*

Argentina
Bolivia
Brazil
British Honduras
British West Indies
Chile
Colombia
Costa Rica
Cuba
Dominican Republic
Ecuador
El Salvador
Guadeloupe
Guatemala
Guiana (British – French)
Haiti
Honduras
Martinique
Mexico
Netherland Antilles
Nicaragua
Panama
Paraguay
Peru
Puerto Rico
Surinam
Uruguay
Venezuela

7. *The Middle East*

Aden (Colony and
   Protectorate)
Bahrain
Cyprus
Egypt
Iran
Iraq
Israel
Jordan
Kuwait
Lebanon
Muscat and Oman
Qatar
Saudi Arabia
Syria
Trucial Oman
Turkey
Yemen

8. *Asia*

Afghanistan
Borneo
Burma
Cambodia
Ceylon
China, Mainland
China, Taiwan
Hong Kong
India
Indonesia
Japan
Korea, North
Korea, South
Laos
Malaya, Federation of
Mongolian People's Republic
Nepal
New Guinea
Pakistan
Philippines
Singapore
Thailand
Viet-Nam (North)
Viet-Nam (South)

9. *Africa*

Algeria
Angola
Belgian Congo and Ruanda-Urundi
British East Africa
British South Africa
British West Africa (incl. Nigeria)
Cameroon
Ethiopia and Eritrea
French Equatorial Africa
French West Africa
Ghana
Guinea
Liberia
Libya
Madagascar
Morocco
Mozambique
Rhodesia and Nyasaland
Somaliland (British - French - Italian)
South West Africa
Spanish North and West Africa
Sudan
Togoland
Tunisia
Union of South Africa

the term best suited to its main purpose. The net *domestic product* is the value of total output, i.e. the total net result of the economic activity within the region in question. It represents the net value of the goods and services produced during a certain period, normally a year. The value of total output being equal to the rewards obtained by individuals (or groups of individuals) for their contributions to production, it follows that the value of total output (less indirect taxes) must equal total *domestic income*. Generally speaking the net domestic product may be regarded as a rough measure of the flow of goods and services that is available for consumption and of the net increase in capital.

This flow may conveniently be expressed in its monetary equivalent. The monetary unit to be used here is the United States dollar at its 1955 purchasing power. Many problems arise when we compare the net domestic products of different countries in terms of this common denominator, because the relative internal purchasing powers of two currencies are not necessarily reflected by the current rates of exchange.

Having shed some light on the situation in or about 1955 we shall proceed to make a forecast of the future development. What changes in the existing balance are likely to take place in the foreseeable future?

This is obviously a question relating to what is now generally termed *economic growth*. Much work has been done in recent years towards the formulation of a theory of economic growth, and some of the aspects of this part of the science of economics will be dealt with in Chapters II and VII. Suffice it here to say that by the economic growth of a certain region will be understood the increase of the net domestic product (as measured in terms of constant prices) of the region during the period under consideration. The main purpose of this book is to contribute to an evaluation of the economic growth that may take place in the various regions on certain assumptions.

An increase of production must of course be compared with the increase of population during the same period. Besides, the increase of population has in itself a certain interest. From a military point of view a large population is usually considered to be an asset and therefore a positive factor in the balance of power. In future, human numbers, however, may be less important than in the past as modern warfare becomes increasingly mechanized. Military potential, therefore, will gradually come to be simply one aspect or part of economic capacity, and though any amount of the economic resources of a state may be devoted to military purposes, it is much easier to build up a strong defence system when total production per capita is increasing rapidly than it would be if productivity were stagnating.

This brings us to an important point. Total production may be considered as a product of two factors. It is equal to total population multiplied by per capita production. Similarly total economic growth may be regarded as having two components. One is the growth of population, and the other is the growth of per capita net domestic product. Both components are intrinsically important and will be given much consideration in the following chapters.

A growing population has traditionally been thought of as adding to the strength of a country if it is accompanied by a substantial rise in per capita production. It will then provide increased wealth for consumption, investment, defence, capital exports or other activities and the country thus increases in power.

On the other hand, in some cases a rapid growth of population may preclude a significant increase in per capita production, and if that is so it may well be that a country is really losing strength—on several scores. At least it is likely to become more vulnerable and more liable to internal political difficulties the moment its economic level deteriorates in relation to that of other nations.

Thus, increase in population and increase in per capita production are equally important aspects of the total of economic growth and are, moreover, interdependent in several ways, as will appear from the following analysis.

There is one point which must be decided before considering the prospects for the future, viz. what should be the length of the period to be considered?

In our present study an analysis covering a space of some few years only would be of little value. No perceptible changes in the existing balance would be likely to take place in so short a period, and, conversely, such a short-term analysis would be liable to register influences which, from our point of view, must be considered fortuitous and irrelevant. There might, by way of illustration, be a boom or a depression in, say, *North America*, the effects of which on other countries might vary to a very large extent. During the American recession in 1957–58 the terms of trade of many Western European countries improved, because the prices of raw materials were falling. For that very reason, however, the terms of trade of some of the underdeveloped countries deteriorated. On the other hand, the economies of the *USSR, Eastern Europe* and Mainland China were hardly affected, because their trade with other countries was relatively insignificant.

This being so, it is impossible to form an impression of underlying general tendencies if the analysis is confined to a short period, one or two booms or depressions being sufficient to distort the picture entirely. On the other hand, if we look too far into the future, we shall soon be out of our depth and unable to gauge the elements which are likely to influence the course of events.

In this book the period marked out for consideration is the twenty-five years between 1955 and 1980. This time-limit will not be observed too strictly, however. To be more explicit, the starting point will be the situation about the year 1955, after which will follow a consideration of the changes that may occur during the period ending somewhere about 1980. As the starting point is already a few years behind us, the end of the period under consideration lies little more than twenty years from the time when the studies contained in the present book were finished.

The main arguments for choosing a period of that length may be summarized as follows.

As for *population,* most of the women that are likely to give birth to children up to 1980, are already living, and their numbers are known, at least approximately. If we take into account what we know about fertility and its trends in recent years, it is possible to form an idea of the number of births likely to take place during the period covered by the present studies. If a longer period were chosen, the degree of uncertainty in this extremely important element would probably be much higher.

From the point of view of *consumption,* the total number of people is of great importance. However, man is not only a consumer, but also a factor of production. Here the decisive element is the number of people fit to work. This is dealt with more comprehensively in Chapter III, but it should be mentioned here that within the rough statistical categories with which we have to operate, 15 years is often chosen as the age of beginning work. That means that most of the men or women who will belong to the labour force during the period ending in 1980 are already born. Concerning this point too, the uncertainty would be appreciably greater if we tried to look, say, ten or twenty years further ahead.

Another important factor of production is the existing stock of *capital.*

The size and composition of that stock is changing continuously, and it is one of our chief concerns to make some estimates of the changes for the span of years we have in mind. The complex problems relating to capital formation are the subject of Chapter IV. One special aspect of these problems, however, has to be taken into account when deciding on the length of the period to be studied, viz. the *technical character* of the various items of capital such as buildings, ships, machines, and so on. Here the fast technical development in our age makes it difficult to make reasonably safe assumptions concerning the character and efficiency of the equipment that will be used in the future.

However, it seems justifiable to add an important qualification to these general remarks on technical change. Most buildings have a fairly long life, and much machinery and transportation material can be used through 10 or 20 years, sometimes even longer. Hence, a substantial part of the capital which will contribute to production during our 25 year period is in existence even now, and therefore its technical character is not unknown.

The capital that will be formed during, say, the nineteen-sixties is likely, to a very large extent, to be of a kind that is not radically different from what we can imagine to-day, especially if we take into account the tendencies of technical change observed during recent years. Concerning such machinery etc. as will come into existence later, the degree of uncertainty must inevitably be higher, but then this capital will only be working through a comparatively small part of our period.

If, on the other hand, we were to extend our considerations some twenty years further into the future, that is to the turn of this century, our speculations concerning the technical forms of capital would bear much less relation to the realities we are familiar with.

One final observation should be made concerning the length of the period. The driving force behind any progress in human history—regardless of the definition of "progress" one prefers—is the activities of men and the *ideas* governing these activities.

Allowing for a multitude of individual variations we may probably say, with some justification, that most people have acquired the bulk of their main ideas in youth. In some cases it may be more correct to say that in their youth they became clearly aware of the ideas, aims or ideals which have been developing in their minds from childhood.

Special attention should be paid to the years of adult education at universities, colleges or technical institutes of many different kinds. Here youth becomes acquainted with the body of knowledge that is the common heritage of its generation, and develops attitudes and working methods with which to meet the problems and difficulties that may arise.

No brief account can do justice to the great variety of problems involved in any estimate concerning the growth of ideas. Still, it seems reasonable to assume that by the age of twenty-five most people have laid the foundation of their future ways of thinking and acting.

Now, to look at the matter from a different angle, we may probably assume that to-day the majority of people in leading positions, whose aims and ideas are of decisive importance, are over forty-five years of age. This again is a very rough indication, but if it contains any truth, it means that the majority of the people who are likely to exert an appreciable influence on the development of the various economies up to 1980, will have acquired a substantial part of their fundamental ideas before 1960.

If we were to push the end of the period under consideration as far forward as 1990 or 2000, we should have to take into account the fact that a considerable part of the development process may be governed by ideas that are unknown to us. If we go no further than about the year 1980, it seems likely that there will be more "knowns" and fewer "unknowns".

It appears from the above considerations that the uncertain factors likely to be encountered would be much increased if the period were lengthened. Within the span of years examined in the following chapters there is at least some reason to believe that development will be governed by factors many of which are not totally unknown to-day.

Even then it is hardly necessary to stress that we are dealing with a vast subject about which no one has an adequate knowledge. One or other of the authors of this book has visited each of the nine regions, and some of them have lived for a time in one or two regions apart from their own. Still they are all West Europeans, and they are fully aware that the total extent of their knowledge is very limited compared with the problems involved.

Nevertheless, it appears to us that these problems are of such importance that an attempt to deal with them requires no apology. On the contrary, as most people to-day are inclined to guesswork on the subject of economic growth and the balance of power, it seems timely to make an effort in the direction of transforming this guesswork into estimates that have at least

2*

some foundation in the knowledge accumulated by science as well as by everyday experience.

It should be remembered at this stage that a task like the present one can be done with varying degrees of success. Of course it is not possible to make anything like an exact statement on the future rates of growth of population or production within the nine regions. It would be of great interest, however, if it were found justifiable to set up some lower and/or higher limits within which it seems more likely than not that the actual growth will take place.

It goes without saying that any such estimates must be based on certain *assumptions*. One general assumption is that no third World War will take place within the period. We do not, of course, know whether this will be so, but it seems to be the only way of confining uncertainty to manageable proportions. Other assumptions of a more special character—and sometimes alternative sets of assumptions—will be stated in the following chapters.

Even when figures cannot be stated with any satisfactory degree of reliability, the possibilities of drawing conclusions are not exhausted. If it can be held with some reason that, e.g. region A is likely to grow faster than region B, this very difference tells us something about the balance.

Finally, if an attempt like the present has no other merits, it may at least serve as a basis and a starting point for further work.

The contents of the eight chapters of this book may be outlined as follows:

Chapter I contains the general survey mentioned earlier of *population, production, etc. in 1955 or about that year*. This chapter also contains a summary account of the development leading up to the situation in 1955. Where it is possible a comparison is made with the situation shortly before the Second World War.

Chapter II deals with the *factors of growth*. Even though no satisfactory theory of economic growth exists as yet, it is argued that the factors influencing the size of production can be grouped in four categories, namely *Labour, Capital, Nature,* and *Culture*. The interdependence of the four factors is outlined in a general way, leading up to the theoretical considerations in Chapter VII.

In *Chapters III–VI* the four factors are treated separately, and attempts are made to estimate their status at the beginning of the period and future development within the nine regions.

In *Chapter VII* the material gathered in the foregoing chapters is used for such considerations concerning future economic growth as are found possible. The chapter starts with a theoretical introduction on models of growth. This is followed by an attempt to project, under alternative assumptions, the growth of each of the nine regions.

Chapter VIII presents some concluding remarks including various proposals for further studies (so badly needed). Finally, in the *Appendix* each of the nine regions have been considered. For each region a short survey as well as a section on future prospects present some few characteristics and potentialities. It goes without saying that within the framework given such regional analyses cannot go into detail and may sometimes appear rather superficial.

CHAPTER I

The Starting Point

——

1. The measure of economic growth to be adopted in this study is changes in the net domestic product. By the *domestic product* is meant the value of a country's total productive achievement in the widest sense. The reason why we talk about production in the widest sense is that production includes not only the manufacture of goods but also the provision of services. The domestic product, however, may be shown either at its *gross* or at its *net value*. The difference between these two is the value of the annual wear and tear on the available capital. Consequently, the *net domestic product* is the value of the production of goods and services minus, on the one hand, the value of the raw and auxiliary materials used and, on the other, the value of the wear and tear on capital (including the value of the maintenance of the capital).

The value of the total production may be calculated in terms of market prices (i.e. the prices at which goods are exchanged), or in terms of factor prices (i.e. market prices minus indirect taxes, but plus subsidies). The value of total production in terms of factor prices will equal the total income paid to the factors of production. In this study the value of production will be measured in factor prices (= factor costs).

In estimating economic growth as measured by changes in the net domestic product at factor costs, our attention is not directed towards the domestic product measured in the prices of the year in question. For this figure may change for two reasons, on the one hand, the prices of the factors of production may change (e.g. when wages and salaries are increased), on the other, the quantity produced may vary. Only in the latter case can there be any question of real growth—economic growth. In order to give special attention to this contingency, we have sought to make allowance for price fluctuations, or in other words, to calculate the domestic product in terms of constant prices, i.e. in such a manner that any changes in it will reflect increases or decreases in the quantities of goods or services produced.

With this end in view, the net domestic product of each country is stated in fixed prices. The method of calculating these has been in principle to multiply each year's output of goods and services by the prices of a certain year. The net domestic product stated in fixed prices (1955) thus indicates the size of production in terms of constant prices.

2. Besides attempting to shed some light on the development of the net domestic product (in fixed prices) in order to measure the growth up to a certain time, it seems also useful to consider—and compare—the net domestic product of the different regions. The figures required are partly the total, partly the per capita figures. From these figures will emerge an impression of the result of the economic activities of the various countries and regions.

However, statements of the domestic product will not allow of any immediate comparison, as they are given in the national currencies of the various countries. In order to make comparisons between countries, it will thus be necessary to state the domestic product of each country in terms of a common unit, e.g. dollars. This has been done for the year 1955 in Table I. 1 in which the official rates of exchange *vis-à-vis* the dollar have been used in the conversion of the national currencies into dollars. In the case of countries on which information regarding the domestic product in 1955 is not available, direct estimates, in dollars, have been made on the basis of such scraps of information as have been obtainable. These estimates cover about 20 per cent of the total net domestic product of the world, which has, in this way, been calculated at about 900 billion dollars. It is important to keep in mind, however, that this is no more than an extremely rough estimate which serves merely to give a vague impression of the order of magnitude of the loose and, indeed doubtful, concept: The world's total product.

As mentioned earlier the figures concerning domestic product should tell us something about the results of the economic activities (the production level) of the various countries and regions. We should be careful, however, not to go further and regard them as indicative of the relative welfare of the countries. For there are many objections to using, say, the real per capita net domestic product for this purpose. In the first place the domestic product tells us nothing about differences of effort in achieving the product. Further, differences in climate and mode of life may mean that a certain per capita national product[1] does not always indicate the same degree of

---

[1] *National product* plus interest and dividends paid abroad minus interest and dividends received from abroad equals domestic product.

welfare, cf. e.g. the fuel and housing problems in different parts of the world.
Nor, of course, does the national product show how much "sense of hap-
piness" the possession of certain benefits implies—or whether the lack of
certain goods is felt to be a definite hardship. Finally, the national product
does not indicate the extent of the cultural achievements of a country which
may also be regarded as a form of "income".

It would thus appear to be particularly difficult to make comparisons
between regions which differ widely as regards climate, culture, and mode
of life. The regions which may be compared with the highest degree of accuracy are probably the following: *North America, Western Europe, Oceania,*
the *USSR* and *Eastern Europe.*

Even when confining the comparison to total production as such, it must
further be kept in mind that the figures compared are broad averages which
tell us nothing about e.g. the composition or the distribution of production
and income within a region.

3. In converting the currencies into dollars the 1955 rates of exchange
have been used. Although we get a common unit by converting the different
currencies into dollars and thus prepare the way for a comparison between
the regions, great care has to be taken in making direct comparisons. The
rates of exchange used need by no means represent rates of purchasing
power, i.e. we have no *a priori* certainty that a one-dollar income has the
same purchasing power in Denmark—converting e.g. 6.92 Danish kroner
into 1 dollar—as in the United States. In fact it is known that the current
exchange rates against the dollar for a number of Western European currencies in this sense undervalue these currencies. Consequently, it is only
with strict reservations that comparisons can be made between income levels
in different regions. To take different or supplementary—and very precari-
ous—lines of approach e.g. by making allowances for the domestic purchasing power would in general be impossible because of the scarcity of the statistical material needed for such adjustments. Some examples are given
below of different purchasing power computations for *Western Europe*
based on current consumption patterns as compared to a conversion by
exchange rates.

If the exchange rate is used for the conversion, and if an attempt is made
to draw conclusions on the basis of such material regarding purchasing
power, the rates of exchange that are used must be in some sense long-term
equilibrium rates. However, it must not be taken for granted that such

equilibrium always obtains, especially with regard to the period following the war, with its extensive restrictions on international trade.

Even if prices in international trade roughly correspond to the exchange rates, the latter cannot be expected to conform with the price levels in all

TABLE I. 1

Population and Net Domestic Product, 1955.

	Population		Net Domestic Product		Net Domestic Product Per capita, (Dollars)
	Total, (Million)	Percentage Distribution	Total, (Billion Dollars)	Percentage Distribution	
North America	182	6.8	342	38.5	1,875
Western Europe	297	11.0	183	20.6	615
Oceania	13	0.5	12	1.4	955
USSR	197	7.3	109	12.3	550
Eastern Europe	112	4.2	51	5.7	455
Latin America	183	6.8	48	5.4	265
Middle East	95	3.5	15	1.7	160
Asia	1,418	52.7	107	12.1	75
Africa	193	7.2	20	2.3	105
Total	2,690	100.0	887	100.0	330

Note : As mentioned in the text the European currencies have in this context been converted into dollars in accordance with the official rates of exchange. This is an alternative to the purchasing power rates applied in the subsequent chapters, cf. e.g. table VII. 2.
Source : United Nations (1958, a) and a number of other UN publications.

of the various countries. Transport and distribution costs alone would preclude any such agreement. Further, a large proportion of the goods and services included in the national income are not subject to international trading, and for this reason also such an agreement is out of the question.

4. The results of the domestic product calculations made for 1955 are shown in Table I. 1. It appears that nearly 60 per cent of the world's population lives in *Asia* and *Africa*; but these two regions account for only 15 per cent of the net domestic product. Conversely, nearly 60 per cent of the net domestic product is at the disposal of the peoples of *North America* and *Western Europe*; but these regions represent barely 18 per cent of the

world's population. The same impression is gained from a comparison of the per capita net domestic product which varies from nearly 2,000 dollars in *North America* to under 100 dollars in *Asia*. Such comparisons between poor and wealthy regions, however, should only be made with caution, as the ways of life of those regions differ so widely.

TABLE I.2

Individual Countries of the Different Regions Grouped According to Per Capita Net Domestic Product.
(Per cent)

Per capita Net Domestic Product (1955 Dollars)	North America	Western Europe	Ocea-nia	USSR	Eastern Europe	Latin America	Middle East	Asia	Africa	Total
Over 1,500	91	–	–	–	–	–	–	–	–	6
1,000–1,500	9	2	89	–	–	–	–	–	–	1
600–1,000	–	59	–	–	52	3	–	–	–	9
300– 600	–	33	–	100	40	28	2	1	7	16
150– 300	–	6	–	–	8	60	27	8	10	11
Under 150	–	–	11	–	–	9	71	91	83	57
Total........	100	100	100	100	100	100	100	100	100	100

Note: The countries appear in the Table weighted according to their populations.
Source: United Nations (1958, a).

The per capita averages stated in Table I.1 above cover wide differences within each region. To illustrate this a grouping of countries according to per capita net domestic product in dollars has been made, as shown in Table I.2. (Cf. the list on page 14). The Table gives an idea of the distribution of the domestic product within the regions, and of the disparities of level between the regions.

In addition to these differences between the countries, there are also within each country great differences in the incomes accruing to individual households. No material is available to enable us to make sound comparisons in this respect. But there seem to be grounds for assuming that the differences in income level are at least as great in the poor areas as in the wealthy ones, and perhaps greater[2].

[2] Cf. Gunnar Myrdal (1957).

5. It was mentioned above that an evaluation of domestic product on the basis of rates of exchange would be subject to certain shortcomings, although such shortcomings may not be very significant in the present context. Nevertheless, it has been thought that other methods of calculation should be referred to here. An example is a purchasing-power calculation[3] referring to eight European countries[4] and the United States in the years 1950 and 1955. The calculations in that study are based on American prices in so far as the quantity of goods included in the national products of eight European countries in 1950 and 1955 have been multiplied by the American prices. Further, the prices in the eight countries taken together have been used as an alternative conversion factor. In turn, the values of the national product as estimated in these two ways are compared with the national product calculated in dollars by applying the official exchange rates to the national product as measured in the national currencies.

The widest differences between the calculations for 1955 made according to the rates of exchange and those based on the purchasing power exchange rates appear when American prices are used. The income level of the eight European countries is then shown to be, on an average, 50 per cent higher than when the official exchange rates are used. If this result is extended so as to include the rest of *Western Europe*—which is, of course, a hazardous step to take—the following figures for the West European net domestic product emerge:

	Billion dollars	Per Capita dollars
(1) According to 1955 exchange rates	183	615
(2) According to 1955 American prices	275	925
(3) According to 1955 European prices	212	715
(4) Average of (2) and (3)	244	820

These calculations show clearly how much the results depend on the methods applied.

In the following chapters the results reached by *Gilbert* and *Associates* have been used in expressing the West European net domestic product in terms of dollars. The average of the purchasing power exchange rates obtained on the basis of the American and European prices respectively are used.

---

[3] Milton Gilbert and Associates (1958).

[4] Belgium, Denmark, France, Holland, Italy, Norway, United Kingdom and West Germany.

An alternative approach (referring to 1950) has been presented by *Colin Clark*[5]. In calculating "real" national product Colin Clark uses two different units, the International Unit (IU) and the Oriental Unit (OU). An "IU of real income" corresponds to the amount of goods which might be purchased with one dollar in the period 1925–34—the equivalent, for the year 1950, of 1.649 dollars. An OU corresponds to the quantities of goods and services which might be bought for one rupee in India in 1948/49.

In using the OU in his reckoning Colin Clark does not take into account the value of transport and the distribution expenses of foodstuffs to the town population, as these figures are fairly insignificant in that context. He also excludes the "Government Sector" for the same reason. This measure should thus be more suitable as regards the underdeveloped countries than the IU.

A comparison between calculations made by the United Nations in dollars for 1949 and 1952/54 on the basis of official rates of exchange—corresponding, thus, to our calculations for 1955—and Colin Clark's OU-calculations shows a positive correlation in spite of differences in the bases and periods of calculation. As might be expected, however, there are notable divergences in the ranking of the countries in these calculations.

6. The picture that emerges from Table I. 1 is the result of a historical process. With a view to evaluating future development it seems expedient to give some indications regarding the development patterns which form the background of the groupings shown in Table I. 2[6].

In the past 200 years *the population increase* has been very high compared to earlier periods. Between 1750 and 1950 the growth rate was 6.4 per cent per decade or 85 per cent per century, whilst in the Middle Ages there seems on the whole to have been no change at all in world population.

A division into periods shows that between 1750 and 1950 the rate of growth has been accelerating. From 1750 to 1850 the rate was 4.6 per cent a decade; from 1850 to 1900 it was 7.6 per cent and from 1900 to 1950 8.9 per cent a decade.

Although the steep population increase has been a general phenomenon the various countries show large differences, particularly as between 'old' and 'new' nations. Thus, the population increase was three times as great in North America as in Europe during the last century.

---

[5] Colin Clark (1957).
[6] The following considerations are based on Simon Kuznets (1956).

In the "new" countries the rate of growth was high in the early days of their development but declined later. Thus in the United States, e.g., the population increased approximately 35 per cent per decade between 1790 and 1860, but only 20 per cent or less per decade after the eighteen-nineties.

In Europe the tendency of the rate of growth to both rise and decline can be discerned. The increase in Europe, including Asiatic Russia, between 1650 and 1750 was 3.4 per cent per decade; from 1850 to 1900 it was 9.1 per cent. It then fell to 7 per cent between 1900 and 1950.

The causes of this heavy and generally rising population increase will not be considered in detail here. Only it should be pointed out that it is not due to an increase in the birth-rate, but to a decrease in the death-rate including the infant mortality rate.

What we have said here applies mainly to the developed regions. In the rest of the world, with high birth and death rates, the population has been fairly constant until very recent times. In the twentieth century, however, the death-rate has fallen considerably in many areas and there has been a sharp rise in population.

Information on domestic and national product, covering a long enough period to shed some light on the question of economic growth, is only available for a limited number of countries—countries that may, with few exceptions, be regarded as economically highly developed and with a high average income per person.

The relevant data available on these countries do not, on the whole, extend further back than 1870. On the basis of more sparse information, however, it is possible to outline the development since about the middle of the eighteenth century.

It looks as though the acceleration in the population increase began before the acceleration in the rise of the per capita national income. Only when the rate of growth of population becomes fairly stable and industrialization is in full swing, will any substantial increase in the per capita national income be achieved.

In Table I. 3 are shown the rates of growth of population and per capita income in the period and in the countries for which information is available. There are fairly substantial differences in the rates of growth of the per capita national income when different countries are compared and also, and perhaps especially, when a comparison is made between the same countries at different times; but on the whole the rates of growth are very high.

TABLE I.3

Rates of Growth of Population, National Product, and Per Capita National Product.

	Average Changes per Decade (Per cent)		
	Population	National Product (Constant Prices)	Per capita National Product (Constant Prices)
Great Britain			
1860–1899	11.5	28.8	15.5
1885–1928	7.8	13.8	5.4
1915–1953	5.2	24.2	18.1
Northern Ireland and Eire			
1860–1903	—6.2	10.5	17.8
1894–1953	—1.6	14.5	16.2
France			
1841–1880	1.6	16.0	13.9
1871–1913	2.1	24.2	21.6
1911–1953	0.3	6.8	6.2
Germany			
1860–1894	9.4	46.5	33.9
1880–1914	13.7	28.2	12.8
Denmark			
1870–1908	10.8	31.3	18.4
1894–1928	14.5	38.0	20.5
1914–1954	10.0	23.5	12.2
Sweden			
1861–1898	6.6	30.9	22.9
1884–1928	7.1	33.8	24.7
1914–1954	6.0	38.6	31.5
Italy			
1879–1913	7.1	19.7	11.7
1899–1933	5.9	25.8	18.8
1919–1954	7.6	10.0	2.2
USA			
1869–1908	22.5	55.0	26.5
1894–1928	18.4	36.9	15.5
1914–1954	11.6	28.6	15.3
Canada			
1870–1909	14.1	40.9	23.1
1895–1929	25.2	41.6	12.7
1915–1954	16.3	42.9	23.2
Japan			
1878–1912	11.4	51.4	36.0
1898–1932	12.3	51.7	35.1
1918–1954	13.1	35.8	19.9

Source : Simon Kuznets (1956).

Thus, in the United Kingdom they represent a threefold increase of the per capita national income over the course of one century, and in Sweden a six- to sevenfold increase.

TABLE I.4

Annual Increase of Population and Domestic Product.
(Per cent)

	Annual Increase of Population			Annual Increase of Domestic Product			Per Capita Annual Increase of Domestic Product		
	1938 -50	1950 -55	1938 -55	1938 -50	1950 -55	1938 -55	1938 -50	1950 -55	1938 -55
North America .	1.4	1.6	1.5	5.3	4.1	5.0	3.9	2.4	3.4
Western Europe .	0.9	0.7	0.8	1.1	4.9	2.2	0.2	4.2	1.4
Oceania	1.7	2.1	1.8	3.1	3.9	3.4	1.4	1.7	1.5
USSR	—0.2	1.7	0.3	6.4	11.1	7.8	6.7	9.3	7.4
Eastern Europe .	—0.2	1.1	0.1	1.5	9.0	3.6	1.7	7.9	3.5
Latin America ..	2.3	2.3	2.3	4.6	4.7	4.7	2.3	2.3	2.3
Middle East	1.6	2.4	1.8	...	...	...	...	...	...
Asia	1.3	1.5	1.4	0.2	6.9	2.1	—1.1	5.3	0.7
Asia without Mainland China .	1.2	1.2	1.2	—0.3	4.5	1.2	—1.5	3.3	–
Africa	1.6	1.6	1.6	...	...	...	...	...	...
Total	1.3	1.5	1.4						

Note : The increase of population and net domestic product have been computed according to the compound interest formula.
Source : Various UN publications and national statistical abstracts.

These very considerable increases in total output and incomes imply that about a hundred years ago international differences in income level were much smaller than to-day. Yet it looks as if the economically developed countries even before industrialization had a higher income level than the underdeveloped areas have to-day. On the other hand, it has been the general opinion in Europe that some of the currently underdeveloped countries, such as China and India, had achieved, before the nineteenth century, a far more advanced stage of development than Europe. Hence, there must have been a fall in the per capita income of these countries—or the income must have increased to a certain degree in Europe prior to industrialization.

7. It is of particular interest to consider the changes in the population

and in the domestic product (as measured in constant prices) in recent years. In Table I.4 is shown the annual increase of the population and of the net domestic product, total and per capita, in the various regions in the period 1938–55.

Of the available figures for domestic product those relating to *North America* and *Western Europe* must be considered the most reliable, and those for recent years more so than those for earlier periods. As regards the *USSR* and *Eastern Europe* there is abundant information, but it may sometimes be difficult to evaluate the available figures because both the underlying method of computation and the definitions employed differ from those applied elsewhere. As far as *Latin America* and *Asia* are concerned information is very scarce and of doubtful reliability. For *Africa* and the *Middle East* the available material is so inadequate that it has not been considered justifiable to base any calculations on it. *Asia* without Mainland China is also included in the Table. This is of some interest, as there is a considerable disparity in the period 1950–55 between the rates of increase in Mainland China on the one hand and the rest of *Asia* on the other. If we ignore the first few years after the end of the civil war in Mainland China and consider the rate of increase of the net domestic product in 1953–55, it seems as if the percentage for that country goes down from 13 to 6.5. If this percentage figure were used as the basis of the calculation in regard to *Asia* as a whole the result would be an annual rate of increase in per capita net domestic product of 3.5 per cent in 1950–55 instead of 5.3 per cent as stated in the Table.

The development from 1938 to 1950 in many countries has been much influenced by the war and the reconstruction after it which probably also affect the figures from the early nineteen-fifties. This suggests that the average rate of growth from 1938 to 1955 gives us a more dependable impression of the long-term trend than the rates during the sub-periods.

In *North America* the growth in population has agreed with the averages of all regions, but here too the rise in the net domestic product has been great. As to *Asia* apart from Mainland China it seems that the increase in the net domestic product in the period 1938–50 has not corresponded to the growth in population. Since the war, however, the increase has been noticeably greater. These differences in the development of the population and net domestic product must of course influence the rate of growth of the per capita net domestic product.

The Table shows, as might be expected, that the annual increase in the per capita net domestic product has on the whole been higher in the period 1950–55 than in the period 1938–50. An exception, however, is provided by *North America* where the rate of increase of the per capita net domestic product in 1938–50 exceeds that of 1950–55.

No matter what periods are selected for comparison, it is apparent that the increase in the per capita net domestic product has been very considerable in the *USSR*, whilst in *Asia* apart from Mainland China it has actually been negative from 1938 to 1950 and only moderate from 1950 to 1955. In Mainland China and the East European countries too the economic growth has been substantial in the period 1950–55. The difference in the increase of the per capita net domestic product between *North America* and *Western Europe* in the two periods was to be expected considering the different ways the war affected the two regions.

As the information available on the *Middle East* and *Africa* is rather scarce, it is not possible on the basis of the domestic products of the countries within the two regions to draw any definite conclusions regarding the development in the net domestic product of these regions as a whole. The development in the two regions has probably run more or less on the same lines as in *Asia* and the rate of increase of the per capita net domestic product in the period 1938–55 may perhaps be put at 1 per cent in both regions.

CHAPTER II

Factors of Growth

A. *The Approach to the Problem*

In Chapter I a summary survey was given of the population and production of the nine regions in 1955, and an attempt was made to put this material into historical perspective by showing in outline the developments which led to the situation existing in 1955.

In this and the following chapters possible future trends will be considered together with the changes that are likely or at least conceivable within the period till about 1980, especially the changes that may be envisaged in the economic balance between the world's main regions.

Obviously the increase in the net domestic product will depend on a great many factors. What are these factors? How will they develop? What are the relationships between the separate factors or groups of factors and the size of production that will result from them?

If a satisfactory answer to these questions could be given, it would mean that a real theory of economic growth had been evolved. Or to go even further: we should then possess essential parts of a more comprehensive theory of the development of human societies. For economic growth should only be regarded as an element in a process involving also a variety of changes outside the sphere usually dealt with by economics. This is especially true when the growth is considered over a lengthy period and within very large areas of the earth. The more the field of inquiry is extended, both as regards time and geographical area, the greater will be the necessity for including, for example, the many differing natural conditions and also the social structure, educational level, and outlook on life of the various nations. Another point to be taken into account is how these factors may conceivably change during the period under consideration.

This would seem to suggest that the number of growth factors will be extremely large. In fact a very long, and yet far from exhaustive list of growth factors may be drawn up. The preparation of such a list is the first task that presents itself. The next will be to make an estimate of the development and size of the more important among these factors during the period under consideration. Finally we must try to get an idea of the main relationships existing between the development of the various growth factors on the one hand and the resulting increase in the net domestic product on the other. Some help is afforded here by the rapidly growing literature on the theory of economic growth, though it must be emphasized that this theory, as it exists today, is far from perfect. It is a tentative approach rather than a coherent system.

Incidentally the three tasks here referred to cannot be entirely separated. We cannot make a list of factors of growth without knowing something about the workings of a process of development. If, for example, invested capital is included in the list, it will be an indication that there is a connection between the investment of capital and the current and subsequent size of total production. Thus the preparation of a list of factors of growth implies certain assumptions which are, in reality, fragments of a theory of growth.

These assumptions, however, do not necessarily have to be of a definite or quantitative nature. We should not hesitate to say that an improvement of public health must be counted among the factors that promote production. On the other hand, it is far more difficult to state how much production would increase if, for example, the number of cases of sickness of a certain kind fell by 40 per cent.

These considerations suggest a classification of the various factors of growth into *direct* and *indirect* factors.

By *direct* factors of growth is here understood those which can be measured or stated in terms of quantity, and whose influence on the size of production can likewise be measured or at least be estimated quantitatively. It will thus be possible to establish quantitative relationships between changes in the amount of direct factors and the corresponding changes in the size of the net domestic product. Although there will often be a considerable degree of uncertainty, the essential thing is that these factors can be directly included in a quantitative treatment of the problems of growth.

Indirect factors will have to be defined in a negative way. They are the factors which do not fulfil the necessary conditions for them to be treated as direct factors. Thus the difference between the two kinds of factor really originates in our inadequate knowledge of the subject. A factor is indirect

3*

when too little is known about its quantity or its significance in economic growth for it to be treated as a direct factor. Gradually, as our knowledge and understanding increase, more factors will become direct. This implies also that the boundary line separating the two categories of factor is not very sharply defined. Indeed, it is sometimes a matter of opinion whether we know enough about a factor to treat it as direct or not.

The direct factors are of course those which attract attention more easily and, for practical reasons also, they must come to the fore in any analysis. The indirect factors thus form a background on which the direct factors have effect. We may try to judge the quantitative effects of changes in each separate direct factor. It should, however, be remembered that the background, also, changes in the course of time, and is by no means the same in each region. The variations to which the background is subject are moreover related to the changes in the direct factors, but must of course be treated far more summarily.

All these facts may be elucidated by means of the so called Cobb-Douglas Function which is often used to illustrate the connection between the factors of production and output. For our purpose there will be advantage in using this function in the following form[1]:

$$P = \beta \ L^{\alpha_1} \ C^{\alpha_2} \ (1 + \gamma)^t,$$

in which P is the net domestic product (e.g. measured in 1955 dollars), L the quantity of labour (e.g. number of man-hours), C the quantity of invested capital (e.g. in 1955 dollars), and t the number of years in the period under consideration. (In the period 1955–80 t thus varies from 0 to 25.)

Among the parameters β is a constant which is different in the different regions and the two exponents α_1 and α_2 indicate how much a one per cent change in labour and capital respectively will change production as measured in per cent. In this case labour and capital are thus treated as direct factors. It is assumed that we at least know something about the amounts of these two factors and the effect of any changes in them.

Finally, γ is a quantity indicating the extent of the increases in production consequent on background changes in the period between junctures 0 and t. The greater γ is over a certain period, in a certain region, the greater will be the share in the rate of growth attributable to the various and often

[1] An application of the function similar, in fact, to this is made by several authors, e.g. Belshaw (1956, p. 59).

imperceptible and indefinable changes in natural, cultural, and other conditions that bring about the continuous variation of the background on which labour and capital operate.

In trying to draw up a list of possible factors of growth or a system of such factors, two things must be taken into consideration. On the one hand we must seek to include all conceivable essential factors. On the other hand it is important that the system should lend itself easily to practical use. The two conditions are not easily fulfilled because the number of factors of growth is so very large. There is hardly any aspect of nature or of human society which is not in one way or another connected with the size of production.

The best way to perform this task will probably be to put the factors into a small number of categories which, taken together, are all-inclusive. Each category may then be treated as a whole, with the reservations necessary to ensure a realistic result.

In the following considerations four such categories will be used, viz. *Labour, Capital, Nature,* and *Culture.* Sometimes when the four factors of growth are referred to, what is really meant is the four categories of growth factors.

By way of a preliminary characterization we may describe *Labour* and *Capital* as the two large direct factors of production and growth. They represent the immediate human contribution to production. Man works for a certain number of hours and utilizes a certain amount of currently and previously invested capital. The result is a production of a certain size. It seems appropriate here to try to establish direct quantitative relationships between effort and result, as is often done.

The result, however, also depends on the background, that is, the indirect factors. The category *Nature* represents the part of these factors resulting from natural sources: soil, climate, raw materials in the earth, marine resources, good sites for building harbours, beauty of scenery, etc.

Finally the word *Culture* here represents that part of the background originating from man's own activities. *Culture is the way in which human beings live.* It includes man's behaviour and habits, his thoughts and feelings, and the ways in which he expresses these thoughts and feelings in art and literature, etc. It also includes the way in which men live and work together in families, associations, religious communities, schools, business concerns, and states, and further it includes the peaceful or hostile interaction between these and other institutions, as well as the various manifestations of the human mind ranging from science to entertainment[2].

In reality human labour as well as capital are also parts of the cultural pattern. In this study they will be given special treatment as direct factors. *Culture,* as the word is used here, must thus be regarded as comprising the sections of culture which are not being given special treatment as direct factors.

There might possibly be other elements in the very complex categories *Nature* and *Culture* which might similarly, with some advantage, be treated separately, but this can only be done if we have a sufficiently clear and well-founded idea as to their size or quantity as well as of their influence on production. Two examples of this will be referred to here, as the items in question are to be included in the following analysis, wherever possible.

Certain elements in *Nature* have a close resemblance to invested capital. This, for example, applies to *farm land.* If a piece of land has been reclaimed it must, by virtue of its origin as farm land, be considered as invested capital. Such land, once it has been reclaimed will, however, usually, from the economic point of view, hold the same position as natural farm land.

If the various types of soil may be graded according to some sort of standard unit, the amount of such *Standard Farm Land*[3] can be included in the analysis in the same way as the amount of invested capital. Especially in dealing with problems of economic growth in countries that are heavily dependent on agriculture can such reasoning be used to good purpose.

The element in *Culture* bearing the most direct relation to the achievement in production is probably the volume of *knowledge* in the widest sense of the word.

The building up of new knowledge by scientific research and practical experiments may in reality be regarded as an investment. The same is true of the propagation of this knowledge by education and publication. Education also includes the training of the labour force in practical skills, by which it increases its efficiency. This investment in knowledge requires a certain share of the annual productive effort just like material investment in ships, machinery, etc. It will always be a matter for consideration which investment will be likely to prove the most advantageous. The choice may

---

[2] This definition of culture is in principle the one adopted by Bagby (1958, p. 84).
[3] *Colin Clark* (1957).

lie between two material investments or between two kinds of investment in knowledge. Of course the choice may also lie between a certain material investment and a certain investment in knowledge. It must be assumed that, consciously or unconsciously, attention will be given to the matter of the return when making investment in knowledge, in much the same way as when material investment is in question.

Hence, it is right to treat investment in knowledge as a direct factor like any other form of investment. The simplest thing to do would in fact be to combine the two kinds of investment but, unfortunately, only very scant information as to the extent of actual knowledge investment is available[4].

B. *The Four Factors of Economic Growth*

Each of the four categories of growth factors has its own characteristics. Some of these have now to be considered by way of an introduction to the analysis in the four following chapters where the status and growth conditions of the four factors in the nine regions are considered.

1. *Labour* can best be measured by the number of hours of work. This measurement, however, gives rise to certain problems.

First of all, the various kinds of *Labour* are of varying quality; hence they cannot be used to perform the same tasks. There are various reasons for these differences in quality and they must be dealt with separately.

a. No two individuals are by nature equipped with the same mental and physical abilities or—more generally—qualities. In this respect there may be great differences even within the population of a minor area. This fact does not, however, cause any particular problems in the present context. There are also a great variety of tasks to be undertaken and consequently a number of very dissimilar forms of education are needed in each community. Economic development promotes these differences so as to create a need for men of widely varying capabilities.

On the other hand, it is very important to know whether there are typical

---

[4] To summarize these reflections, we may express them in terms of the previously mentioned Cobb-Douglas Function (see p. 36), in which may be inserted other direct factors besides L and C, e.g. the amount of standard farm land or of accumulated knowledge investment. The latter factor might also be regarded as a part of C, which would then have to be increased. The parameters indicating the weighting of the indirect factors, i.e. β and γ, would, on the other hand, be reduced accordingly.

differences between populations in different parts of the world. Do certain populations have an *average* or *typical* genotype as regards significant physical or mental qualities in which they differ from certain other populations in a manner relevant to the analysis of the possibilities of economic growth? Of course here we have to take into account especially the qualities which are important with regard to participation in the forms of production for which there will be more demand in the different regions in the period 1955–80.

It will thus be a part of our task to find out whether or not there are such typical anthropological differences between the principal populations of the earth as must be taken into account when comparing possibilities of economic growth in the nine regions. This question is considered in Chapter III, D.

b. The state of health and nutrition, too, plays an important role as regards a man's productive capacity. In many underdeveloped countries the amount and composition of the diet have been unsatisfactory and at the same time certain diseases have afflicted a large part of the population. Improvements in these two spheres would not only increase human well-being, but would enable the individual to do much more work. As long as the state of health and nutrition is bad, on the other hand, it will be difficult for the countries in question to break out of the vicious circle of poverty.

An improvement, especially in the field of nutrition, is hard to bring about until production begins to grow at a higher rate than population. Improved nutrition will then help to accelerate the growth because of the increased working capacity. This is an example of how difficult it can be to set going a process of growth whilst, on the other hand, the process, once the difficulties have been overcome, tends to become self-sustained.

c. A third reason for the differences in men's working capacities is that they have not all had the same education in the widest sense. The number of different forms of education is continuously growing in the communities which are developing economically—this, in fact, seems to be one of the chief prerequisites of growth.

Education will often require a considerable effort and this effort is, therefore, in itself a factor of growth. It is an essential part of what, above, was termed investment in knowledge[5]. The quality of the labour force in a cer-

---

[5] See p. 38–39.

tain region thus depends, among other things, on the investment in know-ledge made in the region.

A prerequisite of any form of education is of course that the persons con-cerned possess the necessary mental and physical qualities to enable them to acquire the knowledge and skill offered them.

In the different regions the demand for education will vary a good deal in the period under consideration, but it is certain to be increasing in all of them. A thing of decisive importance will thus be the typical genotypes of the different populations in relation to the demand for education that may arise in the various regions during the period. Chapter III, D, which deals with the anthropological side of the subject of population and the labour force, should therefore be read with this in mind also.

Moreover, education is, of course, a part of the cultural pattern of a com-munity and will thus be considered in more detail in Chapter VI.

It may seem that to measure *Labour* by the number of hours of work is to over-simplify matters, considering that its quality is subject to such great variations. It would undoubtedly be desirable to formulate a more composite measure, in which the different qualities of *Labour* were assigned different weights. However, for the present this can hardly be done satisfactorily. On the other hand, when considering the figures we must keep the question of quality in mind, and this is true in two respects which are both important.

It should be remembered that there are great differences between the separate regions, especially as far as education is concerned. Indeed this is one of the points with regard to which the differences in development stand out most conspicuously. In some cases may also be added certain anthropo-logical differences.

Secondly, it may be assumed that the composition of the labour force as regards education will change considerably in the regions undergoing rapid economic development. It is perhaps better to reverse the viewpoint and say that a development in education is one of the necessary conditions of such growth. Hence, it will be one of the objects of Chapter VI to appraise the possibilities of development in education in the various regions.

Still another fact concerning *Labour* has to be mentioned. It is the amount of *utilized* hours of work that is of importance as regards the size of production. This brings a number of uncertain factors into the enquiry. For what is, in fact, inferred from a direct appraisal of the population devel-opment is rather the *available* amount of labour force expressed in the number of persons in the age groups fit to work. As to this, readers are referred to Chapter III.

The question arising next will then be, to what extent this labour force is exploited. The length of working hours has been falling in the developed countries in this century. It will be part of our task to estimate what the trend is likely to be in this field in the various regions. The estimate is, however, bound to be of very doubtful reliability.

Another important question is, how large a proportion of the labour force will be unemployed. It must be assumed that unemployment will vary in the future as it did in the past. Over so long a span of time as twenty-five years it appears likely that booms and depressions will to a certain extent cancel each other, so that it would not be unjustifiable to count on the average rate of employment being roughly the same throughout the period.

Finally, we have to take into consideration whether, in certain regions, changes might not conceivably occur in the utilization of female labour in industry, trade, or other branches of production.

2. *Capital* must, as said before, be defined as utilized invested capital, that is *produced* means of production in the widest sense. In this is included not only machinery, factory buildings, means of transport, domestic animals, goods in the process of manufacture and stocks in the wholesale and retail trade, but also houses, schools, churches and temples, hotels and cinemas, as these too contribute to the production of goods and services with which to meet man's demands. All these things are the results of production and they are themselves instruments of future production. They all contribute to the net domestic product.

The most important feature of *Capital,* from the present point of view, is its being dependent, like *Labour,* on the direct effort of men. In the present context the effort consists of *investment.* Part of annual production is not disposed of by current consumption, but is invested, that is to say, used for the enlargement of *Capital,* so that new machinery, ships, buildings, or other capital goods are produced.

It is through the agencies of work and investment that man serves production. The greater the amount of labour and invested capital, the greater the production. Hence, *Labour* and *Capital* are the two great direct factors of production or growth.

Capital goods, however, are not indestructible. They are worn out, some rapidly, others more slowly, and they become obsolete and so lose their value, partially or entirely, before they are finally worn out. In this way, a certain capital consumption takes place every year. In business accounts it appears as depreciation, and in preparing the national accounts a similar figure is tentatively calculated for the community as a whole.

Some of the annual total investment (*the gross investment*) is therefore used to compensate for this annual capital consumption. The figure which indicates this part of the total investment is called re-investment. Only that part of the gross investment which exceeds this amount is the *net investment*. This net investment corresponds to the annual increase of *Capital*. In times when the gross investment is very small, it may not be sufficient to cover the wear and tear of *Capital* so that the net investment will be negative.

It thus appears to be the net investment which concerns us in this enquiry, it being the net investment that determines the increase of *Capital*. The total *Capital* at the end of a year is equal to the *Capital* at the beginning of the year plus the net investment for that year. Hence, it will be one of the main objectives of Chapter IV to estimate the possibilities of net investment in the various regions in the period 1955–80, in order that we may be able to estimate the development of *Capital* as a factor of growth.

Because *Capital* includes so many widely different goods, the only way to arrive at an over-all expression of its size or changes will be to measure it in terms of money, the only possible common measure. Here, as elsewhere in this book, the estimate will be in 1955 dollars.

It must finally be added, of course, that as was the case with *Labour*, it is only the *Capital utilized* that contributes to production. Idle machinery produces nothing.

The degree of utilization of *Capital* is generally less well-known than that of the utilization of the labour force; but it will normally fluctuate *pari passu* with the latter during short-term business cycles. We may therefore refer to what was said above concerning variations in the rate of employment.

3. *Nature,* like *Capital,* is a term common to a great variety of phenomena. This factor, however, confronts us with certain problems which differ from those we encountered in connection with the two first-mentioned factors of growth.

Labour and *Capital* are concepts often dealt with in economic writing. Consequently, they have for a long time been undergoing a process of definition and adaptation to the demands of economic science. The same is true of the concept of production; and a treatment of the relationships between *Labour* and *Capital* on the one hand, and production on the other is a task within the compass of economic theory in the general sense. In making reference to anthropological questions it has, however, been necessary to touch upon another science.

In dealing with *Nature,* on the other hand, we shall have to seek support in various branches of the natural sciences, pure and applied alike. The differences between the nine regions are, to a great extent, due to the very fact that natural conditions in them vary, and it will be an essential part of our task to gauge how much this influences the possibilities for economic growth.

In recent economic writing the question of the relationship between natural conditions and the size of production has occupied, as a rule, a rather modest position. When it is considered in connection with the problem of growth it is usually in order to discuss whether or not the size of natural resources has a decisive influence on over-all production and wealth; and the discussion is often of a somewhat summary character. As an instance, we may mention that *Kuznets*[6] considers natural conditions one of the causes of international differences in income level but does not attach much importance to them in that respect.

The reason for this is probably that economic science in its present form is marked by the conditions and problems current in the countries in which it has developed, that is, first and foremost, the industrialized countries of *Western Europe* and *North America* which, because of big investment and a high technical level, are not so directly dependent on natural conditions as are, for example, the underdeveloped countries.

Conversely, natural conditions have been dealt with thoroughly in a number of books in recent years in which scientists have tried to envisage and discuss mankind's future problems and especially the question of whether it will be possible to maintain a constant or rising standard of living in face of the rapid growth of the world's population[7]. Most of the authors have emphasized the importance of resources as a limiting factor, although some of them incline to think that technological science is capable of meeting

[6] Kuznets (1954, pp. 006 99).
[7] To mention a few: Brown (1954); Darwin (1953); Hoyle (1953); Lee (1957); Osborn (1953); Thomson (1955).

man's requirements, even with the vast human numbers to be envisaged, through exploiting resources by new methods. This, they say, will be the more true the further ahead we look.

These two groups of writings to a large extent deal with the same problems; but wide differences in their basic assumptions are noticeable. Added to this is the fact that the two schools of thought have developed independently, or at least nearly so. Economists seem to have made use of the results gained by scientists only to a very small extent, and the latter have based themselves equally little on the writings of economists.

We are thus in need of a workable analysis of the interaction of natural conditions and economic development. No system of concepts has been formulated which renders terms relating to the factors of *Nature* suitable for the purpose of economic analysis as the concepts of *Labour* and *Capital* have been.

In this connection it should now be stressed, in the first place, that *Nature* is something more than "natural resources". By the latter term is meant, as a rule, a number of concrete physical things like the soil, the sea with its fish etc., the raw materials and fuels contained in the earth, and sources of energy such as waterfalls and the stand of "natural" forests. It has already been said above that these things, viewed as factors of production, offer many points of resemblance to *Capital,* but that their amount as a whole is independent of the investment necessary to the growth and maintenance of *Capital.* The tangible resources might be described as "natural capital" which has, through economic development, been supplemented with a certain amount of produced (and thus invested) capital. As previously mentioned, natural capital and man-made investment are often so closely connected that they can only with difficulty be separated in a concrete analysis.

Besides these material resources, however, nature offers a variety of conditions which can, in a great many different ways, influence production and man's well-being. The most important of these is climate; but the material resources also have a number of qualities which cannot simply be identified with these resources, but which are important in regard to their economic exploitation. Thus, for example, the beauty of mountain scenery may give rise to the building of hotels. The wealth of fish in the oceans is an advantage to adjacent countries. Natural conditions which facilitate the construction of harbours or railways, or proximity to densely populated areas provide the best possibilities for the exploitation of arable land, minerals, etc.

On the other hand, conditions may have a negative influence on production, and particularly on the possibilities of exploiting certain resources. This applies, for example, to an unhealthy climate in a mining area, or a broken terrain making transport difficult from the mine to the nearest harbour. Soil lying on a steep slope is more difficult to work and more exposed to erosion than similar soil on level ground, and so on.

We might then define the growth factor, *Nature,* in a geographical area, as the entire complex of natural (i.e. not man-made) things and conditions which have influence, in a positive or negative way, on production and life in the area.

It is important that we should mention the conditions of life separately because they do not depend on production alone. A mild and pleasant climate, for example, brings immediate well-being, which in colder zones can only be obtained through a certain production of fuel, well-built houses, warm clothes, etc.

In treating *Nature* as a factor of growth the main difficulty is that only certain elements in this many-sided complex of things and conditions can be *measured.* Often an element has certain qualities which can be measured and others which can only be expressed in a more general, verbal description.

Thus, arable land may be measured in hectares; but to what extent do factors like the gradient, the composition of the soil, and the climate determine its productivity? They can be partially described as to quantity (e.g. as regards average temperature and rainfall); but a numerical statement of all relevant facts is not possible. A description of an area in its "Standard Farm Land"[8] equivalent, or in other standardized terms, is thus bound to be an imperfect generalization but it may be useful if applied with caution.

In the same way, to take another example, the reserves of coal, oil, and other raw materials in an area may be stated quantitatively although their size is often known only with a considerable degree of uncertainty. It is more difficult to take into account the differences in quality or other relevant facts which have to be considered. In gaining access to a mineral, for instance, it is of importance whether large amounts of earth or rock must be removed first. Further, it is important whether large quantities of the mi-

[8] See p. 38.

neral will have to be processed in order to obtain a certain amount of metal. A problem that will confront mankind in the coming decades is that for the extraction of many raw materials we shall have to turn to minerals containing a continuously declining percentage of usable material. Location and natural facilities for carriage are also qualities in raw material resources.

If a description of the natural factors in a particular region is required it should be given by means of numerical statements combined with a more general, verbal commentary. The latter must deal partly with the degrees of reliability of the figures, partly with a number of facts pertaining to the natural conditions of the region and which have special economic significance.

Here the question arises of which features should be included and which resources ought to be mentioned and appraised. The things that are relevant to-day are apparently not those that were relevant a hundred years ago. Our increasing knowledge of nuclear energy and electricity has given such things as uranium deposits and water-falls a significance they did not formerly have. On the other hand, other resources may lose some of their importance because new forms of production render them partially superfluous. The general tendency, however, is for technology to create applications for an increasing number of the materials found in nature. It has been said that "technology makes resources"[9].

We are confronted here with a peculiarity as regards *Nature* as a factor of growth. Formerly there was a tendency to consider natural resources as a constant element in production, whereas *Labour* and *Capital* were regarded as variables. Now we have to regard *Nature* too as a factor which is subject to certain variations. This may perhaps be most appropriately expressed by saying that *Nature* itself is virtually unchangeable; changes in climate and geological conditions take place over such lengthy periods of time that they may be disregarded in most economic enquiries. Those elements in *Nature* which are of importance from an economic point of view, however, depend on the stage reached by technology at the time. This is doubtless one of the chief reasons why the economically and politically dominant states in different periods of history have been situated in different parts of the earth. Thus, an American historian has tried to explain historical development in the light of the expanded means of communications[10]. He regards world history as a sequence of four eras, the pedestrian's, the horse's, and

[9] Hoyle (1953, p. 105).
[10] McNeill (1954).

the eras of trans-oceanic shipping and modern mechanized transport. In the time of trans-oceanic shipping, the countries around the Atlantic, especially, were naturally favoured, but the last of the four eras has seen the opening up of the interiors of the large continents to economic development. Hence, a situation close to one of the large oceans will perhaps be a condition of declining importance.

These reflections would seem to lead to the conclusion that the natural conditions in the nine regions must be evaluated in the light of the technological methods which may be expected to prevail in each region in the period 1955–80. This, however, makes necessary a few supplementary remarks.

Technology is one aspect of *Culture* which will be referred to below as the fourth factor of growth. In considering the natural conditions in each region we shall, therefore, have to estimate, among other things, how quickly the technological elements of western culture may spread in areas as yet comparatively untouched by them. This will depend especially on what will be the need to force such a development.

The fact that man's demands are influential in regard to which natural conditions will be economically relevant has been realised for some time. The prairies of *North America*, for example, acquired their great importance only when the immigration of the nineteenth century created a demand for more land; and it is the twentieth century's tremendous demand for transport which has given to the oil fields of the *Middle East* the great value they possess to-day.

In appraising the natural conditions of the nine regions, we have, therefore, to take into consideration not only technical development, but also current demand—and not only in the region in question. On the contrary, in this respect the world is becoming, more and more, a single unit. Thus, it is conceivable that a continued heavy increase in population in the densely populated areas may call for an import of grain requiring, in its turn, an intensified exploitation of farm land in the sparsely populated areas, and so cause the value of this farm land to rise. At the same time it is to be expected that the growing demand of industrial countries for imports of raw materials will give added importance to the mineral resources of some of the countries which are at the moment comparatively underdeveloped.

The foregoing reflections have indicated the way in which the factor of *Nature* will be treated in Chapter V. In the description of the separate regions, the principal aim will be to show in which ways the relative scarcity of resources may possibly restrict the growth which might otherwise, on the basis of more general arguments, be anticipated. In the same context it will be shown what will be the demand for investment the moment the resources are to be utilized more intensively. Current demand will be judged in relation to a few categories of supplies (e.g. food, energy and certain minerals, especially iron ore) and an enquiry will be made as to which regions are best suited to provide the natural basis for the expansion of production that might be expected in these categories.

In this connection another point has, finally, to be mentioned. It was said above that it is the *utilized* amounts of *Labour* and *Capital* that determine the size of current production. The same is true of the factor of *Nature*; but here the term *non-utilized reserves* has a wider significance than it has in relation to the two first-mentioned factors.

At a certain juncture, perhaps 90 per cent of the labour force and 94 per cent of the capital are being utilized. At the same time the annual recovery of a certain raw material may amount to only 2 per cent of the known reserves of high-grade and accessible mineral. The annual exploitation of total known reserves might even be no more than 0.3 per cent.

Likewise, the farm land is perhaps being exploited very extensively in certain geographical areas. It might, if current demand should make it profitable, and if the cultural level were high enough, yield five times as much through an increased application of *Labour* and *Capital*.

These unexploited reserves can be used in the event of increased demand, but, as likely as not, at higher costs than those for the current reserves. Expansion will first take place where it can do so with the highest degree of profit, that is, for example, where *Nature* offers the least resistance.

4. *Culture* is, as said above, a comprehensive term for the way in which man lives; it includes both his thoughts and feelings, his work and his social life. The way in which human life is organized and evolves from an economic point of view, is thus an element of *Culture*; and as was stressed above *Labour* and investment are really elements of *Culture* which are here, for practical reasons, treated separately as direct factors of growth.

Now, it is important to note that groups and communities which have for a long time had contact with one another tend to form a certain cultural pattern which includes a variety of features common to all members of that culture, but different from those of other cultures which are distinguished by other common features.

It is often said that such a cultural pattern is a unity. Researchers have sought, as in other kinds of analyses, to separate from this entity a number of elements. We may mention a great many such *cultural elements,* e.g. the various forms of labour, the social strata, the organization of trade, the political system, language, religion, and, more generally, the entire attitude towards life, including the attitude towards new influences coming from outside. It should be borne in mind here, however, that these elements are closely connected and interdependent. This is one of the reasons why radical changes in the cultural pattern are slow to take place.

A question now arises which is relevant to the problems dealt with in this book, viz., to what extent is it feasible, in a fairly brief span of time, to alter the elements of *Culture* which are particularly important to economic activity, without, necessarily, causing a change which gradually involves the whole cultural pattern and which may not, perhaps, be at all desirable.

There are many different cultures in the world, each with its own history. It is the distinction between primitive cultures and *civilizations* which is relevant to this study, however. By civilizations is here meant, in accordance with *Bagby*'s definition, "those large, complex, urbanized (and usually literate) cultures, whose development embraces most of the events described by the historians"[11]. The modern, highly developed, industrialized economies all number among the civilizations; and the economic growth that has produced this type of economy has been an essential part of the development of such civilizations.

The basis of such a development has usually been a community dominated by subsistence farming. Later, in addition to farming, commerce, crafts, means of transport, banks, administration, and, in our time, industry and mechanical production have grown up. The population then splits up into various occupational groups. Subsistence farming is gradually converted into market agriculture: the farmers selling their products to the other groups. At the same time cities develop. The more advanced this process is, the greater will be the number of people engaged in the so-called secondary and tertiary occupations in comparison with those in the primary ones[12].

One of the necessary conditions of such a development is, and always has been, a considerable investment. Also a willingness to submit to changes seems essential. Further, it appears to be very important that education

[11] Bagby (1958, p. 23).
[12] See Chapter III B, 4 and especially Table III. 5, p. 71.

should develop in such a way that people will be able to perform the tasks set them by the new occupations.

Among the elements of *Culture* mentioned above, education or general enlightenment, that is *knowledge* in the widest sense, is probably the element bearing most directly on economic growth. Indirectly, too, this element is of great importance. Enlarged knowledge, more than anything else, promotes the desire to change the traditional patterns of culture, whenever these tend to obstruct the attainment of the benefits enjoyed by the industrialized countries. The revolutionary element of the peoples of former colonial areas, for example, has often consisted of men educated at Western universities.

In the opening passages of this chapter it was stressed that the building up of a fund of knowledge is really a kind of investment[13]. The amount of knowledge stored at any given time in human minds and in libraries and archives of all kinds represents capital produced by the efforts of men, just as machines, domestic animals, and transportation equipment are produced by material investment. Even depreciation is common to these two forms of capital. Knowledge grows obsolete, like machines, and is forgotten unless maintained through a new effort; and finally it lapses at the death of its holder. In the case of this intangible capital, therefore, we may also speak of gross and net investment.

Unfortunately too little information as to its volume is available. An enquiry carried out in Denmark suggests that gross investment for the year 1955, as reckoned in the traditional manner, must be raised by at least 20 per cent, and net investment by at least 25 per cent when the economic effort expended on the building up and maintenance of knowledge is included[14]. In the absence of similar estimates or other quantitative indicators of the existing volume of knowledge or its annual increase from other countries, some guidance may be obtained from statistics of the number of illiterates, school-children and students.

Apart from this, it is true, of course, of most of the cultural elements referred to, that we may form a general impression only as to their combined importance in bringing about a cultural climate favourable to economic growth. These elements bear the stamp of indirect factors which will, naturally, influence the way *Culture* is treated in Chapter VI.

One other fact of a quantitative nature, however, must be mentioned.

---

[13] See p. 38–39.
[14] Thorkil Kristensen (1959).

4*

Because of the political tension in the world to-day, this being part of the cultural pattern, some states spend very considerable amounts on their defence and thereby engage a part of the annual productive effort which could otherwise have been used for consumption and investment. At present the annual sum of the world's defence budgets is almost of the same magnitude as the annual net global investment (about 100 billion dollars). One of the things which will determine future economic development is, therefore, the increase, or decrease, of this defence effort in the years up to 1980, and its distribution over the various geographical areas.

C. *The Interaction of the Factors*

A region's production is, at any moment, the result of the interaction of all the factors mentioned in this chapter. It would be impossible to say how large a proportion of total output is attributable to any individual factor, just as it would be impossible to attribute one part of the rice crop, for example, to the climate, another to the soil, a third to the labour force, etc. Soil, detached from climate, has no meaning in this connection; and climate detached from soil, as at sea, would produce no rice, nor would labour without soil.

On the other hand, we are able, from experience, to describe how production is affected when one of the factors *varies* while the others remain constant. Our knowledge here is the most certain in the few cases in which it is possible to make experiments. As a rule, however, we must be content with the more approximate knowledge gained by considering historical development. The difficulty is that there are nearly always several factors that vary simultaneously, and consequently nothing definite is known as to how important is each individual factor. Some information, however, may be gained from comparing cases in which a factor grows comparatively fast, with cases in which it grows slowly in relation to the other factors.

The most typical form of economic growth is a process in which not all factors grow evenly and proportionately. As a rule, *Capital* increases faster than *Labour,* while the factor represented by *Nature* is roughly constant for long periods and *Culture* develops in different ways. Further, the growth is slow and fast alternately and at times even negative. There is much material here for comparative studies; and although the historical development is, as we say, a once-for-all process, its very rich pattern contains many regular features, which repeat themselves whenever certain conditions are fulfilled—subject to variations, however, as the conditions are never quite the same. It is on account of these regular features that we are able to pronounce on the future at all; but on account of the variations we can never foretell it completely.

In the chapters following we have to deal with the consequences for production of changes in the factors during the period under consideration. This question falls into two parts: $1°$ How are the four factors of growth likely to develop in the nine regions in the period 1955–80? and $2°$ What will be the connection between the development of the factors and the total production resulting? The first of these questions is the subject of Chapters III–VI. The second is treated in Chapter VII. Some concluding, and more general, remarks concerning the nature of the development will be found in Chapter VIII. Besides, a brief survey and an attempt to indicate the prospects of the individual regions are given in the Appendix.

It would, however, be over-simplifying the issue to describe the relationship between the development of the factors on the one hand and the growth of production on the other as one of cause and effect. The two processes interact to a certain extent; and among the factors also there are certain relationships, so that the development of the individual factor depends on the current or former state of the other factors. The following chapters should be read with these relationships in mind; and we therefore have to illustrate them with a few examples.

Thus, the amount of *Labour* depends in part on economic growth and on certain cultural elements. Improved nutrition and the dissemination of knowledge, modern hygiene and medical science cause the death-rate to fall. Consequently, the size of the labour force towards the end of the period 1955–80 will, to some extent, depend on economic development in the first phase of the period. This applies especially to the poorest countries.

In wealthy countries a continuous rise in the income level will promote a desire for shorter working hours, as has already happened in the industrial states in the twentieth century. Thus, in this instance, economic growth has given rise to counteracting forces.

The efficiency of the labour force depends, among other things, on the climate, as is well-known. It also depends on the anthropological characteristics of the population, which, in their turn are bound up with the climatic conditions, as mentioned in Chapter III, D. The influence of a tropical climate on the working capacity of people who have grown up in a temperate climate, is one of the natural factors which may impede the advance of industrialization in many underdeveloped countries. It may, however, be counteracted by hygienic measures, better houses, etc. Cultural and economic growth may thus, to a certain degree, diminish the influence of the climate and, in consequence, create possibilities for further growth.

This is one of many examples of how a process of growth, once started, shows a tendency to continue. This appears most markedly when we look at the growth of *Capital*. A greater per capita production is apt, for a time at least, to cause increased saving, not only in absolute terms but relatively too, so that the savings quota represents an increasing proportion of total income or production. Even if the savings quota is constant, total savings will grow when production grows. This promotes investment which, in its turn, steps up production. Our modern forms of production are, as we know, distinguished precisely by a large per worker investment in machines, etc.

This tendency to create a self-sustained growth is caused, in no less degree, by the intangible investment in knowledge mentioned above. The greater the wealth, the wider the extent of scientific knowledge and education, and the greater, again, are production and wealth.

There is, however, no hard-and-fast rule that *Capital* should keep on growing *pari passu* with continued economic growth. Thus, the United States has the world's highest income level, but its savings quota is lower than that of some other countries. It would seem that urbanization, advertising, and other features of the structure of highly developed industrial communities are apt to reduce the propensity to save and thus may tend to retard economic growth.

The fact that *Nature*, as a factor of growth, is influenced by technical development which may increase the possibilities of its exploitation, has already been mentioned. We also have to refer to the fact that geological research, in a way, "produces" resources by enlarging known reserves of coal, oil, and raw materials. Economic growth, furthering the demand for such resources, implies, in fact, a tendency to force research in these fields.

On the other hand, economic growth itself may "consume" natural resources. Certain methods of cultivation lead to erosion, for example; industrial development reduces the reserves of raw materials and fossil fuels, especially the richest and most accessible reserves. At the same time the growth of population is, obviously, tantamount to less resources per capita, even when the total amount of the resources is constant. This is especially true of the farm land of certain areas of Asia and Central America.

As regards *Culture,* it has already been pointed out that there is an interrelation between the volume of knowledge and economic growth. Political conditions also are influenced by the latter. A smooth and harmonious economic development promotes political stability, which, in its turn, helps to accelerate the growth. Conversely, poverty and a wide gulf between a minority of wealthy people and the remainder of the population, such as is often found in poor communities, may cause revolutions resulting in a restraint on economic growth.

There is probably also a certain relationship between economic growth and the will to effect such changes in the social structure as will be necessary if the growth is to continue. For it looks as if industrialization and the urbanization following in its wake tend very much to break down the old cultural patterns of the village communities and to form population groups with a spirit of progress.

It must, however, be added here that in the more advanced stages of the economic and cultural development of a civilization there arise, now and then, destructive tendencies in the cultural pattern, and at the same time a lack of stability or a decline in economic development. Here, then, is a retarding force, not unlike the tendencies towards shorter working hours and lower savings quotas mentioned above. The causes of this process are, however, very complicated and explanations of them vary greatly.

The examples given here should throw a certain light on some of the peculiarities of that very complex process, economic growth. We should get an impression of how it comes about that the growth tends to become self-sustained over long periods, once it has started. The explanation of this is that the growth of one of the factors or of production itself promotes the growth of other factors; and this calls forth renewed growth in the first factor or in production. This process has been typical of most western societies in the past few generations.

There are, however, two points in the process which are far more difficult to explain, and which are both important in the context of the present study. They relate to the beginning and the end of the self-sustained process of growth. What makes the process start at all, and what is the reason for the occasional appearance, in a highly developed society, of retarding factors, as just described?

One of the great problems of the next few decades will be whether the world's poorest areas can make the leap from stagnation into a self-sustained process of growth, and whether, perhaps, at the opposite end of the scale, certain retarding factors will emerge in some of the highly developed countries. The present chapter, therefore, concludes with a few remarks about the problems involved in the beginning of the process of economic growth and the possible slowing up of the process.

1. *The beginning.* Many communities, past and present, have been comparatively static through long periods. At certain times and in certain places, however, movements have begun which have gradually gathered momentum through mutual interaction. Often, in this way, a process of growth, of the self-sustaining type, has been started. The problem of what sets this process going has been dealt with by *W. W. Rostow*[15], among others. His analysis, however, concentrates on the beginning of industrial development in a number of communities which have already achieved some development in agriculture, trade, and shipping. As each stage of development is derived from the preceding ones, however, we shall probably have to look further back in time for an explanation.

In the most primitive societies, *Nature* and *Labour* are the only factors of production. The creation of *Capital* and of a *Culture* of any significance can take place only through a process of growth. Hence, it seems probable that the development, in its early stages, gathers speed most easily in areas where natural conditions are favourable to human life and work.

In support of this may be mentioned the fact that the oldest civilizations have all arisen in that part of the temperate zone where the climate makes modest demands on housing, heating, and clothing, and where there are favourable conditions of growth for animals and plants. From this starting point economic and cultural development has gradually spread in two directions, first to the colder parts of the temperate zone and later, sporadically and in the face of many difficulties, to tropical regions and to areas with a polar climate.

In the later stages of this process the real advances seem to have been made most easily where the natural conditions have been favourable, that is, where good or abundant natural resources are found—resources of the type particularly important under the technical and economic conditions

[15] See Rostow (1956, pp. 25–48).

prevailing at the time. The following are a few, briefly described, instances of this:

a. The first civilizations arose in the large *river valleys* of Egypt, Mesopotamia, India, and China, where the natural conditions permitted of intensive agriculture and dense populations. On the other hand, the inhabitants had to learn to co-operate for the purpose of irrigating the land. Often, growth is prompted when *Nature* offers possibilities which can only be exploited by a more than ordinary effort.

b. Gradually, as trade and communications between these civilizations developed, *location* became a factor of some importance. The *Middle East* very early came to have an important function as a link connecting the great civilizations; this function was extended when the Mediterranean became involved in economic and cultural development. The sea traffic from Phoenicia and, later, from Greece promoted a new tendency in economic development, namely *colonialism,* so that the countries which had already attained a certain cultural level, advanced further with the aid of the resources to be found in the colonies. The cities of Northern Italy, in the Middle Ages, and the towns of the Hanseatic League also depended on location for their growth.

c. This development was extended and reached a much larger scale through the great discoveries about the year 1500. The centre of gravity was now moved to *the Atlantic coast of Europe*. Spain and Portugal, and later also France, the Netherlands, and England now took the lead in the greatest epoch of colonization in history. They thus laid the foundation for later, more sporadic growth in various areas of *America, Asia,* and later, *Africa* and *Oceania*. In the first place, however, a fact of more importance was that they themselves developed their trade, shipping, banks, and capital, and, at the same time, an active and experienced entrepreneur class.

d. There is no doubt that these factors contributed to the evolution of the next phase in development: *the industrial revolution* in England. This is probably one of the best illustrations of how the economy of one period has in it the bases of the one following. Another important condition for the rise of industrialism in its first phase was of course England's wealth in the resources that were now to be all-important: coal and iron.

e. The *United States* had the same cultural basis as Europe, and to begin with it possessed less capital per person than England. On the other hand, it had great natural resources, supplying both agriculture and industry, and soon achieved a large per capita production. This first phase in America's progress towards the world's highest income level was thus deeply influenced by *Nature,* partly because this factor offered to entrepreneurs a very good opportunity for their endeavours. The high level of production made possible, in its turn, the creation of the very large *Capital* which has characterized the later phases of America's economic history.

f. The fact that the *USSR* has achieved, over a number of years, a rapid economic growth may have partly resulted from the *USSR* having a natural basis in many respects very like that of *North America.*

g. We might, by analogy, mention also the *Middle East* where the enormous wealth of oil makes possible the creation of *Capital* which can later sustain a more general economic development, but where, however, essential elements of the cultural pattern may be assumed to have a retarding effect. The same applies to several of the countries rich in raw materials which will be particularly in demand in the second half of the twentieth century.

To explain these examples, it must be borne in mind that *Nature* is an *immovable* factor. It has to be exploited where it lies (although raw materials may be carried elsewhere). *Capital,* on the other hand, is fairly easily moved when conditions are calm and stable. The same is true especially of qualified labour which sustains every new forward move. Consequently, the interplay of the factors has often taken the form of a flow of *Capital* and *Labour* towards regions where the natural conditions ensured the highest degree of productivity. The profits derived from the *Capital* have, however, in part at least, returned to owners in the capital exporting countries.

2. *The retarding factors,* which sometimes impede economic growth, are often due to the fact that *Nature* has become impoverished through soil-erosion or the presence of harmful substances in the earth, or because the best raw material resources have been exhausted.

A further, and similar, cause is that the amount of resources per person is reduced through the heavy increase of population. The same circumstance may render it difficult to achieve a larger *Capital* per person, because a relatively large capital formation is required to keep abreast of population. Some of the problems of the densely populated, underdeveloped countries are attributable to these facts.

The retarding factors which it is most difficult to appraise are those deriving directly from economic and cultural development. We have already referred to the tendency to shorten working hours and to reduce, in certain cases, the savings quota. Business cycles are also an offspring of the industrial society; they restrain growth by lowering the degree of exploitation of production factors in the periods of depression—thus retarding *Capital* formation.

There may, possibly, be other retarding factors within the structure of the industrial society[16]. Little, however, is known with regard to the circumstances in which they may appear and the power they are likely to exert. In other words, they constitute an uncertain factor in every long-range economic forecast. On the other hand although they may be decisive in the very long run, they are likely to be of less importance in the period of 25 years considered here.

[16] Cf. for example, Simon Kuznets (1954, pp. 253–74).

CHAPTER III

Population and Labour Force

A. *Prefatory Remarks*

1. The world's population has increased rapidly since the war. According to a report issued by the United Nations the annual growth of population in the period 1950–55 has been estimated at about 1.5 per cent, ranging from 0.7 per cent in *Western Europe* to 2.3 per cent in *Latin America* and 2.4 per cent in the *Middle East*. (See Table III. 1).

At present there is no evidence of any slackening in the rate of increase of population; on the contrary, available population statistics suggest that in the next few years most regions will experience an accelerating increase, so that it does not seem unlikely that a doubling of human numbers will have taken place before the year 2000.

In the event of this twofold increase within the next 40–50 years, serious problems are certain to arise, such as whether the earth can supply food for a population twice as large as at the present time. The answer to this question will undoubtedly be that the earth can feed far more people than twice the present population. However, this answer is not immediately apparent when due regard is taken of the economic and cultural difficulties of applying the most modern techniques everywhere. It would probably not be justifiable to assume that the farming areas of *Asia, Latin America,* and *Africa* will be utilized to the fullest extent technically possible or even to the extent that will have been reached in North West Europe, within the period here considered. The uncertainty prevailing in regard to this problem thus gives rise to another question: is it realistic to imagine that the adoption of measures for the planning of population may, within this relatively short space of time, effectively check the increase of population, in the event of the production of food not being raised at the very fast rate at which population grows?

In the United Nations report referred to on page 61 as the source of Table III. 1 the anticipated annual increase of world population for the next 25 years has been estimated at 1.8 per cent which is tantamount to a twofold total increase in a little under 40 years.

Added to this is the fact that in the years to come, as at present, we shall probably have to reckon with problems of maldistribution of goods which result in the accumulation in certain areas of large surplus stocks of grain,

TABLE III. 1

Population 1955, Increase of Population 1950–55.

	Population in 1955 (Million)	Annual Increase 1950-55 (Per cent)
North America	182	1.6
Western Europe	297	0.7
Oceania	13	2.1
USSR	197	1.7
Eastern Europe	112	1.1
Latin America	183	2.3
Middle East	95	2.4
Asia	1,418	1.5
Africa	193	1.6
Total	2,690	1.5

Source: UN (1958, c).

butter, etc. at the same time as people in other regions go hungry because they do not possess enough purchasing power to import the food stored. In fact, in some countries in economically underdeveloped areas, principally *Asia*, serious food shortages are likely to arise before the end of this century.

2. Available statistics in regard to population are far from sufficient to make possible an exhaustive survey of the present distribution of population according to age or occupation or other relevant criteria. Population statistics are deficient especially as regards *Asia*, the *Middle East*, and *Africa*; hence estimates of future population, no matter how carefully prepared, are, of course, subject to much uncertainty.

On the other hand, our knowledge of population is sufficiently wide for a number of well-founded statements to be made with reference both to the current state of population in the various regions and to the probable main trends during the next 20–25 years. Such a presentation of population statistics is of interest in itself but, also, it is indispensable to an analysis of the problems of economic growth of the various regions of the earth which is the main purpose of the present study.

The size and composition of a country's population is important to the economic development of that country in two ways.

In order to make an estimate of current and future production potentials it is necessary to know the distribution of population according to sex, age, and occupation as the size and composition of the labour force can be deduced from these facts; (the composition as to race may also be of some interest in this context, see pp. 85–103 below). It should be emphasized here that the persons who will constitute the labour force about the year 1980 are, for the most part, already born. It follows, therefore, that a forecast of the size of the labour force can be made provided we consider it justifiable to estimate future trends of mortality rates for the age groups in question[1]. In making forecasts reaching beyond the 20–25 year period it will be necessary to take into account also the anticipated development in fertility, thus considerably increasing the uncertainty in regard to the calculated labour force.

The size and composition of a country's population are also factors that must be taken into account when estimating the development of consumption. Here it is the trend of the population total that is all-important because an increase in population will raise the demand for consumer goods. This growing demand may, in economically developed countries, prove a stimulus to production and consequently to economic growth. If an increase of population, and the resulting growth of the labour force, are to make possible a raising of the standard of living, that is of production per capita, it is, however, necessary that new members of the labour force should achieve an output which exceeds their own consumption and that of their families. This condition may not be fulfilled in underdeveloped countries, where the increase in production consequent on an increase in the labour force will not even suffice to meet the resulting increase in consumption. A growing demand for consumer goods in economically backward countries will thus prove a check to saving and investment or, in other words, to economic growth. These relationships between increase of population and economic

---

[1] On the other hand, it is not easy to predict the development in the number of man-hours worked because in such predictions we must include assumptions regarding trends in the length of working hours in the various regions.

growth will be dealt with in greater detail in Chapter VII, but even the points considered here so far clearly indicate the very close connection that exists between population and economic development.

B. *The Current State of Population*

1. In 1955 world population amounted to about 2,700 million. We do not know the exact figure—in some countries of *Africa* and *Asia* censuses have never been taken and in other countries census results are of very doubtful reliability. According to a United Nations estimate, however, it would seem justifiable to assume that the true figure of world population lies between 2,600 and 2,800 million; and in view of the fact that the estimated annual increase of population amounts to a little below 50 million, the uncertainty with regard to the population total appears to be unimportant.

2. The distribution of the 2,700 million people over the nine regions is very uneven, (cf. Table III. 1). More than one-half of them live in *Asia* (53 per cent), while *Oceania* and the *Middle East* account for only 0.5 per cent and 3 per cent respectively. *North America*, the *USSR*, *Latin America*, and *Africa* each accounts for about 7 per cent, and *Western Europe* and *Eastern Europe* for 11 and 4 per cent respectively.

In considering possibilities of economic growth, the distribution of population over the nine regions compared with their resources will of course be of great interest. It is, unfortunately, impossible to find an all-inclusive measure of a region's resources, partly because our knowledge of several of the regions is very incomplete, and partly because such a measure will depend, among other things, on the technical, economic, and institutional possibilities of exploiting resources at a certain time in a certain region. However, even a comparison of the regions according to *density of population,* that is according to the number of persons per square kilometre, imperfect though it may be for many individual countries, will give an impression of how large the differences in resources per person actually are, cf. Table III. 2.

While in *North America, Oceania,* the *USSR, Latin America,* and *Africa* there are less than 10 persons per square kilometre, the figure for *Asia* is 66, and for *Eastern* and *Western Europe* more than 80. This difference between a group of densely populated areas on the one hand and a group of sparsely populated areas on the other stands out very clearly, also, when we consider only the number of persons per square kilometre of productive land[2] in the nine regions, or the number of persons per square kilometre of *Standard Farm Land*[3]. Especially with regard to the regions in which agricul-

TABLE III. 2

Area and Population.

	Total Area (1000 km²)	Number of Persons per km² 1955	Productive Area (1000 km²)	Number of Persons per km² of Productive Area 1955	S.F.L. (1000 km²)	Number of Persons per km² of S.F.L. 1955
North America .	21,483	8.5	7.300	24.9	10,059	18.1
Western Europe .	3,656	81.2	2,380	124.8	2,908	102.1
Oceania	8,317	1.6	4,190	3.1	1,800	7.2
USSR	22,403	8.8	5,710	34.5	11,089	17.8
Eastern Europe .	1,273	88.0	1,070	104.7	1,124	99.6
Latin America .	20,502	8.9	5,750	31.8	18,346	10.0
Middle East	6,589	14.4	2,680	35.4	1,914	49.6
Asia	21,734	65.2	9,380	151.2	15,271	92.9
Africa	29,132	6.6	10,460	18.5	14,291	13.5
Total	135,089	19.9	48,920	55.0	76,802	35.0

Sources: UN *Demographic Yearbook* 1957, FAO *Yearbook of Agricultural Statistics, Production* (1958) and Colin Clark (1957).

ture is dominant, in *Latin America, Asia,* and *Africa,* a comparison between population and farming area will provide a fairly reliable measure of the relative resources of each region. It will also provide, to a certain extent, an impression of the current conditions of growth in the region, as these are determined, in large measure, by the productive and saving capacity resulting from the prevailing occupational distribution. In relation both to the total area and to the two above-mentioned measures, *Asia* is the worst off of the economically backward regions. At the same time *Asia,* as is well-known, is also short of other natural resources besides farm land; (see Chapter V).

[2] i.e. utilised farm land, pasture, and forest, cf. Table III. 9.
[3] 1 *S.F.L.* = 1 km² of medium-grade farm land in humid subtropical and temperate climates, cfr. Table III. 2.

3. The distribution of a population by age groups is a result of the birth and mortality rates and of migration. Conversely, the prevailing distribution by age groups determines the future birth and mortality rates. To take an example, a population in which the number of women of child bearing age

TABLE III.3

Distribution by Age Groups, 1955.

		0-15 Years	15-64 Years	65 Years and over	Total
North America	Million	52.2	113.6	16.2	182
	Per cent ...	28.7	62.4	8.9	100.0
Western Europe	Million	75.4	193.7	27.9	297
	Per cent ...	25.4	65.2	9.4	100.0
Oceania	Million	3.7	8.1	1.2	13
	Per cent ...	28.7	62.4	8.9	100.0
USSR	Million	62.5	123.9	10.6	197
	Per cent ...	31.7	62.9	5.4	100.0
Eastern Europe	Million	28.5	73.0	10.5	112
	Per cent ...	25.4	65.2	9.4	100.0
Latin America	Million	74.1	102.3	6.6	183
	Per cent ...	40.5	55.9	3.6	100.0
Middle East	Million	38.7	53.9	2.4	95
	Per cent ...	40.8	56.7	2.5	100.0
Asia	Million	570.0	809.7	38.3	1,418
	Per cent ...	40.2	57.1	2.7	100.0
Africa	Million	79.1	109.1	4.8	193
	Per cent ...	41.0	56.5	2.5	100.0
Total	Million	984.2	1,587.3	118.5	2,690
	Per cent ...	36.0	59.0	4.4	100.0

Sourse : UN (1958, c).

is relatively high will, *ceteris paribus,* have a higher *birth-rate,* i.e. number of births per period compared to the total population, than a population which has a relatively small number of women in this age group.

Further, the distribution by age groups has a decisive influence on the number of persons who will be able to take an active part in production and, thus, also on the proportion of the population that is to be supported by them.

These are facts of great importance in any analysis of the prevailing conditions of economic growth.

Adequate information with regard to distribution by age groups is available only for *North America, Oceania,* and *Western Europe.* As to the other regions, more or less accurate estimates can be made on the basis of information from some countries within the regions. In Table III. 3 above is shown the distribution over three age groups: 0–14, 15–64 and 65 years and over in all the regions on the basis of the above-mentioned United Nations report (1958, c). While the figures for *North America, Western Europe,* and *Oceania* may be considered fairly accurate, the figures for the *Middle East, Asia,* and *Africa* have a large margin of error. As to the figures for the *USSR, Eastern Europe,* and *Latin America* they seem to be more accurate than those relating to the latter group of regions, but less accurate than those of the former. It should be stressed that the figures for the regions in the Table cover a wide range of variations within each region.

It is apparent from the Table that a very clearly defined boundary-line separates two groups of regions. In the group which includes *North America, Western Europe, Oceania,* the *USSR,* and *Eastern Europe,* the children, that is to say the 0–14 year olds, make up 25–30 per cent of the population and the age groups above 65 years make up about 9 per cent (in the *USSR,* however, only about 5.5 per cent), while the children in the regions of *Latin America,* the *Middle East, Asia,* and *Africa* represent more than 40 per cent of the total population and the old people of over 65 years of age only from 2.5 to 3.6 per cent.

The productive age groups, i.e. those from 15–64 years old, do not show similarly wide variations. They make up from 62.4 per cent to 65.2 per cent in the five first-mentioned regions and from 55.9 per cent to 57.1 per cent in the four last-mentioned.

It may, however, be questioned whether this grouping according to age indicates precisely the distribution of the economically active persons of the regions as opposed to the persons whom the community has to support as is suggested by the use of the term "productive age groups" for the group from 15 to 64 years of age.

It is a well-established fact that young people are incorporated in the labour force at an earlier age in the economically backward regions than they are in those that are more developed and where increasingly complicated production techniques call for ever longer training courses. If this fact is taken into account it will be seen that the ratio of the number of economically active persons to the number of those they have to support may well be the same in the two groups of regions mentioned, cf. Table III. 4 below.

As regards the 0–14 years old, the great difference between the two groups of regions will, however, be most important to the future trend of mortality, and particularly perhaps to birth-rates and thus to the rate of population growth in the two groups of regions. With fertility remaining unchanged and with falling mortality (which appears to be the most likely trend in the next few years in most underdeveloped countries), there will occur a bulge in the annual number of births in the four regions *Latin America,* the *Middle East, Asia,* and *Africa* when the 0–14 years age group reaches child-bearing age in 10 to 15 years' time. This will be discussed in more detail in section C, which deals with the expected future development in population.

The figures in Table III. 3 do not, however, as has already been mentioned, throw much light on the question of the size of the labour force as there are considerable differences between the regions in regard to the employment of both young and old people. Also, as is well-known, the extent to which women take part in production is not the same in all of the nine regions.

In Table III. 4 below is shown the proportion of the total population which is economically active. The Table also shows, for each sex separately, how many persons in each age group are economically active.

The Table has been prepared on the basis of information in the Yearbook of Labour Statistics for 1958. For the *USSR* no information is available. With regard to the other regions, apart from the last three in the Table, the figures cover practically the entire population. As regards the *Middle East, Asia,* and *Africa,* however, the figures cover only about one-half (or perhaps a little more) of the total population. It should be emphasized that the reliability of the figures does not depend solely on how large a proportion of the population they include but also on the fact that it is very difficult to make a fairly accurate estimate of the number of *economically active persons* in a country.

The definition used by ILO is: "The total of employed persons (including employers, persons working on their own account, salaried employees and wage earners and, so far as data are available, unpaid family workers) and of persons unemployed at the time of the census. The economically

5*

active population does not include students, women occupied solely in domestic duties, retired persons, persons living entirely on their own means, and persons wholly dependent upon others"[4].

However, it is very difficult to apply this definition particularly with regard to the under-developed countries. The size of the group of unpaid

TABLE III.4

Economically Active Men and Women in the Various Age Groups as Per cent of Total Population in the Same Groups.

	Men				Women				Men and Women
	15-19	20-64	65-	All Age Groups	15-19	20-64	65-	All Age Groups	All Age Groups
N. America	49.2	93.3	36.3	57.0	30.9	39.4	9.7	24.9	40.8
W. Europe	73.3	93.7	39.8	63.8	51.8	33.0	8.3	24.5	44.6
Oceania	75.6	95.7	31.5	61.5	65.2	25.6	4.7	19.0	40.3
E. Europe	56.7	94.3	60.9	60.8	58.1	59.9	24.4	42.0	49.7
Lat. America	76.1	95.2	75.2	56.7	26.8	23.1	12.7	15.0	35.6
Middle East	82.8	95.7	82.6	64.7	42.5	41.7	31.0	30.9	40.5
Asia	56.2	92.6	51.3	54.4	46.8	52.4	19.2	32.9	39.3
Africa	66.4	94.1	72.6	61.3	27.1	31.4	18.8	19.3	44.5
Total	65.3	93.8	51.9	59.5	41.6	37.8	13.8	25.5	41.1

Source: ILO (1958).

family workers, for example, is hard to estimate with any degree of certainty. This group is encountered mainly in the backward regions and is represented by women of all age groups and by 15–19 year old men.

Certain trends, however, may be discerned from the Table:

a. In all regions about 94 per cent of all men in the 20–64 years age group belong to the economically active part of the population. This proportion varies but little from region to region (from 92.6 per cent in *Asia* to 95.7 per cent in the *Middle East* and *Oceania*).

b. In the developed regions, in which special measures for the support of the aged are often taken, only one-third of the men and less than one-

---

[4] ILO (1958, p. 2).

tenth of the women of over 65 years of age belong to the economically active population (excepting *Eastern Europe,* where 61 and 24 per cent respectively of the men and women in this age group are members of the labour force). In the less developed regions, on the other hand, a considerably larger proportion of old people belong to the labour force. (It might be added here that in the last-mentioned regions only a very small part of the population is included in the group of persons of over 65 years of age).

c. There seems to be a tendency for that part of the 15–19 years old group, who on account of studies or other forms of training or education are not included in the labour force, to increase *pari passu* with the development of the regions. However, the information available on this point is somewhat confused by the uncertainty prevailing with regard to the group of family workers, as the 15–19 year olds often, in the backward regions, belong to this group.

d. In the three most developed regions, *North America, Western Europe* and *Oceania,* a little less than 25 per cent of the women are included in the economically active population, but there are marked differences between the three regions with regard to the distribution by age groups of the economically active women. In *Western Europe,* and to an even greater extent in *Oceania,* it is the very young women especially who participate in production, whilst those slightly older (after marrying) do not. In the United States, on the other hand, the reverse is the case. The very young, on account of being trained in one way or another, are not members of the labour force. On the other hand, a larger proportion of the slightly older (married) women are in the labour force.

e. In *Eastern Europe,* and probably also in the *USSR,* a comparatively high percentage of the women are economically active.

f. In *Latin America* only very few women belong to the labour force. Available information concerning the remaining underdeveloped regions does not allow of any reliable evaluation of women's contribution to the labour force. Here again uncertainty with regard to the classification of the unpaid family workers makes itself felt. It appears, however, that a great many more women in the other underdeveloped regions take an active part in work outside their homes than is the case in *Latin America.*

4. It is evident that the composition of the labour force as regards occupation has its own significance in much the same way as has the size of the

labour force. The industrialization of a community causes many difficulties and problems. One of these problems is the scarcity of industrial workers. In a community in which, for example, 80 per cent of the total population earn their living by primary production (i.e. either by agriculture or fishing) the creation of a class of industrial workers takes a long time. First of all, the workers have to acquire technical skill and also, to a very high degree, accustom themselves to new working and housing conditions. The drastic change from the village community to the industrial quarters of a large city may prove extremely difficult especially to people living in the economically underdeveloped regions in which village communities are still often completely isolated.

While variations from region to region in the ratio of the labour force to the total population were found to be moderate, the distribution according to occupation proved to vary greatly although the available information, it is true, is very slight. For many of the countries in the underdeveloped regions we have virtually no statistics of the distribution by occupational groups, and the reliability of such figures as are available is not very great. On the other hand, the countries for which such statistical material has been obtained show marked deviations from the state of things in the advanced regions.

In Table III. 5 are shown, for certain countries, per cent figures for three main occupation groups, primary occupations (agriculture and fishing), secondary occupations (industry, crafts, mining), and tertiary occupations (trade, administration, professions, etc.).

While in the industrial countries of *North America, Western Europe,* and *Oceania* the primary occupations include from 5 to 20 per cent of the populations only, the corresponding percentage for a number of countries in *Asia* and *Africa* is as much as between 70 and 80. Further the Table shows, as might be expected, that there are very wide variations in the distribution of occupation groups from country to country within each region. In *Western Europe* only 5 per cent of the population of Great Britain are in primary occupations, whereas for Italy the figure is 42, and for Spain 49. In *Eastern Europe* the percentages for primary occupations are 29 for East Germany and 67 for Yugoslavia. In *Latin America* the percentage are 25 for Argentina and 72 for Bolivia.

5. In Table III. 6 are shown average birth- and death-rates, according to United Nations estimates, for the various regions. The *natural rate of*

TABLE III.5

Distribution of Economically Active Persons in Main Occupational Groups, about 1950.

(Per cent)

	Year	Primary Occupations	Secondary Occupations	Tertiary Occupations	Occupations Unknown
North America					
Canada	1951	19.0	34.3	45.2	1.5
United States	1950	12.2	34.7	50.4	2.7
Western Europe					
Belgium	1947	12.1	48.8	36.3	2.8
France	1954	26.6	34.4	36.0	3.0
Holland	1947	19.3	32.3	45.8	2.6
Italy	1951	42.2	31.6	26.2	–
Spain	1950	48.8	24.6	25.0	1.6
Sweden	1950	20.4	39.7	39.2	0.7
United Kingdom	1951	4.9	47.5	47.2	0.4
West Germany	1950	23.2	41.6	33.1	2.1
Oceania					
Australia	1947	15.6	35.2	42.0	7.2
Eastern Europe					
Czechoslovakia	1947	37.7	37.3	24.6	0.4
East Germany	1946	29.2	41.2	29.6	–
Hungary	1949	52.9	23.2	17.4	6.5
Yugoslavia	1953	66.8	15.4	6.0	11.8
Latin America					
Argentina	1947	25.2	27.9	41.1	5.8
Bolivia	1950	71.6	13.2	13.9	1.3
Brazil	1950	57.8	15.9	26.1	0.2
Chile	1952	30.1	28.4	38.0	3.5
Haiti	1950	83.2	5.5	8.5	2.8
Mexico	1950	57.8	15.5	21.6	5.1
Peru	1940	62.5	19.0	18.5	–
Venezuela	1950	41.3	18.1	32.2	8.4
Middle East					
Egypt	1947	53.6	5.5	29.8	11.1
Asia					
Ceylon	1946	52.9	10.3	26.1	10.7
India	1951	70.6	10.7	18.7	–
Japan	1950	48.4	21.4	30.0	0.2
Malaya	1947	64.9	10.6	24.3	0.2
Pakistan	1951	76.5	7.3	12.5	3.7
Philippines	1948	65.7	8.2	17.1	9.0
Thailand	1947	84.8	2.3	11.7	1.2
Africa					
Algeria	1948	80.8	6.4	10.7	2.1
Mozambique	1950	75.4	5.9	18.7	–
Union of South Africa	1946	46.9	20.2	28.1	4.8

Source: UN *Demographic Yearbook 1956.*

growth, i.e. the difference between birth-rate and death-rate, is also shown. The *Middle East* and *Asia* have here been considered as one region, as also have *Western* and *Eastern Europe.*

In making forecasts concerning the population of a country, knowledge of the fertility and mortality pattern is essential. Although a knowledge of

TABLE III.6

Annual Birth-rate, Death-rate, and Natural Increase, 1951–55.
(Per Thousand Persons)

	Birth-rate	Death-rate	Natural Increase
North America	25	9	16
Oceania	25	8	17
Europe	20	11	9
USSR	26	9	17
Latin America	40	19	21
Asia	46	33	13
Africa	47	33	14

Note : The figures for *Latin America, Asia,* and *Africa* are very uncertain estimates prepared by the United Nations. The figures for the other regions are based on available
population statistics.
Source : UN (1958, c).

the current birth- and death-rates does not provide a sufficient basis for a population forecast, it gives some indications of the probable development of population in the next few years.

Table III. 6 provides a kind of explanation of the dividing line we noticed between two groups of regions with regard to distribution by age groups (page 66). The same dividing line, it appears, is applicable to birth- and death-rates. While the five economically developed regions have a birth-rate of 20–25 per thousand and a death-rate of about 10 per thousand, and thus an annual growth of population of 9–17 per thousand (neglecting migra-tions), the birth-rate for the economically backward regions is 40–47 per thousand, the death-rate from 19 in *Latin America* to over 30 in the other regions, and the natural increase 13–14 per thousand in *Africa* and *Asia* and 21 per thousand in *Latin America.* Again there are wide variations within each region especially as far as *Europe* and *Latin America* are concerned. Thus in *Europe* the birth-rates vary from 15 to 30 per thousand (United Kingdom, West Germany about 15, Spain and Czechoslovakia about 20, Poland and Yugoslavia about 30) and the death-rates from 7 to 12 per thousand. In *Latin America* the birth-rate is as small as 20 per thousand in some countries in the temperate zone (Chile, Argentina), whereas certain other countries in that region have a birth-rate of more than 45 per thousand. Also in the other regions, however, there are a few countries which deviate markedly in this respect from the average of the region. Among the larger nations there is particular reason to mention Japan, where the birth-rate is now less than 20 per thousand and the death-rate less than 10 per thousand against the regional average for *Asia* of 46 and 33 per thousand respectively.

6. In very large parts of the world birth-rates have been at the present level as far back as information on the subject is available. This applies to nearly all the countries in the so-called backward areas, viz., *Africa, Asia,* the *Middle East,* and to a certain extent *Latin America* (Central America and the northern part of South America). Experience with regard to countries in which birth-rates have undergone major changes would seem to suggest that profound social and economic changes are necessary if the level of the birth-rates is to be disturbed.

In *North America, Western Europe,* and *Oceania* the fall in the birth-rate began as early as about the turn of the century, whereas Eastern and Southern Europe, the southern part of *Latin America,* the *USSR,* and Japan did not experience a similar fall until the inter-war era. Indeed, in the case of Japan and to a certain extent also the *USSR* the change only became apparent towards the end of the nineteen-thirties.

7. The mortality rate has proved to be more susceptible to change. Since 1945 death-rates in nearly all backward countries, with the main exception of certain areas of *Africa,* have been falling rapidly. The adoption of new remedies to combat and prevent disease has made it possible to achieve, through fairly moderate economic efforts, a considerable reduction in death-rates. In some countries, e.g. Ceylon and Formosa, the death-rate has been reduced by one half in the post-war period, and in many other countries it has been lowered by more than 25 per cent. Consequently there are to-day populations which experience an annual increase of over 30 per thousand. In the foreseeable future this may be the case with other populations too.

8. As appears from the following section, which deals with future population development, such information as is available to-day suggests that the natural rate of growth in the next 25 years will be rising in *Latin America* and *Asia* and will remain at its present high level in the *Middle East* and *Africa*. This quite naturally raises the question of whether population policies will be introduced for the purpose of lowering the birth-rate. For the fact that the resources of these regions are often very slender makes it seem rather hazardous simply to await a more or less automatic adjustment of the birth-rate which, it appears, occurs only at a rather late stage of economic development.

An analysis of the current situation in the backward regions shows that, except in a few countries, there is no very strong inclination to take measures for population adjustment. Results achieved through such measures, therefore, can only be judged to a limited extent. Among the larger nations only Japan has so far achieved any notable results in this field—but these results are striking. In a little over 10 years the Japanese birth-rate has been halved. It should, however, be stressed that we cannot infer from this that similar results can be achieved everywhere. On the contrary, Japan is probably exceptional among the nations faced with serious population problems in that the Japanese can read and write and are accustomed to interference on the part of the state authorities in their daily life.

The political leaders of *India* are in favour of introducing a population policy which will reduce the growth rate of the Indian population. They think it necessary, however, to await the evidence of a very thorough enquiry into the suitability of such a policy under given social and cultural conditions before deciding how this step should be taken[5].

In *China* certain measures in the direction of a population policy, or rather, a family policy were introduced a few years ago. The main purpose of these measures was, officially, to give the women a freer choice between either looking after their children or taking an active part in economic life, but in reality they constituted a programme for birth control. It is too early to evaluate the effect of them; the more so as the official attitude towards the population problem in recent years seems to have been marked by uncertainty. It appears, however, that the measures already taken have been fairly widespread throughout the country[6].

[5] See Gopalaswami (1953, Vol. I, pp. 207–226).
[6] Cf. Sauvy (1957) and Pressat (1958).

9. An undesirably heavy population increase in a single country may, of course, theoretically be countered by a policy of encouraging emigration.

TABLE III.7

Immigration into Some Typical Immigration Countries, 1955.

From	To	Canada	United States	West Germany	Australia and New Zealand
North America		11,497	110,093	276	4,368
Western Europe ...		89,966	129,654	3,339	127,161
Oceania		1,700	1,232	29	9,589
Eastern Europe ...		724	1,219	187,873	1,294
South America		1,654	8,494	595	99
Asia		3,724	13,092	57	6,704
Africa		548	1,112	49	2,250
Total		109,813	264,896	192,218	151,465

From	To	Argentina	Israel	Belg. Congo, Kenya Rhodesia and Nyasaland Union of South Africa
North America		115	308	1,046
Western Europe ...		46,468	529	49,470
Oceania		8	16	266
Eastern Europe ...		888	967	74
South America		3,298	617	111
Asia		1,942	1,207	6,116
Africa		64	32,553	16,642
Total		52,783	36,197	73,725

Source: UN *Demographic Yearbook* 1958.

Such a policy, however, is scarcely practicable to-day in the same way as it was in the second half of the nineteenth century when *Western Europe* experienced a great increase in its population.

Even if it were possible to induce the surplus population of the most densely populated areas to leave their homes (and this is very doubtful; see below), there are no "New Worlds" to-day in which room could be found for these emigrants. Added to this is the fact that in the countries which might conceivable accept immigrants in large numbers (such as those of *North America, Oceania*, the *USSR*, and certain parts of *Latin America* and *Africa*) there is scarcely any political possibility of the frontiers being opened to immigrants from countries with a lower educational standard. Finally it should be mentioned that many instances may be quoted to show that migrations from densely to sparsely populated areas may fail to take place even if these migrations do not involve crossing any frontiers. On balance we may therefore conclude that migration is not a means of solving the population problem of a whole region. In Table III. 7 is shown the extent of real immigrations into a few countries that are typical receivers of immigrants. The statistical material on the subject does not permit us to prepare a table showing all migrations between the nine regions. The present Table reveals the fact, however, that, in view of the relatively small number of people involved, migration is a factor of little significance in relation to the population problem as a whole. The Table also shows that emigrations nearly always start from economically highly developed regions. (It goes without saying that the migrations actually taking place are important in many other respects, e.g. politically, socially, etc.).

C. *The Development of Population 1955–1980*

1. As a rule enquiries into future trends in economic growth are prefaced by some form of estimate of the future development of population, it being assumed that such estimates will be more reliable than those of development in other spheres.

The present book is no exception to this rule. It should, however, be emphasized that even a population estimate can be little more than a rough approximation. This is due to the uncertainty prevailing with regard, on the one hand, to the current structure of population which is made the starting point of the whole undertaking and, on the other, in regard to the birth- and death-rate assumptions. The latter element of uncertainty will of course increase with the length of the period under consideration. Further it should be noted that the assumed birth- and death-rates will depend on the trends in social, political, and cultural development—a fact which increases the difficulty of the task.

However, by selecting a period of moderate length many obstacles may be overcome. Experience seems to show that birth- and death-rates are very slow to change. It has often been maintained that it takes at least one generation for any radical change in a nation's birth-rate to take place. Consequently, for the period of 25 years at present under consideration no great problems of calculation should arise. On the other hand, it may be claimed that the theory of the slowness of changes in birth- and death-rates is based upon conditions in an age when broadcasting, films, aeroplanes, and other means of communication, in the widest sense, were not yet commonly used. To-day, tendencies towards declining birth-rates, for example, are far more likely to spread rapidly, especially if policies are launched for limiting the population in this way.

2. Economic development in the post-war era has nearly everywhere been characterized by more or less extensive planning projects of varying success usually covering periods of five years or more. Hence, since the war, far more effort has been devoted to preparing estimates of future population, national as well as international, than before. The Department of Economic and Social Affairs of the United Nations has done much work in this field and the statistical material here presented concerning the anticipated development of population in the various regions till the year 1980 is based almost exclusively on reports issued by the United Nations[7]. In some cases forecasts for a particular country, prepared by that country's own population statisticians, are more accurate than those of the United Nations because they are based on wider knowledge of the special conditions existing in the country. The present study uses the United Nations' figures, however, because they have the advantage that estimates of future population for the various regions may better be compared with one another.

The above-mentioned United Nations report contains a number of forecasts of the development of population in each continent reaching as far ahead as the year 2000. For each region estimates have been prepared according to maximum, minimum, and medium assumptions. The difference between the three assumptions becomes apparent in the various hypotheses with regard to the development of birth and death rates. Estimates on the basis of medium assumptions have been used in the following text.

The method employed by the United Nations in calculating such population estimates has to be briefly described. On the basis of available population statistics the earth has been divided into 19 areas. Thus, countries

---

[7] Especially the report previously referred to, UN (1958, c).

included in the same area have common demographical features. Following a careful study of the growth of population in those regions[8] various *models* demonstrating the growth of population have been prepared. The models are characterized by certain figures for gross *reproduction rate* (i.e. the total

TABLE III.8

The Development of Population 1955–80. Population Figures (in Millions).

	1955	1970	1980	U.N. Report 1980	2000	Annual Increase (Per cent)		
						1955 -70	1970 -80	1980 -2000
North America	182	238	280	254	375	1.8	1.6	1.5
Western Europe ...	297	320	343	352	390	0.5	0.7	0.6
Oceania	13	17	20	20	27	1.8	1.6	1.5
USSR	197	247	286	297	360	1.5	1.5	1.2
Eastern Europe	112	132	143	143	170	1.1	0.8	0.9
Latin America	183	275	365	348	600	2.7	2.9	2.5
Middle East	95	134	169	173	275	2.3	2.3	2.5
Asia	1,418	1,866	2,326	2,342	3,650	1.8	2.2	2.3
Africa	193	244	289	290	450	1.6	1.7	2.2
Total	2,690	3,473	4,221	4,219	6,297	1.7	2.0	2.0

Source: UN (1958, c).

number of girls that 1000 women will bring into the world assuming a certain fertility) and for the *average expectation of life* of a new-born child (the average duration of life of a new-born child at given death-rates in the various age groups) and by a certain annual growth (positive or negative) in these figures. The method of choosing a model of development for a given area consists in finding other regions which have previously shown the same demographical features as that area. The characteristic features of the development of population in the "model region" are then used as a guide in estimating the future development of population of the area considered.

3. In Table III.8 is shown the development in population in the nine regions from 1955 to 1980 and as far ahead as to 2000, as they appear in

[8] See UN (1953,b).

the above-mentioned United Nations report. In the case of some of the regions minor corrections have been made. These corrections are based partly on the comments of the United Nations report on the figures calculated (migrations, for example, have not been taken into account) and partly on a general evaluation of the figures contained in the report in the light of national forecasts. As regards *North America* the series of population projections released by the Bureau of the Census on November 10, 1958 has been used as a major source. The uncorrected figures of the United Nations report, however, are also stated for comparison in the Table.

It appears that for the population of the earth as a whole an increase of about 1,500 million is anticipated in the period 1955–80, which means an annual rate of growth of 1.8 per cent. For the period 1980–2000 an increase of another 2,000 million, corresponding to an annual rate of increase of 2 per cent is estimated. With regard especially to the last-mentioned period, however, the estimates are of doubtful reliability. In the period 1950 –55 the annual rate of increase was 1.5 per cent. In the two preceding periods of 25 years, 1900–25 and 1925–50, the annual rates of increase were "only" 0.8 per cent and 1.1 per cent respectively.

For the whole of the period 1955–80 the annual increase is, as stated above, expected to amount to 1.8 per cent, if estimated according to the medium assumption. If this period is subdivided into two periods, 1955–70 and 1970–80, the annual increase during the first sub-period will be 1.7 per cent and during the second 2.0 per cent, or the same as the anticipated rate of increase for the period 1980–2000. The acceleration of growth experienced since the beginning of this century is thus expected to continue in the period under consideration.

The figures in this Table have, as already stated, been calculated on the basis of the estimate according to the medium assumption of the United Nations report. The estimate according to the maximum assumption of the report is only 2 per cent higher than the medium estimate, while the minimum estimate is about 10 per cent lower. The difference between the minimum estimate and the medium estimate is usually accounted for by the assumption that birth-rates in the densely populated countries of *Asia* have already started to fall now rather than in 1975 as envisaged in the medium estimate.

A closer examination of the forecasts for the nine regions shows that the population increase of 1,500 million will fall very unevenly on the various regions. While the increase in *Western Europe* during the period of 25 years is estimated at about 15 per cent and in *Eastern Europe* at about 28 per cent, the increase in *North America,* the *USSR, Africa,* and *Oceania* is estimated at about 50 per cent and in *Asia* and the *Middle East* at 64 per cent and 78 per cent respectively. At the top of the list is *Latin America* with an estimated increase of 100 per cent.

The assumptions with regard to the trends in birth-rates and death-rates on which these calculations are based have to be briefly described. For *North America, Oceania, Western* and *Eastern Europe,* and the *USSR* a continued slight fall in the death-rate and unchanged fertility are anticipated. For these five regions the difference between maximum and minimum estimates is very slight and the trend in the rate of increase for them will, it is assumed, be close to the medium estimate here stated.

As regards the other regions there is a wider range of possible variations and there is probably a correspondingly greater likelihood that the medium estimate will prove to be wrong.

As for *Latin America,* the *Middle East,* and *Asia* it is the anticipated trend in birth-rates, especially, that is uncertain. Will the current high birth-rates remain unchanged, and if not, when may a decrease be expected to commence?

The medium estimate is based on the assumption that the birth-rate will remain unchanged until 1975 and then decrease slightly. The maximum estimate assumes that the current high birth-rate will remain constant till the end of the period; the minimum estimate that it will decrease all through the period.

As no country in these regions (except Japan) has, so far, consistently taken measures for birth-control, the authors of the United Nations report are probably right in maintaining that there is little chance that the assumptions of the minimum estimate will, in fact, eventuate. On the other hand it might be held that in certain countries there is a real chance that a decline in the birth-rate may occur before 1975. The assumptions of the maximum estimate, however, can by no means be rejected as unrealistic.

The authors of the United Nations report are of the opinion that there is every likelihood that the decrease in mortality which has already begun in *Latin America,* the *Middle East,* and *Asia,* will continue at an even rate throughout the period. In view of what is said later, in Chapters IV, V, and VI of this book, this assumption may, however, be questioned. In the event, mentioned at the beginning of this Chapter, of acute food shortage in the countries where the pressure of population is heaviest—and this is a very real danger—starvation will raise mortality and bring about a tragic situation in which people may be relieved of the most common epidemic diseases only to be faced with famine.

As far as *Africa* is concerned all three estimates assume that the birth-rate will remain constant; mortality is, however, considered to be less predictable here than anywhere else. In the medium estimate the present high death-rate is assumed to remain unchanged until 1975 and then to fall. The maximum estimate assumes a falling death-rate and the minimum estimate an unchanged death-rate throughout the period.

If the medium estimate for the nine regions is accepted (with minor corrections), the distribution by age groups shown in Table III. 9 (below) will result. (It should be noted, however, that *Eastern* and *Western Europe* are included in the same population model. Consequently in the Table the two regions have the same distribution by age groups. In reality there is a certain difference between the two regions especially with regard to persons of over 65 years of age, of whom *Eastern Europe* has rather fewer and *Western Europe* rather more than shown in the Table).

Apart from the fact that persons of over 65 years of age will form a growing proportion of the population of all regions and especially of those that are economically developed there will only be very small fluctuations in the three age groups within the period. The productive age groups (15–64 years of age) of the nine regions will grow at much the same rate as the population generally, but it is doubtful whether or not the number of economically active persons will grow proportionately. This will depend partly on the number of women doing non-domestic work and partly on the future status in the labour market of elderly and very young people. We may perhaps say that in the event of the total demand for labour rising steeply there will be a reserve which may be utilized as required, while, on the other hand, a less pronounced increase in the demand for labour will not necessarily cause these population groups to be registered as unemployed.

In order to provide a simple quantitative measure of *Labour* as a factor of production to-day and in the time up to 1980 we may use the number of man-hours worked by the economically active population of the nine regions in one year.

It should, however, be emphasized that this measure of the amount of

TABLE III.9

The Distribution by Age Groups, 1955, 1970, and 1980.

		Under 15 Years			15-64 years		
		1955	1970	1980	1955	1970	1980
North America	Million	52.2	66.7	83.3	113.6	145.9	165.7
	Per cent	28.7	28.0	29.7	62.4	61.3	59.2
Western Europe	Million	75.4	75.5	82.7	193.7	206.1	214.4
	Per cent	25.4	23.6	24.1	65.2	64.4	62.5
Oceania	Million	3.7	4.6	5.7	8.1	10.6	12.0
	Per cent	28.7	27.1	28.4	62.4	62.1	60.2
USSR	Million	62.5	74.9	84.4	123.9	154.6	178.5
	Per cent	31.7	30.3	29.5	62.9	62.6	62.4
Eastern Europe	Million	28.5	31.2	34.5	73.0	85.0	89.4
	Per cent	25.4	23.6	24.1	65.2	64.4	62.5
Latin America	Million	74.1	113.9	153.7	102.3	150.1	196.4
	Per cent	40.5	41.4	42.1	55.9	54.6	53.8
Middle East	Million	38.7	56.3	71.3	53.9	74.1	92.6
	Per cent	40.8	42.0	42.2	56.7	55.3	54.8
Asia	Million	570.0	766.9	963.0	809.7	1,043.1	1,286.3
	Per cent	40.2	41.1	41.4	57.1	55.9	55.3
Africa	Million	79.1	100.8	120.2	109.1	136.9	161.0
	Per cent	41.0	41.3	41.6	56.5	56.1	55.7
Total	Million	984.2	1,290.8	1,598.8	1,587.3	2,006.4	2,396.3
	Per cent	36.6	37.1	37.9	59.0	57.8	56.8

		65 Years and over			Total		
		1955	1970	1980	1955	1970	1980
North America	Million	16.2	25.4	31.0	182	238	280
	Per cent	8.9	10.7	11.1	100	100	100
Western Europe	Million	27.9	38.4	45.9	297	320	343
	Per cent	9.4	12.0	13.4	100	100	100
Oceania	Million	1.2	1.8	2.3	13	17	20
	Per cent	8.9	10.8	11.4	100	100	100
USSR	Million	10.6	17.5	23.1	197	247	286
	Per cent	5.4	7.1	8.1	100	100	100
Eastern Europe	Million	10.5	15.8	19.1	112	132	143
	Per cent	9.4	12.0	13.4	100	100	100
Latin America	Million	6.6	11.0	14.9	183	275	365
	Per cent	3.6	4.0	4.1	100	100	100
Middle East	Million	2.4	3.6	5.1	95	134	169
	Per cent	2.5	2.7	3.0	100	100	100
Asia	Million	38.3	56.0	76.7	1,418	1,866	2,326
	Per cent	2.7	3.0	3.3	100	100	100
Africa	Million	4.8	6.3	7.8	193	244	289
	Per cent	2.5	2.6	2.7	100	100	100
Total	Million	118.5	175.8	225.9	2,690	3,473	4,221
	Per cent	4.4	5.1	5.3	100	100	100

Source: UN (1958, c).

Labour is subject to certain serious defefects. Most important among these is the fact that the man-hours worked are not comparable either within a single country or a single region, nor, especially, between regions. It is evident, for example, that the yield per hour of an American car factory worker cannot be compared with that of an Asiatic agricultural labourer. Further problems arise in connection with overt or hidden unemployment. Are the "hours of work" of wholly or partially unemployed workers to be included or not? In the calculations below they have been included, but it is obvious that objections to this procedure may, with some justification, be raised.

Subject to these reservations, the following survey has been prepared of the number of man-hours worked in 1955, cf. Table III. 10. Maximum and minimum estimates of the total number of man-hours that will be worked in 1980 have also been made. The figures for 1955 are based on the ILO Yearbook of Labour Statistics 1958, cf. Table III. 4. The information provided by the yearbook with regard to the economically underdeveloped regions, however, is very slight and the figures given are to a great extent based on rough estimates.

In calculating maximum and minimum estimates for 1980 certain assumptions have been made.

A growing number of persons from 15–19 years of age is expected to be non-members of the labour force because the length of time needed for their education, especially in the economically developed areas, will increase. With regard to women, however, this tendency may be neutralized by an increasing number of them working outside their homes.

An unchanged proportion (90–95 per cent) of the men from 19–64 years of age are expected to be in the labour force. Whilst it is far more difficult to make reasonable estimates with regard to the corresponding age groups of women an unchanged or slightly higher share in the labour force has been assumed. (This share may, however, increase slightly in *Latin America,* the *Middle East,* and *Africa,* where in 1955 it was very small in comparison with the other regions).

As regards the groups of those over 65 years of age two conflicting tendencies are becoming apparent. Whilst the expected increase in average life expectancy may well result in fewer persons retiring from their work at 65, on the other hand the anticipated rise in the standard of living may pave the way for more far-reaching pension arrangements. It has therefore been

84   POPULATION AND LABOUR FORCE

assumed that the share in the labour force of those over 65 years of age will remain more or less unchanged; the figures for the backward regions, however, have been altered slightly from those for 1955.

As regards the length of working hours a slight fall has been anticipated

TABLE III. 10

The Supply of Labour 1955 and 1980.

	Hours of Work per Week		Weeks of Work per Year		Total Man-hours Available per Year (1000 Million Hours)		
	1955	1980	1955	1980	1955	1980 Min.	1980 Max.
North America	41	35	47	45	143.2	156.3	182.5
Western Europe ...	47	40	49	47	304.6	245.9	290.1
Oceania	45	38	48	46	11.3	12.0	14.0
USSR	48	40	49	47	232.2	223.7	271.5
Eastern Europe	49	45	50	48	136.9	139.1	171.1
Latin America	50	48	51	50	165.8	268.1	328.8
Middle East	51	48	51	50	99.7	144.2	176.9
Asia	52	48	51	50	1,478.1	2,012.4	2,464.6
Africa	52	48	51	50	228.1	290.1	346.1
Total	...	...	...	...	2,799.9	3,491.8	4,225.4

Note: The 1955 figures for hours of work per week are based partly on information provided by the ILO *Yearbook of Labour Statistics* (1958) and partly on estimates. The number of weeks of work for 1955 has been estimated on the basis of scattered information. The hours of work totals have then been calculated on the basis of information obtained with regard to the size of the labour force. For 1955 this information is given in Table III. 4. For 1980, see text.

for all the nine regions, but especially for the economically most advanced. For *North America* the working hours per week have been put at 35 (45 weeks per year), for *Oceania* at 38 (46 weeks per year), for *Western Europe* and the *USSR* at 40 (47 weeks per year), for *Eastern Europe* at 45 (48 weeks per year) and for all the other regions at 48 (50 weeks per year).

The expected development in the supply of *Labour* may be summed up as follows: in the economically more advanced regions, viz. *North America, Western Europe, Oceania,* the *USSR,* and *Eastern Europe,* the number of persons in the productive age groups will only increase slightly. At the same time there is, in these regions, a tendency in the direction of shorter working hours and longer holidays and more time-consuming education so that the number of man-hours worked may, on the whole, be expected to remain constant. In the other regions, however, there will be a marked increase of population, also in the 15–64 year groups, and a tendency towards shorter hours and longer holidays cannot be expected to show itself. There is also a possibility that women will be more extensively engaged in productive work. It may therefore be concluded that the supply of *Labour* in the latter regions will increase very much.

Besides the question of the total size of the labour force the shortage of skilled labour[9], already apparent, (cf. what was said above regarding the composition of the labour force) should be mentioned. The problem of education also, will be very pressing everywhere, and especially in the regions that attempt to transfer labour on a large scale from primary to secondary and tertiary occupations. This problem is already among the gravest of those of the industrialization now taking place in the backward countries. It will be dealt with in more detail in Chapter VI.

D. *Races and Climate*

1. The contribution that mankind is able to make to total world production depends not only on the number of human beings in the world but also on their acquired and hereditary characteristics in relation to the tasks they are required to perform. Their acquired characteristics are more particularly dependent on education and the general cultural level—subjects which will be dealt with in Chapter VI. We shall, however, conclude this chapter with some remarks concerning the distribution of the population in the various regions from the anthropological point of view in so far as this may be assumed to have any bearing on the possibilities of economic growth in the period under review. What is of particular interest is to try to form some idea of the extent to which the various races will be able to adapt themselves, in the biological sense, to such climatic, living and working conditions as may be foreseen during a period when it may be taken for granted that the tropical regions will also, to an increasing extent, be introducing similar methods of production etc. as are at present in use in the industrial countries.

[9] Including especially the supply of experienced leaders in the various branches of production.

Our knowledge of these conditions is founded on many different and sometimes very vague sources of information, which make it impossible to draw any definite conclusions on some important points. Nevertheless, as they are essential for the study of the conditions for economic growth in the different regions they will have to be taken into consideration as far as the material permits.

That the human species—*Homo sapiens*—belongs to one of the most recently developed groups of creatures in the earth's history may be taken for granted from the fact that the earliest forms of modern man appeared about 100,000 years ago, which is a very short period compared with the 5,000 million years or so that the earth is believed to have been in existence. Even if we include extinct near-relations such as the Trinil Man from Java, *Homo erectus* (originally taken to be of a separate genus and called *Pithecanthropus erectus,* which died out about 250,000 years ago), the human genus is very young from the geological point of view. *Homo erectus* was first discovered in Java, but many more fossils have been found of Peking man, who was originally called *Sinanthropus pekinensis,* and as there is a good deal of similarity between the fossils of Java man and those of Peking man they are usually both now referred to as *Homo erectus.* In this connection it is interesting to note that the human genus, *Homo,* can not only be defined in terms of zoological characteristics but also in accordance with mental capacity, as together with Peking man various stone implements have been found which demonstrate how man, the tool-maker, has become singled out from all other animals. As *Oakley*[10] remarks, "the systematic making of tools implies a marked capacity for conceptual thought".

Whereas from the biological point of view it may often be difficult to distinguish accurately between different species, there are no such difficulties in the way of proving that human beings all belong to one single species—because, *inter alia,* there is complete fertility in the offspring of all combinations of the human races. (The word *race* is here used in the same biological sense as that in which *Barnett*[11] uses it when he defines it as "a group which shares in common a certain set of genes, and which became distinct from other groups as a result of geographical isolation".) In spite of the fact that this word is often misused it has been used here partly because it is relevant from the biological point of view and partly because it illustrates

[10] Oakley (1958, p. 3).
[11] Barnett (1957, p. 149).

the diversity of man—however little we may know as yet about this subject —and is, therefore, significant to the argument put forward in this book.

The oldest fossils of *Homo sapiens* have been found in the Mediterranean area, but so far insufficient research work has been done in large parts of *Africa* and *Asia* to determine how far the human species was spread over the globe and whether there was any kind of geographical division into races as at the present time. Some 100,000 years ago the earth was at a stage between two ice ages when conditions were presumably largely the same as at the present time. This period was followed by another ice age that lasted until probably between 15,000 and 10,000 years ago. During this last ice age about 27 per cent of the total surface of the earth was covered with ice compared with about 10 per cent at the present time. Climatically this meant that large areas of the earth gradually became too cold for human habitation, whilst other parts such as the present-day sub-tropical desert areas became habitable, as the effect of the ice age on them was to produce a pluvial climate. It may also be mentioned that the sea-level was then about 100 meters lower than at the present time, and many areas of the earth were connected by strips of land which are now submerged by the sea—which incidentally found its present level about 8,000 years ago.

The coming of the ice age compelled both human beings and animals to migrate southwards and created new opportunities for them to spread to areas which, when the ice age came to an end, became separated by isolating barriers in the form of either straits at sea or deserts on land—and these barriers so contributed to creating geographical speciation of animals and undoubtedly also lead to the diversification of the human species. This division of the human species into geographical races has become a permanent feature owing to these isolation barriers.

It should also be remembered that, in any case, up to a few thousand years ago—and indeed in large parts of the globe to the present day—the evolution of man was largely subject to the same conditions as those of other mammals, i.e. it was a question of the survival of the fittest in the struggle against hunger, illness or enemies of the species. It is such factors that are at work in the process of selection in a population and which naturally vary considerably from one geographical region to another as well as from one age to another in the same region.

2. Now, for the purpose of studying the races of mankind in relation, particularly, to the problems dealt with in this book it will perhaps be most

appropriate to start by considering the situation a few hundred years ago, i.e. before the last great migration, which started with the world discoveries about the year 1500 and which is still in progress.

The picture, as here presented, is somewhat simplified as some populations that are small numerically are only briefly mentioned, although they are very important for a full study of the human race.

a. *Numerically Small Race Groups.* The original inhabitants of Australia were probably no more than about 150,000 in number when James Cook arrived in Australia in 1770. A comparison between the skeletons of ice-age man in Europe and the Australiforms shows several obvious similarities. It is not known how long these Australiforms lived in Australia isolated from the rest of humanity, but the mere fact that their only domestic animal, the dingo, is quite different from all other races of dog in the world is proof of a very long period of isolation.

Apart from the Australiforms there are several other numerically small races to be found as widely dispersed populations, each of which has certain primitive physical characteristics but no important common features. Most of them are very small, the men being less than 150 cm and the women averaging less than 140 cm in height. Their distribution is reminiscent of many races of animals that have been forced out to the periphery by stronger races and which, now, only exist as the last remnants of races which formerly peopled much larger and inter-connected areas of land. This applies to various Asiatic races in New Guinea, Malaya and neighbouring countries, the Philippines and the Andaman Islands as well as to the Pygmies in the rain forests of the Congo, to the Bushmen in the Kalahari Desert and to the Hottentots in South Africa.

b. *Negriforms.* Until a few centuries ago the races in this group mainly existed in Africa south of the Sahara Desert, and also in a large and remote area, viz. Melanesia. There are also certain tribes in South East India and Ceylon that are reported to have negriform characteristics. This again would seem to point to their formerly having populated a much more extensive and connected area of the earth. Later on the Caucasiforms of Western Asia and India and the Mongoliforms of South-East Asia pushed southwards, only to be more or less halted in their migrations by deserts and the sea.

In Melanesia a distinction is made between the old Melanesian type which is found on the periphery—New Caledonia, New Hebrides and the

Bismarck Islands and more characteristically formerly in Tasmania—and a younger Melanesian type which predominates in New Guinea and the immediately surrounding islands. Similarly a distinction is made in *Africa* between the old Negriform type which predominates in the rain forest areas and a young Negriform group, of which the Sudan negroes are typical.

c. *Mongoliforms*. At the time of the great world discoveries this group of races, which is said to have originated in South China and in the northern parts of South East Asia, populated by far the largest area of the earth, i.e. they were spread from the White Sea over the Ural Mountains and the Caspian Sea in the West and as far as North and South America in the East and Indonesia in the South-East. It goes without saying that as they were spread over such a huge area with almost insurmountable natural barriers to inter-breeding the result was the creation of a number of smaller populations, which, however, it can scarcely be doubted belong to the Mongoliforms. This group can also be divided into the old Mongoliforms, which are mostly to be found in the South-East and more particularly in Indonesia (incl. the Philippines) and which can be traced both in the Micronesians and the Polynesians whilst also constituting a large part of the Satsuma type (the old lower classes) in Japan. The other extreme of the Mongoliforms is represented by the Tungusians and related types living north of China proper in the Amur country, by Lake Baikal, in Manchuria and as far as the Arctic regions.

It may also be mentioned that the special type of Mongoliforms found in North and South America, the Indians, can likewise be divided into an older and a younger type. The younger type is mainly to be found in the Southern States of North America, Mexico, Central America and the Western parts of South America far down into Chile and thus includes the old civilised peoples such as the Mayas, the Incas and the Aztecs. The old type, on the other hand, is mainly located in the rain forest areas of tropical South America.

d. *Caucasiforms (Europiforms)*. The area inhabited by the Caucasiforms originally comprised the whole area West of the Mongoliform populated area, i.e. from India in the South to Scandinavia in the North and as far as the Atlantic Ocean, plus all Africa north of the Sahara. There were also more or less doubtful elements such as the Polynesians and the Ainus of Japan, which are not numerically important.

In the case of the Caucasiforms a fairly definite line can be traced back to the ice-age race in Europe, Cro-Magnon man, whom it is thought can be recognized almost unchanged among the present population of certain areas.

e. Since the great voyages of discovery began about the year 1500 considerable changes have taken place in the composition of the populations in large areas of the world. The most important of these was the great migration from *Europe* which resulted in the Caucasiform type now being predominant in *North America, Oceania* and also in the southern, temperate and subtropical part of South America. More scattered groups of this type are also to be found in many other areas.

Another migration of considerable size was the compulsory transference of Negriforms from *Africa* to *North America* and Central and South America which took place during the days of the slave trade. In the same way in which the European emigrants from temperate climates chiefly settled in temperate areas, the negroes from tropical *Africa* mainly remained in the tropical and subtropical parts of the *Americas*. It is only in recent centuries that certain population groups have settled down to a limited extent in considerably different climatic conditions from those to which they had adapted themselves over the space of many centuries.

An indirect result of these and other migrations has been an increase in the intermingling of the races, more particularly in Central and South America, where the three main types of race are mixed in many different combinations. Intermingling has, however, also taken place to a lesser extent in other areas.

For the purposes of the particular analysis that is the subject of this book it may be useful to survey in broad terms the numerical distribution of the various racial groups in the different regions of the earth. It may, also, be useful to examine these figures in relation to climatic conditions, as it is undoubtedly precisely on account of the necessity of adapting themselves to different climatic conditions that the various branches of the human species have developed and divided into the particular types that are characteristic of them today.

A survey showing these points will be found in Table III. 11. As far as climate is concerned, this has been compiled on the basis of *Lee*[12], and as

---

[12] Lee (1957, pp. 1–2).

Table III.11

Races and Climate.

	Area (Mill. km²)		Population 1955		
	Total	In the Tropics[1] (approx.)	Total (Mill.)	In the Tropics[1] (Mill., approx.)	Distribution of Races
North America	21.5	–	182	–	Mainly Caucasiforms. Just under 10 per cent Negriforms and racial mixtures.
Western Europe	3.7	–	297	–	Mainly Caucasiforms.
Oceania	8.3	3	13	5	Mainly Caucasiforms. Small groups of Australiforms, etc.
USSR	22.4	–	197	–	Mainly Caucasiforms.
Eastern Europe	1.3	–	112	–	Mainly Caucasiforms.
Latin America	20.5	14	183	130	Very mixed. Mainly Caucasiforms in the South, considerable Negriform elements in tropical regions, otherwise Mongoliforms and racial mixtures.
Middle East	6.6	1	95	10	Mainly Caucasiforms.
Asia	21.7	6	1,418	450	Approx. ⅔ Mongoliforms and ⅓ Caucasiforms with other small groups and racial mixtures.
Africa	29.1	21	193	140	Mainly Negriforms south of Sahara, Caucasiforms in North Africa, plus small groups of other races and racial mixtures.
Total	135.1	45	2,690	735	

[1] The "Tropics" is taken to include the countries mentioned by *Lee* (1957) and which correspond roughly with the area between the Tropic of Cancer and the Tropic of Capricorn. On Lee's List B the following countries are referred to as being "substantially within the tropics", i.e. they may be taken as tropical as regards both area and population: half of Mexico, two-thirds of Burma and India and five-sixths of Bolivia and Brazil. The figures for the area and population in the tropics are rounded off very roughly. Estimates are also included for *Oceania,* which is not mentioned in Lee's list. Lee states that "roughly one-third of the land area of the earth is in the tropic zone. About thirty per cent. of the world's population lives there". On the basis of the approximate figures in the table the tropics cover one-third of the land area and 25–30 per cent of the world's population.

Source: Lee (1957, Table 1, p. 2) and available information concerning the distribution of races.

far as racial distribution is concerned on available statistical material, including various estimates.

Practically the whole of the tropical zone comes into the under-developed regions. The climate in these regions is either tropical or, in the case of parts of *Latin America,* the greater part of the *Middle East,* a broad belt of *Asia* and the parts of *Africa* north and south of the tropical zone, sub-tropical. Temperate climates are, however, to be found in the southern parts of *Latin America* and in the north of Japan (which cannot on the other hand be called under-developed), as well as in northern China, where Manchuria is relatively industrialized.

To a large extent the distribution of races coincides with climate zones. It may roughly be estimated that in 1955 there were somewhat more than 200 million Negriforms in the world, about 170 million of which lived in tropical *Africa* and the remainder in tropical and sub-tropical *America.* At the same time there were about 1,400 million Caucasiforms who, apart from the previously mentioned small scattered groups, all lived in the temperate zone with the exception of one important group, i.e. the population of India and Pakistan. These people have been living for a long time in tropical or sub-tropical climates and have, among other things, darker skin which makes them better adapted to these areas than the Caucasiforms of more northern areas who constitute practically the whole of the population of the vast, highly-developed regions in the temperate zone, viz. *North America, Western Europe,* the *USSR,* and *Eastern Europe.*

The Mongoliform population comprised about 1,000 million people, about 950 million of which lived in Asia and the remainder—apart from smaller groups in *North America* and elsewhere—in *Latin America.* This race of mankind is divided into several varied, even if not highly differentiated, groups with special characteristics which enable them to adapt themselves to greatly varying climatic conditions, ranging from the Eskimoes in the north to the "older" groups in the South American and Indonesian rain forest areas mentioned under *c.* The adaptation referred to is probably mainly biological adjustment to the varying natural conditions while the pattern of culture may also play an important role.

The rest of the world's population—between 50 and 100 million people—consisted of racial mixtures and small groups of races such as have been mentioned earlier.

It should be added that in the mountainous districts of the tropic zone the climate is more favourable to agriculture than in the plains and more particularly in the great river basins. It is in the latter areas especially that the typical tropical climate is to be found, i.e. with heat and humidity all the year round. The most important of these areas are the three large rain forest belts in South America (the Amazon country), the western part of Central Africa (the Congo basin) and in and around the Indonesian archipelago. It can hardly be a mere coincidence that it is precisely in these areas that we find the "older" branches of the Negriform and Mongoliform racial groups mentioned earlier. After long periods of isolation these peoples have become adapted to this particular type of climate, in which other people find it very difficult to live and work. On the other hand they have survived with a relatively primitive form of economy; nature having provided them both with heat and a rich plant and animal life in proportion to the density of the population.

3. It will be seen from Table III. 11 that practically all the tropical areas are within the four underdeveloped regions, whilst most of the temperate areas have attained a higher state of development. Japan, which has a Mongoliform population of the younger type, has now entered into a similar period of growth. One of the most important problems in the period under consideration will be to try to estimate what are the possibilities of the tropical countries reaching a similar stage of development.

This is largely a question of the availability of *Capital,* but at the same time it is very much dependent on what is demanded of the people in the process. Either it will be necessary for people from industrial countries in the temperate zones to work to an increasing degree in the tropics, or the native populations of the tropics will have to adopt new ways of life and undertake on a big scale quite different tasks from those to which they are accustomed. In either case there will be problems of adaptation, and the question is whether the various races of mankind possess the necessary conditions for solving these problems.

It is an established fact that the blood groups are very differently distributed in the various races. Recent research[13] has shown that certain illnesses occur more frequently among persons of a certain blood group than among persons of other blood groups. Other investigations have proved racial differences of a physiological nature such as for instance various ways of reg-

[13] Ford (1957).

ulating the temperature of the body in relation to the surrounding temperature[14]. There is not much doubt that there are physiological differences between the various races in certain areas, although we are far from being able to determine their exact importance.

Our knowledge of these conditions is limited, but even now we know a good deal about the special problems and difficulties that the Caucasiforms from the less warm countries come up against when they are required to live and work in the tropics.

The black or brown skin that predominates among the peoples of the tropics and sub-tropical areas is caused by the presence of melanin and it has the effect of affording protection against the harmful effect of *an excess* of ultra-violet rays; *vice versa* the paler skin of the inhabitants of northern countries allows the more scarce ultra-violet rays existing here to exercise a beneficial effect on the body. In other words, a pale skin is less suited to life in the tropics.

In Queensland (North-East Australia) there are conspicuously high figures for the occurence of skin cancer, whilst cancer of the inner organs is no more frequent than in Europe. *Cooper*[15] attributes this to the strong sunlight as the cancer mostly occurs on exposed parts of the body such as the face, neck, hands and lower arm on outdoor workers and appears to be more frequent among blondes than among darker-skinned people.

The death-rate for skin cancer in Australia is as follows:

Queensland	23 deaths per million per year
New South Wales	17 – – – – –
West Australia	15 – – – – –
South Australia	13 – – – – –
Victoria	8 – – – – –
Tasmania	8 – – – – –

From the fact that the death-rate from skin cancer is greatest in the tropical parts of Australia the conclusion may be drawn that it is in areas towards the equator that Caucasiforms encounter the greatest difficulties when attempting to re-settle.

As regards the effect of tropical climate on mental ability, *Ladell*[16] sums up the situation by saying that certain experiments "lend some weight to

[14] Echolander, Hammel, Hart, de Messurier and Steen (1958).
[15] Cooper (1957, p. 75).
[16] Ladell (1957).

Critchley's suggestion that mental capacity is greater in a temperate than in a hot climate" (p. 71), and later on (p. 77), "It seems, then, that there are undoubtedly undue psychological stresses on the settler in a hot climate, if less for the indigeneous inhabitants. It is all the more important therefore, as Huntington has pointed out, that only men and women of the "right type" should attempt to settle in hot climates".

Regarding *Lee*'s[17] treatment of this subject it may be mentioned that in his resumé he speaks of reduced effectiveness but also more particularly of an increased disinclination to work among people who are not used to a tropical climate. As regards the mental aspect he says that "some loss of mental initiative is probably the most important single direct result of exposure to tropical environment".

Certain people appear to be able to overcome these difficulties when they become acclimatized. On the other hand an investigation of European children in inner Queensland, representing three generations on the spot, would seem to point to an unfortunate long-term effect. A report on this subject[18] says: "We found that there was a definite deterioration in the physical condition of those children who were of the third generation ... In the three generation groups the intelligence quotients of the children who had come from outside averaged 99.4, and those of the third generation 92, again showing that something is going wrong".

In other words, many different kinds of difficulties seem to be encountered by people from temperate zones—and more particularly the Caucasiform type—when they attempt to adapt themselves to life in a tropical climate, and reduced effectiveness is a factor that must be expected in many such cases of transplantation.

It is much more difficult to arrive at any definite conclusions concerning the other main problem in connection with the relationship between race, climate and economic growth, viz. to try to discover to what extent particularly the "older" tropical racial groups have the capacity to adapt themselves to a modern economy with its need for systematic work, precision, leadership and initiative. There is no basis of past experience on which to form an opinion on this, and although it is easy to point to many external differences between the races too little is known about the connection between these and mental capacity.

[17] Lee (1957, pp. 96 and 100).
[18] Brown (1957, pp. 80–81).

The physical basis for intelligence in mammals, in so far as it is developed at the present time, depends on both the absolute and the relative size of the brain (in relation to the size of the body). This has been clearly demonstrated by *B. Rensch*[19], among whose conclusions we (translate and) quote the following as of specific importance to our argument:

TABLE III.12

The Endocranial Volume of Apes and Men in cm³. Adults, Males and Females.

Species	Mean	Standard Deviation	Standard Error of the Mean	Number of Measurements
Gorilla	510	69.1	6.5	113
Homo erectus	1026	128.1	34.2	14
Homo sapiens				
Australian Aboriginal .	1230	133.7	11.9	127
British (17th century)	1380	165.1	13.4	151

Source: Ashton & Spence (1958) and Ashton (1950).

"A comparison of the brain capacity among related species or races of large and small animal forms shows that those forms which have the largest brain, in the absolute sense, are able to learn more tasks as well as more complicated tasks, to remember for a longer period of time and perhaps also to recognise alterations in the tasks learnt, i.e. they have a better capacity for abstraction. Apart from the fact that the speed of learning simple tasks is presumably greater among the smaller forms, the general brain capacity is greater among the larger forms." It is also of particular interest to note that the purely quantitative increase in the number and structure of brain cells runs parallel to the increase in mental capacity.

As an addendum to the conclusions reached by Rensch it might be mentioned that it is not known to what extent the absolute and the relative size of the brain are of importance. It is generally assumed, though, that in the case of human beings the two coincide to a large extent.

Regarding the question of variations—relative and absolute—in the size

[19] B. Rensch (1958, p. 179).

of the brain in the different races of mankind little research has been done, in addition to which the different methods of investigation make comparisons very difficult. We have selected a few examples showing the racial diversity in the absolute size of the brain.

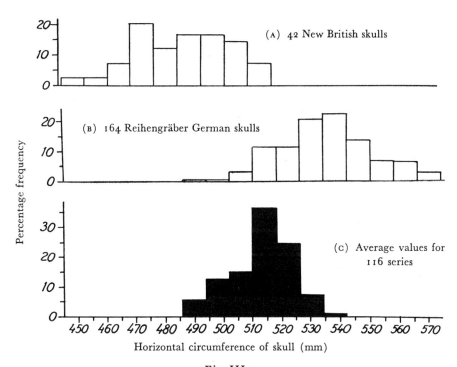

Fig. III. 1

Distributions of Horizontal Circumferences of Skulls for:

(A) The one among 116 male adult series having the smallest average (489 mm for 42 natives of New Britain).
(B) The one having the largest average (535 mm for 164 Reihengräber Germans).
(C) The average values for the 116 series.

It can clearly be seen from Table III. 12 for instance that the size of brain of Australiforms is considerably less than that of younger races; this also corresponds well with the results of investigations into the anatomy of Australiforms, which generally speaking shows them to approximate to extinct races of mankind. In other words, the Australiforms have retained characters typical of other races who lived many thousands of years ago.

Ashton and *Spence* have also given figures for a group of West Africans

(Negriforms) and for an isolated group from Tibet and Nepal (Mongoliforms). The size of these brains was between the Australian and the British, but the material is not sufficient for any definite conclusions to be drawn.

The second example is taken from *Morant*[20], showing the variation in the horizontal circumference of the skull, cf. Fig. III. 1. The conclusion may justifiably be drawn that this linear measurement expresses an equally big difference in the volume of the skull, as old races of humanity—such as the Melanesians from the Solomon Islands mentioned here—often have proportionately thicker skulls than younger races, i.e. a smaller volume of brain in proportion of the circumference.

The distribution of these measurements are shown both for the series (among 116) which has the smallest average and for the series which has the highest average. The ranges for these extreme distributions overlap considerably. The distribution of the *average* horizontal circumference for the 116 series is also shown, and it is clear that most pairs of the series must have distributions which overlap to a marked extent, as is typical of the racial characteristics of any mammal.

There seems no doubt that the brains corresponding to these measurements must vary considerably in volume, but at the same time no definite conclusions may be drawn as to their potential intelligence capacity.

After a discussion on previous race theories, Morant himself sums up his investigations by saying[21]: "It almost looked as if the ultimate solution of the problem might be a denial of the existence of any racial differences. But this conclusion is manifestly untrue in the case of physical characteristics, and in the writer's opinion is very unlikely to be proved in the case of mental qualities".

As it is, however, none of the investigations mentioned are such that they permit definite conclusions to be drawn as to the importance of the rôle played by racial differences in relation to economic growth, quite apart from the fact that there are also considerable variations within the scope of each of the races. A more reliable method would be to undertake actual intelligence tests, but other investigations along these lines have shown how difficult it is to distinguish between the reactions caused by different cultural backgrounds and those caused by hereditary biological differences, i.e. racial differences.

[20] Morant (in UNESCO (1956, b), pp. 309–10).
[21] Morant (in UNESCO (1956, b), p. 324).

The past civilizations of history have, however, emerged from the specialized activities of the various racial groups, including their struggles to overcome climatic and other natural difficulties. A study of the development of these cultures may therefore be expected to throw some light on the relation between climate, race and intellectual capacity.

4. The human genus, *Homo,* has elsewhere been characterized as the tool-maker, but many hundreds of thousands of years went by before *Homo sapiens* emerged and gradually evolved a higher culture on the basis of the palaeolithic implement culture. There are, however, still communities living at the stone-age stage of culture in our own century. It may therefore be useful to investigate whether the differences as to biological development, which are the basis of the division into older and younger races, can also be traced as a pattern for the development of culture.

The first thing that strikes us is that all the oldest racial groups—Bushmen, Congo pygmies, the Andamanese, Negritos, Australiforms and Tasmanians—were, and in many cases still are, food gatherers and primitive hunters. Among the Tasmanians and Andamanese dogs were not used as domestic animals, whilst the dog used by the Australiforms, the dingo, is a very old and quite unique offshoot from the general and otherwise very varied race of domesticated dog to be found all over the world. Leaving out of account the transition from primitive hunters to skilled hunters it may be useful to trace the line of development from the food gatherers through the stage of primitive agriculture to the highest stage of agricultural development which employs the plough, draught animals and other domestic animals.

The digging-stick used by the women for gathering food is retained as a useful implement in primitive agriculture, or it may be replaced by a hoe; and to this day we find that in the parts of *Africa* south of the Sahara there are huge areas that are still cultivated with the hoe and where the plough—which marks a decisive stage in the development of higher agriculture—is unknown.

Irrigation is one of the factors that has contributed most to making the soil usable over long periods of time, and it is therefore regarded by many as being the first step towards the development of modern agriculture. From early days it has been employed in the areas around the Nile, the Euphrates and the Indus, but it is possible that the rice culture of East Asia—which has also existed through the ages—may have been introduced independently, as may artificial irrigation in South America.

7*

Among the Negriform populations in *Africa* artificial irrigation was only known as far south as Tanganyika in East Africa, but it never attained the same admirable levels here as in the Mediterranean countries, the Far East or Peru.

It would take up too much space to try to cover the history of the many different kinds of cultivated plants, but it is generally believed that tropical Africa has contributed only very few types of plants, and these are mainly cultivated in Africa itself, viz. primarily durra (*Andropogon sorghum*), or guinea corn, and pearl millet (*Pennisetum typhoideum*).

We have already mentioned the oldest form of domestic animal, viz. the dog. On the basis of information available so far it is probably not possible to trace the exact chronological order in which the other domestic animals were taken into use by mankind, but none of them has been tamed for more than about 10,000 years (that is fairly recently in terms of the history of our species) and most of them for less than that period.

The dog accompanied human beings up to the polar regions and acquired new functions as a transport animal and as a watch-dog for the new domestic animal that was tamed there, the reindeer—which is directly descended from the wild reindeer. It was the ancient population of the polar regions that enlisted one of the native species of animals into the service of mankind.

Whilst the reindeer became—and still is—the characteristic domestic animal of the arctic nomads, the horse was tamed and became the most important animal for the nomads on the steppes of Central Asia and *Eastern Europe*. Again it was a question of enlisting the help of animals to be found in their immediate surroundings, viz. the European equine species (*Equus gmelini*) and the closely related Asiatic wild horse (*Equus ferus*) in the West and East respectively.

The sheep and the goat have a varied background and both originated in *Europe-Asia*.

The origin of the camel and dromedary is very obscure. It is not certain whether any wild form of this peculiar species exists anymore; possibly they may just be two cultivated forms of the same species. The oldest traces of them would seem to point to South-West Asia and North-East Africa, i.e. the great continuous expanse of desert.

Whilst the yak (*Bos grunniens*) in the mountain regions of Central Asia belongs to a nomadic culture, the domesticated ox in all its manifold types has been specially developed into the farmer's domestic animal. It is undoubtedly a descendent of the aurochs (*Bos primigenius*) that was native to Europe, North Africa and West Asia, whereas the zebu cattle of the tropics "probably come from a different, tropical Asiatic ancestor" [22].

The water-buffalo has been tamed and kept as a domestic animal in the most varied types of culture from the Mediterranean to Japan.

The elephant occupies a special position as a domestic animal in that it still has to be caught and trained for service, as only a very few elephants are born in captivity. The exploitation of the elephant dates back, however, to the old Indus culture.

The Mongoliforms of the new world, the Indians, have tamed the llama and the alpaca, which are South American versions of the family of camels.

The pig is another domestic animal the forbear of which is known, viz. the wild boar (*Sus scrofa*) which is found from West Europe to East Asia.

This survey covers the principle domestic animals, and it will be realized from the foregoing that it was the European-Asiatic peoples that first had the vision to tame animals for the purpose of long-term exploitation of them—otherwise these wild animals would have to be hunted continually. There is no doubt that in particular the ox family and the pig family must have been hunter's prey for many thousands of years before they became domesticated. This can be seen from the fact that the human being is the only normal final host for two species of tape-worm which in their primary stages are the larval beef tapeworm and pork tapeworm respectively.

It is a remarkable fact that Negriform in *Africa* with its wealth of mammals suitable for domestication (e.g. elephants, water-buffalos, zebras and various species of the pig family) has not got a single domestic animal that it has tamed itself but has acquired all its domestic animals through cultural currents from North-East Africa. For instance it may be mentioned that in modern times the African elephant has proved to be capable of taming by Indian elephant tamers in an experiment that was made in the Congo.

Finally it is apparent that all the highest civilizations have been attained among the Mongoliform and Caucasiform peoples. It is these two races that have developed the arts, sciences, architecture, the art of writing with its manifold alphabets, technology, etc., etc. Furthermore, these two racial groups have shown an eminent capacity for absorbing and adapting all the

---

[22] Darlington (1957, p. 406).

different cultural elements that they found to be useful to them under their very different living conditions.

5. On the basis of the foregoing sections a picture of the races of mankind may be briefly drawn as follows:

From the purely physical point of view each of the races shows a certain ability to adapt itself to its natural surroundings, this capacity being most marked among the oldest types such as Bushmen and Australiforms etc. who in relation to the age of the human species as such have lived isolated for a long period of time in a particular spot. On the other hand there are the younger races—i.e. more particularly the young races among Mongoliforms and Caucasiforms—who have been subjected to such a large range of temperature fluctuations within the total area they have occupied that they simply have not had time to adapt themselves to the changing conditions by means of the constant but slow process of the pressure of selection.

Admittedly they have had to learn to adapt their surroundings to their needs by means of an economic and cultural development which reduced their dependence on nature; but this has required vision, imagination and a sense of planning.

It is an easy matter to prove that the oldest races, such as the Tasmanians, Australiforms and Bushmen did not have the same potential degree of intelligence that allowed other people at the stone-age stage of development such as the New Zealand Maories to slip into modern industrialized civilization without any special difficulty. Extreme cases like this should, in any case, serve as a warning against the opinion that any and every racial group ought to be able to adapt itself equally easily to an industrialized form of society.

It should be added that many of the opinions in this chapter are the result of investigations based on rather slight material or material which may be questionable for other reasons. At the same time, when taken as a whole the material includes a great number of observations in a variety of different fields, and when these are viewed together they seem to form a pattern which may perhaps have a greater value than might be thought from a separate study of each element.

Finally it should be mentioned that it is often difficult to distinguish between the differences in behaviour and in suitability for certain tasks caused by hereditary racial characteristics and those brought about by cultural environment and tradition. Races that have been isolated, in the genetical sense, have also been isolated culturally. It is essential, therefore, that this chapter should be studied in conjunction with Chapter VI, which deals with the cultural aspects. Only a joint study of the two aspects can provide a true picture of the special characteristics and the future possibilities of the various populations.

CHAPTER IV

Capital

—

A. *Prefatory Remarks*

1. The differences in the amount of *Capital* available in each of the regions determines in great measure the differences in the income levels between them. Also, the increase which can be expected in the amount—and "quality"—of capital is of vital importance to the growth of a region. There is thus on the one hand, a close connection between *Capital* and income, and on the other, a no less intimate relationship between the level of income and the potential increase in the amount of capital goods. The poorer the region, the harder will it be for it to secure a production surplus that can be used for increasing its *Capital*. Even when saving is comparatively high in comparison with consumption, the total capital increase will only be modest if production is small. In the wealthy regions, however, even moderate saving may result in a considerable total increase in the amount of capital goods on account of the large production. In trying to envisage the possibilities of economic growth there arises, therefore, the question as to the extent of the economic aid which the poor regions may expect to receive from the wealthy regions. In the event of their having more goods at their disposal than they can produce themselves, they will be better able to increase the amount of their capital.

2. In estimating the future economic growth of the regions it is therefore necessary to start by making certain assumptions regarding the development of investment. This development depends on the opportunities for saving as well as the propensity to save in each region, and on such capital movements as may take place between the regions. Saving, however, as mentioned earlier, is related to the income level and thus to economic growth; they cannot actually be considered separately. In spite of their close relationship we may, however, on the basis of our knowledge of the past and present relationships between income and saving, make an estimate of the *probable* future trend in the various regions, at the same

time, of course, taking into account in our considerations the other factors of growth.

Greater difficulties, in fact, confront us when we try to forecast capital movements between the regions. For it may be assumed that these will depend not only on the return that may be obtained on the *Capital*, but also on political considerations. Thus, if the task of gauging future capital movements is difficult when these are determined by economic factors alone, it will be even more so when political thinking wholly or partly influences the extent of the movements.

3. Any evaluation of the growth of *Capital* in the various regions is thus subject to much uncertainty and indeed no such evaluation would be possible if our knowledge of current investment, saving, etc. in the region did not provide a background for it. In these fields a certain amount of information is now available and will be utilized in the following analysis. With regard to present conditions, however, the analysis should be regarded with some reserve. For some countries, especially in the most backward regions, the information available is indeed of very poor quality. Consequently, it has been necessary to assume that the per capita investment, saving etc. in these countries is the same as in countries that are in a similar situation economically and for which better information is available. Further we may say that, generally speaking, figures of the kind we are dealing with here are not to be relied upon too much. The statistical material available from even the most advanced countries is often deficient and estimates with regard to the underdeveloped areas must, therefore, be relatively less reliable. In these areas the subsistence economy is important, and often estimates of investment —as well as estimates of the domestic product—do not include this part of the economy. This will not normally influence the total amount of investment very much, because investment in this sector is insignificant. It will, however, probably give the estimated *investment quota* (i.e. the investment as a per cent of the net domestic product) an upward bias. Therefore, if what is known about the net domestic product and investment is applicable to that part of society which has a market economy, the same investment quota related to the regions as a whole will be too high. A similar problem will usually arise when the trend in investment quotas for a particular, developed, country is considered over a long span of years, as the subsistence economy will appear to have played an increasingly important role the further back we go in time.

Comparisons between investment and investment quotas in various countries are rendered difficult by another problem, viz. that of the differences in the price relationships between investment goods and other goods. Such differences probably exist between most of the regions (and also between the countries within the regions). In this context, however, there is particular reason to emphasize the differences as regards the fixing of prices between communities with a planned economy and those with a freer economy, though it is impossible to say in general terms how the various price fixing systems affect the price relationship between investment goods and other goods. Yet, as far as Mainland China is concerned, the price structure, it may be mentioned, causes the investment quotas to be overvalued in comparison with those of *Western Europe*, for example[1].

Comparisons of investments in the *USSR, Eastern Europe* and Mainland China with those of other areas are also made difficult by the fact that the definitions of investment and net domestic product are not identical in the two groups of countries. Finally, to this may be added the difficulties which arise when a conversion to a common monetary unit is required.

4. The term *Capital* has been referred to in detail in Chapter II, B[2] and the definition given there will be used in the following text. Generally the term *Capital* refers to the stock of capital goods, i.e. buildings, machinery, transport equipment etc. However, in certain cases *Capital* is referred to as if it were an amount of, say, dollars. This is for instance the case when we speak about capital transfers between regions. Even in this case, however, the capital transfer is effected by a flow of goods and services between the regions. The terms gross investment, capital consumption, and net investment have also been dealt with in Chapter II. B. In the following pages *Capital* in 1980 means, for each particular region, *Capital* in 1955 plus net investment during the period 1955–80. *Capital* as well as investment will be expressed in 1955 dollars.

The purpose of the present chapter is thus firstly to estimate the amount of *Capital* in or about 1955. This has been attempted in section B. Further it will be necessary to have some idea of the net investment, and consequently of the growth of *Capital,* in the period 1955–80. This task, which is even more difficult than the former, will be undertaken in section C.

A necessary condition for the actual occurrence of net investment is, of

[1] See UN (1958, f, p. 106).
[2] See page 42.

course, that income or, in other words, the value of total annual production is not all used in consumption. That part of income which does not go into consumption is usually called *saving*. For the world as a whole, therefore, the annual saving will be equal to the annual net investment. The same would be true of each separate region if there were no trade connections between the regions. When such connections exist it may happen that a region, through a surplus of exports of goods and services over imports of goods and services, puts some of its annual income—and thus of its saving —at the disposal of other regions and so enables them to make a larger net investment than they could with their own saving alone.

5. There is thus a close affinity between investment and saving; *the investment* of a certain region being equal, according to the definition used here, to the saving of the region, provided that the region's imports of goods and services are exactly as large as its exports of goods and services. If, on the other hand, the value of exports and the value of imports do not correspond to one another, the investment and the saving of the region are not similar. If the region has an import surplus, a transfer of *Capital* to the region has taken place, whilst if it has an export surplus, there has been a transfer of *Capital* from the region to other regions. In the event of a region having received *Capital* from other regions, the investment of that region will be equal to its own saving plus the *Capital* from abroad, whereas if *Capital* has been transferred from the region in question to other regions, the saving of the region will equal its investment plus the *Capital* transferred.

B. *Capital To-day*

6. Estimates of *the size of capital* are available for only a few countries. In any case available estimates are not normally included in official statistical publications. For this reason it is not possible to make actual calculations of the size of *Capital* for areas that together cover the entire land surface of the earth. In addition there are a number of very intricate problems in connection with the assessment of *Capital* which make it difficult to apply any clear-cut interpretation to such assessments. *Capital*, as will be seen from the definition above, has a very complex structure. On the one hand it consists of a great many different goods, on the other hand these goods have been used in production over greatly varying periods. For these

and a number of other reasons it is very difficult to appraise the value at any given time of these different elements of *Capital*.

The size of *Capital,* however, is a subject which plays a very important part in this book, as will be shown in greater detail in Chapter VII. With *Nature* and *Culture, Capital* combined with *Labour* determines the growth of the regions. In Chapter VII an attempt has been made to describe this connection by means of the Cobb-Douglas formula [3]. A necessary condition for the application of this formula is that we are able to appraise the size of *Capital* in the various regions. This has been attempted below in spite of the great difficulties and the very considerable uncertainty prevailing in this field.

Only as regards *North* and *Latin America* are over-all evaluations of *Capital* for whole regions available. For *North America* [4] *Capital* may be put, in 1955, at a little over 1000 billion dollars, whilst for *Latin America* [5] it amounts to about 140 billion dollars. This is tantamount to a capital value per person of about 5,600 dollars and 750 dollars respectively.

With regard to the other regions estimates of *Capital* are available for comparatively few countries within the regions. In estimating the total *Capital* of the various regions it will be useful to consider the so-called average *capital/output ratio.* As is suggested by the term, this is the ratio of total *Capital* to total output (for example as measured by the net domestic product).

By application of the capital values mentioned above for *North* and *Latin America* and the figures calculated in Chapter I for the net domestic product, there emerges a capital/output ratio of about 3 for both regions. Ratios of about 3 are fairly common for the countries for which it has been possible to obtain estimates of *Capital* in 1955 or thereabouts. In the United Kingdom the ratio is between 2.5 and 3, in Western Germany about 3, in Japan a little over 3, and in Australia and the Union of South Africa about 3.5. In Norway the ratio is a little higher, viz. between 3.5 and 4, whilst in India it is probably as low as about 2.

Besides these figures for the average capital/output ratio about 1955, figures are also available for particular countries showing the average capi-

[3] See pp. 226 ff.

[4] *Statistical Abstract of the US 1957,* and Anthony Scott (1959).

[5] In UN (1958, e) *Capital* in Latin America in 1955, as measured in 1950 prices, is put at 123 billion dollars.

tal/output ratio over a number of years (see Table IV. 1 below). These figures are not quite comparable with the figures mentioned above for 1955 because other concepts than that of net domestic product have generally been used for expressing total output. On the other hand, it will hardly affect the *trend* demonstrated by the figures whether one concept or another is used, as long as the same one is used all the time. It may further be mentioned that the level of the capital/output ratios depends on the prices of *Capital* relative to the prices of output. For example, a considerably lower 1955 ratio for the Union of South Africa emerges when the 1938 and not the 1955 price level is used (as is seen in Table IV. 1). The application of the 1955 price level will result in the above-mentioned ratio of about 3.5. This is a consequence of a change in the system of relative prices from 1938 to 1955.

In estimating the trend in capital/output ratios we have to bear in mind that no correction has been made in regard to the varying intensities of exploitation of *Capital* at different times resulting from changes in economic activity—whereby the capital/output ratio is altered. The errors that this is likely to cause could, however, be avoided, at least to a certain extent, by calculating the ratios for years in which the degree of exploitation of *Capital* is about the same.

With regard to the trend in the size of the capital/output ratios over a number of years these seem very often to be comparatively low in the earliest stages of economic development. This probably applies to both the average and the *marginal capital/output ratio* (i.e. the ratio of the growth of capital to the growth of total production). When *Capital* is scarce it must be expected to give a relatively good yield. The acquisition of fairly simple investment goods, such as agricultural tools, may result in a quite substantial increase in production. If economic growth is to continue, however, a change must take place in the nature of the investment. Investment which has a less immediate influence on production will come to play a greater part; the transport network will have to be extended, power stations must be erected, schools, hospitals, administration buildings, etc. must be built and housing provided for the process of urbanization which is a consequence of and a necessary condition for economic growth. The time required for building such investment is long and it is generally some time before its capacity can be fully utilized. With the increasing importance of such investment the marginal capital/output ratio will rise and will cause the average capital/

TABLE IV. 1

Average Capital/Output Ratios.

	Period			Period	
United States[1]	1805	0.8	United Kingdom[1]	1865	3.1
	1850	1.6		1875	3.5
	1880	2.5		1885	4.0
	1890	3.4		1895	3.7
	1900	3.3		1905	3.8
	1912	2.8		1909	3.8
	1922	3.2		1914	3.4
	1929	3.0		1928	3.5
	1939	3.4		1938	2.7
	1948	2.5		1953	2.6
Canada[1]	1914	2.6	France[1]	1893	3.9
	1929	3.8		1913	4.8
Australia[3]	1903	4.3	Germany[3]	1913	3.7
	1915	3.9		1929	3.9
	1929	3.6		1939	3.2
	1947	2.8		1948	3.4
	1956	3.0		1950	2.6
Union of S. Africa[2]	1919–28	3.5		1955	2.3
	1924–33	3.5	Norway[4]	1900	4.1
	1929–38	3.4		1916	3.8
	1934–43	3.0		1930	3.6
	1939–48	2.8		1937	3.5
	1944–55	2.6		1950	3.0
				1955	3.4

[1] Capital in relation to net national product at market prices.
[2] Capital in relation to domestic product.
[3] Capital in relation to gross national product at market prices.
[4] Fixed capital in relation to net domestic product at market prices.
Sources: Colin Clark (1957), Garland and Goldsmith (1959), Franzsen and Willers (1959), Grünig (1959) and Aukrust and Bjerke (1958).

output ratio to do likewise. (In general, the variations as between regions of the capital/output ratio, and also variations in time, may be taken as clear demonstrations of the fact that production depends on a great many factors besides *Capital,* cf. Chapter VII, A).

Although these considerations are to a certain extent speculative the figures in Table IV. 1 seem to indicate such a trend. The figures also suggest that at some point in the development the increase will stop and a tendency to decline, even, may become apparent. When the full influence of investment in the transport network, power supply, etc. is brought to bear on production, it might be expected that at least the increase in the capital/ output ratio would cease. As a general rule, however, the greater the size of a production factor in relation to other production factors, the less will be the effect on production of any increase in it. On the other hand technical development, rationalization, etc. have in recent years caused this rule to be less generally applicable.

Though a development of this kind is perhaps common to all areas, there may well be differences from area to area in the level at which the capital/ output ratio fluctuates. There may be especially good reason to assume that a connection exists between the level of the ratio and the wealth, or poverty, of the area in resources. This may show itself in such a way that the larger the resources the smaller will be the ratio. It will be recalled that *Capital* only includes the means of production produced by man and in areas where natural resources are plentiful a large yield might well be expected from a relatively small application of the means of production. It does not, however, seem to be possible on the basis of the information available either to confirm or to refute this assumption.

Because capital/output ratios change in the course of economic development comparisons may only be made between areas that have reached the same stage of development. This can scarcely be done on the basis of the material available at present; quite apart from the fact that it would be very hard to decide whether the condition has been fulfilled or not. Further, it appears that owing to the statistical difficulties of estimating capital/output ratios, comparisons between different areas would have to be made with great care.

Although the basis upon which estimates of *Capital* in the various regions must be made is very slender, it has been found, as mentioned above, that such estimates do serve a purpose. The estimates of *Capital* have been shown in Table IV. 2. For some of the regions, viz. *North America, Oceania,* and *Latin America* it has been possible to make direct estimates of *Capital,* as information is available for almost the whole of the regions. In the Table is also shown the ratio of these capital values to the net domestic product of the regions.—i.e. the average capital/output ratio. For the other regions an estimate of the total capital/output ratio has been attempted on the basis of the scant information available. The capital value has then been estimated by means of these ratios and the figures for the net domestic product shown in Table I. 1, the amount of *Capital* being found by multiplying capital/output ratio by net domestic product. In Table IV. 2 figures are also given for the capacities of power plants as well as for steel consumption. These

TABLE IV. 2

Capital/Output Ratios, Capital, Power Station Capacities, and Steel Consumption 1955.

	Average Capital/ Output Ratio	Capital		Power Plant Capacities Per capita (KW)	Steel Consumption Per capita (kg/annum)
		Total (Billion Dollars)	Per capita (Dollars)		
North America	3.0	1,015	5,600	0.79	591
Western Europe	3.5	850	2,900	0.37	241
Oceania	3.3	40	3,100	0.38	305
USSR	3.0	325	1,650	0.19	220
Eastern Europe	3.5	175	1,550	0.16	144
Latin America	2.9	140	750	0.06	42
Middle East	2.5	35	350	0.03	22
Asia	2.5	270	200	0.02	11
Africa	2.5	50	250	0.03	27
Total	...	2,900	...	...	...

Note : The figures for power plant capacities and steel consumption have been taken from the UN *Statistical Yearbook* 1957. For the remaining figures, cf. the text.

are used for comparison with the capital value and as evidence in support of the estimates made. Power plant capacities and steel consumption are fairly well known factors and give a comparatively reliable idea of the stage of development that the regions have reached. The figures reflect the very great differences in power plant capacities, steel consumption, and *Capital* that exist between the regions.

7. The preceding paragraph dealt with the amount of *Capital* in the various regions and its influence on production. In the present paragraph the actual growth of *Capital*, i.e. the *net investment*, will be considered. In addition to what has been said in the prefatory remarks of this chapter about the uncertainty of figures generally, there may be reason to make some

further comments on the difficulties that must be overcome before net investment can be assessed.

Calculations as to the extent of investment must generally be based upon the figures for gross investment. Consequently a figure for net investment must be obtained by means of an estimate of capital consumption. An obvious way of making such an estimate is to consider business depreciation accounts. The amounts that are set aside annually for depreciation in business accounts will not, however, meet the definition of capital consumption used in the present book[6]—and in national accounts generally. As a rule values used as a basis for calculating depreciation by business concerns do not correspond to the cost of re-acquiring the capital goods. Further, such concerns may want depreciation to be determined by other factors than the estimated wear, tear and obsolescence. If, therefore, these depreciation accounts are used as indications of capital consumption, errors will arise which will influence the size of net investment. Another method that may be followed is to calculate capital consumption on the basis of the amount of capital and the assumed life of the capital goods. On account of our very inadequate knowledge of these facts, however, such calculations can only be very approximate and this latter method will also increase the uncertainty with regard to net investment as determined from gross investment.

Further, it should be emphasized that the figures for investment given in this chapter can provide only a very general impression of the growth of *Capital*. First, it is not possible, in view of the wide scope of the present study, to give a detailed account of the nature of the various types of investment. It is probably a matter of some importance to economic growth, however, whether investment is made in factories, farming machinery, power plants, schools, museums or churches. Some investment, e.g. agricultural machinery, may be assumed to have a more immediate effect on production than, for example, investment in power plants. On the other hand the latter is necessary in order to ensure lasting economic growth. The same applies to investment in schools and educational institutions—whereas the effect of investment in churches is very hard to evaluate. It might also be mentioned that whether an office building, for example, gets a more or a less expensive finish is of little consequence to the economic growth of a community as long as the practical installations of the building are the same in both cases.

[6] See page 43.

Anyhow it is necessary to assume that investment, first and foremost, involves economic growth. On the other hand there is no possibility of judging how effectively investment is being utilized, e.g. due to inadequate training a worker may prevent a machine from being used effectively, or cause a considerable reduction in its life.

TABLE IV.3

Net Investments 1954–56, Annual Average.

	Total Net Investment (Billion Dollars)	Investment Quotas (Per cent)
North America	38	about 11
Western Europe	31[a]	about 13
Oceania	3	about 25
USSR	25	20–25
Eastern Europe	9	15–20
Latin America	5	11–12
Middle East	2	10–12
Asia	12	10–12
of which:		
Mainland China & Japan	9	15–20
Other areas	3	6–7
Africa	3	about 15
Total	128	...

a Converted into dollars on the basis of special investigations of the purchasing power of European currencies against dollars, see Chapter I.
Source: Various United Nations Surveys and UN (1958, a) and (1959, e).

It is, therefore, with many reservations that estimates of total net investment in each of the nine regions have been made. The figures should be read with this in mind. The estimates arrived at, which appear in Table IV. 3, refer to the period 1954–56.

A little over 55 per cent of total net investment in this period was made in *North America, Western Europe,* and *Oceania* and a little over 25 per cent was accounted for by the *USSR* and *Eastern Europe,* leaving 15–20 per cent for the rest of the world, or in other words for about 70 per cent of the total world population.

The large part of total investment that was located in *North America* and *Western Europe* was not due to particularly large investment quotas there (i.e. net investment as a percentage of the net domestic product) as these were a good deal lower than those of the *USSR* and *Eastern Europe* and similar to those of several of the economically backward areas. Production is so large, however, in the two first-mentioned regions that even when only a comparatively small proportion of it is used for investment, the total investment is very high.

In considering the relatively low investment quota of *North America* it must be borne in mind that capital consumption in this region is high in consequence of the very large *Capital* (previously) invested. Further it should be noted that defence costs take a share of United States production equal to its net investment. (Total expenditure on defence is considered as governmental consumption).

A similar situation to that in *North America* obtains in West European countries, especially the United Kingdom, whilst other countries, e.g. West Germany, Holland, and Norway, have investment quotas of the same level as those of the *USSR* and the East European countries.

In Table IV. 3 the investment quotas for the *USSR* and the East European countries are given within very wide margins. This is due to the uncertainty that arises because, as previously mentioned, these regions—as, incidentally, does Mainland China also—use other definitions of domestic product and investment than the rest of the regions. Nevertheless there can be little doubt that net investment quotas are very high in these regions. It is also probable that in these regions capital consumption accounts for a smaller proportion of gross investment than it does in the United States, for example, while, on the other hand, defence consumes a large part of production, as in the United States. The fact that the government is able to guide production factors into whatever channels it wishes has brought about not only a high investment quota but also the situation that investment is made in fields where it is likely to prove most conducive to economic growth. Thus heavy industry, especially, has been consolidated through the rapid increase of *Capital*.

Investment quotas as high as those of the *USSR* and *Eastern Europe* occur in Japan and Mainland China, whereas in the rest of *Asia* the level of investment is very low. The price structure in Mainland China causes the investment percentage of that country to be overestimated (see page 106), but there can be little doubt that the investment quota is high especially in comparison with the quotas of other countries with similar production figures. In India, admittedly, the investment quota is a good deal lower, viz. about 7 per cent. It reached this level in the course of the first five-year plan, at the start of which in 1951 it was 5 per cent. During the period of the second five-year plan it is expected to reach 10–11 per cent.

For the *Middle East* the investment quota is thought to be between 10 and 12 per cent. This is a very uncertain estimate, however, as little information is available. The investment quota for Turkey, whose share in the total regional net domestic product is a little over 40 per cent, is about 12 per cent, in Israel it amounts to over 25 per cent, whereas in Egypt it is a little below 10 per cent.

For *Africa,* also, the available material is slight but it seems to indicate that the investment quota is fairly high. In the Union of South Africa the investment percentage is very high, viz. about 20, which greatly affects the total, as one-fourth of *Africa*'s total domestic product is accounted for by this country.

In *Latin America,* following a great increase in investment immediately after the war, there seems to have been a slackening in the rate since 1953 and the investment quota is probably a little lower for 1954–56 than for the years preceding 1953.

In order to supplement this information, investment quotas for a few countries over a long span of years are given in Table IV. 4. The net investment has been calculated as a percentage of the net national product at market prices. This means that investment quotas generally appear to be a little lower than when they were calculated, as above, as a percentage of the net domestic product at factor cost.

The investment quota has been, on the whole, rather higher in recent years than in the inter-war period. In fact we have to go as far back as the years preceding the First World War to find quotas as high as those about 1955. Further the figures shown for Sweden indicate the very considerable increase in investment quotas in a country which, after being economically relatively backward, experienced a rapid growth. On the other hand, in the United Kingdom investment quotas were fairly stable in the years stated prior to the First World War, the country having already at that time reached a high level of development.

8. As mentioned earlier there is a very close relationship of definition

TABLE IV.4

Net Investment as Percentage of the Net National Product in Market Prices[1].

	Period	Investment Quota (Per cent)		Period	Investment Quota (Per cent)
United States	1869–1878	13.9	United Kingdom	1870–1879	8.7
	1879–1888	13.8		1880–1889	7.4
	1889–1898	14.6		1890–1899	7.9
	1899–1908	12.8		1900–1909	8.8
	1909–1918	10.7		1904–1913	7.6
	1919–1928	8.8		1924–1930	5.4
	1929–1938	2.3		1954–1956	8.3
	1939–1948	11.4	France	1853–1878	8.5
	1954–1956	9.6		1878–1903	4.6
Canada	1901–1910	19.4		1903–1911	5.6
	1911–1920	14.1		1927–1930	7.0
	1921–1930	10.2		1954–1956	10.1
	1926–1930	12.5[a]	Sweden	1861–1870	3.8
	1931–1940	4.2[a]		1871–1880	5.8
	1941–1950	9.9[a]		1881–1890	7.1
	1954–1956	16.0		1891–1900	8.6
Union of S. Africa	1919–1928	13.3		1901–1910	12.2
	1924–1933	8.7		1911–1920	14.1
	1929–1938	11.9		1921–1930	11.9
	1934–1943	12.2		1954–1956	about 13
	1939–1948	15.2			
	1944–1955	21.9			
	1954–1956	20.3			

[1] All ratios are based on annual averages for the periods indicated, and the underlying totals are in current prices.

[a] Excluding changes in inventories.

Sources: Kuznets (1956), Franzsen and Willers (1959) and UN (1958, a).

between *investment and saving*; the two factors being equal if we consider the world as a whole. The same need not be true for individual regions, because a region may use part of its saving for lending or as a gift to some other region thus enabling the latter to dispose of more goods and services and consequently to invest more than it saves.

The figures shown above for investment in the various regions will therefore have to be supplemented by information about capital transfers taking place between the regions in order to provide an impression of the saving of the regions. As mentioned in the paragraph dealing with investment, the estimates of investment are based on information obtained for the years 1954–56. In the course of so brief a period there may be quite considerable differences between investment and saving. This need not, however, indicate a lasting trend but may be due to short-term capital movements including the utilization of foreign balances. In trying to appraise trends such transactions need hardly be taken into account, as is evident from the words "short-term" which indicate their temporary nature. On the other hand it must be admitted that if a region is able to replace short-term loans with new short-term loans or if it has an abundance of foreign exchange reserves which it may draw on, these short-term capital movements are as likely to promote economic growth as the raising of long-term loans or increasing the region's own saving. The effect of short-term capital movements, however, cannot easily be judged in an attempt to make projections for economic growth. In the following enquiry only reflections on saving in the various regions and on long-term capital transactions between the regions have been given.

In view of the large margin of error involved, the investment quotas in Table IV. 3 have largely been given in round figures. Consequently the task of giving figures for saving with any greater certainty has been almost impossible. On the other hand the level of *the savings quotas* (the net saving as a percentage of the net domestic product) can be estimated on the basis of the investment quotas in the period 1954–56. In the following paragraphs, therefore, the saving of the regions will be described by indicating the difference between investment and saving quotas. Just as both investment and saving are expressed as a percentage of the net domestic product so the difference between them will be expressed. The figures are shown in Table IV. 7, column 3.

In *North America* the saving quota exceeds the investment quota, the difference being between 0.5 and 1 per cent of the net domestic product. In this context it should, however, be remembered that donations under military aid schemes are not included as part of the United States' saving but as part of its public consumption.

In *Western Europe,* also, saving is slightly higher than investment, but the difference between the quotas probably does not exceed 0.5 per cent of the domestic product. Here too donations from the United States play a certain role. In the period under consideration these donations were in the nature, mainly, of military aid. Although they are not actually included in the savings figures for *Western Europe* their influence is felt indirectly in the savings total. If *Western Europe* were to defray expenses for defence of the same magnitude as the United States' aid granted to it, saving would, *ceteris paribus,* be proportionately smaller.

A fairly large proportion of the considerable investment made in *Oceania* has been financed by means of loans raised abroad or by the utilization of foreign balances. The saving quota is probably 3 to 4 per cent lower than the investment quota.

In *Latin America,* also, saving has been lower than investment. The difference between the quotas is probably between 1 and 2 per cent.

With regard to the *Middle East* an evaluation of saving is scarcely feasible because for a number of important oil-producing countries no information is readily available. While saving is a good deal lower than investment in Turkey and Israel, for example, there can be little doubt that the opposite is the case in the countries rich in oil where income from oil concessions is very high.

In *Asia* the saving quota is lower than the investment quota; the difference is probably about 1 per cent of the net domestic product. As there does not seem to be any difference between investment and saving in China and Japan, the saving quota in the rest of the region is about 2 per cent lower than the investment quota.

Africa also belongs to the capital-importing regions, the saving quota presumably being 1 to 2 per cent lower than the investment quota.

An estimate of the relationship between saving and investment in the *USSR* and *Eastern Europe* is not considered feasible. If the two regions are regarded as a whole, however, there does not appear to be much difference between the two quotas.

As may be gathered from the above, it is mainly *North America* that exports *Capital.* Most of the other regions are importers of capital. The United States at present holds the position of principal exporter of capital and has thus assumed the rôle formerly played by the United Kingdom.

From the beginning of the industrial revolution up to 1914 the United Kingdom was the principal supplier of *Capital.* In 1913 British capital interests abroad made up nearly half of the total "foreign capital", about 18 billion dollars in all or, according to 1950 prices, about 50 billion dollars.

France, Germany, Holland, Belgium, and Switzerland also had considerable capital interests abroad. The sum of their foreign capital, in fact, equalled that of the United Kingdom.

It should, however, be emphasized that the extensive capital movements that took place before 1914 were due to very special circumstances which are unlikely to recur. Prior to 1914 the creditor countries were at the same time suppliers of labour, in the form of emigrants, and of machinery and technical skill to the debtor countries. They also formed natural markets for the export of raw materials and food from the debtor countries. It was quite natural, therefore, that the process of economic growth in overseas areas, which was made possible by European, and especially British, emigrants, engineers, and machinery should also be financed with European, and largely British, capital.

It is obvious that this situation does not exist to-day. There are no unpopulated territories rich in resources, and the United States is not, to the same extent as the United Kingdom was in 1914, a natural purchaser of the goods that the underdeveloped countries are able to export. At the end of the First World War the earlier pattern of capital movements came to an end. Europe had been impoverished by the war and the economic structure of the United States was not of a nature to promote any considerable export of capital. After a spell in the twenties of fairly large United States capital exports, partly prompted by speculation, the international capital market suffered a complete collapse. The latter part of the inter-war period was marked by trade restrictions, devaluation, and political upheavals.

As late as 1939 the United States was a net debtor to Europe. This was due, however, to considerable United States capital investment in *Latin America* and Canada, and to the fact that the foreign capital in the United States consisted, to a great extent, of "escape capital" from countries with less valuable currencies, e.g. France.

Before the Second World War the countries of Europe were thus net-creditors of the rest of the world. The flow of *Capital* was stagnating, however. If inter-European debts are excluded, West European capital interests in other regions in 1938 amounted to about 30 billion dollars.

The debtor countries were more evenly distributed over the various regions than the creditor countries. The British dominions and colonies accounted for a very substantial part of total foreign capital, but considerable *Capital* was also located in *Latin America,* China, and Indonesia.

The *Middle East,* on the other hand, had attracted *Capital* only to an insignificant extent.

During and since the Second World War the United States has come to the fore as a capital exporter. At the end of the war the United States was still to all appearances, it is true, a net debtor. This was due partly to the influx of "escape capital" from war-stricken European countries and partly to American purchases of war supplies (mainly from *Latin America*) which resulted in 4.2 billion dollars of foreign claims against the United States when the war was over. After the war this amount was soon paid back and at the same time a considerable additional capital export took place.

Table IV. 5 shows the public loans and grants made by the United States in the years following the war. Initially, the purpose of this aid was to promote reconstruction, but later the bulk of it came to be used for defence purposes. About 60 per cent of the loans and grants were made to *Western Europe* and its dependencies. This percentage is roughly the same for both civil and military aid. In the last few years *Western Europe* has continued to receive a similar share of United States military aid, but civil aid, to a great extent, now goes to other regions.

United States direct investment in foreign countries has also played an important rôle in the post-war years, as can be seen from Table IV. 6. Interest on *Capital* that has remained in the countries in question is included in the figures. In the course of a decade the average capital export has been about 1.5 billion dollars per annum and the rate of export is growing rather than diminishing. As can be seen from the Table, about one-third of the increase is in respect of Canada and thus does not leave the region of *North America.*

The figures given in Table IV. 5 do not include United States loans etc. to the International Bank of Reconstruction and Development. Up to the middle of 1958 the loans granted by the Bank amounted to 3.7 billion dollars, of which a considerable part was financed by the United States.

At the same time as *Western Europe* has been receiving grants and loans from the United States, some West European countries have themselves been exporting capital, especially to their overseas territories. No complete survey of these capital movements is available, but a report issued by OEEC[7] contains figures that give some idea of them. Under the Colonial Development and Welfare Acts, for example, the United Kingdom has made grants

[7] OEEC (1958).

TABLE IV.5

United States Public Grants and Loans 1945–57.
(Billion Dollars)

	July 1945–Dec. 57	1953–57
Military Grants:		
Western Europe (excl. Greece and Turkey)	12.31	9.19
Near East (incl. Greece and Turkey), Africa and South Asia	2.93	1.88
Other Asia and Oceania	5.20	3.60
Latin America	0.36	0.23
Other countries	0.21	0.12
Total	21.01	15.02
Other Grants and Credits:		
Western Europe incl. dependent areas	25.51	2.48
Oceania	0.17	0.11
USSR	0.43	–
Eastern Europe	1.50	0.30
Latin America	1.38	0.85
Asia	9.09	3.71
Middle East and Africa	1.89	1.34
Various International Organizations and Unspecified Areas	1.16	0.32
Total	41.13	9.11
of which:		
Grants	32.19	8.76
Credits	8.94	0.35
Grand total, annual average	4.97	4.83

Source: *Statistical Abstract of the United States 1958.*

and loans amounting to about 525 million dollars in the period 1946/47–1956/57. About 60 per cent of this sum has been received by countries in *Africa*. Further, the British territories have had grants-in-aid from the United Kingdom to the value of 175 million dollars in the period 1951/52–1955/56. Similarly, during the period 1948–56 there has been a capital

export of about 125 million dollars by the Colonial Development Corpora-
tion, an institution whose purpose is to assist the colonial territories in the
development of their economies. The governments or other public bodies of
these territories have raised loans on the British capital market to a value of

TABLE IV.6

United States Direct Investment in Foreign Countries 1946 and 1956.
(Billion Dollars)

	End of 1946	End of 1956	Increase
Geographic Distribution:			
Canada	2.47	7.48	5.01
Western Europe	1.04	3.49	2.45
Latin America	3.05	7.41	4.36
West European "dependencies"	0.15	0.82	0.67
Others	0.52	2.92	2.40
Total	7.23	22.12	14.89
Distribution by Industry:			
Oil	1.40	7.25	5.85
Manufacturing	2.37	7.09	4.72
Mining	0.83	2.39	1.56
Public Utilities	1.34	1.69	0.35
Trade	0.41	1.44	1.03
Other	0.88	2.26	1.38
Total	7.23	22.12	14.89

Source: *Statistical Abstract of the United States 1958* and D. McDougall (1957).

about 425 million dollars during the period 1949/50–1956/57. There is
little information to be had concerning private capital transactions. It has
been estimated, however, that private capital export to the dependent areas
of about 525 million dollars has taken place in the years 1954–56. France's
export of public capital for purposes of investment in her overseas territories
amounted to over 1,800 million dollars in the period 1952–56. The bulk of
this export has gone to *Africa*. Besides this there has been an export of
private capital from France to her overseas territories. Information con-

cerning this is far from complete, but for the period 1952–56 the recorded capital export was about 400 million dollars.

Since the war the *USSR* has also played the part of capital exporter mainly to *Eastern Europe* and the countries under communist rule in *Asia*, but also to some other countries in *Asia*, the *Middle East* and *Africa*. The

TABLE IV.7

Investment, Saving, and Capital Influx 1954–56, Annual Averages.

	Net Domestic Product (Billion Dollars)	Per cent of Net Domestic Product		
		Investment	Saving Exceeding Investment	Long-term Capital Influx
North America ...	342	about 11	0.5 to 1	—1.0
Western Europe .	244	about 13	0 to 0.5	–
Oceania	12	about 25	—3 to —4	1.2
USSR	109	20–25	...	—0.3
Eastern Europe ..	51	15–20	...	0.5
Latin America ...	48	11–12	—1 to —2	1.8
Middle East	15	10–12	—1 to —3	2.1
Asia	107	10–12	about —1	1.1
of which: Mainland China and Japan	55	15–20	–	0.3
Other Areas	52	6–7	about —2	2.0
Africa	20	about 15	—1 to —2	5.0

Source : cf. Chapter I, Table IV. 3 and text.

total loans received from the *USSR* by communist countries in the period 1945–55 is estimated to have been about 2 billion dollars. The total loans promised to non-communist countries by the *USSR* up to the middle of 1959 amounted to about 3 billion dollars, of which about 1 billion dollars were granted in 1958.

In Table IV. 7 are shown all the capital transactions mentioned above. The aim has been to provide an impression of capital movements between the regions and to compare them with what is known about investment and saving there. The figures for capital movements between the regions are not strictly accurate although a reasonably close approximation has been made.

In drawing up the Table, United States military aid has not been included, and for this reason *Western Europe*'s imports of long-term capital appear to be very modest. United States aid may be regarded as an influx of *Capital* just as much as any other capital import provided the countries that receive it would maintain the same military equipment if they had not received aid as they do with it. Because the reactions of different countries to the prospect of increased expenditure on defence may vary, however, and as the information available on United States military aid does not allow of an analysis by regions it has been omitted from Table IV. 7.

There is a fairly close agreement between the figures for investment on the one hand and those for saving and capital export or import on the other, though the differences are not entirely negligible. Besides other long-term capital movements than those stated in the Table, as for example from the United Kingdom to *Asia* in connection with the Colombo Plan, short-term capital movements, as mentioned above, may also have taken place.

The total capital movements between the nine regions shown in Table IV. 7 amount to a little under 4 billion dollars. This is a fairly small amount compared with the total net domestic product of *North America* and the *USSR*, the principal capital exporting regions, and in fact it is less than 1 per cent of the net domestic product. On the other hand, these capital movements are of considerable importance to the recipients of the *Capital*. The capital import of *Latin America* represents about one sixth, and that of *Africa* and *Asia* (excluding China and Japan) about one third of investment in those regions.

C. *Future Development*

9. The main objective of the present section is to estimate, for the period ending in 1980, *the increase of Capital,* i.e. net investment, in the various regions.

The amount of investment, however, is not independent of the size of production. This is obvious as far as total investment is concerned, as big production allows of big investment. It also applies, however, as far as the investment quota is concerned. When the development in investment is estimated it will thus be necessary to take account of the development in production—which is, indeed, the subject of the present book.

With regard to no other factor of growth is there such a clear relationship as between *Capital* and the growth of total production. This fact, therefore, decides the procedure to be adopted in any estimate of future capital formation, i.e. of net investment. In the foregoing paragraphs two terms have been used to relate the annual net investment to certain variables expressing the extent or growth of production. These terms are *the investment quota* and *the marginal capital/output ratio*. They are defined as follows:

$$\text{Investment quota} = \frac{\text{net investment}}{\text{net domestic product}} \qquad (1)$$

$$\text{Marginal capital/output ratio} = \frac{\text{net investment}}{\text{increase in net domestic product}} \qquad (2)$$

It is useful to relate these formulas to a third which expresses the growth of production, viz. the *rate of growth*, defined thus:

$$\text{Rate of growth} = \frac{\text{increase in net domestic product}}{\text{net domestic product}} \qquad (3)$$

By dividing (1) by (2) we get:

$$\frac{\text{investment quota}}{\text{marginal capital/output ratio}} = \text{rate of growth} \qquad (4)$$

(4) is a term denoting the relationship between the growth of *Capital* and the growth of production, as also in (2). In Table IV. 8 figures are given for the three factors included in (4) on the assumption of, respectively, a relatively small and a relatively large rate of growth in each region. These two assumptions are discussed in more detail in Chapter VII B[8]. The two rates of growth shown in Table IV. 8 are identical with those of Table VII. 2.

It should also be mentioned that the three factors considered here are so arranged in Table IV. 8 that they conform to formula (4) both when the minimum and when the maximum rate of growth is applied. In practice this is done by estimating the value of each of the three factors separately and then applying and adjusting them so that they conform to the relationship expressed in (4). In this way each factor is not only required to be

---

[8] See pp. 249–251 and especially Table VII. 2.

reasonably likely in itself but is made to conform to "reasonable" values for the other two factors.

Further, it may be said of the *rates of growth* shown in the Table that they have been estimated in accordance, partly, with the growth up to 1955 and, partly, with an over-all estimate of the relationship between the four

TABLE IV.8

Investment Quotas and Capital/Output (c/o) Ratios 1955–80.

	1955 (1954-56 Average)		1955-80 Min. Rate of Growth			1955-80 Max. Rate of Growth		
	Inv. Quota (Per cent)	Average c/o Ratio	Inv. Quota (Per cent)	Marginal c/o Ratio	Rate of Growth (Per cent)	Inv. Quota (Per cent)	Marginal c/o Ratio	Rate of Growth (Per cent)
N. America .	about 11	3.0	10	3.33	3.00	14	3.11	4.50
W. Europe .	about 13	3.5	9	5.14	1.75	13	4.00	3.25
Oceania	about 25	3.3	12	3.43	3.50	16	3.56	4.50
USSR	20–25	3.0	15	3.75	4.00	20	3.64	5.50
E. Europe ..	15–20	3.5	11	4.40	2.50	15	3.75	4.00
L. America .	11–12	2.9	10	2.67	3.75	14	2.95	4.75
Midd. East .	10–12	2.5	9	2.75	3.25	12	2.82	4.25
Asia	10–12	2.5	6	3.43	1.75	11	4.00	2.75
Africa	about 15	2.5	8	3.20	2.50	12	3.43	3.50

Source : cf. Table IV. 2 and IV. 3 and text.

factors of growth as it may be expected to evolve during the period. In the following paragraphs a few remarks are made about the considerations which have determined the way in which the above survey of investment quotas and marginal capital/output ratios has been prepared.

Thus, the two *investment quotas* for the years 1955–80 have been estimated in the light of what has been said above on this subject. Therefore the quotas for 1954–56 (see Table IV. 3) are shown for comparison. In view of the close relationship that exists between investment and economic growth the investment quota has been assumed to be comparatively low at the minimum rate of growth and comparatively high at the maximum rate. The difference between the maximum and the minimum investment quotas has been made fairly large in most of the regions.

The investment quotas depend, as previously explained, partly on the saving quotas of the various regions and partly on capital movements between the regions, both of which are difficult to estimate. In the following paragraphs a few examples of the problems of making such estimates will be mentioned.

What will be the development in saving quotas in the advanced areas? In recent years, saving it would seem, has been a good deal higher than in the inter-war period. Will it remain on this rather high level or will the quotas begin to fall? What assumptions can be made with regard to defence costs and what influence are these costs likely to have on saving? Will the pressure for a higher standard of living exerted by the population of the *USSR* and *Eastern Europe* cause a reduction of the saving quota there?

In Table IV. 8 the investment quotas for the two last-mentioned regions have been reduced substantially compared with the quotas for 1954–56, partly, because of the likelihood of higher consumption, and partly in view of the increasing importance of wear and tear on capital as the active capital advances in age and size. A large reduction has been made for *Oceania* as the figure for 1954–56 is probably abnormally high. The higher quota in 1954–56 for *Western Europe* than in *North America* is probably due to the fact that during those years *Western Europe* was undergoing reconstruction facilitated by capital import from the United States. Another reason may be the large American defence budget and the military aid given to other countries. For 1955–80 the investment quotas have been assumed to be slightly lower in *Western Europe* than in *North America*.

As regards the underdeveloped areas it is particularly difficult to estimate future investment quotas. Many countries in these regions wish, in order to promote their plans for development, to pursue a policy that will lead to an increase in saving. Their very low income level, however, will often make this difficult. *Latin America* has the best chance of doing so because here the income level is rather higher than in the other backward regions. The same applies to those countries of the *Middle East* which receive large revenues from oil. In *Asia* and *Africa*, on the other hand, the difficulties will be very great if the two regions are to manage with the saving they can produce themselves. We should probably expect a considerable flow of capital to these regions from *North America* and presumably also, to an increasing extent, from the *USSR*. Finally, the countries of *Western Europe* which have territories in *Asia* and *Africa* (especially the United Kingdom, France, and Belgium) are likely to continue to export capital to those territories. This export will probably be furthered indirectly by a continuous flow of *Capital* from *North America* to *Western Europe*.

A large part of the capital movements dealt with here will, however, depend on political considerations and it is therefore impossible to estimate them with any degree of certainty. It should also be mentioned that in large parts of the underdeveloped regions it will only be possible to utilize effectively an increase in investment if political stability can be assured and considerable progress in education and general enlightment be achieved.

The *marginal capital/output ratios* for 1955–80 shown in Table IV. 8 are in most cases rather higher than the corresponding average ratios for 1954–56. As said above, it is normal for the capital/output ratio to rise when the amount of *Capital* invested increases at a greater rate than that of the other factors of production employed, especially *Labour* and *Nature*. This may be of particular importance in the case of *Western Europe*. Even so the marginal capital/output ratio assessed for this region may tend to exaggerate the influence of this effect. It should be pointed out here that the increase in invested capital in the period 1955–80 is likely to be very great, as far as can be judged from the current trend. As appears from Table IV. 9 there will be, roughly, a doubling of *Capital* if the minimum rate of growth obtains and a trebling if the maximum rate obtains for the regions considered as a whole.

The tendency towards higher capital/output ratios is counteracted by technical progress. On the other hand, investment which only affects production in the long run may be expected to become increasingly important in the period under consideration. In the underdeveloped regions such investment is first and foremost that made in power plants, railways, roads, harbours, schools, etc., whereas investment in nuclear research and utilization, space exploration, etc. will probably make increasing demands on the capital budgets of the other regions.

It appears that in most cases the marginal capital/output ratios remain practically the same whether maximum or minimum rates of growth obtain. The fact that the growth of invested capital is so large at the maximum rate of growth might suggest that capital/output ratios generally are largest at the maximum rate. However, a large increase over so long a period is only possible we may assume, provided there are such favourable circumstances as, for example, the maintenance of a high and stable level of employment, a high rate of technical progress accompanied by a speedy rise in the level of education, new possibilities of utilizing natural resources, etc. which will at the same time contribute to greater achievements in production in relation to invested capital.

10. In Table IV. 9 is shown how invested capital will grow in the period reviewed if the same assumptions as those employed in Table IV. 8 are

TABLE IV.9

Capital in 1980.
(Billion Dollars)

	Capital 1955	Min. Growth			Max. Growth		
		Growth of Net Domestic Product 1955-80	Growth of Capital 1955-1980	Capital 1980	Growth of Net Domestic Product 1955-80	Growth of Capital 1955-1980	Capital 1980
North America	1,015	374	1,245	2,260	686	2,133	3,148
Western Europe	850	132	678	1,528	299	1,196	2,046
Oceania	40	16	55	95	24	85	125
USSR	325	182	683	1,008	307	1,117	1,442
Eastern Europe	175	44	194	369	85	319	494
Latin America .	140	72	192	332	105	310	450
Middle East	35	18	50	85	27	76	111
Asia	270	58	199	469	104	416	686
Africa	50	17	54	104	27	93	143
Total	2,900	913	3,350	6,250	1,664	5,745	8,645

Source: cf. Table IV. 2 and text.

made. The Table also shows *Capital* in 1955 (see Table IV. 2) and *Capital* in 1980 as it will be on these assumptions.

The figures for the growth of *Capital* in the period 1955–80 have been calculated by multiplying the marginal capital/output ratios shown in Table IV. 8 by the total increase in the net domestic product in the same period. The marginal capital/output ratio is defined, as mentioned earlier, as the growth of capital divided by the growth of total production.

The increase in the net domestic product from 1955 to 1980 may be deduced from Table VII. 2 in which the total net domestic product is shown for 1955 and for 1980 assuming both the minimum and the maximum rates of growth.

Finally it should be added that it has been necessary in the present chapter to confine all estimates to *Capital* and investment in the ordinary sense of the words. The *investment in knowledge*[9] mentioned in Chapter II could not be included in the tables, partly because too little is known about its size —not to mention the problems of trying to give a quantitative value to this factor. There can be no doubt, however, that the sum of accumulated knowledge even in 1955 represented intangible capital of very great importance to production especially in the developed regions. This is particularly true of that part of it which, in the form of education, is "invested" in the labour force, mainly among its best qualified groups.

In the period 1955–80 we may expect a rapid increase in intangible investment on account of research, education, and general enlightenment. This will probably apply more and more to the underdeveloped regions or certain parts of them. If it were possible to evaluate this accumulation of knowledge, in all its forms, the figures for *Capital* and its increase would be higher. Consequently the capital/output ratios shown in Table IV. 8 would also be greater. This is presumably true, especially, under the assumption of maximum rates of growth, a necessary condition of which is that there should be great strides forward in research and education.

[9] See pages 38–39.

9*

CHAPTER V

Nature

—

A. *Prefatory Remarks*

It was stressed in Chapter II[1] that in estimating the position of the nine
regions with regard to *Nature* as a factor of production and growth, both
the technical development and the current demand during the period should
be taken into account. The size of the population and the size of its income
are factors that play a particularly important rôle in determining the amount
and nature of the total demand. Again, it is this demand, together with the
technical methods employed, that determines which of the gifts of *Nature*
will be used. The demands made on *Nature* will thus depend on the total
economic growth.

Conversely, the natural conditions partly determine how large this growth
can be. If the provision of energy and primary products engages a large,
and perhaps increasing, amount of economic activity in a certain area this
may have a retarding influence on total growth. The rates of growth for
total production shown in Chapter VII (Table VII. 2) have therefore been
estimated in accordance, *inter alia,* with what is said in that chapter about
the natural conditions of the separate regions.

As mentioned in Chapter II, the world is gradually becoming a unity
with regard to demand. Certain natural resources, e.g. hydro-electric power,
would be too expensive to use far from their location. Most primary
products, however, can be carried over great distances. For many of them
increases in production will tend to take place, especially in areas where
conditions for production are most favourable, and not always where the
primary products are to be used. It seems probable, therefore, that trade
in primary products between the regions will increase considerably during
the period under review.

Thus if a region is, in certain respects, richly endowed by nature, its pro-

[1] See pages 47–49.

duction of primary products may exceed its own consumption and it may, therefore, become an exporter of them to other regions. The income from this export may then enable the region, or parts of it, to increase its imports of machinery, etc., and thus to promote general economic growth. On the other hand other regions may have to import, to an increasing extent, certain primary products. The consequent strain on their balance of payments may then compel them to invest less than they would otherwise be able to.

In view of the rapidly growing world population a great increase in the demand for *food* may be expected. An attempt is made in section B of this chapter to examine the natural conditions of food supply which is based, largely, on the limited, but usually renewable resources of farm land and the sea.

The supply of energy, on the other hand, which is dealt with in section C, is based, to only a slight extent, on renewable resources, such as forests and waterfalls. On the whole the supply of energy, which is so closely connected with the process of economic growth, is based on expendable resources of mineral fuels, especially coal, oil and natural gas.

Among the many metals and other minerals which are used in industry, *iron ore* is by far the most important. Further, it is closely related to investment in, for example, machinery and means of transport, and therefore, like energy, with the expansion of production. Section D thus deals mainly with iron ore.

Finally, section E contains some concluding remarks meant to summarize, as far as this is possible, the main ideas of the chapter.

B. *Food*

1. *Food Consumption and Production 1955*

Food consumption is normally expressed in terms of calories per person per day[2]. In the following text food consumption is given for the populations of the various regions.

The food consumption of the people of a certain region is calculated in calories on the basis of information regarding the "food basket" available to this population during the period under consideration.

---

[2] The calorie used here is that normally used in physiology, the kilocalorie, *kcal,* being equal to the energy required to raise the temperature of 1 kg. of water one degree centigrade.

In the first stage of the calculation an attempt is made to estimate the quantities of animal and vegetable foods the people of the regions have consumed. The figures for consumption used below are mainly those which appear in the FAO Food Balance Sheets. In these the progress of each crop in the different countries is followed from the harvest to the subsequent applications, viz. exportation, food, sowing, trade and industry, changes in stock piles, waste, etc. up to the point when the foods are placed on the shop-counter. Thus it is the consumption of the various foods at retail level that is being examined. Such food balance sheets, however, have not been prepared for every country. It will be necessary, therefore, to deal largely with rough estimates. Added to this is the fact that the calculations of food consumption are very uncertain, even in the case of countries for which such balance sheets have been prepared. It goes without saying that great difficulties are encountered in estimating the harvest itself as well as in the following stages of its handling. This applies particularly to the estimate of fodder consumption.

Further, the second stage of the calculation, viz. the conversion of food quantities to calories creates more uncertainty. The quality, and thus the calorie content, of the different foods varies a good deal from country to country, but the same factors of conversion are used everywhere. The conversion factors employed in the present chapter are those recommended by FAO[3].

In estimating the food supplies of a region it is important to know not only the total calorie consumption, but also the quality of the food consumed. To provide satisfactory nourishment food must contain at least certain minimum quantities of the various substances of which the human body consists. The consumption of protein, especially, is of great importance in this connection. Consequently, in the following paragraphs figures are given for the protein content, both animal and vegetable, of the food. What has been said about uncertainty with regard to the estimated consumption of calories applies equally to protein consumption.

In Table V. 1 the calorie value of average per capita food consumption thus calculated is shown for the nine regions. In addition the total protein consumption and the part of it which is animal in origin is given. In Table V. 2 the percentage of carbohydrates in the food of various countries is

[3] FAO (1949).

shown. This Table reveals, as might have been expected, that the countries in the regions which have a small consumption of protein are those in which the food has the highest carbohydrate content.

TABLE V. 1

Food Consumption in 1955.

	Calories per capita per day (kcal.)	Protein per capita per day (grammes)	Animal Protein per capita per day (grammes)
North America	3,150	95	67
Western Europe[1] ..	2,950	84	43
Oceania	3,200	91	59
USSR[2]	3,000	90	34
Eastern Europe	2,950	86	34
Latin America[3]	2,500	67	26
Middle East[4]	2,600	82	13
Asia[5]	1,925	52	8
Africa[2]	2,300	70	11
Total	2,325	66	21

[1] Among the larger countries Spain is not included.
[2] These figures are ad hoc estimates.
[3] Among the larger countries Cuba, Mexico, Columbia, and Venezuela are not included.
[4] Includes only Israel, Turkey, and Egypt.
[5] Includes only Ceylon, India, Pakistan, and Japan.
Sources: UN (1957, d). FAO *Yearbook (Production)* 1957. UN (1959, a).

The figures of Table V. 1 refer largely to the year 1955, in some cases to 1954 or 1953, and for most of the East European countries to a more recent year. In most cases they are based on estimates for individual countries made by FAO. As far as the East European countries are concerned they are, however, from ECE sources (see references at the food of the Table).

The figures for *North America, Western Europe, Oceania,* and *Eastern Europe* include practically all the countries in them. *Latin America* is covered to the extent of 60 per cent of its population, the *Middle East* and *Asia* only to the extent of 50 per cent. The available figures for *Africa* include only those for the Union of South Africa and the Central African

Federation and cannot, therefore, be considered a very reliable guide as far as *Africa* as a whole is concerned. The figures in the Table, therefore, are estimates. Only incomplete information is available for the *USSR*, where food consumption is probably a little higher than in *Eastern Europe*.

The information contained in Table V. 1 should, of course, be read with the important reservations mentioned above in mind. Despite these it would seem possible, however, to discern from the Tables certain characteristic differences between the regions. Above all, the Tables reveal a very big difference between the developed regions, viz. *North America, Oceania, Western* and *Eastern Europe* and the *USSR* on the one hand and the four underdeveloped regions, viz. *Latin America*, the *Middle East, Asia,* and *Africa,* on the other. *Asia's* per capita calorie consumption is, in fact, according to the Table, less than two-thirds of that of the developed regions.

Whether this difference is sufficiently large for the conclusion to be drawn that a large part of the population of the underdeveloped regions is permanently undernourished—as has often been maintained—seems doubtful, however, in view of our limited knowledge of the requirements for food in the various regions. The differences in climate between the two groups of regions, and the distribution of population by age groups, race, average height and weight, and especially the differences in the kinds of physical activity undertaken during and outside working hours are so great that they may well account for a great difference in food requirements. No accurate information on the relation between the food requirements and these factors is available[4], however.

On the other hand, although no widespread famines have occurred since the war we should not, for that reason, conclude that the calorie requirement has everywhere been fully met. An insufficient supply of calories in the human body shows itself, initially, in loss of weight, reduced working capacity etc., i.e. symptoms which very frequently occur in the populations of underdeveloped countries. These symptoms of undernourishment, however, are probably rather due to the quality of the food, particularly as regards the small protein content, than to lack of calories. It is noteworthy, in this connection, that a low protein content is often indicative of other deficiences. Table V. 1 shows large differences between the regions with regard, also, to the consumption of protein. The consumption of animal pro-

---

[4] See FAO (1957).

TABLE V. 2

Food Carbohydrate Content.
(Average Per cent of Total Calorie Consumption)

	1948/49–1949/50	1952/53–1953/54
North America		
Canada	45	44
United States	43	42
Western Europe		
Austria	65	58
France	60	57
West Germany	68	54
Greece	66	64
Italy	70	68
Netherlands	58	51
Portugal	64	65
Sweden	50	48
United Kingdom	52	50
Oceania		
Australia	51	50
New Zealand	47	43
Latin America		
Argentina	56	50
Brazil	66	66
Chile	74	69
Colombia	68	63
Mexico	72	72
Uruguay	48	49
Middle East		
Egypt	78	78
Turkey	79	77
Asia		
India	75	76
Japan	81	78
Pakistan	80	78
Africa		
Southern Rhodesia	80	79
Union of South Africa .	76	76

Source : UN (1957, d, page 54).

tein, especially, is very small in the underdeveloped regions as compared with that of the developed regions. Although the two kinds of protein may, to a certain extent, replace each other, a certain minimum quantity of animal protein is necessary for the formation of the amino acids in the human body. A figure for this minimum requirement cannot be given, but when the intake of animal protein approaches its minimum, a greatly increased amount of vegetable protein is required if the total protein need is to be satisfied. When the carbohydrate content of the food approaches 80 per cent, which is the case in some countries, cf. Table V. 2, it is doubtful whether this protein need is satisfied.

On balance the two Tables seem to show that even to-day there is a major problem with regard to meeting the food requirements of the underdeveloped regions, and that it is particularly urgent as far as the requirement for animal protein is concerned.

A necessary condition for a realistic appraisal of the development of *agricultural production* is a knowledge of current conditions. First of all it is necessary to know the total vegetable production as this forms the basis of the total food supply (apart from fish, see page 156 below), either as vegetable calories for human consumption directly, or as fodder for animals which provide meat, etc.

Further, it is important to know the conditions prevailing in animal production, and especially how many vegetable calories are required for making the various animal products. Only thus can the consequences of possible changes in protein consumption in the various regions be estimated.

Unfortunately, the available statistical material regarding food production is as scanty as the consumption statistics. With regard to the yield per unit of fodder used in animal production, especially, calculations have to be based on rather arbitrary estimates.

The total "vegetable production", by crops, is not known for the whole world and FAO has not so far published estimates. The estimates given below, which are based on calculations specially made for this book, can therefore at the most, provide only an idea of the order of magnitude of the "true" figures. Even such an incomplete estimate of the level of total vegetable production in the nine regions may, however, be of some interest.

Total vegetable production may be measured in two ways, viz. by a direct survey of the harvest or by using food consumption as a basis and then calculating how large a quantity of vegetable produce has been used for the total food supply. If this method is used it will be necessary to make adjustments for that part of vegetable production which is used for sowing, as fodder for draught animals, and in industry, as well as that part which has been wasted at the various stages of production.

Direct data for vegetable production are only available for a few countries and even for these the grass crops have been estimated residually, i.e. on information about animal production based on grass fodder. Thus an artificial agreement is created between the direct and the indirect methods of calculation. Independent estimates can only be made with difficulty.

On certain very rough assumptions, however, a direct estimate of vegetable production may be made. In 1955 the total cultivated area of the earth amounted to about 1,400 million hectares whilst the area of permanent grass land amounted to approximately 2,400 million hectares. The area under cultivation has for some years been steadily increasing.

The acreage laid to grains, pulses, oil seeds, potatoes and other roots, fruit, and certain fibres is known, but how much is sown with turnips, green fodder, beets, various seeds, etc. is only known for some countries and at intervals of several years. The acreage of fallow land has not been recorded except in a few countries.

That part of the cultivated area which has been specified has presumably been considered the most important being mainly that under crops which can be used directly as human food.

In Table V. 3 below the world's farming area is shown. It should be noted that the figures for fallow land etc. are partly calculated figures, and those for fodder crops have been calculated residually.

As grain is the most important crop and probably the one which has been most accurately measured it is shown in Table V. 4.

The crop average is given in *crop units* per hectare. This units is defined as the fodder value of 100 kg of barley. It should be pointed out that the figures in Table V. 4 for the various crops do not include the yield of straw. In certain areas, especially in *Asia*, straw is an important livestock fodder.

As the acreage devoted to grain amounts to about one-half of the total cultivated area, and as the grain yield is generally a fair indication of the size of other crops, it seems reasonable to use the grain yield in the various regions to calculate the total yield of all crops. There is reason to believe, however, that the hectare yield, in crop units, of the fodder crops in *Europe* is higher than the grain yield. This is certainly true of north-west Europe.

TABLE V.3

The World's Farming Area About 1955.

(Million hectares)

	Grains	Sugar	Potatoes and Other Roots	Pulse	Oil Seeds	Fruit and Vegetables	Beets, Other Fodder Crops, Certain Vegetables (calculated)	Fallow Land, Seeds, etc. (partly calculated)	Tobacco, Coffee, Tea, etc. Fibres	Cultivated Area, Total	Permanent Grass Land	Total
North America	98.7	0.6	0.8	0.8	18.0	0.6	74.5	34.4	0.7	229.1	279.0	508.1
Western Europe ...	41.4	1.4	4.4	2.8	0.8	6.0	28.7	9.5	0.3	95.3	64.9	160.2
Oceania	6.5	0.2	0.1	–	–	0.1	13.5	3.6	–	24.0	377.0	401.0
USSR	125.0	1.8	9.1	1.4	8.9	1.5	35.7	42.6	2.6	228.6	259.0	487.6
Eastern Europe	33.9	1.2	4.9	2.5	2.4	1.0	3.1	5.5	0.2	54.7	20.1	74.8
Latin America	33.2	2.9	3.0	4.8	7.5	1.1	26.4	15.3	6.7	100.9	368.0	468.9
Middle East	23.1	0.3	0.1	0.8	2.6	1.2	19.9	8.5	0.2	56.7	158.0	214.7
Asia	251.7	2.2	13.8	27.0	51.7	0.5	20.1	–	4.3	371.3	276.0	647.3
Africa	46.6	0.2	6.8	2.8	8.0	0.6	129.7	34.9	2.8	232.4	594.0	826.4
Total	660.1	10.8	43.0	42.9	99.9	12.6	351.6	154.3	17.8	1,393.0	2,396.0	3,789.0

Sources: The *FAO Yearbook (Production)* 1957 and the authors' own calculations made on the basis of among others: Leo Ranek (1959) and K. Wittern (1954).

TABLE V.4

The World's Grain Crop in 1955.

(Million crop units)

	Wheat	Rye	Barley	Oats	Mixed Grain	Maize	Millet and Sorghum	Rice	Total	Crop Units (Hectare)
North America	395.7	11.1	142.3	234.2	10.0	872.9	61.6	20.8	1,747.6	17.7
Western Europe	354.9	64.4	143.5	121.0	27.7	61.2	0.2	13.0	785.9	19.0
Oceania	53.9	0.1	9.9	8.8	—	1.4	1.4	0.9	76.4	11.8
USSR	460.0	...	...	...	...	...	...	...	1,070	8.6
Eastern Europe	143.1	115.0	55.5	46.7	10.2	157.8	1.2	1.2	530.7	15.7
Latin America	95.1	6.9	17.0	8.0	—	200.6	5.4	45.8	378.8	11.4
Middle East	119.5	6.5	50.5	3.0	3.4	31.6	8.5	14.6	237.6	10.3
Asia	390.2	0.3	194.8	15.0	—	212.7	403.1	1,562.9	2,779.0	11.0
Africa	39.2	—	29.9	2.1	—	92.5	127.1	23.7	314.5	6.7
Total	...	...	...	...	...	...	...	...	7,920.5	12.0

Note: In converting to crop units the following factors of conversion have been used: Wheat, rye, barley, millet and sorghum, 1.0, oats 1/1.2, mixed grain 1/1.1, maize 1/0.95, rice 1/1.22.

Sources: FAO *Yearbook (Production)* 1958 and, for the *USSR*, FAO, *The State of Food and Agriculture* 1959.

In a world-wide survey, however, it is reasonable to assume the same yield per hectare for that part of the cultivated area which does not lie fallow and which is not used for stimulant plants, fibre plants, grass seeds, etc., as for grain.

If we assume that 1,220 million hectares are sown with grain and other food plants and that each hectare yields 12 crop units, the result is 15 billion crop units.

There then remain the grass crops from 2,400 million hectares of permanent pasture. These crops have been used solely for animal fodder—in so far as they have been used at all. Some grass crops have not been utilized, but the area covered by them is not known. Further, the degree of utilization that has been achieved in the areas which have actually been used for pasture in uncertain. It might be mentioned in this context, however, that the amount of grass crops yielded by the areas which cannot, for various reasons, be used for pasture, is immaterial because it cannot be used in food production. As it may probably be assumed that the grass areas which can be used for pasture have, as a rule, been used for this purpose already, the yield of grass may, very roughly, be said to be the amount of grass consumed by animals in the grazing period. Thus only the degree of exploitation of various forms of pasture (for example whether the animals are grazing during the whole growing season, etc.) is left out of account.

By the indirect method of measuring vegetable production the total consumption of fodder, including that for draught animals, is estimated to be about 15 billion crop units (13.7 plus 10 per cent waste, cf. Table V.7). The amount of grass fodder may roughly be put at one-half of this amount, that is 7.5 billion crop units or about 3 crop units per hectare. This is tantamount to a crop unit per hectare yield of 25 per cent of that obtained from arable land. This result does not seem at all improbable. It must be emphasized, however, that in this field our knowledge is very slight. On the other hand, the use of the grass yield estimated by the indirect method as a standard brings about an artificial agreement between the results obtained from the two methods of measurements. Independent evaluation of the two estimates can, therefore, only be achieved by inserting direct estimates of the grass yield. Little is known as to whether the grass yield mentioned above is reasonable but it must be assumed, as already said, that the grass yield from areas with permanent pasture does not differ much from the estimated 25 per cent of the yield per hectare of the cultivated area.

By this method we arrive at a figure for total vegetable production of between 20 and 25 billion crop units.

In the indirect method of calculating the starting point is the use of vegetable products. Part of the vegetable production is consumed directly and for this the information provided by the Food Balance Sheets may be used directly. The greater part of vegetable production, however, is used as raw material for the production of animal foods for human consumption. The total production of animal foods can be reckoned fairly accurately but it is very difficult to get any idea of how large are the quantities of vegetable products consumed by animals in the various regions.

With regard to *Europe* a group of experts have prepared estimates for 1955[5] of fodder per kg of the various food products of animal origin and have established the following standards:

For 100 kg of beef or mutton 17 crop units are required
 — 100 — — pork   6 —   —   —   —
 — 100 — — milk   1 —   unit is   —
 — 100 — — eggs   6 —   units are   —

These standards have been used below also in dealing with the other regions, although, in this way, the consumption of fodder will undoubtedly be underestimated for most of the underdeveloped regions. Special mention should be made of the fact that the large stock of oxen in *Asia,* and especially in India, appears to account for a considerably larger consumption of fodder per kg of milk than that for the cattle of the more developed regions in the temperate zones. Added to this is the fact that Indian oxen are not used for human consumption.

In Tables V. 5 and V. 6 below are shown figures for the consumption of fodder. These figures have been calculated in accordance with the standards referred to above. It has been necessary, however, to add a few items which were not included in the publication referred to above. These items are horse meat, poultry, waste meat, tallow, and a certain amount of lard. For poultry 6 crop units per 100 kg have been used and for horse meat and the other products 10 crop units per 100 kg. Lard is included under pork. It should be noted that in the *Middle East* all waste meat etc. is considered as originating from horned cattle and sheep and that the factor 17 has consequently been used for that region.

[5] FAO (1955).

TABLE V.5

The Production of Animal Products in 1955.
(Million kg)

	Milk	Meat of Cattle, Sheep, Goats	Pork and Lard	Poultry	Waste Meat, etc.	Eggs
North America ...	63,800	7,760	6,730	2,810	2,380	3,940
Western Europe .	90,000	4,910	5,695	640	1,580	2,640
Oceania	11,300	1,740	143	50	270	150
USSR	43,200	3,005	2,530	...	785	1,080
Eastern Europe ..	22,200	1,600	2,845	330	230	630
Latin America ...	18,200	5,410	1,410	293	1,136	780
Middle East	7,900	970	–	62	138	165
Asia	32,200	3,740	6,272	679	1,151	1,810
Africa	10,600	1,970	145	96	255	255
Total	299,400	31,105	25,770	4,960	7,925	11,450

Note : Poultry in the four last regions is distributed in relation to egg production. Waste meat in the four last regions is distributed in relation to beef, pork, etc. For the *USSR* waste meat includes poultry.

Sources: Det Statistiske Departement (1957). FAO *Yearbook* (*Production*) 1957. Swedborg (1959).

TABLE V.6

Fodder Consumption for the Output Stated in Table V.5.
(Million crop units)

	Milk	Meat of Cattle, Sheep, Goats	Pork and Lard	Poultry	Waste Meat, etc.	Eggs	Total
North America ...	638	1,319	404	169	238	236	3,004
Western Europe .	900	835	342	38	158	158	2,431
Oceania	113	296	8	3	27	9	456
USSR	432	511	152	...	79	65	1,239
Eastern Europe ..	222	272	171	20	23	38	746
Latin America ...	182	920	85	18	114	47	1,366
Middle East	79	165	–	4	23	10	281
Asia	322	636	376	41	115	109	1,599
Africa	106	335	8	6	25	15	495
Total	2,994	5,289	1,546	299	802	687	11,617

Source : Table V.5 and the conversion rates given in the text.

The total production of the nine regions in 1955 has been calculated (see Table V. 7) partly on the basis of information obtained from FAO Food Balance Sheets regarding the amount of directly consumed crop units of vegetable products, and partly from the figures shown in Table V. 6. In

TABLE V.7

World Yields in 1955.
(Million crop units)

	Direct Consumption of Vegetable Products	Livestock Products (Fodder Consumption)	Exports (+) Imports (−) (Plant Products)	Fodder for Draught Animals	Seeds	Total
	(1)	(2)	(3)	(4)	(5)	(6)
North America	357	3,004	+188	100	160	4,266
Western Europe ...	640	2,431	−335	200	110	3,412
Oceania	25	456	+ 37	20	15	619
USSR	519	1,239	−	300	280	2,619
Eastern Europe	289	746	− 13	160	90	1,425
Latin America	364	1,366	+114	650	60	2,860
Middle East	243	281	− 9	110	45	750
Asia	2,748	1,599	− 27	430	310	5,667
Africa	442	495	+ 54	170	90	1,401
Total	5,627	11,617	−384 +393	2,140	1,160	23,019

Note: The "Total" is the sum of the five first columns in the Table to which 12 per cent has been added (10 per cent for waste and 2 per cent for use in industry. These are items that are assumed to be included in the Food Balance Sheets, and consequently not included in "direct consumption of vegetable products").
Sources: Table V. 6. FAO (1959). FAO *Yearbook* (*Trade*) 1957.

this calculation exports and imports of vegetable products have also been taken into account. Among these grain predominates, but for some countries the import of oil cake is also of considerable importance. On the other hand, the fact that a certain amount of animal products are moved from one region to another before being consumed has been neglected as irrelevant to the subject of plant production. In Table V.7 are also given figures for fodder for horses, mules and donkeys, and for seed as well. With regard to the latter item, only grain, potatoes, pulses, and oil seeds have been taken into account. These, however, comprise the bulk of the crops of which the seed represents a considerable amount of crop units. Due consideration has been given to the fact that rice and maize require a good deal less seed per hectare than other grains.

According to this indirect reckoning the total amount of crop units available in 1955 appears to have been 23 billion. The two methods of reckoning thus lead to roughly the same results. The conclusion cannot be drawn, however, that the actual yield has amounted to the same number of crop units as there is much uncertainty in both cases and especially as an artificial agreement between the results of the two methods may occur in consequence of the way in which the grass yields have been estimated.

In making this comparison it should, further, be remembered that the direct calculation of vegetable production did not include the output of straw, although this is an important fodder, especially in the rice areas of *Asia*. The underestimate of the yield implied by the direct method of calculation is offset by a similar underestimate resulting from the indirect method of calculation, viz. the figures for livestock fodder. These figures, to all appearances, have been put too low, e.g. because the fodder consumption in the underdeveloped regions has been underestimated, especially as regards the fodder consumption of the indian oxen, a consumption which has been calculated on the basis of the, very low, yield of these oxen.

2. *Food Consumption and Production about 1980*

Food consumption in the nine regions in 1980 will be largely determined by the development in population on the one hand and the flow of real income on the other. Any estimate of the development in population and purchasing power, however, is subject to a high degree of uncertainty. Some of the problems of population have been dealt with in Chapter III, which provides projections for changes in population for 1955–80 for the various regions. The estimate of how much purchasing power will be expended on food depends, of course, partly on the development in the total per capita income, and partly on the proportion of such income that is spent on food. In Chapter VII an attempt has been made to form a numerical framework for the development in income in the regions with an indication of maximum and minimum figures for each region. These income figures have been used in the calculations below.

The part of total consumption accounted for by food consumption and the latter's relation to income may probably be determined with greater accuracy than may (future) income itself. In this field a good deal of information, based on experience, is available either in the form of (1) consumer survey data at a particular time which show the relation of expenditure on food to total expenditure on consumption of the families included in the surveys, or (2) time series which indicate over a period, for whole populations, the development in income per capita and the development in food expenditure per capita, or (3) the development as shown in the food balance sheets referred to earlier (see page 134). Such balance sheets are available for 38 countries and state the *quantity* of food consumed. These quantitative figures may easily be combined with figures for the per capita income of the countries in question. In the two former cases the figures for expenditure on food will have to be converted, as far as possible, into quantitative food figures before estimates can be made of the trend in consumption. In the latter case indications of quantities can be obtained directly. On the basis of the estimated income figures it will be possible to calculate the corresponding figures for food consumption, assuming that the relationship which has been found to exist between income and food consumption will not change.

It should, however, be kept in mind that a limit has to be put on the estimates for food consumption in the nine regions inasmuch as consumption, taken as a whole, can never exceed the total food production. On the other hand, the world's food production is not a given factor which imposes a fixed ceiling on consumption. In fact, total output will largely depend on the demand for food, especially if periods of five years or more are considered. It is obvious, however, that the extent of the possibilities of production limits the expansion of consumption. If, therefore, the calculations made here concerning the trend in consumption result in a total consumption estimate larger than the estimated potential production, it will be necessary to modify the assumptions with regard, especially, to population and income per capita on which such calculations have been based. This, again, means that the trends in food consumption, income, and population respectively cannot be calculated separately, but must be calculated simultaneously.

Despite these necessary and major reservations, a numerical estimate of food consumption in 1980 may still be of some interest as it may help us to decide whether the various regions will be able to meet the implied production requirements.

TABLE V.8

Per Capita Calorie Consumption and Protein Consumption per Diem in 1955 and 1980.

	Population		Per Capita Income			Per Capita Consumption per diem						
				1980		1955			1980			
									Min.		Max.	
	1955 (Million)	1980 (Million)	1955 (Dollars)	Min. (Dollars)	Max. (Dollars)	(kcal)	Protein (grammes)	Animal Protein (grammes)	(kcal)	Animal Protein (grammes)	(kcal)	Animal Protein (grammes)
North America	182	280	1,875	2,550	3,670	3,150	95	67	3,100	75	3,100	85
Western Europe	297	343	820	1,100	1,580	2,950	84	43	3,000	50	3,000	60
Oceania	13	20	955	1,400	1,800	3,200	91	59	3,200	70	3,200	80
USSR	197	286	550	1,020	1,450	3,000	90	34	3,150	48	3,200	58
Eastern Europe	112	143	455	665	950	2,950	86	34	3,100	43	3,200	52
Latin America	183	365	265	330	420	2,500	67	26	2,550	31	2,700	37
Middle East	95	169	160	195	250	2,600	82	13	2,650	15	2,800	19
Asia	1,418	2,326	75	70	90	1,925	52	8	1,875	7.5	2,050	9.5
Africa	193	289	105	130	165	2,300	70	11	2,400	14	2,500	17
Total	2,690	4,221	350	440	620	2,325	66	21	2,300	22	2,425	27

Source: FAO, The State of Food and Agriculture (1957), Table III. 8 and Table VII. 2.

The basis of the estimates of food consumption in the nine regions in 1980 given below, which consists partly of the consumption of calories, partly of the consumption of proteins, is a survey, published by FAO, on the relationships between income and food consumption[6]. These relationships are expressed by means of, among other things, a number of curves showing (in the cases of 38 countries) values for calorie consumption on the one hand and per capita income on the other, as well as protein consumption and per capita income. The regional figures for income and food consumption in 1955 shown in Table V. 8 respectively correspond well with these curves. The estimates given in Chapter VII of per capita income in the nine regions in 1980 have then made possible a reading of the calorie and protein consumption of the regions for that year from the curves. It has here been assumed that the relationship existing in 1955 between income and consumption will remain unchanged until 1980. In making these estimates, however, due regard has been given to the question as to whether the level of consumption of the regions in 1955 was above or below the "normal" curve: in the regions where consumption in 1955 was large in relation to income, consumption for 1980 has been put at a similarly high estimate and *vice versa*. These preliminary calculations have been made for both a maximum and a minimum estimate of income in 1980.

It appears that the per capita calorie consumption will remain almost unchanged in the developed regions, as the curve showing the connection between income and calorie consumption is almost horizontal from the point where it reaches a per capita/per annum income level of about $ 500; from the $ 1,000 level it even shows a slight fall. The consumption of animal protein, on the other hand, is more sensitive to changes in income, even for populations with a high income average, although this curve, too, levels off as soon as it reaches the top income group.

In the underdeveloped regions calorie consumption as well as protein consumption will show a comparatively large increase when there is an increase in income. When the standard of living of a population is so low that the consumption of food, quantitatively as well as qualitatively, touches the lower limit of food "demand"[7], it seems probable that a raising of the

---

[6] FAO, *The State of Food and Agriculture* (1957).

[7] In this context, a person's "demand" for food is (vaguely) to be understood as the quantity of calories, proteins, etc. that is required if the person, while keeping up his "normal" physical activity, is to maintain his "normal" physical condition.

income level will show itself in considerable changes in food consumption, including the consumption of foods rich in protein. With regard to *Asia,* however, the per capita income, on the minimum assumption, is expected to fall slightly. In this case a decline in per capita food consumption will consequently occur.

When the increase in population is also taken into account the total food consumption in the various regions can be calculated on the basis of the figures for per capita consumption in 1980, as these appear from Table V. 8. The total food consumption is shown in Table V. 9, which also gives, for each region and for the world as a whole, the annual rate of growth of calorie and animal protein consumption, both on the minimum and the maximum assumptions for the development of income.

The calorie consumption has been estimated to increase by a minimum of 1.8 per cent per annum and by a maximum of 2.0 per cent per annum for the world as a whole. The consumption of animal protein, a factor which is of great importance in the calculation of the plant production required to meet the estimated food consumption, shows a greater increase, viz. 2.2 per cent per annum and 2.9 per cent per annum respectively. For both calorie and protein consumption there are large differences in the rates of growth from country to country. *Western Europe* is lowest with an increase in calorie consumption of 0.6 per cent per annum on both maximum and minimum assumptions for the development in income and a minimum and maximum increase in the consumption of animal protein of 1.2 and 1.9 per cent per annum respectively. *Latin America* is highest with an increase in calorie consumption of 2.9 and 3.1 per cent per annum and an increase in animal protein consumption of 3.5 and 4.3 per cent per annum. It appears to be characteristic of the underdeveloped regions, where the increase in population is large and the demand for food very great, that they show the greatest increase in caloric consumption, whilst the consumption of live-stock products seems to be rising steeply in all regions. In the developed regions this is due, first and foremost, to the rapid growth of per capita income and in the underdeveloped regions to the rapid increase in population.

How correct are these consumption figures? Nothing can, of course, be said with any certainty on this point. In describing the methods that have been used to prepare Tables V. 7, V. 8 and V. 9 it was emphasized, as will be recalled, that the calculations were subject to a high degree of uncer-

TABLE V.9

Total Calorie and Animal Protein Consumption 1955 and 1980.

| | Total Consumption 1955 | | Total Consumption 1980 | | | | Rate of Growth between 1955 and 1980 Per cent per Annum | | | |
| | | | Min. | | Max. | | Min. | | Max. | |
	1000 Mill. kcal	1000 Mill. grammes Protein	1000 Mill. kcal	1000 Mill. grammes Protein	1000 Mill. kcal	1000 Mill. grammes Protein	kcal	Animal Protein	kcal	Animal Protein
North America	209,254	4,451	316,820	7,665	316,820	8,687	1.7	2.2	1.7	2.7
Western Europe	319,813	4,661	375,585	6,260	375,585	7,512	0.6	1.2	0.6	1.9
Oceania	15,184	280	23,360	511	23,360	584	1.7	2.4	1.7	3.0
USSR	215,715	2,445	328,829	5,011	334,048	6,055	1.7	2.9	1.8	3.7
Eastern Europe	120,596	1,390	161,804	2,244	167,024	2,714	1.2	1.9	1.3	2.7
Latin America	166,988	1,737	339,742	4,130	359,708	4,929	2.9	3.5	3.1	4.3
Middle East	90,155	451	163,447	925	172,718	1,172	2.4	2.9	2.6	3.9
Asia	996,304	4,140	1,591,838	6,367	1,740,430	8,065	1.9	1.7	2.3	2.7
Africa	162,024	775	253,164	1,477	263,712	1,793	1.8	2.6	2.0	3.4
Total	2,296,033	20,330	3,554,589	34,590	3,753,405	41,511	1.8	2.2	2.0	2.9

Source : Table V.8.

TABLE V.

Calculated Sup

		Per Capita Consumption per Day (in kcal)						
		Total Calories		Fish etc. Calor- ies	Animal Calorie Consumption		Vegetable Consumption	
		Min.	Max.		Min.	Max.	Min.	Ma
North America		3,100	3,100	35	1,500	1,700	1,565	1,3
Western Europe		3,000	3,000	90	1,000	1,200	1,910	1,7
Oceania		3,200	3,200	30	1,400	1,600	1,770	1,5
USSR		3,150	3,200	20	960	1,160	2,170	2,0
Eastern Europe		3,100	3,200	20	860	1,040	2,220	2,1
Latin America		2,550	2,700	20	620	740	1,910	1,9
Middle East		2,650	2,800	20	300	380	2,330	2,4
Asia		1,875	2,050	20	150	190	1,705	1,8
Africa		2,400	2,500	20	280	340	2,100	2,1
Total		2,300	2,425	27	450	540	1,830	1,8

[1] 1 crop unit = the feeding value of 100 kg of barley i.e. the equivalent of about 340,000 k
Source : Table V. 8, Table V. 9 and text.

tainty. It goes without saying that this uncertainty cannot be entirely eliminated, but one can inquire whether the consumption figures can be met by the possibilities of food production, however, and thus, to some extent, form an opinion on the likelihood of the figures.

By analogy with the indirect method, referred to above, of calculating the plant production corresponding to food consumption in 1955, estimates can be made of the volume of production that will be necessary in 1980 if the consumption estimates for the nine regions are to be realized. By relating the vegetable production in 1980, thus calculated, to that in 1955 and by comparing it to existing possibilities of increasing production, it will be possible to get some idea of the reliability of the figures for consumption (and in turn income). This applies to the figures for the world as a whole, but especially to the individual figures for each region. In such appraisals the trade in agricultural produce between the regions must be taken into account.

BLE V.10

quirements 1980.

Consumption per Annum for the Whole Population (Million Crop Units)										
Direct Consumption[1]		Indirect Consumption		Draught Animal Fodder	Seed	Industry, Waste etc.		Total 1980		Total 1955
Min.	Max.	Min.	Max.			Min.	Max.	Min.	Max.	
470	410	4,509	5,110	50	175	624	689	5,828	6,434	4,266
703	630	3,682	4,419	100	120	553	632	5,158	5,901	3,412
38	34	301	344	10	20	44	49	413	457	619
666	620	2,947	3,561	150	300	488	556	4,551	5,187	2,619
341	329	1,320	1,597	80	100	221	253	2,062	2,359	1,425
748	760	2,429	2,900	325	70	429	487	4,001	4,542	2,860
423	435	544	689	55	50	129	147	1,201	1,376	750
,257	4,594	3,745	4,744	215	350	1,028	1,188	9,595	11,091	5,667
652	664	869	1,055	85	100	205	228	1,911	2,132	1,401
,298	8,476	20,346	24,419	1,070	1,285	3,721	4,229	34,720	39,479	23,019

In Table V. 10 the result is given of the calculation of production in 1980. The consumption figures shown in Table V. 9 form the basis of this calculation, which is on the same lines as the calculation of production in 1955 referred to on page 145. In the present case a detailed analysis, however, is not possible. For the year 1955 we know not only the consumption of food measured in calories and grammes of protein, but also the consumption of each particular food. It is important to know this, especially as far as the consumption of protein is concerned, as the conditions of production vary a good deal for the different animal foods.

It has not, however, been considered feasible to calculate the consumption in 1980 of single items such as milk, butter, meat, eggs, etc. Estimates of the total consumption of calories and protein only have been made. Consequently, it has been necessary to make the conversion from protein consumption as a whole to vegetable production requirement.

Animal protein consumption, measured in grammes, as shown in the

Table, can be converted to animal calorie consumption by multiplying by twenty (the average conversion factor for the various livestock products in 1955) and the consumption of vegetable calories can then be calculated as the difference between the estimated calorie consumption and the consumption of livestock calories. A further, separate estimate, however, of the consumption of fish has been made. The vegetable calorie consumption per person per day thus calculated can be converted directly into total annual consumption by multiplying by the 1980 population figure and by 365 (days). The fodder consumption which corresponds to the consumption of animal calories, calculated in a similar way, is provided by multiplying by the conversion factor 10. This stage in the calculation is the one that is most difficult to explain, because whether the factors of conversion in the various regions are to be greater or smaller than 10 will depend partly on what livestock products gain most ground in consumption, as the fodder consumption per livestock calorie varies a great deal from one product to another (see page 143 above). It will also depend on the conditions to which livestock production is subject in the nine regions. In fact, the factor applied in the present context, i.e. 10, is slightly higher than the factor as observed for the developed regions in 1955. This is due to the rapid growth of meat consumption expected in the period up to 1980 which will create a need for large quantities of fodder. On the other hand, the factor used is smaller than the conversion factor valid for the underdeveloped regions in 1955. This is because of an expected increase in livestock production and of the assumption that the products which require relatively small quantities of fodder, viz. milk, pork, poultry, and eggs will predominate among the items of consumption.

The assumption that there will be a marked increase in productivity in the underdeveloped regions may perhaps be questioned. Should such an increase fail to occur, or should it be only slight, the factor used will have been too small and the demand for fodder will be correspondingly underestimated. The assumption that there will be an increase in productivity in the underdeveloped regions is founded on the belief that the extended animal production assumed in the forecast for these regions cannot in future be based on that part of vegetable crops which would not otherwise have been used. It must, in fact, be assumed that domestic animals in the underdeveloped regions to-day are nourished by grazing areas which are not arable. The limit of the domestic animal production which can be achieved in this way, however, has probably already been reached so that further increase will only be possible if crops grown on arable land are also used. This extension of production may, with some justification, be expected to require fewer vegetable calories per animal calorie.

Fodder for draught animals (horses, mules and donkeys) is estimated at only one-half of the fodder total for 1955 on account of increasing mechanization, whereas the quantity used for sowing is estimated to be 10 per cent higher than in 1955. This is in accordance with the estimated extension of land under cultivation as the necessary increase of vegetable production cannot, it is assumed, be achieved merely by a change in the amount of seed per hectare of arable land. To the sum of these items, viz. direct consumption of vegetable products, indirect consumption, draught animal fodder, and seed is finally added 12 per cent. Of this, approximately 2 per cent corresponds to vegetable calories used in industry (beer, spirits, etc.) whilst the remaining 10 per cent is understood to include the waste in the preparation of food products for the consumer at the retail level.

Finally in the last column of Table V. 10 is shown the requirement of vegetable products measured in millions of crop units (one crop unit = the feeding value of 100 kg of barley) which will result from the estimated food consumption of the nine regions in 1980.

Can this requirement be supplied? The answer to this question is of fundamental importance for this book.

It should, first of all, be emphasized that the question cannot be satisfactorily answered by means, only, of an estimate of potential production in the world as a whole, as it is possible that the world's total requirements could be supplied through a substantial increase in production in some of the "surplus" areas, whilst production in certain "deficit" areas might remain unchanged or rise slightly. If, however, the "deficit" areas are not in a position to make good the shortage by purchasing from the "surplus" areas, the requirements cannot be met in the "deficit" areas and the estimated consumption figures in 1980 for these areas must be reduced accordingly. In order to answer the question under consideration we are thus compelled to take into account problems of *distribution.*

Furthermore, the question cannot be satisfactorily answered simply by taking into account the technical possibilities of increasing vegetable production. It is beyond all doubt that the use of the most effective means of cultivation, including the introduction of new seed strains, the elimination of plant diseases and full exploitation of the possibilities of irrigation and of fertilizers, would make it possible to raise vegetable production to a level substantially above the estimated requirements in all regions but, in fact, many factors, particularly those of *Culture*, will hinder the application of the most effective methods of cultivation. We must try to judge whether land reforms may be expected in the underdeveloped regions in the period up to 1980, whether traditional, obsolete methods of cultivation are likely to be changed by the education of the peasants, and whether it will be possible to improve the poor marketing conditions that prevail in many underdeveloped areas. Last but not least we must try to forecast price development for vegetable crops, as the necessary increases of production are more likely to come about if prices for vegetable products rise.

Before trying to throw some light on these requirements it is appropriate to comment briefly on column 3 of Table V. 10, which shows the estimated consumption of *fish* etc. The consumption estimates for the world as a whole are about 85 per cent higher than actual consumption in 1955. This represents a considerable percentage increase. The absolute increase, however, is only slight. The estimate for fish consumption in 1980 is still not much more than one per cent of the total calorie consumption, and is about 5 per cent of the total consumption of animal protein. It is, however, often thought that the sea contains very large food reserves which could be exploited if it should prove difficult to meet the demand for food production in other ways. On the other hand it may be argued that though the annual production of organic matter from the flora of the sea may be estimated to be of the same magnitude as that obtained from the land, viz. about 40,000 million tons[8], the possibilities of exploiting it are very limited. By far the largest part of the plants are microscopic and live scattered in the layers of the sea lighted by the sun, down to from 300 to 600 feet below the surface. In reality the production of organic matter by these plants can not be exploited directly as human food, but only at a later stage of the so-called food-chain of the sea. Microscopic or small macroscopic animals are nourished on these plants and in this way 90 per cent of the solar energy absorbed by the plants is lost. Nor can these animals be used directly in food production as they are too small and too scattered to be easily gathered. Only the two following links of the chain (herring etc. and cod, mackerel

[8] Steemann Nielsen (1959).

etc.) lend themselves to such use; but they amount to less than 1 per cent of the total organic production of the sea.

It may be mentioned that the actual catch of fish in the North Sea, which is already being intensively exploited, amounts to about 0.2 per cent of its organic production. If we imagine similarly intensive fishing taking place in all seas the total catch would be about 80 million tons a year, against an actual catch of about 30 million tons in 1955. It does not seem reasonable, therefore, to assume that the consumption of food from the sea will rise very much more than is indicated in Table V. 10.

For a preliminary study of the figures for requirements shown in Table V. 10 it may be useful to make some simple assumptions with regard to the relationship between the rates of growth in the vegetable production of the various regions. In the following it is assumed at first the same rate of growth in production will obtain in the period 1955–80 in all regions. One reason for this assumption is that the plant production of the highly developed regions has become subject to the law of diminishing returns so that an anticipated intensive application of fertilizers and improved methods of cultivation there will not bring about a higher rate of growth than will result from a relatively moderate application of these factors which may be expected in the less developed regions.

If the calculated requirements are to be met there will have to be an increase in vegetable production in all regions corresponding to the world average, or 1.66 and 2.18 per cent per annum for the minimum and maximum growth respectively in the period under consideration (see Table V. 12). The possibility of realizing such growth percentages may be evaluated partly through a comparison with the development up to now and partly through an analysis of the consequences for the trade in food between the regions that the achievement of these rates of growth in production will have.

The trend in the world's vegetable production cannot be determined, even roughly, over long periods. If, however, grain yields alone are considered, and this may be regarded as reasonable for the present purpose, the rates of growth for the two periods 1909/13 to 1934/38 and 1934/38 to 1957 shown in Table V. 11 will result. During both of these periods a world war occurred, but it is not clear *a priori* whether they accelerated or retarded production, if the latter is considered over a long span of years. It appears that the rates of growth for the two periods, for the world as a whole and for most of the regions, are a good deal lower than those required for the next 25 years. It must be borne in mind that the area which has been used for growing grain may have varied through the years. In the two periods covered in the Table, however, the grain area has increased relatively more —62 per cent in the first period and 17 per cent in the second—than has

TABLE V. 11

Annual Rates of Growth for Grain Production.
(Per cent)

	1909/13 to 1934/38		1934/38 to 1957	
	Total Yield	Yield per Hectare	Total Yield	Yield per Hectare
North and Central America .	—0.46	—0.90	2.51	2.54
Europe	—0.09	0.33	0.85	1.12
Oceania	1.55	—0.28	1.23	—0.74
South America	2.33	0.83	0.79	0.30
Asia	4.11	—0.31	1.37	—0.08
Africa	3.92	—1.38	1.59	0.54
USSR	1.89	0.95	0.14	...
World Total	1.61	—0.10	1.34	0.74[a]

a excl. *USSR*.

Note: The division by regions in this Table differs from that otherwise used, in conformity with the arrangement of the source material.

Sources: International Institute of Agriculture (1931), and FAO *Yearbook* (*Production*) 1954 and 1958.

the total agricultural area, and also more than the total agricultural area may be expected to increase in the period 1955–80 (see below). This implies that the yield per hectare has increased less than total grain production (see Table V. 11).

To assume that the total world demand as shown in Table V. 10 is satisfied in the sense that total world production is increased *pari passu* with the requirements calculated, is tantamount to assuming a growth in output over the period of 50 and 72 per cent respectively (for minimum and maximum growth). These rates of growth are, as mentioned, assumed to hold true in each region. In this way the total output of each region is arrived at as shown in Table V. 12. When this is related to the projections for demand of the individual regions as shown in Table V. 10 and Table V. 12 each region is shown to have a surplus or a deficit, cf. the last two columns of Table V. 12.

TABLE V. 12

Estimated Supply Requirements, Harvest, Imports and Exports in the Nine Regions 1980.

(Million crop units)

	Estimated Supply Requirements in 1980		Total Harvest at Common Rate of Growth		Exports (+) Imports (−)	
	Min.	Max.	Min. 1.66 (Per cent pro anno)	Max. 2.18 (Per cent pro anno)	Min.	Max.
North America ..	5,828	6,434	6,439	7,322	+ 611	+ 888
Western Europe .	5,158	5,901	5,150	5,856	— 8	— 45
Oceania	413	457	934	1,063	+ 521	+ 606
USSR	4,551	5,187	3,941	4,481	— 610	— 706
Eastern Europe ..	2,062	2,359	2,154	2,449	+ 92	+ 90
Latin America ...	4,001	4,542	4,308	4,898	+ 307	+ 356
Middle East	1,201	1,376	1,140	1,296	— 61	— 80
Asia	9,595	11,091	8,547	9,718	—1,048	—1,373
Africa	1,911	2,132	2,107	2,396	+ 196	+ 264
Total	34,720	39,479	34,720	39,479	+1,727 −1,727	+2,204 −2,204

Sources: see text.

It appears that certain regions will have very considerable surpluses (*North America, Oceania*) and others large deficits (*Asia, the USSR*). Certain corrections, however, of the porduction figures given will have to be made, in view of the anticipated extensions in area, before the trade pattern referred to is examined more closely.

Table V. 12 has in fact been prepared on the same assumptions as Table V. 7. The export and import that has been calculated as the difference between requirements and production is thus only that of vegetable products, and especially, grain. Whether some of the animal foods produced in a region are afterwards exported to other regions is not taken into consideration. It may be said, however, to have been indirectly assumed that the interregional trade in livestock products will not differ much in 1980 from what it was in 1955. The increase in fodder consumed in livestock *production* in each region is based on the expected increase in the *consumption* of livestock products in that region (see Table V. 10). This implies that the

TABLE V. 13

The Present and the Future Agricultural Area.

	Cultivated Area			Total Agricultural Area				Estimated Increase 1955-80 Net (Per cent)		
	1955	Possible Increase[1]	Probable Increase[2]	1955	Possible Increase[3]					
					Gross	Net[4]	Net Per cent of 1955-Area		Min.	Max.
	Million Hectares									
North America	229	79	22	508	78	70	14		0	0
Western Europe	95	5	4	160	12	7	4		0	0
Oceania	24	5	2	401	11	9	2		0	0
USSR	229	...	(25)	488	247	185	38		10	15
Eastern Europe	55	3	2	75	8	5	7		0	5
Latin America	101	54	17	469	127	114	24		10	15
Middle East	57	54	3	215	45	33	15		7	10
Asia	371	63	25[a]	647	105	79	12		7	10
Africa	232	98	10	826	217	173	21		7	10
Total	1,393	375[b]	110	3,789	850	675	18		8	12

[1] FAO *Yearbook* (*Production*) 1955.
[2] FAO (1954).
[3] Guerrin (1957).
[4] i.e. gross values reduced with regard to soil and climate.
[a] Excl. China.
[b] Incl. the *USSR*.

difference between a region's production and consumption of livestock products remains unchanged throughout the period.

Table V. 12 was drawn up on the assumption of the same annual rate of increase of vegetable production in all nine regions. This assumption is scarcely justified. It is more realistic to count on wide variations from region to region, although such variations will be hard to measure with any accuracy.

To throw more light on this important question it will be necessary, it seems, to consider the more important factors which determine the size of the harvest and its increase. In Table V. 15 a distinction is made between, (1) area increase, (2) increase in the use of fertilizer, (3) improved water economy, (4) other factors. Further, certain estimates have been made of the effects that these groups of factors may have on the increase in the harvest in the period 1955–80 assuming minimum and maximum economic growth respectively.

(1) Table V. 13 should, by way of introduction, provide some idea of the possibilities of *extending the agricultural area*.

These have been examined by international organizations (FAO) and by some private persons. The results of these enquiries vary a good deal, due to the complicated nature of the subject and the lack of information. The enquiries made by FAO mainly concern the cultivated area and allow a fairly wide margin between the possible and the probable increase, without indicating how long a period is likely to elapse before either of these may occur. The possibilities of extending the total agricultural area have been examined by André Guerrin who, on the basis of estimates for individual countries, has arrived at the figures shown in Table V. 13. The figures are given both gross, i.e. showing the real increase, and net, i.e. showing the area increase converted to soil of the same average quality and subject to the same amount of precipitation as the present agricultural area. It will be seen from the Table that a large increase may take place in the *USSR, Latin America* and *Africa,* and that in *North America* and *Asia* a rather smaller increase may be expected. The global increase may amount to as much as 675 million hectares, that is 18 per cent of the present agricultural area.

It is unlikely, however, that the total area of 675 million hectares will in fact be made into farm land, particularly in the developed regions where the income which may be obtained in other occupations is high and an increase in the agricultural labour force cannot be expected. Even a change in the terms of trade in favour of agricultural products may do little to counteract the tendency for agriculture in the developed regions to be an industry which is being deserted. It has, therefore, been assumed that in *North America, Western Europe,* and *Oceania* no extension of the agricultural area will take place. In the case of the other regions the maximum estimate corresponds to between two-thirds and one-half of the theoretically possible increase, and the minimum estimate to between one-half and a quarter. It should be added, however, that in the case of *Asia* the maximum estimate corresponds to five-sixths and the minimum estimate to a little over one-half of what is theoretically possible. Provided the new land is under similar cultivation to the old as regards fertilizers, water, etc. the increase in area alone should result in a production increase which can be measured by means of the percentage figures shown in the last column of Table V. 13.

(2) An even more important condition for an increase in agricultural production than the extension of the area under cultivation is, however, an increase in the *consumption of fertilizer* per hectare. From 1938 to 1955/56 the fertilizer production rose steeply (cf. Table V. 14) ; nitrogen and potash fertilizers more than twofold. Moreover, the increase in consumption has been largest in *Western Europe, North America*, and *Oceania*, whilst in *Asia* it has been slight.

Investigations made in various parts of the world show that a very considerable harvest increase may be expected as a consequence of the growing consumption of fertilizers. The largest increase in harvest in relation to the increase in the amount of fertilizers may be anticipated in areas where consumption of fertilizers is still insignificant, but in the developed regions, also, much improved results may still be achieved. A number of experiments carried out in the United States indicate that a threefold increase in the consumption of fertilizers will result in a production increase per hectare of between 25 and 100 per cent, according to crop. In the United States it has, also, been ascertained that such a production increase will be possible in warm and humid climates as well as in dry, temperate areas. It is reasonable to assume a general increase in the consumption of fertilizers which will be largest in the developed regions where such an investment is not of decisive importance, whereas in the underdeveloped regions it may be assumed that the shortage of capital will restrain the production and the import of fertilizers.

The difference between the two estimates for 1980 in Table V. 14 is due mainly to alternative assumptions about the increase in income (and in turn consumption) in the developed regions. It is assumed that in the underdeveloped regions fertilizer consumption will in any case rise rather steeply.

(3) An increase in agricultural production in consequence of improved *water economy* should, in theory, have the greatest effect in the subtropical zone and parts of the tropical zone, i.e. largely the underdeveloped regions. When, nevertheless, the estimated increases in percentages for these regions have not been set very high in Table V. 15 it is because irrigation is expen-

sive and the possibilities of extending it are greatest in the most sparsely populated regions.

In this case also it must be assumed that a greater effort will be made in the under-developed regions to improve the water economy than is the case in the developed regions. With regard to extension of the irrigated areas and limitation of areas exposed to flooding, major improvements can be effected

TABLE V.14

The World's Fertilizer Consumption.
(Million tons, excl. the *USSR* and China)

	Nitrogen (N)	Phosphoric Acid (P$_2$O$_5$)	Potash (K$_2$O)
1938	2.5	4.1	2.7
1955/56	6.3	7.1	6.1
1980 minimum .	12	12	12
1980 maximum .	16	16	15

Source: FAO *Yearbook* (*Production*) 1957.

with a relatively small expenditure on materials. On the other hand, the fact that a considerable amount of *Labour* will be required both to create the irrigation systems and to cultivate the areas reclaimed is of little importance in view of the labour force at present available in these areas.

(4) The increase in production that may be expected as a result of *other measures,* as for example the selection of more productive strains, and the fight against vermin etc., can only be estimated on the basis of varying information. The same applies to a number of other factors which should be taken into account in estimating future agricultural production, for example improvements in machinery and cultivation methods, and in land tenure etc. Improvements in marketing systems should also be mentioned in this connection.

Further, it should also be underlined with regard to all factors which influence agricultural production that improvements cannot be carried out quickly; there are both economic and human problems to overcome.

In Table V.15 the increase in area is put alongside the factors mentioned above which are likely to cause the yield per unit area to rise. The figures should be read on the assumption that current knowledge about fertilizers etc. will be applied to the reclaimed areas also, and that the increase in the use of fertilizers will be so great that this factor alone will result in the harvest increase per hectare (of old as well as of new land) stated in columns 3 and 4. If the effects of an increased area under cultivation and the use of

TABLE V.15

Increase of Vegetable Production 1955–80.

	Per cent Increase of Agricultural Area (net)		Per cent Increase of Production per Hectare in Consequence of					Production 1980 (Index 1955 = 100)		Annual Rate of Growth (Per cent)	
			Increased Use of Fertilizer		Improved Water Economy	Other Measures[1]					
	Min.	Max.	Min.	Max.		Min.	Max.	Min.	Max.	Min.	Max.
	1	2	3	4	5	6	7	8	9	10	11
N. Amer. .	0	0	30	40	10	7	13	152.7	174.0	1.71	2.24
W. Europe	0	0	20	30	5	7	13	134.6	154.2	1.19	1.74
Oceania ..	0	0	30	40	5	7	13	145.7	166.1	1.52	2.05
USSR	10	15	30	40	10	7	13	168.0	200.0	2.09	2.81
E. Europe	0	5	20	30	5	7	13	134.6	161.9	1.19	1.94
L. Amer. .	10	15	30	40	10	7	13	168.0	200.0	2.09	2.81
Midd. E. .	7	10	20	20	10	7	13	150.9	159.5	1.66	1.88
Asia	7	10	20	20	10	7	13	150.9	159.5	1.66	1.88
Africa	7	10	10	20	10	7	13	138.3	164.0	1.31	2.00
Total	8	12	...	...	...	7	13	150.9	171.6	1.66	2.18

[1] The exact figures are 6.7989 and 12.955, cf. the text.
Sources : See text.

fertilizers alone are considered, there should result, e.g. for the *USSR*, at a minimum rate of growth, a production of 100 × 1.10 × 1.30 (harvest in 1955 = 100). The remaining factors are treated in the same way. With regard to water economy it is not considered necessary to distinguish between maximum and minimum growth. The percentage for "other improvements" has been calculated as a residual item so that total output will increase in accordance with the estimates shown in Table V. 12. This being assumed, the share of the increase to be explained by "Other Measures" is what remains for the world as a whole after due allowance is made for the influence of the agricultural area, an increased use of fertilizers as well as the effect of an improved water economy. The percentage increase due to "Other Measures" has been assumed to be the same for all regions as no information allows for a differentiated distribution according to regions.

In colums (8) and (9) of Table V. 15 index numbers have been calculated for the harvest in 1980 (1955 = 100). For the *USSR* at a mini-

TABLE V. 16

Estimated Supply Requirements, Harvest, Exports and Imports 1980.
(Million crop units)

	Estimated Supply Requirements		Total Harvest at the Rates of Growth Given in Table V. 15		Exports (+) Imports (—)	
	Min.	Max.	Min.	Max.	Min.	Max.
North America ..	5,828	6,434	6,515	7,421	+ 687	+ 987
Western Europe .	5,158	5,901	4,592	5,261	— 566	— 640
Oceania …………	413	457	902	1,028	+ 489	+ 571
USSR …………	4,551	5,187	4,386	5,223	— 165	+ 36
Eastern Europe ..	2,062	2,359	1,920	2,310	— 142	— 49
Latin America …	4,001	4,542	4,795	5,709	+ 794	+1,167
Middle East ……	1,201	1,376	1,139	1,204	— 62	— 172
Asia …………	9,595	11,091	8,541	9,033	—1,054	—2,058
Africa …………	1,911	2,132	1,930	2,290	+ 19	+ 158
Total …………	34,720	39,479	34,720	39,479	+1,989 —1,989	+2,919 —2,919

Sources: See text.

mum rate of growth, for example, the result is $100 \times 1.10 \times 1.30 \times 1.10 \times 1.06799 = 168.00$. In columns (10) and (11), the corresponding annual rates of growth calculated for the period 1955–80 are given on the basis of the figures in columns (8) and (9).

Finally, in Table V. 16, the figures for total production in 1980 which emerge from the index numbers arrived at in Table V. 15 are compared with the figures for supply requirements (as shown in Table V. 12). The two Tables thus correspond to one another. Table V. 16 may probably be assumed to possess the higher degree of reliability because of the adjustments made to the figures for output for the individual regions. In spite of the serious limitations, it may, nevertheless be possible to draw some conclusions on the basis of this material.

Firstly, if a *global* view is taken it should again be emphasized that very considerable rates of growth will have to be achieved in vegetable production if requirements are to be met. In fact such an increase might already have taken place if the demand had required it. We might then say that the increased demand will come to be a driving force in vegetable production of far greater importance than it has been so far. The reasons for this are, of course, the rapid increase in population and the expected rise in the income level in large parts of the world.

It is difficult to state whether the demand for food will rise more than the demand for other goods. The relatively high rate of growth of income per capita which is foreseen in the developed regions (see Chapter VII B) will presumably give rise to a demand for industrial products rather than for food, as the demand for the latter is already nearly satisfied in these regions. In the underdeveloped regions, on the other hand, the considerable growth of population which is foreseen, in conjunction with the modest growth of income per capita, will involve a rise in demand for food rather than for other goods.

More important, however, for the development of terms of trade for these categories of goods are the conditions of supply. In this respect the agricultural production, as has been shown in this chapter, meets serious problems.

First of all, increases in agricultural production are limited by the scarcity of land. Lack of water for irrigation purposes as well as difficulties arising from the introduction of new production methods will also play a rôle in this connection.

As regards industry, lack of *resources* will not make itself felt seriously in the period under consideration, and although lack of *Capital* and of skilled labour may raise difficulties, especially in the underdeveloped regions, the production capacity in the industrial sector in the developed regions will be able to meet steeply rising demands.

This would seem to suggest that the prices of agricultural products will rise in relation to the prices of other goods and so attract the necessary *Capital* and retain the required *Labour* until the great increase in agricultural production referred to above is brought about.

In this connection it should be borne in mind that livestock production must rise even more steeply than vegetable production if the calculated supply requirements are to be met. Whilst the calculated annual global rates of growth for the harvest are, as stated above, 1.66 and 2.18 per cent (minimum and maximum) the corresponding rates for animal protein consumption are 2.2 and 2.0 per cent respectively (see Table V. 9). Livestock production must, therefore, be assumed to require an increasing proportion of the world's agricultural capital and labour. This serves to emphasize what was said above about the likelihood of increasing, relatively, farm product prices, though no conclusions can be drawn from it with regard to the price relationship between animal and vegetable foods.

It is well-known that for a long time past agriculture has represented a diminishing proportion of the national product of most countries. This will probably be the case also in the period under consideration here. It appears, however, that for agriculture and especially animal husbandry the rates of growth will be closer to the total rates of growth than they were in the decades immediately preceding. Further, should it prove that steeply rising production requires proportionate increases in agricultural prices, we may assume that agriculture will play a more prominent part in the development plans of many countries than it seems to have done in recent years. The fact that it may be difficult, even in the event of increasing prices, to meet the demand in certain regions is referred to below.

This may be expressed in another way by saying that *Nature* will probably, as far as soil and the natural supply of water are concerned, tend to retard global growth—especially if all the other factors of growth should permit the maximum rates of growth. A considerable proportion of total available *Capital* will in fact be employed in agriculture in order to achieve the calculated increases in cultivated area, in the use of fertilizers, in irrigation, in improved strains and breeds, etc. In several regions much will have to be done in the cultural field, also, if the necessary change of attitude is to be brought about and the knowledge disseminated for these great innovations in agriculture to be achieved within a comparatively short space of time.

Of both global and regional interest is *grain trading and carriage* between the regions which seems to be about to rise steeply. The + and — figures in Tables V. 7, 12 and 16 represent exports and imports of grain especially. While the carriage of grain between the regions in 1955 amounted to about 0.4 billion crop units, it will, according to Table V. 16, run to a minimum of about 2.0 and a maximum of about 2.7 billion crop units in 1980. This will create a considerable capital demand because, among other reasons, the grain will probably have to be carried long distances, e.g. from both North and South *America* to *Asia*.

Further, it is characteristic of Table V. 16 that the rates of harvest growth, on the given assumptions, seem to vary greatly from one region to another. At the minimum growth *Western Europe* and *Eastern Europe* are lowest with 1.19 per cent annually, whilst the *USSR* and *Latin America* are highest with 2.09 per cent. At the maximum growth the corresponding figures vary from 1.74 in *Western Europe* to 2.81 in the *USSR* and *Latin America*. The latter rate of growth is very high. It represents, in fact, a doubling of the harvest in the 25 year period under consideration. It should here be remembered, also, that on the assumption made livestock production in the two regions will rise even higher. According to Table V. 9, it would seem that the consumption of animal protein at the maximum growth will increase by 3.7 per cent annually in the *USSR* and by 4.3 per cent annually in *Latin America*. When these figures are compared with the agricultural growth rates of earlier times it is apparent that the difference between the possibilities of growth in the various regions emphasizes the fact, mentioned above, that the increase in agricultural production will probably make such heavy demands, in many places at least, that economic growth as a whole will be retarded.

With regard to the trade between the individual regions Table V. 16 indicates that *Western Europe* will be, as it is now, a grain importer, whereas *North America* and *Oceania* will remain exporters of grain and will perhaps increase their exports, possibly by exporting to *Asia* also. The large surplus calculated for *Latin America* may be an overestimate; indeed the figures for this region are probably even more uncertain than those for the other regions. In *Latin America,* in fact, very considerable cultural progress will be required if the much increased efforts assumed in Table V. 15 are to be successfully made. As mentioned earlier, the assumed rate of growth for agriculture in this region is also very high. Further, it has to be remembered that a large proportion of livestock production in *Latin America* consists of beef and mutton. In the case of these products a conversion factor considerably higher than 10, which has generally been applied here, should be used (as mentioned on page 154) in calculating fodder consumption. The supply requirements in 1980 should, therefore, perhaps be raised if meat production plays an equally important part at that time.

The most remarkable item of Table V. 16 (and indeed of Table V. 12

also) is, however, the very large import requirements of *Asia*. For this region, which already has a very large population in comparison to its area, a heavy population increase is anticipated according to Chapter III. If the food situation is to be improved at the same time, as is assumed in the case of the maximum rate of growth, the supply requirements will be very great. Here again it has to be remembered that there is a great deal of uncertainty in these considerations. When it is borne in mind, however, that the price of one crop unit in 1955 was 6–7 dollars and that it may be expected, as already mentioned, to rise a good deal, it will be apparent that, on the assumptions made, there will be a grain import requirement of the magnitude of 10 billion dollars or more even if it should be found that the figure stated in case of maximum growth may be reduced. In 1955 there was no grain import of importance into *Asia*. A change may, therefore, possibly take place which will drastically upset the balance of payments of that region. 10 billion dollars would be about 5 per cent of *Asia's* net domestic product in 1980—a large amount compared with the figures given in Chapter IV for *Asia's* supply of capital.

Added to this is the fact that agricultural production itself will make heavy demands in *Asia* even if it is supplemented with the imports referred to. On the assumptions made here, total agricultural production (including livestock production) in the region will rise, in the case of maximum growth, by a little over 2 per cent per annum in the period considered. This will require, among other things, a considerably increased use of capital. Only very sparse information is available with regard to capital/output ratios in agriculture. Some material from Denmark[9], however, points in the direction of 3 to 4, both on an average and marginally. If 3 is reckoned on for *Asia*, we get a net investment requirement of a little over 6 per cent of agricultural production which, in large parts of the region, represents about one-half of the total net domestic product. Thus an investment quota for agriculture alone of about 3 per cent does not seem improbable.

If this is considered in the light of the large import requirements and the comparatively large investment requirement which the increase in population alone will create for housing, schools, etc., even the moderate per capita rate of growth assumed here[10] would seem difficult to realize. A slower population increase than that assumed here, and a large capital influx might

[9] Landøkonomisk Driftsbureau (1958).
[10] See Table VII. 2.

change the picture. The enquiries made in this book, however, scarcely suggest that such supplies of *Capital* may be counted on with any certainty. A change in the existing cultural pattern rendering it possible to exploit the very large reserve represented by India's livestock, will considerably increase, at least for a time, the possibility of meeting the protein requirements. Unforeseen technical improvements may, of course, take place. Even the application in large parts of *Asia* of the techniques now at our disposal, however, would involve very difficult cultural readjustments.

With regard to this region, especially, the facts described above thus seem to suggest that soil and the supply of water will, in consequence of their limitations in relation to population, have a retarding effect on economic growth and also on the standard of living as compared with that of other regions.

C. *Energy*

1. *Consumption*

The greater part of the world's supply of energy is based on the utilization of mineral fuels, which constitute, together with water-power, what is normally termed commercial fuels.

These sources of energy, coal, oil, natural gas, and water-power produce about 85 per cent of primary energy, whilst non-commercial fuels, especially all vegetal fuels, produce the rest.

The total output of primary commercial fuels in 1953 was the equivalent of the heating value of about 3 billion tons of coal. Coal and lignite accounted for about 50 per cent, oil and natural gas for about 44 per cent, and water-power for about 6 per cent[11] of this consumption.

By far the greater part of energy is consumed in the developed regions. *North America* thus accounts for over 40 per cent of total consumption of commercial fuels, and *North America, Western* and *Eastern Europe,* the *USSR,* and *Oceania* between them for about 85 per cent. These regions contain only 30 per cent of the population of the world. The annual per capita consumption thus varies greatly—from the heating value of about 8,000 kg of coal in *North America* to the heating value of only 200 kg of coal in the *Middle East, Asia,* and *Africa. Western Europe* and the *USSR*

---

[11] This figure is based on the assumption that 1000 *kwh* of electric power is equivalent to 0.6 ton coal.

lie between the two extremes with an annual per capita consumption equi-valent to 2,500 kg of coal.

In some regions the so-called non-commercial fuels[12] still play a vital part. This is especially so in the under-developed regions where nearly one-half of total energy consumption about the year 1950 was based on these fuels.

TABLE V.17

The Consumption of Primary Commercial Fuels in 1955,
Rates of Growth and Consumption in 1980.

	Consumption 1955 (Million tons of coal equivalent)[1]	Average Annual Rates of Growth (Per cent)		Consumption 1980 (Million tons of coal equivalent)[1]	
		Min.	Max.	Min.	Max.
North America	1,482.8	2.5	3.8	2,750	3,800
Western Europe	787.6	1.9	3.4	1,250	1,800
Oceania	44.6	3.3	4.4	100	130
USSR	439.3	4.3	5.8	1,250	1,800
Eastern Europe	236.9	2.6	4.4	450	700
Latin America	101.3	4.1	5.4	275	375
Middle East	25.3	3.8	5.4	65	95
Asia	266.6	1.7	2.7	410	525
Africa	52.7	2.6	4.1	100	145
Total	3,437.1	2.7	4.1	6,650	9,370

[1] Coal, lignite, crude oil and natural gas, and hydroelectric power are converted into coal equivalent, so that 1 ton of crude oil is taken to correspond to 1.3 tons of coal; 1000 m³ of natural gas to 1.33 tons of coal; 1000 kwh of hydroelectric power to 0.6 ton of coal, assuming that the production of 1000 kwh electric power requires on average 0.6 ton coal.
Source: UN *Statistical Yearbook* 1957 and Tables VII.2 and III.8.

On the other hand, the consumption of non-commercial fuels is rapidly declining and is being replaced by an increasing consumption of commercial fuels, especially oil.

The fact that the consumption of commercial fuels seems to be related to economic development is the basis of the following projections of energy consumption in the period 1955–80.

[12] Fuelwood, bagasse, and various vegetal fuels.

There can be little doubt that there is some connection between the size of the net domestic product and the consumption of energy. In its simplest form this connection would imply that a certain specified increase in the net domestic product per capita would result in a certain increase in per capita consumption of primary commercial fuels. Such a relationship, it is assumed, will prevail until 1980. On the basis of observed per capita income and consumption (production) of primary fuels in 1955 the relationship between income per capita and consumption of energy per capita has been calculated. Future energy consumption has thus been projected by linear interpolation using the income projections of Chapter VII B. The total regional requirements for primary fuels in 1980 are then set in accordance with the estimates of the trend in population given in Table III. 8. The results of these calculations are shown in Table V. 17. As in Chapter VII B two estimates, a minimum and a maximum, are included in the calculations.

Objections may probably be raised on grounds of principle to the assumption of a proportionality between the development of the net domestic product and the consumption of energy. To compensate, however, for errors in the model the figures for consumption in 1980 have been corrected by the same percentage as that by which the regions deviate from the proportionality in 1955. If a region's energy consumption in 1955, for example, is 10 per cent larger than the consumption thus calculated, consumption in 1980 has also been set 10 per cent higher than the consumption calculated.

The estimate for *North America* has been further corrected as there is some reason to believe that the future expansion of the national income will be due to increased activity in the tertiary occupations rather than in agriculture, mining or industry. This may lead to changes in the relationship between energy consumption and per capita income, as the former may possibly increase relatively less at such a mature stage of economic development than at earlier stages which are characterized by a large expansion in the industries requiring energy. In view of this consideration the rates of growth for energy consumption in *North America* have been made slightly lower than they would have been according to the model.

It is clear from Table V. 17 that the estimate of consumption does not imply any major changes in the relationship between energy consumption in the economically developed regions on the one hand and in the underdeveloped regions on the other. The former five regions will continue to account for nearly 90 per cent of total world consumption, and this conclusion appears to be reasonably in agreement with other forecasts[13].

It should perhaps be mentioned that the estimates of consumption do not include an appraisal of the trend in the relationship between consumption of primary fuels and the consumption of *useful energy*. In the event of the fuel efficiency undergoing major changes during the period the consumption of primary fuels may, of course, be reduced.

There are a number of opinions on this complicated subject. *Putnam*[14] thinks that the technique of fuel utilization will be further developed and thus ensure an increase in the average efficiency of extracting energy, which, it must be admitted, is, as yet, rather low in terms of the ratio of input of fuels to output of useful energy, which was, about 1955, 20–25 per cent for the world as a whole[15]. Putnam is of the opinion that it will be possible to increase the average efficiency to 35 per cent by the year 2000 in consequence of improved techniques. If we assume that the average efficiency will be increased by, say, 5 per cent by 1980, it follows that the consumption of primary fuels in that year will be 20 per cent lower than it would have been under existing conditions of utilization of fuels.

Finally, the future energy consumption of the underdeveloped regions poses problems which have been disregarded in the model used. The fact that a shift is taking place, and will continue to take place, in energy consumption from non-commercial to commercial fuels can hardly be attributed entirely to the trend in income, as the shift will probably continue even if the increase in per capita income is slight. It is almost impossible, however, to measure quantitatively the possible effect of this shift.

2. Energy Resources

Irrespective of which of the two consumption estimates in Table V. 17 is used—the maximum or the minimum—there seems to be good reason to believe that there will be no world-wide shortage of energy resources within the period considered here. But before this aspect of the matter is dealt with in detail it would seem appropriate to mention that the energy resources of the nine regions vary a great deal.

---

[13] UN (1956, c).

[14] Putnam (1953).

[15] In 1950 the average efficiency was about 30 per cent in the United States, but only 6 per cent in India, cf. UN (1956, c).

This point may be illustrated by Table V. 18 showing the magnitude of regional per capita resources of energy in 1953.

Even though the regions rich in oil appear to have been put at a very low estimate, the main impression is that the resources are unevenly distri-

TABLE V. 18

Regional Capita Resources of Energy 1949–53.
(World Average = 100)

North America	525
Western Europe	100
Oceania	150
USSR	375
Eastern Europe	100
Latin America	30
Middle East	25
Asia	25
Africa	75
World	100

Note : As a criticism of the estimate may be adduced the fact that only proved, and not possible, oil resources are included, whilst for other fuels possible resources are also given. This of course results in a somewhat distorted impression of resources in areas rich in oil where only a small proportion of the oil resources are "proved". In general, knowledge about the resources of under-developed areas is imperfect. This gives the figures a further bias.

Source : UN (1956, c).

buted. *North America,* the *USSR,* and to a certain extent *Oceania* and *Western* and *Eastern Europe* seem to be amply supplied with energy resources, and the underdeveloped regions, on the other hand, seem to be relatively poor in this respect. The fact that the resources are unevenly distributed becomes even more apparent if we look a little further ahead; for the populations of the underdeveloped countries increase much more rapidly than those of the well-supplied, economically developed regions. This is so, especially, in *Asia* whose per capita energy resources are likely to be modest in the future, unless new and very considerable reserves of coal, oil, etc. are found.

For the period under review, however, the total resources seem to be sufficient in each region. This conclusion might be drawn on the basis of

TABLE V. 19

Resources of Fuels and Total Fuel Requirements 1955–80.
(Approximate figures in billion tons of coal equivalent)

	Exhaustible Resources			Inexhaustible Resources	Accumulated Energy Repuirements 1955-80[5]	
	Coal and Lignite Potential Resources[1]	Crude Oil Total Potential Resources[2]	Natural Gas Total Potential Resources[3]	Hydro Power Annual Capacity × 25 (1955-80) i.e. Total Potential Use of Hydro Power in the Period[4]	Min.	Max.
North America .	1,551	50	50[a]	6.7	51.9	62.6
Western Europe	465	2[c]	...	7.2	25.3	31.1
Oceania	30	...	...	1,0	1,7	2.0
USSR	1,306	25	20[b]	7.2	19.8	24.8
Eastern Europe .	173	...	...	1.9	8.4	10.9
Latin America...	21	12	...	7.2	4.4	5.4
Middle East	4	26	...	1.4	1.1	1.4
Asia	395	9	...	16.8	8.4	9.7
Africa	77	1	...	22.6	1.9	2.3

[1] Compiled from UN (1956, c).

[2] The Joint Committee on Atomic Energy (1956) p. 84; conversion to coal equivalent by multipliation. [c] Including Eastern Europe.

[3] [a] The Joint Committee on Atomic Energy (1956) p. 83; [b] Emelyanow, UN (1958, b).

[4] Same source as 1). Water power based on capacity at Q 95 assuming annual utilization of about 8000 hours. Annual capacity in kwh thus arrived at has been converted into c.e. by dividing by 1667 (0.6 ton c.e. = 1000 kwh). Q 95 means that the potential is estimated on the basis of the amount of water that is present during 95 per cent of the period.

[5] Estimated on the basis of rates of growth assumed in Table V. 17.

the figures in Table V. 19. They show the estimated total or potential resources of coal, oil, natural gas and water-power in each of the nine regions —and for comparison, the total requirements which may arise in the period 1955–80 if the trend in consumption assumed in Table V. 17 is applied.

If the resources are considered as a whole we may say that there seems to be little likelihood of regional shortages arising. For a certain expenditure each region will be able to enjoy the consumption estimated, through the utilization of its own exhaustible or inexhaustible resources (mainly water-power).

On the other hand this conclusion is hardly relevant here inasmuch as the prices of the energy which can be recovered from the resources have a decisive influence on the pattern of utilization. Accessible high-grade resources will be utilized sooner than inaccessible inferior resources, in the same way that some types of fuel will be preferred to others because the current technique and consumers' habits limit the actual possibilities of substituting one fuel for another.

These circumstances seem to restrict the *utilization* of resources in certain regions—and to increase the possibilities of utilization in others. *Western Europe,* for example, has large potential coal resources, but the utilization of them *pari passu* with the increase in energy consumption seems to involve comparatively steeply rising costs. This fact, together with the apparent poverty of the region in other energy resources, is one of the reasons for *Western Europe's* "exploitation" of the rich and easily accessible oil resources of the *Middle East.*

It may be argued, however, that the problem of availability of regional resources is not so important, at least as long as the necessary fuels can be procured through international trade at "acceptable" prices. This view is probably of some importance in the period considered here. On the other hand, the actual scarcity or abundance of desired and *suitable* resources at least influences the balance of payments in the nine regions—in a negative or positive way as the case may be—and thus the stock of resources is of some significance as regards the general possibilities of economic expansion in the regions.

It is necessary, therefore, to find out how each *type of energy resource* is distributed by regions, and also to enquire as to the rate at which the regions may draw on the various types of fuel. A study of this should provide a basis for an appraisal of the need for inter-regional transfers of fuels in the period —and thus for an evaluation of the importance of energy resources to the possibilities of economic growth.

Coal is available in far greater quantities than other conventional fuels, as will be seen from Table V. 19, but is also the source of energy most extensively used.

Other and scarcer fuels, however—especially oil— are now competing with increasing intensity with coal. In all parts of the world the general trend in total fuel consumption is thus that oil and natural gas consumption is rising far more rapidly than coal consumption; the latter, in fact, shows a tendency to remain constant.

At the turn of the century coal provided 90 per cent of the world consumption of energy from primary commercial fuels. In 1955 the percentage for coal was 50, whilst oil and natural gas accounted for about 44 per cent.

The share of coal in the total consumption of fuels varied, of course, from region to region. In *Western Europe*, the *USSR*, *Eastern Europe*, *Asia*, and *Africa* it was about 70 per cent or more. In *Oceania* it was about 60 per cent, in *North America* about 30 per cent, and less than that in the *Middle East* and *Latin America*. In the first-mentioned regions coal was thus definitely the principal fuel, whereas in the two last-mentioned regions, which incidentally are poor in coal, oil was predominant. In *North America* coal, oil, and gas contributed fairly evenly to the total consumption of fuels.

In recent years the consumption of coal has increased by hardly more than one half to one per cent annually. The consumption of oil and gas, on the other hand, has mounted by 5–7 and 7–10 per cent respectively. The consumption of hydro-electric power has also increased at a rate of about 5–7 per cent. The three last-mentioned fuels, together, are thus steadily gaining ground from coal.

There are many reasons, of course, for this development, two of which should be mentioned as being of particular importance, viz. that oil and natural gas seem to be able to compete with coal as regards price and that oil has been found to be technically suitable and convenient for the development of transport and the improvement of heating methods.

The ability of coal to compete is influenced by the fact that in most of the principal producing areas coal has had to be extracted at a rising cost. This applies especially to *Western Europe* where it has been necessary to go ever deeper underground to reach the coal. Also, provision of the necessary labour force for the mines is becoming increasingly difficult—not only in Europe, but also in the other coal producing areas.

Coal prices appear, therefore, to be increasing in relation to the prices of other fuels, and it is generally recognized that coal extraction will have to take place under increasingly difficult conditions. Whether the competitiveness of coal will be further decreased in consequence depends, of course, on the prices at which other fuels can be supplied in future.

It should also be remembered that the future consumption of coal is partly determined by the technique employed in using the coal. The possibility cannot be ignored that improved mining techniques, underground gasification, or improved heating methods in power plants and other coal-using industries may bring a relative increase in coal consumption. But in the short term it appears that technical development in the fields of heating, industry, and transportation are likely to favour the liquid fuels and gas at the expense of coal.

In some fields, however, coal can hardly be replaced, practically or technically. Many countries will probably seek, for financial or political reasons, to utilize their own resources to the greatest possible extent. It should also be borne in mind that coal is, for the present, the most important source of heat in pig iron and steel smelting. If the world's total steel output is 500 million tons, for example, in 1980, it is quite possible that the production of this amount will require about 500 million tons of coking coal. A considerable proportion of coal consumption will, in any case, be accounted for by iron and steel production, so that a certain output of iron and steel will require a certain amount of coking coal. It being generally assumed, furthermore, that iron and steel production is increasing steadily, it may be expected that the consequent coking coal requirements will counteract tendencies towards a stagnation or decline in coal consumption.

It is difficult, of course, on the basis of these general observations, to give figures showing the possible trend in coal consumption, but it does not seem unlikely that consumption may grow by between 0.5 and 1 per cent annually in the period. Total consumption being 1700 million tons in 1955, this rate of growth should result in a maximum consumption of 2200 million tons in 1980, or a little under one-third of the total fuel consumption estimated for that year. Within these limits coal will account for a maximum of 40 per cent of total energy requirements in the whole period.

North America and the *USSR* will be able to meet fully any demand for coal that may arise in the period in the two regions. Both regions, as appears from Table V. 19, have very considerable resources of coal and these are fairly easily accessible and include both coking, and other types, of coal in sufficient quantities. At present *North America* has, and is likely to continue to have, an export surplus.

Western Europe has considerable coal resources. Nevertheless, production difficulties hinder the full utilization of these resources, especially as regards coking coal. As a result *Western Europe* has for a number of years been compelled to meet part of its demand for coal by imports—mainly from the United States.

Latin America apparently lacks coal resources and it is not unlikely that this shortage may restrict the industrial development of those Latin American countries that otherwise seem to have passed the primary stage of economic expansion. Brazil, for example, has ample resources of iron ore, but lacks coking coal for smelting the ore. Consequently it may prove difficult for the basic industries to develop. Coking coal is not easily accessible in sufficient quantities anywhere else in *Latin America* and therefore has to be brought from the United States or *Western Europe*. In either case transport costs are high because of the long hauls.

Asia and *Africa* are not yet fully surveyed as regards the amount and quality of their resources. But the geological structure of *Africa* does not give promise of large potential coal resources. North Africa and South Africa have coal deposits that are being utilized for industry, but tropical Africa will apparently have to import part of its, no doubt modest, coal requirements.

There are probably considerable coal resources in *Asia,* but whether these suffice to meet the demand of the region is hard to say. Mainland China, it appears, will require particularly large coal resources in order to realize its industrial targets. The coal resources of China are not known although they are frequently claimed to be very large—500 billion tons or perhaps more [16].

On the other hand it is difficult to maintain the regional viewpoint with regard to this extremely varied region. The political and economic differences between the countries of *Asia* are so great that it is hardly appropriate to speak of "the coal resources of the region" as a whole. It would, for example, be difficult to imagine that the discovery of new large coal resources in the interior of China might benefit Japan or Indonesia under the present political and economic conditions. Those parts of *Asia* that are not so rich in resources, such as Japan, will be compelled, when sufficient resources are not available near the coasts, to procure coal from other regions.

This fact reflects an important aspect of the problems connected with the exploitation of coal deposits. Compared with oil, coal is not a particularly

---

[16] Barnett (1959) quotes a Chinese estimate according to which the coal resources of Mainland China amount to somewhere between 1000 and 1500 billion tons.

12*

easily moved source of energy, and anyhow its movement requires a well
developed transport system. Such a system does not exist in the interior of
Asia and it is therefore doubtful whether the coal resources there are of more
than local importance—at least for the present.

Oil and natural gas, together, provided about 44 per cent of the world's
demand for primary commercial fuels in 1955, and as mentioned in the
previous paragraph, the share of oil and natural gas in the supply of energy
is increasing steadily. In the period between 1929 and 1950 the total consumption of commercial fuels rose on average by 2 per cent annually. Oil
consumption, however, increased by 4.7 per cent, and natural gas consumption by 6.3 per cent per annum. About 1955 two-thirds of energy consumption in *North America* was based on those two fuels, which took a similar,
or even larger share of the energy consumption of *Latin America* and the
Middle East. In the other regions oil and natural gas accounted for much
smaller percentages—from 30 downwards. But in all the nine regions
the consumption of these two fuels is rising relatively faster than, for example, the consumption of coal.

The reasons for this trend have already been touched upon in the section
dealing with coal. There might be grounds, however, for emphasizing that
oil may easily be moved, which implies that it lends itself, as distinct from
other fuels, to transport across great distances, by ship, pipeline, or train.
Furthermore the mobility of oil favours it in many underdeveloped countries where energy consumption is being switched from non-commercial
to commercial sources.

Forecasts of the trend in energy consumption, generally, assume that the
consumption of oil and gas will increase more rapidly than that of commercial fuels collectively, and there may be some grounds for assuming that
this increase will be in the neighbourhood of 5 per cent annually in the
period 1955–80 for both fuels. With an annual average rate of growth of
this magnitude the consumption of the two fuels will be more than trebled
by 1980, and will then correspond to about 5 billion tons coal equivalent or
more than two-thirds of the calculated total consumption in that year. On
the assumptions made this will mean that oil and natural gas will be able to
meet a little over one-half of total consumption of primary fuels in the
period 1955–80.

This very considerable increase in consumption does not imply any exhaustion of the world's oil and gas resources which are, as shown in Table

V. 19, believed to be at least 200 billion tons (coal equivalent). On the other hand, the consumption of oil and natural gas during the period 1955 –80 might well reach the level of the so-called "proved reserves"; but these are a stockpile for production in the next few years and should not be taken to indicate the total amount of exploitable resources. Most estimates of "proved reserves" are of the order of approximately 45 billion tons c.e. of oil[17] and 13 billion tons c.e. of natural gas[18]. This, then, is only the equivalent of less than one-third of the resources which can, eventually, be extracted from the ground; the greater part of which are not yet being exploited.

The estimates of both "proved reserves" and potential resources show that oil resources are very unevenly distributed among the nine regions. Contrary to the case of coal resources, the greater part of oil resources appear to be located in the underdeveloped regions, whereas the economically developed and high consumption regions have only a modest share of them.

As is only partly apparent from Table V. 19, the *Middle East, Latin America*, and *Africa* have large oil resources—between them probably more than two-thirds of all "proved reserves", and undoubtedly also a considerable proportion of all potential resources. The greater part of consumption, about 80 per cent, takes place, however, in *North America, Western Europe*, the *USSR* and *Eastern Europe*. The very fact that the first two of these four regions consume a rapidly increasing amount of oil, but have barely sufficient resources to meet the demand for it, seems to imply a problem closely related to the general problems dealt with in this book. For it seems fairly certain that *Western Europe* and *North America* will have to satisfy a steadily growing part of their demand for oil through imports from the *Middle East* and *Latin America* (Venezuela). This will, of course, have repercussions on the balance of payments of the importing regions.

Of more far-reaching consequence will be the income which will be received by the oil producing countries from their oil exports which may reach such proportions that it will be able, in view of the otherwise limited possibilities of capital formation in those regions, to contribute greatly to their economic growth.

A necessary condition of this is, of course, that the income from the export of oil should be beneficial to the region which possesses the resources.

The next question to be asked is: what magnitude will these inter-regional

[17] *World Petroleum Report* (1959).
[18] W. Pratt in The Joint Committee on Atomic Energy (1956).

transfers of oil reach? This depends, of course, on the trend in consumption in the importing regions.

As far as *North America* is concerned, *Aubrey*[19], basing himself on the report of the Paley Commission[20], seems to incline to the view that about 1975 the United States will require oil imports of between 1460 and 1650 million barrels annually[21], the equivalent, approximately, of 50 per cent of the expected crude oil output of the United States at that time. In 1953 dollars the cost of this import is estimated to be between 5 and 6 billion dollars. Part of the import is expected to be intra-regional, as Canada is assumed to deliver oil to the United States to a value of about 1.3 billion dollars. The rest is expected to be distributed among *Latin America* (about 2.5 billion dollars) and the *Middle East* and others (between 0.6 and 1.5 billion dollars). Aubrey's estimate, however, is probably rather too conservative. If we adopt instead the estimates in Table V. 17 rather higher import figures for 1980 than those given by Aubrey will probably emerge.

That *North America* thus appears to be a potential net importer of oil is due particularly to the fact that the exploitation of United States' oil resources is becoming more and more expensive[22], and, to a lesser extent, to the fact that these resources are becoming exhausted. It seems possible that the very fact that increasing production costs in the United States make imports desirable from regions where the resources are easily accessible, and where production costs are therefore lower, may increase the drain on the resources of these regions to such an extent that they too will have to be exploited at growing costs. Should this entail relatively increasing import prices it might possibly be more rewarding to utilize America's own resources again thus diminishing the rate of increase of imports. For this reason, *inter alia*, it would seem that the import figures should not be given too much importance.

[19] Aubrey (1957).

[20] The President's Materials Policy Commission (1952).

[21] Barrels may be converted, roughly, into tons of coal equivalent by division by 5.

[22] Thus, in the *Petroleum Press Service* (April 1957) it is stated that *exploration costs* in the United States have risen by 100 per cent in the period between 1948 and 1957. *Development* costs have risen by 40 per cent and production costs by 36 per cent. The share of the three cost groups in the total recovery costs is 38, 29, and 33 per cent respectively.

The 100 per cent increase in exploration costs is due to the fact that more and more drills are required to keep proved reserves at the desired level (the equivalent of about 12 years' output of the current magnitude).

In this context it should be remembered that *North America* has large resources of oil shales and tar sands. These may possibly be exploited if the price of oil shows even a slight tendency to rise, and may possibly increase *North America's* recoverable resources of liquid fuels by 20 billion tons coal equivalent—or more.

Another fact to be taken into account is that improved techniques of oil recovery may increase the available resources of oil. At present the extraction efficiency is only 30–40 per cent. A good deal more is likely to become accessible, however, in the next few years in consequence of improved techniques.

With regard to *Western Europe* the problems are of a different nature as it is very doubtful whether that region holds any significant oil resources although it is often thought that the geological structure of the region gives promise of considerable potential resources. On the other hand it seems to be generally agreed that whatever resources may be available, they are not proportionate to the anticipated demand for oil. This view is based on estimates of the future demand for primary fuels in relation to the regional output potential made by OEEC in 1955 and in 1959 [23]. According to these estimates *Western Europe* must expect "an increasing gap between indigenous production and consumption of primary energy".

According to the OEEC forecasts there will be, in 1975, a difference of 380 to 580 million tons coal equivalent between the demand for primary fuels and the regional production of these. This implies that around 35 per cent of the anticipated total demand will have to be met by imports of primary fuels from other regions and by the use of atomic energy. If the development continues along the lines suggested in Table V. 17 the import requirement may be even greater than that foreseen in the OEEC paper. It is generally assumed that oil imports will fill most of the gap thus arising.

The greater part of this oil will be brought, we must assume, from the *Middle East,* while the rest might be imported from *Latin America* and from North Africa (Algeria, Libya). This latter area may be able to meet a very considerable part of the demand for oil imports.

Opinion, however, is still divided on this question; but in so far as the fields in the Sahara and Libya may be made to yield the qualities of oil that *Western Europe* particularly requires (viz. fuel oils), they should be a good deal cheaper to carry to Europe than oil from the *Middle East.*

[23] OEEC (1956 and 1960).

This possibility does not only imply that future profits from oil from the *Middle East* may be jeopardized somewhat, but also that the consumption of oil might be further increased at the expense of other fuels—coal and atomic power.

As for the *USSR* and *Eastern Europe* it must be assumed that the *USSR* has such plentiful oil resources that the requirements of the two regions will be satisfied irrespective of the fact that these requirements will presumably be increasing steeply. In the light of current developments it is also likely that the *USSR* will be able to spare considerable quantities of crude oil for export not only to *Eastern Europe,* but also to other regions.

The demand for crude oil and petroleum products in the other regions, *Oceania, Asia,* and *Africa* in the period 1955–80 will hardly give rise to major problems as regards resources. *Oceania,* it is true, has no very large resources, but is capable, on the other hand, of procuring the necessary, and comparatively modest, amount of oil and petroleum products from regions with a surplus.

Parts of *Asia* and *Africa* appear to have considerable resources[24]. Other factors, however, especially the prevailing political unrest, seem to limit, anyhow for the time being, the economic advantage to be gained from these resources.

The oil resources of such important countries as Japan and India, on the other hand, appear to be quite insufficient. Mainland China's resources are presumably considerably larger, but whether they are sufficient is doubtful, especially in view of China's rapidly growing population and the expansion of its industrial capacity[25].

Much of what has been said about oil applies to *natural gas* also. Some further remarks, however, would seem appropriate.

Crude oil and natural gas are often found in the same deposits and, in recent years, when drillings have tended to become deeper and deeper, the amount of natural gas in the oil deposits seems to have increased.

The world's actual resources of gas are quoted with even more uncertainty than are the oil reserves, but the Report of the Panel on the Impact of the Peaceful Uses of Atomic Energy[26] declares that the total gas resources may amount to 250 billion tons coal equivalent.

[24] Algeria's oil resources are thus quite considerable.

[25] According to Barnett (1959), Mainland China has claimed its oil resources to be about 5 billion tons coal equivalent.

[26] The Joint Committee on Atomic Energy (1956).

In 1955 only *North America* consumed considerable amounts of natural gas. At that time gas accounted for nearly 30 per cent of the total consumption of primary fuels and its use in the United States is expected to increase for a number of years yet. The very steep increase in the consumption of natural gas involves, of course, a considerable drain on the resources. It has in fact been held that these will be exhausted within comparatively few decades and that increasing recovery costs have to be reckoned with in any case, *pari passu* with the increased drain on the gas resources. Such a trend may be counteracted through inter-regional transfers, if the technical and economic conditions of its utilization and transport are changed so that, for example, the gas located in *Latin America* can be used in *North America*.

At present, however, natural gas, unlike oil, can hardly be conveyed from one continent to another at a reasonable cost. Much of the gas resources are not, therefore, yet being utilized. Neither the *Middle East* nor *Latin America* have, themselves, needed to use the gas for the production of useful energy.

The gas resources of both the *USSR* and *Western Europe*, (and, to a certain extent, of *Asia*) on the other hand are about to be used, it appears, far more extensively than hitherto. In many of these areas gas is an inexpensive alternative to other kinds of primary energy. The *USSR*, at least, has very large resources of natural gas[27] and the utilization of the gas resources of European Russia will probably imply that this part of the *USSR*, a part which seems to be relatively poor in energy resources, will have its energy problems solved far more easily and cheaply than formerly expected.

Water power is the third and last of the conventional commercial "fuels". In the total balance of energy water power plays a rôle much inferior to that of coal, oil, and natural gas. Yet the output of energy from water power has been increasing steeply in recent years. Between 1929 and 1950 the production of hydro-electricity rose by 5 per cent per annum, measured in kwh, and this form of energy contributed about 6 per cent of the world's total supply of primary energy about 1955.

Water power is utilized almost exclusively for the production of electricity, and this very fact imposes a limit on the possible modes of its utilization. On the one hand such utilization presupposes a certain technical capacity, in the form of transmission lines, power consuming industries, etc., and on the other hand it has certain geographical limitations, the cost of conveying the

[27] See Table V. 19.

generated power for distances exceeding 1000–1500 kilometres being pro-
hibitive. It follows that water power resources are of much greater importance in economically developed areas than in backward areas where the
demand for their use is limited.

The total water power resources of the regions are shown in Table V. 19.
From this it appears that water power is a marginal source of energy in
comparison with coal and oil. Water power is, however, inexhaustible.

North America, Western Europe, and the *USSR* all possess relatively
large resources of water power, and it may be taken for granted that an
important part of them will have been put to use by the end of the period
here considered. In this connection it should be mentioned that the estimates
in the Table are based on the so-called Q 95 computation, which means that
the potential is estimated on the basis of the amount of water that is present
during 95 per cent of the period. This form of calculation does not, therefore, allow for the fact that further energy can be recovered from the source
—for example by installing a generator capacity so large that the maximum
flow of water may be utilized, or by increasing the potential by means of
dams etc.

Africa has the largest regional water power resources, probably more
than one-fourth of the world's total resources. A large part of them are
located in tropical Africa (the Congo) where the technical and economic
conditions necessary for their utilization have not existed and it is doubtful
whether this state of affairs will change very much in the next few decades.
On the other hand it must be admitted that the presence of other resources,
viz. considerable deposits of ore in West Africa (e.g. bauxite), increases the
chances that the Congo water power resources will be utilized. A possible
consequence of this would be that the smelting of, for example, aluminium
ore, on the basis of hydro-electric power, would give rise to other forms of
economic expansion so that the utilization of water power in one field would
prove a stimulus to a more general process of development.

On the whole the relative importance of water power compared with
other energy resources is not likely to change very much in the period up
to 1980. If we imagine that the amount of generated hydro-electric power
increased, for example, by 5 per cent per annum during those 25 years, its
contribution to the world energy supply will still hardly exceed 10 per cent
in 1980.

Atomic Energy. The increasing shortages of conventional fuels which must inevitably make themselves felt sooner or later are the reason for the great interest in utilizing the energy available in the atomic nuclei of uranium and thorium[28]. The time when nuclear energy will be utilized on a larger scale will, however, be determined by the economic competitiveness of nuclear power in relation to conventional power.

Generally, the immediate future of atomic energy as an economic source of energy is viewed with rather more pessimism to-day than it was four or five years ago. The conventional fuels, it seems, will be fully competitive for some time yet. This is particularly true of oil.

There is general agreement that the construction of relatively large atomic power plants provides the best conditions for the exploitation of atomic energy. The competitiveness of atomic energy is, furthermore, at its highest when such plants can be fully utilized. In other words, at the present stage of technical development, atomic energy is barely competitive in areas with small energy requirements because they only need small power plants. This does not apply, however, where special conditions prevail, as, for example, in isolated mining areas. But on the whole, in underdeveloped areas where the markets for electric power are usually small nuclear power will not be economic.

The use of atomic energy in large power plants is possible especially in industrial *Western Europe* where such plants can probably be almost fully utilized. Atomic energy will thus be more competitive in this region than in most others—and all the more so as *Western Europe*'s fuel resources are relatively small.

In some ways there seems to be an analogy between atomic energy and water power. The exploitation of both presupposes a certain level of economic and technical development, which in its turn involves a considerable consumption of electric power.

The form of nuclear energy produced at present is based on the use of uranium minerals, and the amount of these available in workable deposits, thus sets a limit to the amount of nuclear power that can be produced.

According to *J. C. Johnson*[29], the directly accessible uranium reserves of the world (excluding *Eastern Europe*, the *USSR*, and Mainland China)

[28] See, for example, in the UN (1956, c) and (1958, b), and The Joint Committee on Atomic Energy (1956).

appear to be at least 1.5 million tons of uranium oxide. At three to six times the cost it would probably be possible to recover more than 20 million tons from lower grade ores, and at still higher costs probably considerably more.

At the present stage of reactor technique 1.5 million tons of uranium oxide correspond to the energy that may be recovered from about 15 billion tons of coal (it being assumed that 1 ton of uranium may yield 3000 mega-watt days of thermal energy). Seen in this light these accessible uranium resources appear to be fairly modest; the equivalent of less than one per cent of the coal resources stated in Table V. 19. On the other hand reactor technique is still developing, and if the so-called breeding process can be successfully introduced it may well be possible to derive, from the said 1.5 million tons of uranium oxide, an amount of energy equalling that of several hundred billion tons of coal. Further, the lower-grade ores are also expected to lend themselves, in the long run, to being exploited. In addition there are thorium resources, and these may possibly also be utilized through breeding.

It should be noted that uranium occurs in most of the regions, but that *North America, Africa* (the Belgian Congo and South Africa), *Oceania* and *Western* and *Eastern Europe* seem to have the greater part of the known reserves. For countries such as South Africa and the Belgian Congo the uranium reserves appear to be a trade asset capable of providing a considerable income.

D. *Metals*

The increase in the world's population during the next 20–25 years will create an increasing need for metallic and non-metallic raw materials of mineral origin. Furthermore, the per capita consumption of these raw materials is likely to increase with the rise in the income level. This applies, first of all, to the countries whose manufacturing output represents, or is likely to represent, a substantial part of their national product. For the consumption of mineral raw materials depends mainly on the size of the manufacturing output. On the other hand, it is hardly possible to find, for *each* metallic and non-metallic mineral, a simple relationship between consumption and, for example, per capita income or per capita industrial output.

[29] UN (1958, b).

Many metals can to a great extent be replaced by others and, furthermore, changes are always taking place in technology which effect the amount and consumption of the minerals consumed in industry.

In the period considered here, however, iron and steel are likely to retain their predominant position in all manufacturing industry. The following paragraphs, therefore, deal first and foremost with the position as to resources of iron and steel production in the nine regions.

Iron and steel consumption vary widely from region to region. The five most highly industrialized regions, *North America, Western Europe, Oceania, the USSR* and *Eastern Europe* thus consumed more than 90 per cent of all crude steel in 1955. The differences in consumption as between regions are apparent from Table IV. 2 which shows per capita consumption of crude steel in 1955.

North America, and particularly the United States, had a per capita consumption at least twice as large as that of the other economically developed regions, and 10 to 50 times as large as per capita consumption in the underdeveloped regions.

The trend in consumption during the next 20–25 years should, of course, be viewed in the light of these very large regional differences. These could hardly be levelled out very much in so short a time, even if it were assumed that steel consumption would be subject to a slightly larger percentage increase in those countries that are about to undergo a process of industrialization than in the countries that have reached a "mature" industrial level.

It is, therefore, to be expected that the five developed regions, and especially *North America, Western Europe,* and the *USSR,* will account for the greater part, by far, of total steel consumption in 1980 also.

In the course of the last fifty years the world production of crude steel has increased by an average of 4 per cent annually, and this rate is usually expected to persist for some years to come. There appears to have been some relationship between developments in income level, industrial output and steel consumption, although the view can hardly be held that a linear relation will obtain between per capita steel consumption and per capita net domestic product in all regions[30]. But the estimates of the trend in income

---

[30] Thus we must assume that the increase in the income level of the United States will be connected with "services" rather than with "material production".

appear to give some indication of the trend in steel consumption. If the rates of growth of income shown in Table VII. 2 were used in calculations of a similar nature to those that led to the estimates of consumption given in Table V. 17, the conclusion might be drawn that the need for crude steel would amount to between 500 and 730 million tons in 1980 against 270 million tons in 1955. A little more than one-third of this amount would be for *North America*, about one-half for *Western Europe, Oceania*, the *USSR*, and *Eastern Europe*, and the rest, about one-sixth only, for the other regions.

Although too much importance should not be attached to these estimates, they do seem to express a truth, namely that the greater part of steel consumption will still be for the five most highly developed regions, and that their, already considerable, need for iron ore, coking coal, and ferrous-alloy metals will be greatly increased in the period 1955–80.

The resources of *iron ore* are very large, and most regions seem to be fairly richly endowed with them, if they are estimated according to their total iron content.

In *North America, Western Europe, Latin America,* and *Asia*[31] the "proved reserves", measured by iron content, seem to amount to 6 billion tons or more in each region. In the *USSR* and *Africa* they are from to 2 to 8 billion tons, and in *Oceania* and *Eastern Europe* about 0.5 billion tons. Only the East European resources appear, from this standpoint, to be insufficient[32].

The value of these resources appears somewhat different if we consider the location and quality of iron ore and coking coal deposits that are available for smelting in the various regions.

In Table V. 20 the quality of the potential iron ore resources and indications of resources of coking coal in eight regions (i.e. disregarding *Oceania*)

---

[31] These figures are taken from three publications: UN (1950, b), UN (1955) and Hagen (1954).

[32] The production of 1 ton of pig iron usually requires, according to its iron content, 2–3 tons of iron ore, and 1 ton of coal or ¾ ton of coke. The production of steel involves pig iron, scrap, ferrous-alloy metals and varying quantities of fuels. The total amount of iron ore required for the production of 1 ton of crude steel thus depends on the amount of scrap used in the process. If scrap is abundant and cheap, a charge will often consist of 70 per cent of scrap and 30 per cent of pig iron. Where scrap is not abundant, however, the percentages will be 20–30 and 70–80 respectively.

are illustrated by means of a few figures taken from the *Paley Report* and the United Nations publication *World Iron Ore Resources and Their Utilization* (1950, b).

TABLE V. 20

Potential Iron Ore Resources.
(Billion tons)

	Ores with 50 Per cent Iron Content or more	Ores Containing 35-50 Per cent Iron	Ores Containing 25-35 Per cent Iron	Proportion of Coking Coal to Total Coal Reserves[1] (Per cent)
North America	6	5	75	High (above 15)
Western Europe	3	11	10	High (above 15)
USSR	–	11	2	High (above 15)
Eastern Europe	–	–	–	Moderate (5–15)
Latin America	21	15	1	Low (below 5)
Middle East	–	4	–	...
Asia	22	12	2	Low (below 5)
Africa	2	–	117	Moderate (5–15)

[1] Estimates of coal resources are shown in Table V. 19, and may probably, with some reserve, be compared with the per cent figures given here, although the latter do not originate from the same source or computation.
Source: UN (1950, b), *The Paley Report.*

The iron ore consuming regions thus have limited resources of high-grade ore, but large resources of lower-grade ore. This applies to *North America, Western Europe* and the *USSR*. On the other hand these regions possess considerable resources of coking coal. With regard to resources the three regions should thus be relatively better off than *Latin America* and *Asia* which may have very considerable resources of good iron ore, but small reserves of coking coal.

The fact that *North America*'s resources of *good* easily accessible iron ore are limited has confronted the United States steel industry with supply problems. The better part of the Lake Superior ore is nearly exhausted and although this deposit, the most important in the United States, still contains vast reserves of low-grade ore (60 billion tons of taconite) it will probably be necessary to import increasing amounts of iron ore from Canada and *Latin America,* where good ore is accessible in considerable quantities.

Aubrey[33] says, on the basis of a Bureau of Mines estimate, that the United States may need to import as much as 35–40 per cent of its total iron ore requirements for 1975, or approximately 70 million tons, against an import of 20 million tons in 1955. About one-half of these imports may be supplied from Canadian deposits, the rest primarily from Venezuela and other Latin American countries, and to a less extent from West Africa and Asia. Aubrey further states that this import may cost about 500 million 1953 dollars f.o.b., assuming slightly rising iron ore prices.

Other estimates put the import requirements higher, and envisage that about 1980–85 they may amount to approximately 100 million tons, one-half of which will have to be procured from outside *North America*.

In any case there are many indications that, owing to decreasing resources of high-grade ore, *North America* will be in need of considerable imports which may largely be supplied by utilizing Latin American resources.

Like *North America*, *Western Europe* has large iron resources, a considerable part of which, however, can only be utilized at increasing costs. There is some reason, therefore, for assuming that *Western Europe*, like *North America*, will seek to meet an increasing proportion of its ore requirements through imports. It is true that a substantial part of the iron ore needed by the principal European industrial countries could be procured on an intra-European basis, but it must be assumed that the West European iron and steel industry will be tempted to utilize West and North Africa's iron ore resources to a much greater extent than now.

The *USSR*, presumably, has plentiful iron ore resources especially in the Asiatic part of the Union. *Eastern Europe*'s iron ore resources, on the other hand, appear to be quite insufficient and the region depends for its supplies on imports from the *USSR*.

Latin America, as mentioned earlier, has large resources of high-grade iron ore, and of other metals necessary to the iron and steel industries. On the other hand the resources of coking coal, as well as those of other types of coal, seem to be very small indeed. The necessary natural conditions for local iron and steel industries are thus, apparently, poor—a fact which is of some importance if it is assumed that *Latin America* is about to enter an era of comparatively rapid economic growth.

These conditions will, of course, become less important to the extent that

---

[33] Aubrey (1957).

coking coal can be dispensed with in steel production and be replaced by other local fuels or by oil. The production of pig iron by the use of other fuels, however, does not seem to be profitable at present, and is hardly likely to become so through the progress of technology in the immediate future. Though the scarcity of coking coal is thus a possible handicap for *Latin America*'s basic industries, its wealth in iron ore on the other hand should improve the possibilities of expansion in some Latin American countries. Thus the chances of economic development in Venezuela and Brazil are likely to be affected somewhat by the increasing payments that the United States will presumably make for the use of their iron ore resources.

In *Asia* both India and Mainland China have very substantial resources of iron ore. China has quite large coal deposits also, whereas India's coal resources are comparatively small. In *World Iron Ore Resources*[34] it is stated that each of these countries will be able to maintain a steel production of about 20 million tons annually on the basis of local resources, which would be sufficient to meet probable consumption in the period under consideration here. It must further be assumed, at least as far as China is concerned, that the extent of both coal and iron resources is not fully known. Recent investigations in Central and Western China suggest that these areas have considerable potential resources of coal and iron although at present there is hardly any basis for utilizing them in these remote and backward areas. On the other hand China is perhaps one of the few underdeveloped countries whose economic development might conceivably be so rapid that the large potential mineral resources would become economically relevant within the period considered here. If a high rate of industrial expansion is maintained the coal and iron resources of the western and central parts of China may be utilized even within the next 10–15 years.

Japan, on the other hand, is relatively poor in both iron ore and coal. It is largely compelled to supply its not inconsiderable iron and steel industry with raw materials by imports, partly from other countries in *Asia*.

Africa, like *Latin America*, has large iron ore resources—but small resources of coal. South Africa has iron and coal located together and is one of the few areas in *Africa* where such economic and social conditions prevail that it has been possible to establish a steel and iron industry at all. It is doubtful whether there will be any basis, in the near future, for local utiliza-

[34] UN (1950, b).

tion of iron ore resources in more than but a few other places in *Africa,* and Southern Rodesia and Algeria are, for the present, the only areas that seem to have both sufficient resources and the necessary economic and technical basis for developing an iron and steel industry.

In North and West Africa, on the other hand, there is scope for exploiting the good iron ore deposits located near the coast for export to *Western Europe* and the United States as, in fact, is already the case. If, however, the world demand for high-grade iron ore is increasing it may well be that the rich deposits of North-west Africa will be more intensively exploited. The most easily accessible iron ore deposits, it would appear, may thus become economically important—in the same way as the resources of the northern part of *Latin America*—with the result that the ore-exporting countries will have an opportunity of using part of their export earnings for investment. However, even though the export of ore implies a possibility of indirect advantage through foreign investment in transport and other public utilities, its importance for the economic development of the exporting countries should not be exaggerated as it is unlikely that it would be able to increase the supply of *Capital* and stimulate growth in the same way as oil has done in the *Middle East.* It will be too limited for that.

Industrial development has resulted in more and more *metals* being utilized. Although these metals are very important to modern industry they are used in much smaller quantities than the mineral fuels and iron. In 1955 world production of crude iron was thus about 190 million tons, whereas the output of manganese, copper, aluminium, lead, and zinc was between 2 and 4 million tons in each case. The total cost of procuring many of these raw materials is, therefore, despite all, smaller than the cost of utilizing mineral fuels and iron deposits because they are used in small quantities; unit cost is, however, very often greater as the recovery of many of them is expensive. Consequently the fact that many industrialized countries have insufficient resources of ferrous-alloys, bauxite, etc., does not give rise to any serious economic or foreign exchange problems.

More than 80 per cent[35] of the chromium, cobalt, and tin of the world (excluding the *USSR* and *Eastern Europe* and Mainland China) is produced on the basis of deposits in the underdeveloped countries. The same

---

[35] These figures have been compiled from Yates (1959).

is true of about one-half of the world's production of copper, aluminium, and tungsten. The resources of these countries, moreover, provide about one-third of the world's output of zinc and lead. On the other hand, about nine-tenths of these metals are consumed by the economically developed regions. Of this quantity *North America* consumes between one-third and one-half, and *Europe* and the *USSR* the rest.

This pattern will probably be even more clearly outlined in the course of the next few decades, for both *North America* and *Europe* have already used up the best and most easily accessible ore resources, and are, therefore, compelled to obtain an increasing proportion of their needs through imports. The *USSR,* on the other hand, has sufficient resources of most metals for some time to come.

With regard, especially, to the important *ferrous-alloy metals, North America* and *Western Europe* will have to depend more and more on the resources of other regions. This applies to alloy metals such as manganese, chromium, vanadium, and tungsten. Although these metals may be replaced, to a certain extent, by other metals, they are as a whole essential to modern steel production. The consumption of alloy metals appears to be rising, and although this may be counter-balanced by better techniques and larger supplies of scrap, it is probable that tropical *Africa*'s abundant resources of these metals, especially, will be utilized in the coming decades.

The resources of copper ore, aluminium clays (bauxite) and lead and zinc ores are rather more evenly distributed among the nine regions than are the ferrous-alloy metals. It is true of these metals also, however, that a steadily increasing consumption of them in the already highly industrialized countries will result in a growing drain on the resources of the underdeveloped regions. On the basis of our current knowledge of the reserves of these metals there seem to be grounds for believing that tropical *Africa,* and in certain cases *Asia,* with their considerable untapped resources will be able to meet the demand for these metals for many years to come.

While *Asia*'s known reserves of ferrous alloy metals are comparatively modest it has important deposits of tin and the world's tin consuming industries will have to obtain the greater part of their requirements of this metal from there.

E. *Conclusion*

The above considerations cannot, of course, be claimed to provide a basis for a comprehensive survey of the situation of the regions with regard to natural resources. Other raw materials than those mentioned here may well be of such importance that they ought to be included in an appraisal of the influence of the factor *Nature* on the economic growth of the regions.

Thus the resources of sulphur, phosphate, potash, and other salts form the basis of the chemical industry. The *forest resources* occupy a similar position as regards the timber, cellulose and paper industries. None of these resources, however, seem to give rise to problems comparable to those relating to fuels and metals. In section B, *water resources* have been sonsidered in connection with agriculture. It is likely, however, that water will, in fact, confront industry also with great problems in many areas. If, for example, the production of 1 ton of steel requires more than 200 tons of water, it is evident that the iron and steel industry is very dependent on easily accessible and plentiful resources of water. Generally, the consumption of water appears to increase sharply when industrialization and urbanization take place. Even areas endowed with relatively large water resources may thus have difficulties in satisfying the need for further supplies of water for industrial purposes. This applies to parts of *North America* and *Western Europe,* but will, of course, apply particularly to the large arid and semi-arid tracts of *Asia* and *Africa* if extensive industrialization should take place there.

On the other hand there is little reason to deal with the so-called *synthetic materials* such as plastics etc., as these are often made from oil, coal and other minerals or cellulose and must thus be considered largely as by-products—and not as raw materials in the sense used here.

The fact that the consumption of practically all important minerals is rising rapidly implies, of course, the eventual exhaustion of the resources that we know and use to-day. From the point of view of this book this fact is not so important, as it is unlikely that in 1980 there will be any serious shortage of important minerals. Consequently, there does not appear to be a "problem of resources" in this sense, facing the nine regions collectively. The problems of the exhaustion of important basic materials are bound to arise one day. But it will not be in this century.

As will be seen from the above observations, however, raw materials are not all equally mobile. Their mobility is limited by geographical, economic, technical and political factors. Furthermore the resources are not evenly distributed among the regions. Some regions will, therefore, have to envisage a shortage of raw materials, whereas others are likely to be favoured with a surplus which may either be used in other regions or remain unexploited.

This conclusion refers to the nine regions as they are defined in this book. It should be emphasized, however, that the characterization of each region as such is in very general terms which obscure many of its significant characteristics. Each region is here, for example, viewed on the basis of its possible resources of a particular mineral. In many instances this is hardly sufficient. In the developed regions "the reach of resources" is perhaps, in some cases, so wide that deposits in one part of the region may be used with advantage in the most distant part of it. This may be due to the elimination of geographical, commercial, economic and transport difficulties. In the underdeveloped regions the "reach" of the resources is probably much shorter because such obstacles persist. For instance, the coal deposits of the interior of Mainland China are a part of *Asia's* total coal resources, but it is doubtful whether such coal is sufficiently mobile to eliminate shortages in other parts of the region. For this reason the viewpoint adopted here with regard to regional resources is not completely satisfactory.

On the other hand the regional viewpoint is probably relevant in so far as it is applied to elucidate certain simple inter-regional relations between the consumption of raw materials and the distribution of them and also in making more summary comparisons between the regions with regard to the supply and demand for food.

In attempting to form a general impression of the position of each particular region the fact may, firstly, be stated that as far as food, oil, and a number of mineral raw materials are concerned, growing import surpluses in some regions, and, therefore, growing export surpluses in others are to be expected. The consequent effects on the balance of payments of the regions will have a limiting effect, *ceteris paribus,* on the general economic growth of the importing regions and a stimulating effect on the exporting regions. These effects will be intensified if, at the same time, prices of food and primary products should tend to rise more than the prices of manufactured articles and services. Such a development in prices is probably most likely to take place if the general growth is great. This is because *Nature* must then be vigorously exploited; inferior and less accessible resources will have to make a larger contribution to the world's output of agricultural products and raw materials, a process which involves higher costs, though this trend, of course, may be counteracted by changes in techniques in general.

It appears, incidentally, from Table III. 2 that the regions fall into two distinct groups with regard to density of population. Three regions are densely populated, viz. *Western Europe, Eastern Europe,* and *Asia,* all of which had over 65 inhabitants per square kilometre in 1955. The remaining six regions are all sparsely populated with under 15 inhabitants per square kilometre. Although there are great differences in natural resources per square kilometre in the regions it is probable that the densely populated regions will be most likely to require increased imports of primary products. In *Western Europe* this probably applies to both food, fuel, and various raw materials. In *Asia* it applies mainly to food. Here, however, a very heavy strain may possibly be put on the region's balance of payments, and thus on its growth potential. When the rates of growth for those two regions are put at a relatively low estimate it is due, partly, to the state of *Nature,* and, in the case of *Western Europe,* the slow increase in population, in consequence of which this region experiences a greater per capita growth than several of the other regions.

Eastern Europe is very like *Western Europe,* as regards both density of population and natural conditions, but the level of income and production, and thus the need for primary products, are a good deal lower. The import problem is therefore less pressing and will presumably be solved, to a great extent, by imports from the *USSR.*

Among the sparsely populated areas both *North America* and the *USSR* have large natural resources. At present these are being exploited most intensively in *North America.* The high income and production level of this region involves heavy requirements with regard to fuel and raw materials, especially, of course, if the rate of growth is high. A considerable increase in imports is, therefore, to be expected there, especially oil and certain metals, and also tropical products such as coffee and cocoa. On the other hand Table V. 16 seems to suggest that the region will export considerable amounts of food, especially grain. The total effect on *North America*'s general growth potential brought about by these natural factors can be assessed only with difficulty and will depend on the trend in prices, changes in techniques, etc. The position can perhaps best be described by saying that in this respect *North America* will take up an intermediate position between

Western Europe, where imports of primary products will be a "handicap", and *Latin America* where improved export possibilities will be a stimulus to development.

The *USSR* will probably be self-supporting in all important raw materials for many years to come, and may even have some important export surpluses e.g. of oil.

Oceania may possibly achieve a quite considerable export of food compared with its (small) population. The *Middle East* may have large earnings from the extensive oil production there, but these will be very unevenly distributed over the various parts of the region.

Latin America and *Africa* also seem to have a chance of profiting from exports of primary products. They will be able to supply, *inter alia,* certain metals and tropical farm products to the highly developed regions. *Latin America* may also expect considerable earnings from exports of oil and non-tropical foods.

The seemingly slender reserves of coal in those two regions and in the *Middle East* may prove a handicap. This is particularly true of *Latin America* where there are large quantities of iron ore and where other prerequisities for a development of the iron and steel industry are also present. On the other hand this region has large resources of other commodities, and *North America*'s growing import of primary products is expected to be supplied mainly by *Latin America.*

The state of resources, as it might conceivable be about 1980, is, indirectly, of importance in the context of the present book and a few observations on this topic and also on development after that date, may serve to round off the considerations in the foregoing paragraphs.

The resources of *oil and natural gas* will probably be noticeably diminished. It is probable that the world will experience an increasing shortage of these fuels in the period following the year 2000, especially if consumption continues to increase after 1980. At a rate of growth of a mere 3 per cent annually consumption will be doubled every 25 years. If the equivalent of consumption in 1980 is 5 billion tons coal equivalent, it will be in the neighbourhood of 10 billion tons about the year 2000. It was about 1.5 billion tons in 1955. Consumption requirements of this magnitude can hardly fail to exhaust, in the decades following year 2000, the total oil and gas resources that are thought to be recoverable to-day.

The consumption of *other minerals* in the period 1955–80 will probably not result in quite so serious shortages in the years immediately after 1980. It should be kept in mind, however, that the drain on resources implies that the most easily accessible resources of the highest grade will be exhausted to a more or less considerable extent. Consequently a continued increase in the demand for minerals will have to be met through the utilization of remote deposits of lower grade at higher cost.

A trend in this direction will presumably leave those countries that are poor in resources and *Capital* in a relatively unfavourable position in the struggle for raw materials. What, for example, will be *Asia*'s chances of satisfying its need for raw materials under such conditions?

This problem of *Asia*'s is likely to become even more serious than it is now because, if for no other reason, with a population of 2300 million people (the figure estimated for 1980) it will have a very great need for food, fuels, and metals, even if the per capita consumption remains comparatively small.

The importance of the question depends, of course, on whether it will be possible to develop substitutes for the fuels and minerals which will then be running short.

With regard to *food,* the issue will mainly be whether a clear tendency towards a slower increase in population will make itself felt in the years around 1980, especially in *Asia.* If the rate of increase in population does not slow down, it seems most likely, at present, that the problems outlined at the end of section B will be further intensified towards the close of this century.

CHAPTER VI

Culture

———

1. In Chapter II were provided a definition and a provisional characterization of *Culture* as one of the factors which influence the processes of economic growth. The aim of the present chapter will be, in the first place, to give a more detailed account of the principal elements of the cultural patterns and of their significance. This is done in *Section 2* below. In *Section 3,* an attempt is made to express "quantitatively" the state of knowledge in the various regions; this, as was stressed in Chapter II[1], is the element of *Culture* which has the closest direct relationship to economic growth. The other elements of *Culture* cannot be dealt with in a similar "quantitative" way. Moreover, they are interwoven and form a cultural pattern which is subject to constant changes. In *Section 4* an attempt is made to treat some of the very difficult problems relating to the character of these processes of change, and especially to those aspects of them which are thought to be of primary importance to economic growth in the main areas of the earth within the period under consideration. Finally, *Section 5* contains concluding remarks about some characteristics of the problems confronting us with regard to *Culture* as a factor of growth in the various regions. These remarks, together with the statements made in Chapter III–V concerning the other factors of growth, should be borne in mind when studying the projections of total growth contained in Chapter VII B.

The general significance of cultural factors depends on the fact that they are interwoven, in varying measure, in nearly all aspects of economic growth. This means that most material factors can only be estimated, as far as their influence on economic growth is concerned, by their relationships to cultural factors.

At this juncture, however, a number of fundamental difficulties arise and limit the possibilities of reaching more comprehensive or general conclusions.

---

[1] See page 51.

The cultural factors, whether they be religious, social, or political, cannot, by their nature, be measured and are very difficult to compare. This applies particularly when we consider the same factor in different regions, as, for example, the condition and importance of religion in various parts of the world.

Thus, Catholicism and the Catholic Church do not exert the same influence in each of the countries where they are dominant, either politically, economically, or socially. In some areas Catholicism promotes economic growth, in others it retards it. This depends in large measure on the periods of time and the social patterns within which the Church works, and the opposition, or adjustment, of the Church to these patterns. The Catholic condemnation of birth-control, except through the use of the woman's "safe" period or the exercise of restraint by the husband, in many places influences the factor of population. It is difficult to say, however, with any certainty what is the extent of the influence of the Catholic Church at present or what it is likely to be in the future because the degree of acceptance of the Church's teachings by the population varies greatly even in preponderantly Catholic areas.

2. The following survey of cultural factors includes only those that are generally considered to be essential to economic growth during the next generation. It should be pointed out, however, that the survey uses concepts which lack scientific precision and which have been artificially severed from their contexts or "patterns".

a. *Religious belief and religious organization* influence, sometimes in a fundamental way, the other cultural factors in large parts of the world. It should be emphasized that this factor is, itself, under the influence of other factors of growth (see, for example, section e). Many religious practices and teachings may be shown to be derived from economic, technical, or other origins, that have later received religious sanction, which has often remained even after the disappearance of the original motive. In this context, however, religion must, generally speaking, be regarded as an institutionalized expression of the experience, in the widest sense, of a community, and may thus be said to have had, and in many places to have retained, a fundamental importance as far as the subject of the present book is concerned.

Also with regard to areas where traditional religions no longer play an important part in people's lives, or where they have been "adapted" to economic conditions it must be assumed that the generally accepted norm of behaviour is a factor in economic development. This norm will not be uniform during the period dealt with here in areas of any considerable size although modern economic development will tend to eliminate existing cultural differences.

Special importance attaches to the views of the various religions on economic activity in one form or another, such as agriculture, trade, industry, interest, etc. This applies both generally within a whole community, as, for example, with regard to the attitude of Islam to interest, and within certain groups of society, such as the Hindu division of trades among the various castes by which India has long maintained a rigid pattern of trades, which may in earlier centuries have had a stabilizing effect on economic and social life, by ensuring, *inter alia,* an appropriate distribution of manpower. When, however, external or internal conditions destroyed the basis of this structure, as happened as a result of British policy in the nineteenth century for instance, the system became a serious obstacle to adjustment to the new conditions, and a hindrance to economic growth. The division into castes, and thus into trades, corresponded to a social grading which placed some of the most productive trades—as we regard them to-day—low down on the social scale.

In the matter of the attitude of the human race to birth-control, religion has had, and still has, a similar influence. Most of the world's great religions still consider a large family to be a blessing.

In many parts of the world, and especially in the underdeveloped areas, the teachings of religion may to-day be an impediment to economic development. Most of the great religions arose in the old agricultural communities and many of their attitudes, which directly or indirectly influence economic or social life have, of course, been determined by, and have remained connected with, the interests and viewpoints of such communities. This is one of the reasons why, in these parts of the world, many revolutionary governments attempt to create a secular state in which economic activities, politics, and social conditions are separated from religion (the USSR, Mainland China, Turkey, and India for example), as has already happened in the Western World. The influence of religion on economic development is enhanced by the fact that it expresses or influences the attitude or "spirit" of a community towards many of the conditions or values which in part determine the forms and the intensity of economic activity.

b. This *attitude* or *spirit* is expressed in *standards of value* which, in many places, still hinder economic development as they have done in *Western Europe, North America,* and Japan during the past century. There are great differences in the social esteem of the various forms of material and non-material activity. Similarly, there are big differences in the evaluation of the purposes of life now and hereafter. It should be kept in mind in this context, also, that a relatively uniform economic development does not necessarily lead to the same "cultural pattern", and this, in its turn, will further influence economic development.

From these differences have sprung significant divergences or contradictions in the attitude to modern economic activity, ranging from the European and North American *spirit of enterprise,* originally interwoven with a Puritan-Calvinist background, to, for example, the "passive attitude" of Hinduism. It should, however, be emphasized that there are other considerable differences in attitude, in people's receptiveness or conservatism, as the case may be, which result from physical environment, from living conditions, and similar factors. The demands vary greatly, and estimates of the goods with which to meet the demands vary accordingly.

c. Another significant cultural factor is *the social organization and structure* of a community. To this factor belong, for example, the organization of the family, the systems of family law, the division of the community into social groups, including age groups, and the rôle played by these age groups. Further, the criteria of social prestige (for example the social evaluation of the various types of economic activity), racial conditions, and divisions into castes should be mentioned. These phenomena may often impede the mobility which is so important to the development of modern industrial communities.

d. The development and maintenance of a civilization depends very largely on the ability of a community to co-operate within a given framework. In this context *the political organization* is also of importance in relation to economic development. It should contribute to ensuring co-operation in one form or another.

Such organization requires, *inter alia,* an effective administration which demands able officials and acceptance by the population which is normally called "public spirit" or "loyalty". This may not be present in some parts of the world, particularly in the underdeveloped countries.

This is apparent when we consider that there is not only a need for economic changes proper. The education of both officials and the population as a whole and the necessary profound changes in the social organization are very difficult tasks for the new states. Further, there are cultural contrasts, between, for example, political groups struggling for power while they are themselves undergoing changes, and between groups of leaders that have suddenly come into power.

A new regime may be confronted with many internal and external pressures which compel it to make extensive and economically "unwise" investments. These may confine much activity to "unproductive" fields and thus diminish the possibilities of growth. Even very small and poor countries seem to consider it essential to have their own national airlines, for example. Military expenditure for defence or agression, for maintaining order or for achieving national unity may require vast sums of money. Awareness of higher standards of living in other areas, the so-called demonstration effect, works in this direction. The same applies to expenditure for the purpose of achieving political prestige at home and abroad. Important opportunities of investment in economic development may thus be lost.

The former colonial powers, as well as the rest of the world, are aware of the need for rapid social improvements. Especially in the underdeveloped areas is it necessary that an early effort should be made in the field of welfare, partly for the reasons given above, and partly because the collapse of the older cultural patterns leads to radical changes in the familiar social order. The development of a modern economy intensifies this process from the outset and involves large social expenditure. This may for a time divert economic investment, although, in the long run, such social expenditure may create new possibilities of continued economic development by spreading purchasing power and thus extending the local marketing possibilities for new products. As often as not, however, this situation strains the means of the poor countries to the utmost and may compel their governments to embark on a policy which ruins, or at any rate considerably diminishes, the possibilities of economically decisive investment.

International tension also interferes with and limits investment even within economically productive fields. This injures the poorer areas relatively more than it does the highly developed countries which are better equipped to bear it and at the same time continue their economic expansion.

e. Among the political factors wich, also, at present influence economic policies and investment are *national currents,* including *the struggle for national independence.* These include, above all, the relationships between the

"Old World" and the former or present-day colonies and semi-colonial areas, and the internal strains of the newly independent areas.

Widely differing forces underlie these national currents. There is the struggle for freedom against foreign rule and against direct or indirect "exploitation" which has been led and pursued by nationalist leaders who have, in many cases, been educated at the universities of the colonial powers or the Communist Bloc on the lines of thought and by methods prevailing in the developed countries.

These peoples, however, fight for a triple purpose, namely that of eliminating foreign rule, taking power into their own hands and abandoning part of the heritage of their country in order to introduce modern conditions. In this they are opposed, both before and afterwards, by the leaders of the older cultural tradition which is threatened by the new rulers. The latter come to be regarded as "Europeans" in the eyes of their countrymen and in the struggle between the old groups and the new the possibilities of ensuring the necessary acceptance from the population are diminished or destroyed until major changes have been carried out. This is illustrated by developments in the *USSR* in the nineteen-twenties and thirties and by the situation in a number of the new countries at the present time where the conflicts that take place may well have seriously delayed economic development along modern lines.

Both nationalism, which is directed against foreigners, and internal struggles between the old and the new ruling classes, which tend to make nationalism more radical, are expressions of a desire for greater independence. This sometimes leads to a refusal of aid from the technically advanced areas and to an exaggerated desire to conduct investment policy alone even when this is against sound economic sense and based on wrong ideas about possibilities and aims.

f. The last factor to be mentioned here is *education* in the widest sense, and primarily *elementary literacy*. This cultural factor probably exerts the most powerful single influence in the transformation of cultural patterns, and, as we shall see in section 3, most clearly indicates the development of a community over and above what is indicated, for example, by investment. Among the cultural factors literacy, generally speaking, is the cultural factor which lends itself most easily to being expressed in quantitative terms.

Education aims, first and foremost, at creating the fundamental conditions for developing a modern community of the sort described earlier. These conditions are: the ability to make oneself understood everywhere within a community and the ability to read and write the common language of the community. The fulfilment of these conditions is often made extremely difficult by linguistic and other major cultural differences within the area as for example in many new countries such as Mainland China, India, Indonesia, and a number of African states.

Secondly education implies higher education continuing to highly specialized vocational training. How quickly and how far the advance can be made depends not only on the economic possibilities of building up education, but also on the attitude of the older cultures towards such education. Much depends on the ways in which the thoughts and ideas of the people have evolved and in which direction scholarship has moved. An example of this is the influence of the mathematical and scientific traditions of imperial Russia on technical development in the *USSR*.

Education is necessary not only if a new attitude is to be created towards modern techniques and modern economy generally. It contributes to the break-down of the older cultural traditions and clears the way for the new. It is surprising to see how quickly, if a systematic effort is made, as it has been in the *USSR*, literacy in its elementary forms may be achieved—almost within a single generation. Further development, however, depends on a number of other factors.

3. Among the elements of culture dealt with above *education* is, as already mentioned, the one which can most easily be expressed quantitatively. Further, together with other forms of propagation of knowledge in the widest sense, it is the cultural activity which is most directly connected with economic growth. It is therefore important that we should have some idea of the position of each region as far as education is concerned.

Unfortunately the information available is slight and partly uncertain, one reason being that a particular term does not always refer to the same facts. Thus "illiteracy" may be considered more or less narrowly. The universities and other places of learning that are included in the concept of "higher education" represent, of course, education at much different levels.

The following is based mainly on the publications of UNESCO on illiteracy and education and thus on the definitions used in these publications. This means that we have figures which, as a result of being adapted by UNESCO, have been made as comparable as possible. Nevertheless, it must be emphasized that the figures shown in the tables should be read with many reservations. On the other hand they should contribute towards understanding the situation, partly because their probability may be tested through independent channels.

The principal element among the factors of *Culture* is the ability of the population to read and write and thus to make possible the adjustment to

TABLE VI. 1

Illiteracy.

	Percentage of Illiteracy	Per cent of Population Covered
North America	3	100
Western Europe	8	100
Oceania[1]	12–13	100
USSR[2]	5–10	100
Eastern Europe	17	100
Latin America	43	99
Middle East	73	58
Asia	62	95
Africa	79	52
Total	44	92

[1] UNESCO (1956, a, p. 9).
[2] UNESCO (1957, b, p. 42).
Sources: Calculations made from UNESCO (1956, a) and (1957, b).

a modern economy as well as to the other modern social conditions, administration, etc. A comparison of the regions in this respect is therefore of great importance.

With this in view a survey has been provided, in Table VI. 1, of *illiteracy* in the nine regions. The percentages given represent, in most cases, the number of illiterates in relation to the number of persons of over 15 years of age (in some countries of over 10 years). As a general rule the figures have reference to a year about 1950. For some countries, however, they refer to earlier years. For the year 1955 the figures would on the whole have been a little lower.

There are, of course, considerable variations within some of the regions. In the case of the five developed regions illiteracy may now be considered to have almost entirely disappeared except in certain areas which are, incidentally, also economically retarded. These areas are the southern part of *Western Europe,* the Pacific islands of *Oceania,* certain regions of the *USSR,* and the southern part of *Eastern Europe.* Reciprocal influences are undoubtedly at work here as economic growth makes it easier to provide more education which in its turn renders the population better able to take part in further economic development.

This impression is confirmed if we turn to the four underdeveloped regions. They all have far more illiteracy than the developed regions. *Latin America,* however, which has advanced the farthest economically, has also made the greatest strides in the elimination of illiteracy. It may seem surprising, on the other hand, that *Asia* appears to be a good deal better off than the *Middle East.* This is due to the fact that there are large differences within the vast area of *Asia.* In Japan, which has also reached a high level of development, there is practically no illiteracy, and for Mainland China the percentage is stated to be 50–55. The southern parts of the region, on the other hand, are largely on the same level as *Africa* and the main part of the *Middle East.* In the latter region the percentage for Israel is as low as 5–10. For Cyprus it is 35–40, for Lebanon 50–55, and for Turkey 65–70, whilst for the other countries the percentages are generally very high.

The art of reading and writing is but the most elementary form of that *education* which is one of the necessary conditions of economic growth. Within education a very obvious distinction can, incidentally, be made between primary schools, which provide the general basic instruction of children, secondary schools, which give further instruction, often of a specialized kind, and finally higher education, which includes universities and colleges which provide general as well as special training. A survey of these institutions is given in Table VI. 2.

The number of pupils has here been compared to the population. With regard to primary schools, and probably also to secondary schools, it would have been more appropriate to compare them to the number of children and young people in the age groups in question. The necessary information for this, however, is not available. If the number of primary school pupils is compared to the number of children aged 0–15, the figure for *Western Europe* will be comparatively larger as this region has a slow rate of population increase and therefore comparatively few children in relation to its adult population. Conversely, the figures for the four underdeveloped regions

would be considerably reduced relatively as a very large percentage of the
population of these regions is in the 0–15 age group. (See Table III. 3).

If these reservations are taken into account it may be said, on the basis
of Table VI. 2, that *North America* is above the other regions, especially
with regard to the higher and highest levels of education. The other deve-

TABLE VI. 2

Pupils and Students.
(Per 1000 inhabitants)

	Primary Schools	Secondary Schools	Higher Education
North America	164	44	14
Western Europe	103	22	3
Oceania	112	23	4
USSR	123	26	9
Eastern Europe	124	28	3
Latin America	93	7	1
Middle East	56	6	1
Asia	75	15	1
Africa	37	2	—
Total	88	17	3

Source : Calculations made from UNESCO (1956, a).

loped regions are roughly on the same level with the exception of the *USSR*
which is particularly advanced as regards higher education although it has
not quite caught up with *North America* in this field.

In evaluating these figures we shall probably have to include under the
heading "higher education" in *North America* and the *USSR* some courses,
which are a good deal more elementary than those which are normally
included in higher education in *Western Europe,* for example. The superiority of the two former regions is, therefore, perhaps not as great as the
figures might seem to indicate.

In the underdeveloped regions the number of primary school pupils compared to the total number of children in the 0–15 years' age group is between one-half and one-fourth of those for the developed regions (apart
from *North America*). As is the case with the general level of economic

development, *Latin America* is highest and *Africa* lowest. *Asia,* however, stands comparatively higher than might be expected. The reason for this is, to some extent, the rather high level in Japan and China. Further, there is the fact that since the time of British rule India has had a school system (especially secondary schools) which partly explains why *Asia* is highest among the underdeveloped regions as far as this level of education is concerned.

In addition it will be seen that the four last regions in the Table are relatively lower with regard to secondary and higher education than with regard to elementary education. In any future industrialization and consequent division of labour in these communities they will be in great need of increased intake into secondary and higher education as there will be many more technical, commercial, and administrative tasks to be performed than hitherto. The number of competent teachers available may prove to be a bottleneck in the advanced stages of education.

It would be desirable to supplement the figures for education with some information regarding *research.* It is not possible to make comparisons between the regions in this way, however. Information from the United States, though, shows how great may be the investment in building up "knowledge capital" by research. Expenditure on basic and applied research (excluding market research, sales promotion and so on, and excluding also research in the social sciences and psychology) totalled some $ 8 billion in 1957 [2]. This is more than 20 per cent of total annual net investment in *North America* about 1955. In Chapter II it was mentioned that total gross investment in Denmark would probably have to be raised by at least 20 per cent when investment in knowledge is included. The greater part of it, however, was allocated to education and publishing. It must therefore be assumed that investment in knowledge in the United States is larger in relation to tangible investment than in Denmark when, as mentioned above, research alone takes more than 20 per cent. The figures for education are also, as will be remembered, very large for *North America* (see Table V. 2).

4. *a.* As mentioned above, it is impossible to foretell the weight that the various factors of *Culture* may have, either in relation to one another or jointly against the other factors. History, however, clearly shows us that the existence of natural resources and capital for investment alone have not

[2] Fabricant (1959).

14*

been sufficient to account for the economic development, and the subsequent changes in the social structure, which has been experienced in large parts of Europe and in some other areas during the past few centuries.

A number of cultural factors among those referred to above are, in part, responsible for this particular development (see 2 *b*). These have developed in some West and Central European countries under certain historical conditions and have continued to exist not only in *Europe* but also in *North America,* parts of South America and *Oceania* and in some isolated areas of other continents through the agency of *European* peoples who have brought to these countries their habits, views and knowledge. The indigenous populations were expelled, exterminated, or suppressed so thoroughly that their traditions have virtually had no influence on the development in these areas.

In the rest of the world the basic conditions have been very different from those obtaining in *Europe.* In parts of South America, *Africa,* and *Asia* European individuals or groups have started a similar development, but not under the same conditions as in *North America* and *Oceania.* In the former areas large indigenous communities continued to exist as a large majority and it was within these communities that the "European" development took place. It depended on a limited number of European leaders and on large numbers of unskilled indigenous workers who belonged to entirely different cultures. Extensive cultural clashes and an ever increasing europeanization took place and continued to make themselves felt within the indigenous communities. Those who have been involved in this process have gradually become detached from their customary ways of life and their former cultural pattern has disintegrated. Cultural and tangible factors have operated jointly in this process in the indigenous communities. The Japanese seem to be the only non-European community which has achieved a modern economy under its own leaders. Mainland China and India seem likely to be the next to do so.

A particularly unfortunate aspect of these cultural clashes is the racial conflicts that occur within some communities. South Africa is the most notable example. Here the price of racial discrimination has been even higher because of the conscious division of work, wage rates, housing, social organization and political and other cultural structures. The fact that the economic development of South Africa—and of Algeria—has advanced so far in the European communities, and also within certain groups of the indigenous population, is due partly to the ample natural resources and partly to the availability of cheap unskilled labour and the existence of a community of European immigrants in all strata of society who have become leaders of all kinds as well as skilled workers. Thus wealthy enclaves have been created in these areas and also, to a lesser extent, elsewhere in *Africa* and *Asia* which, as mentioned earlier, are based on European settlement of varying duration.

Once European cultural or economic factors are able to influence the indigenous population directly—which means that they are *involved in European activity*—the older culture disintegrates, often very quickly.

In many of the underdeveloped countries certain cultural patterns have existed for a very long time. The main reason for changes in them, when these have occasionally occurred, has been, at least in more recent times, immigration by people from other cultures. The changes have seldom taken place from internal causes. From this fact alone, however, no conclusions can safely be drawn with regard to the power of resistance of these cultural patterns in modern times. When, on the whole, they seem to be static this is probably due rather to the fact that no major assaults have been made on them, apart from the incursions of foreign cultures already referred to.

In reality such cultural patterns have often stagnated in various respects. They have gradually lost their practical background and are only maintained by tradition, sometimes becoming apparently meaningless. After the first serious incursions from outside these sections of the culture may relatively easily collapse. There can be no doubt that this is what is happening in certain parts of the Hindu culture of India and in the Buddhist culture of Southern and Eastern Asia. The great reforms regarding land, family and inheritance law, the status of women, and the low castes have already revealed how much exaggerated the belief in the power of the older patterns has been. On the other hand, in many places opposition to reforms has been stubborn and there are still large areas in which they have not been established.

It should be added here that economic development, as well as cultural development, follow the main paths, that is to say, they are confined to the areas with the best growing conditions whilst the hinterland will often for long remain untouched. This may, even before the end of the period considered here, lead to *new* antagonisms arising from differences in standard and way of life which, in their turn, will act as a growth-retarding factor (see above concerning enclaves of wealth in underdeveloped areas).

The hinterland is generally to be found in the world's large agricultural areas. It has proved an much harder task to improve methods of cultivation than to create a basis for modern industry. In many countries agriculture is likely to prove the principal bottleneck and a more permanent check to economic development. Political and cultural clashes will also have to be envisaged between townspeople and industrial workers on the one hand and the more conservative peasant workers on the other as the latter will find it hard to accept the organization and ethics of the new community.

Reactions may already be observed in this part of the world (se section 2 e). Nevertheless the over-all impression of the development in the areas in which *direct* action has been possible is one that gives warning against overestimating the retarding force of the older patterns of culture in face of modern economic and political activity, and against underestimating the latent possibilities which may be released when the old patterns disintegrate (cf. Japan, the *USSR,* and Mainland China).

It seems that *economic* and *technical* factors are far more influential in *destroying* a cultural pattern than any cultural factor—apart from *literacy.* This applies mainly to the consequences of industrialization and the separation of the individual from family and the old village community. Their repercussions are usually more powerful than political and other reforms and they may run counter to other cultural factors without losing much strength and importance if such factors are applied against them.

Some of the clearest illustrations of this can be obtained from two of those communities whose racial and class distinctions are thought to be particularly significant, viz. South Africa and India. Long before the Indian reform acts were passed in the wake of independence it was noticeable in Indian industrial centres how quickly and irrevocably the caste system collapsed *within* the industrial organization itself. In South Africa, it has similarly been observed that whereas racial discrimination can, on the whole, be maintained in the older sectors of the South African economy, such as the mining industry in which *unskilled* labour may be used, it has gradually been weakened in the new industries. This applies to the discrimination concerning labour, education, wages, working hours, and the employment of female labour. This is one of the reasons why the racial struggle has been intensified by the Nationalists, whilst the parlamentary opposition, which to a greater extent represents the industrial leadership, has called for a moderation of *apartheid* and an "elastic" policy which meets the demands of industry for skilled labour and so adjusts itself to actual conditions.

With regard to population it may likewise be stated that in the groups in which wealth and modern types of economic and social activity have gained a foothold the average number of children in each family has decreased—at least for a time. This happened in the industrialized countries and is about to happen in some of the areas of the newly-independent countries where industrialization has made headway since the Second World War. It occurs in Catholic, Moslem, and Hindu communities alike.

b. In this enquiry one of the principal dividing lines is that which separates the *technically highly developed part of the world from the underdeveloped.* It is the same line which, roughly speaking, divides the world both economically and as regards illiteracy and other cultural elements.

It may therefore be of importance to outline the economic and cultural relationships in the regions on either side of this boundary line and to compare their development. The particularly important phases of development are those which have been observed throughout the past 150 years in the most highly developed countries and in a number of underdeveloped countries before and since their independence. As to the last-mentioned fact the following observations should be made.

Before independence: Apart from subsistence agriculture and trade the development of resources and their application by modern methods was due mainly to foreign investment and leadership which concentrated on raw materials of high value on the international market, whereas modern large scale industry did not, on the whole, come into existence in these countries. What inspired investment was the dividend which might be earned in the area and remitted home. The construction of roads, bridges, railways, harbours, etc., and the maintenance of law and order (including the observance of agreements), that is to say, effective administration to permit of these activities, was left in the hands of the European administrators. They interfered but little with the culture of the indigenous population and were often unaffected by the disintegration which the economic activity directly and indirectly caused in the local tribal communities. Imperial Russia behaved in a similar manner in its dealings with the Asiatic parts of the realm, whereas the *USSR* has pursued a quite different policy, namely that of attempting to promote a modern economy among non-Russian nations without relinquishing its own political power.

After independence: From the moment independence is secured a number of new problems will arise in the relationship between the former colonies and the rest of the world. Economic activity in former colonial areas, for example, will be influenced by the endeavours of the new rulers to change the cultural factors, in order to ensure, *inter alia,* the development of a modern economy.

During such a change a new régime is confronted with a number of difficulties, economic and others, some of which are described in the present chapter. These are partly due to the fact that a new state has to take a number of economic decisions for non-economic reasons, partly to the fact that they must meet the expenses involved in changing the cultural factors to accomodate the new economy, and finally to the fact that they must take the social (and economic) responsibility for the collapse of the existing patterns which are likely to take place to an increasing extent—often as a result of the state's initiative.

In such a situation the régime of some of the new states will, naturally, tend towards dictatorship or at least towards a high concentration of power; the state playing an important part also in the social and economic field (cf. the USSR, Mainland China, South America, the Middle East, India, and Indonesia). The state must make a number of extraordinary investments, must plan and carry out the mobilization of resources and of population and, as mentioned earlier, take the social responsibility for these changes. This takes place in countries whose economies are very backward. The alternative to such a régime, in most of these countries, would be anarchy.

The said tendency is not surprising. It prevailed during the transition of the countries of Europe to a modern economy in the seventeenth and eighteenth centuries. As mentioned earlier, the European colonial powers were active in the economic development of their colonies. The public authorities in *Africa* are supposed to have made about one-half of total investment in the last third of the nineteenth century and the first third of the twentieth. The development of the Japanese economy in the years 1870–1914 was largely achieved through investment by the state itself or through other forms of state initiative in the economic field.

At present the world may be divided into three groups according to the economic-political systems in operation, extending on either side of the boundary line between developed and underdeveloped areas. *Group 1* consists of countries with a form of democratic rule and largely based on private capital investment economies. *Group 2* includes communist-governed states with economies financed almost entirely by state-owned capital. Group 3 comprises the remainder of the countries of the world:

1) The majority of the *West European* states, *North America, Oceania,* Japan, and a few *Latin American* states.
2) The *USSR, Eastern Europe,* and Mainland China.
3) The rest of the world taking up some intermediary political position between 1) and 2).

This division, which, in many respects, runs counter to the regional division used in this book, is of particular importance in this chapter because the criterion of division is of a cultural nature inasmuch as the definition of culture here used includes political structure. It must be anticipated that, within the period considered economic development will be affected by the rivalry between the countries of groups 1 and 2 as to who is to exert influence on the aid programmes for the countries in group 3.

As regards cultural factors many underdeveloped areas are in a *first phase* in which traditional cultural factors put serious obstacles in the way of modern economic development and in which the question arises as to how far such development might be facilitated by the disappearance of the traditional factors of *Culture*. The *second phase* is the formation of new patterns of culture that are more in harmony with the demands of a modern economy.

c. There remains then the task of attempting to answer the difficult question of what will be the *possibilities* and the *rate* of development in the various regions when they are considered in relation to one another. It should be pointed out here that the forecasts to be attempted relate to a period of only *20–30 years*. The considerable difficulties encountered in making such a prognosis would be different in nature if the period were longer, for example, one hundred years. This is due to the fact that the world situation since the Second World War, and the special combination of factors which prevails to-day, at least within the period under consideration, will be decisive.

As far as the cultural factors are concerned, it is fairly clear that we must distinguish *at least* between the two phases mentioned above within the next two or three decades.

During the *first phase* strong repercussions from the first purposeful and *direct* effort may be expected in some of the underdeveloped countries. It is a question of what may be termed the *primary investment* in the cultural factors—corresponding to primary investment in the economic sphere. Like economic investment it may sometimes give a surprisingly large yield. This applies especially to the disintegration of the older cultural patterns. As was mentioned above, the resistance of these to direct attacks has often been somewhat overestimated as it is quite certain that they disintegrate quickly in places where they are attacked by a combination of modern economic factors. The mobility of the individual and his freedom to change occupation, the development of modern agriculture, trade, and fishing together with industrialization are among the chief of these factors. The same applies also to the growth of literacy wherever a direct effort may be made. It may not take very long as its power to destroy the older cultural patterns may be very strong.

In this phase it is of little importance that the first offensive penetrates only to certain parts of the population. Even in some of the highly developed communities, to say nothing of those that have reached an intermediate stage of development, there are large parts of the population which have not yet been affected very much by this development. Older cultural patterns survive here and even where the new factors of *Culture* actually triumph they find no practical application.

If only the primary investment is made very considerable results may, as has already been pointed out, be achieved in the first instance, in the sense that the older cultural patterns may be modified or adjusted so that their institutions may not generally impede a further development.

Thus we reach the *second phase,* i.e. the period in which, on the one hand, the disintegration of the old cultural pattern and the development of elementary literacy are to continue, and in which, on the other hand, the actual *formation* of new patterns—accompanying further economic growth— is to begin. The investment and the demands made on the population are so large that major difficulties will probably be encountered within the period.

In the cultural sphere it is a question of higher education, the training and selection of officials and leaders, the development of a new political organization, of a new attitude towards life, an ethic which meets the demands of the new techniques and the new economy, the development of political and social acceptance or loyalty, etc. It is clear that the disintegration of the older pattern of *Culture* prepares the way for the new pattern, but does not in itself result in a rapid formation of a new pattern. In many cases it leaves a vacuum or chaos—the quite familiar "state of transition"–which can only later be replaced by, or develop into a new pattern. What new forms may develop is hard to say in general terms. In many cases some of the old cultural traditions may be expected to survive with a force great enough to leave their stamp on the new traditions.

The recruitment of leaders is one of the essential prerequisites of economic development all over the world, and especially in the underdeveloped areas. A modern industrialized community requires highly qualified leaders, even at the first stage. The growing need of engaging individuals of the highest intelligence in the leadership of a country will probably require a more widespread recruitment than has hitherto taken place. This is a very costly process, partly because it generally requires a higher degree of literacy and, as far as higher education is concerned, it will probably encounter resistance from those classes which by virtue of their birth have a monopoly of higher education and therefore of the top executive posts. Within the period here dealt with no fundamental changes are likely to be felt although a prompt effort is required, and has already been made, as the education of the new class of leaders will take at least one generation. With regard to the full acceptance of empiricism as known in Europe, which is very remote from the original culture of many countries, the adaptation will take even longer.

To illustrate the importance of educational systems we may compare the systems of India and Mainland China. As far as can be seen (see also section 3), higher education in India is largely formed on the British pattern of some generations ago. Even at the present day this results in a rather narrow, but very discerning recruitment for higher education. In consequence a relatively large proportion of those selected for such higher education complete their studies. In China, since 1949, a much wider recruitment has been made. The results achieved, however, cannot yet be evaluated. Time will show whether the Chinese will surpass India in making leaders by virtue of their educational system.

With regard to both the disintegration of the old cultural pattern and the formation of a new the importance of such factors as modern means of communication and propaganda is hard to appraise as we have no historical standards of comparison. The development in Mainland China after the Second World War, however, suggests that radical changes in the cultural pattern, through the systematic application of such means, may be achieved sooner than had hitherto been thought possible.

Another example of the significance of modern means of communication is provided by the fact that in the highly developed Western democracies "public opinion", the moral principles of the population, are formed, to a great extent, through the influence of the press, the radio, television, etc. Public opinion may prove of importance, especially in the relationship with the underdeveloped countries, as a factor both retarding and promoting economic growth.

5. With regard to *Culture* as a factor influencing the economic growth of the regions it may be said, to summarize, that there are considerable differences within some of the regions and that, owing to the nature of the factor *Culture,* all estimates in this field will be even more uncertain than those relating to the other factors of growth. The elements of *Culture* can only to a limited extent be described quantitatively, as has been done in section 3, and the complicated changes in the cultural patterns mentioned in section 4 cannot be exhaustively characterized or expressed in a few categoric sentences.

This, however, by no means diminishes the actual importance of *Culture*. Its relevance to economic forecasts is obvious. Ethnologists have shown how deeply *Culture* influences all fields of human activity. They have further shown how dangerous it is to interfere with such a pattern without a knowledge of its whole structure.

It must, however, be our task in conclusion to supplement the survey given with a few words regarding the *trends* that are noticeable, in order to gain some impression of the possibilities of development and of the problems to be anticipated in the various regions of the earth.

Enquiries seem to suggest that the increase in the net domestic product of the developed areas in the past few decades considerably exceeds what is directly accounted for by increase in *Labour* and tangible *Capital*. This is in accordance with the projections given in Table VII. 3, as the parameter γ represents a very considerable proportion of total growth. As mentioned in Chapter II [3], γ corresponds to the effects of the changes taking place during

[3] See page 37.

the period considered in the background of production constituted by *Nature* and *Culture,* including, above all, progress in technical and other forms of knowledge and changes in the cultural patterns which render the latter more susceptible to innovations. Great importance therefore attaches to the prospects for the elements of *Culture.*

As was mentioned in section 3, *North America* spends very large sums on research and has substantially higher figures for all levels of education than the other regions. A large investment in knowledge is thus made there which will have to be taken into account when, as appears from Chapter IV, tangible investment in *North America* is in fact relatively smaller than might be expected from the income level. This is thus part of the reason for the comparatively large rates of growth which have been projected for *North America* in Chapter VII B.

The *USSR* also has relatively large figures for higher education. It is well-known that large sums are being expended on research in certain fields. Although it is uncertain how broad is the basis of this research work, it may probably be said that, in relation to its present economic level, the *USSR* spends more on investment in knowledge than does *Western Europe, Oceania,* and *Eastern Europe. North America* and the *USSR* are therefore the two regions in which the factor of knowledge may be assumed to be most conducive to growth.

In the underdeveloped regions the widespread illiteracy, the limited education, and the traditional, static patterns of culture seem to be factors which may retard the growth in the net domestic product which might otherwise be possible on account of the extent of the natural resources. The situation is relatively favourable in *Latin America* (especially in Argentina, Chile, and Uruguay) and in the northern part of *Asia* (Mainland China and especially Japan). It is in the tropical and subtropical regions of the *Middle East, Asia,* and *Africa,* particularly, that difficulties arise.

In this connection the UNESCO investigations of the trends in illiteracy [4] are of particular interest. Development since 1900 has been examined for a number of countries, and the intervening period has been divided into sub-periods of about 10 years each. For the last of these sub-periods the following, very summary, figures are given for the development in 40 countries (arithmetical averages):

[4] UNESCO, (1953).

Illiteracy in Per cent of Adult Population.

	Group A 26 countries	Group B 14 countries
At the beginning of the period	32.0	73.3
At the end of the period	22.7	67.4
Per cent decrease in the period	29.1	8.0

Group A includes those countries in which illiteracy was below 50 per cent at the end of the period, Group B all other countries.

It appears that progress was relatively greatest where the greatest strides had already been made, so that the distance between the two groups has increased. This can easily be explained inasmuch as the countries with much illiteracy, as a rule, have few schools and teachers. A calculation of the same summary nature as the above-mentioned shows[5] that for 16 countries with an illiteracy percentage of over 50, average illiteracy was 72.4 per cent. In these countries 26.4 per cent of all children went to school. In the remaining 23 countries average illiteracy was 27.3 per cent and 60.6 per cent of the children went to school. We may therefore say that in the first group there are many who are in need of education and few to teach them. The reverse holds true in the other group. It is thus difficult to get started but once this has been done the improvement in this field, as well as in many other fields of the social development, tends to become self-sustaining.

To-day such facilities as wireless, films, etc., are available to education. These facilities, however, may probably be used most effectively in countries where some progress in education has already been made.

If we consider the change in the cultural patterns there is reason to emphasize, besides the general attitude of the population, the importance of creating effective political and administrative systems, it being often incumbent on the State to undertake tasks which are normally, in some of the developed regions, executed by private persons. It is significant that in *Latin America* the formation of independent states virtually came to an end a long time ago. In the *Middle East* it was largely carried out between the

[5] Calculated on the basis of UNESCO figures for 39 countries, UNESCO (1957 b, p. 166).

two world wars. In *Asia* the process really began only after the Second World War, but is now practically completed. In *Africa* it has started only in very recent years. There are still very large areas of this continent which have not yet obtained full political independence. As the establishment of new states, the consolidation of their rule, and the building up of their administration often involves considerable difficulties, it should be pointed out that these problems will be particularly significant in *Africa* and perhaps to some extent in *Asia*.

Another problem to be encountered by the new countries arises when their populations hear more about the consumption habits of the industrial countries and desire to posses the same. This may contribute to a quicker increase in consumption than is actually warranted by the relatively large need for investment.

It is, of course, especially in the large isolated agricultural areas away from the industrial centres and the main paths that illiteracy prevails. This appears from the figures issued by UNESCO and conforms with what was said above concerning the cultural patterns, which remain longest in agricultural areas. When these facts are compared with the conclusions arrived at in Chapter V B which show that in these very areas there will be a demand for a large increase in agricultural production in the period considered, and that this will require a great capacity for and a positive attitude towards innovations, it will be seen that the effort that can be made in these areas with regard to cultural development and adjustment will greatly influence economic development.

CHAPTER VII

Models of Growth

A. *On the Theories of Growth*

1. It was mentioned in Chapter II that the growth of the net domestic product depends on a great variety of factors. Among those that will influence the growth of a region are, to mention a few at random: the development in population and its distribution by age groups, the amount of real capital and changes in it, the quality and quantity of natural resources, the trend in prices in general and, in particular, in the relationship between export and import prices, the level of general education, people's attittude to economic incentives, the organization of the economy of the region, and national policies. As has also been emphasized in Chapter II, this catalogue may be very considerably extended without even then being complete.

Certain factors, however, are distinguishable as not only being of special significance but also of a nature that particularly attracts attention in the course of an economic study. These are *Labour* and *Capital* which with *Nature* constitute the basis of all material production. They were dealt with in Chapters III–V, and, in Chapter VI, an analysis of their cultural foundation was added. This foundation is a necessary condition of growth and influences, and is influenced by, the process of growth. In dealing with *Culture* we have also to deal with the effects of changes in production techniques. Such changes are of vital importance in an analysis of growth. To take a traditional but questionable line, the effects of technical changes will not be considered until the effects of changes in real capital, labour and resources have been dealt with.

The aim of Chapters II to VI was to give a description and analysis of the various factors. It is a characteristic fact, however, that all production is carried out through a combination of a variety of factors of production. The present chapter is an attempt to throw some light on the relationship of the factors of production and to examine the probable trends of development in the nine regions during the years to come.

2. Whether production is described as taking place through the application of human labour and (produced) real capital to natural resources—such as earth, water, air, minerals, etc.—or whether the process of production is said to consist in the extraction of raw materials from nature and their transformation into a form suitable for human consumption, the crux of the matter is, still, the fact that production is achieved through the joint employment of the various factors of production. This applies also to intangible production, e.g. teaching and services in general.

If a particular production process is considered it may sometimes appear as though the composition of the factors of production is predetermined. Examples of this may easily be found, e.g. in the chemical industry. It is nevertheless, on the whole, characteristic of some communities that a certain production level can be achieved with varying amounts of factors of production. A certain quantity of goods—e.g. a certain amount of agricultural products—may thus be produced through a relatively moderate use of natural resources (earth) but, at the same time, through a relatively extensive use of other factors, such as labour and fertilizers. In other words, it may be established that factors of production may to a very large extent replace each other. Indeed, if production is considered as a whole, the possibilities of substitution will probably be almost unlimited.

Another important fact is that when the input of a particular factor is increased output will also increase. This is due to the possibility of substitution, just referred to. If the input of *Labour* in agriculture is increased, agricultural production will increase; an increase in the real *Capital* invested in the extraction of natural resources will lead to an increase in production, and so on. On the other hand, if we keep on increasing the input of a factor in a production process the resulting increase in output will grow continuously smaller—at any rate after a certain level of output has been reached. Agricultural production will grow as the input of *Labour* is increased, but if we go on employing more and more persons we shall increase production, but at a diminishing rate. Although the same applies, perhaps, in only limited measure to industrial production it would seem that for production as a whole a decreasing return will result[1].

---

[1] These relations may be expressed in a number of formulas. If the factors of production are specified as $F_1, F_2, \ldots, F_k$, the return, P, will be a function of the input of F_i $(i = 1, 2, \ldots, k)$:

$$P = P(F_1, F_2, \ldots, F_k).$$

(*Footnote continued on page 226*)

Economists express the facts relating to these general limitations by saying that *the marginal productivity of a factor of production,* that is the production increase achieved by increasing the input of the factor by one unit, will be positive but will decrease as the amount of the particular factor is increased. On the other hand it will increase with an increasing input of another factor.

If the process of agricultural production is considered, on the lines mentioned above, it will be possible to visualize the relationship between input of labour and output to be as follows:

Labour Input (e.g. man-years)	Output (e.g. tons of wheat)	Marginal Productivity
1,000	20,000	
		17
1,001	20,017	
		16
1,002	20,033	
		15
1,003	20,048	
		13
1,004	20,061	

If, however, the amount of fertilizer is increased, the marginal productivity of labour will be increased. The sequence of figures may then, for example, be 25, 23, 21, and 18.

These relationships between input and output have been tentatively expressed in various forms in production functions. In Chapter II the *Cobb-Douglas function* was mentioned in which the relationship was specified as:

$$P = \beta \ L^{\alpha_1} \ C^{\alpha_2},$$

P, L, and *C* being indices for output, manpower, and real capital respectively, while α_1, α_2 and β are parameters, α_1 and α_2 having values between

(*Footnote continued from page 225*)

From what was said above it follows that within "reasonable" limits we may assume that

$$\frac{\delta P}{\delta F_i} > o \ (i = 1, 2, \ldots, k)$$

whereas
$$\frac{\delta^2 P}{\delta F_i^2} < o \ (i = 1, 2, \ldots, k)$$

Further, it may be assumed that $\dfrac{\delta^y P}{\delta F_i \ \delta F_j} > o \ (i \neq j).$

o and 1. It appears that this function, which will be considered in detail below, at least fulfils the general requirements mentioned above[2].

It has been stated, on the one hand, that these characteristic features in the production function may be assumed to be valid only within certain limits, just as it has been argued that other rules apply in certain sectors, e.g. manufacturing industry. On the other hand it should be emphasized that irrespective of what may or may not obtain in a particular production process, the present account refers to a total production function, i.e. a community as a whole. The facts stated may thus be assumed to be generally applicable to macro-economic analysis of this kind. It must, however, once more be underlined that the relationships stated assume that no change in techniques takes place.

From the theory of production outlined above it follows that when there are clearly perceptible differences in production level and in the increase in production in the various regions of the earth these differences may be attributed to:

(1) differences in the quantities of factors of production employed in production processes, including differences in the quantities of natural resources and (2) differences in the "productivity" of the factors (which may, in the present context, be regarded as the production return achieved in different places with the same inputs of production factors). As will appear from what follows, these "explanations" are not, however, by any means independent of each other.

3. In Chapters III–VI the differences in the supply of factors of production, in the widest sense, were analysed and described. In Chapter I the differences in production of the nine regions about 1955 have similarly been

[2] This is seen by considering the derivatives:

$$\frac{\delta P}{\delta L} = a_1 \ L^{(a_1 - 1)} \ C^{a_2} \ \beta = a_1 \ \frac{P}{L} > o \text{ and}$$

$$\frac{\delta P}{\delta C} = a_2 \ L^{a_1} \ C^{(a_2 - 1)} \ \beta = a_2 \ \frac{P}{C} > o;$$

$$\frac{\delta^2 P}{\delta L^2} = (a_1 - 1) \ \frac{1}{L} \ \frac{\delta P}{\delta L} < o,$$

$$\frac{\delta^2 P}{\delta C^2} = (a_2 - 1) \ \frac{1}{C} \ \frac{\delta P}{\delta C} < o, \text{ and}$$

$$\frac{\delta^2 P}{\delta L \ \delta C} = a_2 \ \frac{1}{C} \ \frac{\delta P}{\delta L} = a_1 \ \frac{1}{L} \ \frac{\delta P}{\delta C} > o.$$

examined. In the light of the general remarks made above about the effects of variations in factors of production and the relationship between resources generally and output will now be examined more closely.

Such an examination will as far as is practicable lead to an "explanation" of present conditions, i.e. the world economic balance of to-day as well as explaining the possible changes. In other words, it will lead to an analysis of growth essential to any attempt to envisage the economic future.

Thus is established the connection to the theory of economic growth which has been developed since the war and which has as its background the crises and stagnation of the thirties, the (politically inspired) pre-occupation with the underdeveloped countries in the post-war era, and also the competition as regards growth which has started in recent years, e.g. between the USSR and United States and between China and India.

The task to be undertaken would have been comparatively easy and much more clearly definable if we had at our disposal a theory of economic growth which was, if not actually "complete", then at least so far advanced as to be in an appropriate form. This, however, is very far from being the case—as has already been mentioned in Chapter II. The literature dealing with growth has, it is true, been expanding rapidly. Yet it is still of a tentative nature and far from perfect—which this literature itself makes abundantly clear.

If the nature of the problem is kept in mind we could scarcely expect anything else. It should especially be emphasized here that an analysis of economic growth, which must inevitably refer to a comparatively long period of time, will have to include a great many facts which are normally left out of account in economic analyses. While, in an examination of a trade cycle, we may thus reasonably suppose that, for example, the general attitude towards leisure time as opposed to working hours will remain practically unchanged, such an assumption will scarcely be tenable in an analysis of growth covering a much longer period. More generally, it seems that it will be necessary to take into account a number of facts which are usually, in economic analyses, referred to as the boundaries, viz. technology, psychology, and sociology. A realistic theory of economic growth must, in other words, deal with things that are not normally thought to belong to the field of economics. It is significant that several of the contributions that have been made to a theory of economic growth are the work of men who were not merely economists, e.g. *Adam Smith, Karl Marx, Joseph Schumpeter* and

W. W. Rostow. The difficulty of the task becomes more apparent when it is considered how a number of related sciences, such as psychology and sociology, are in much the same state as economics, viz. one which may, without reservation, be called backward.

4. An attempt to prepare a general theory of growth which will be satisfactory in the sense that it will "describe" the process of economic history in different countries and explain the differences in standards of living and production levels that are indisputable, is probably the most ambitious task that economic research can set itself. In view of the intimate connection between economic development on the one hand and political and cultural development on the other it will be realized that such a task is really, in the last resort, a search for a general, and deterministic, theory of history.

If the purpose of the theory of growth is expressed in this way we shall, presumably, be compelled to declare the problem insoluble, or at least we shall recognize that, in order to make a start on such a theory, we must limit it[3].

It has therefore been assumed—often, it is true, only implicitly—by most authors on the subject that the models set up refer only to communities of the *West European* (or even north-west European) and *North American* type. In adapting these theories to other communities—or to other historical periods than the present—it is thus necessary to make a number of reservations. When it is possible, nevertheless, with some advantage to argue from certain simple basic points in these theories with regard to, for example, large parts of the undeveloped areas of the earth, it is probably due mainly to the fact that the problem confronting us in these areas is generally accepted to be: in what circumstances will the development change so that a process of growth similar to that of *Western Europe* and *North America* is experienced?

We may, however, react against the entire set of problems involved on the grounds that (even with the said limitations imposed on the theory) the part of the behaviour and condition of mankind which is made the subject of such theories is so small that if a forecast of the future of mankind is seriously attempted the models used will be far too narrow. This fact, it may

---

[3] Karl Marx is probably the only economist who, in the doctrine of the class struggle as the motive power, has attempted to formulate such a theory in entirely general terms. Even with Marx, however, the special theory of growth is confined to the problem of the trends in "modern Capitalism", i.e. capitalism about the middle of last century!

be argued, however, is taken into account, to a certain extent at least, inasmuch as the limited scope of the analysis has been emphasized. The consequence of this, on the other hand, is that the theory of growth in its present form can provide, at the most, what is known in American terminology as projections, and not predictions or forecasts as such.

From what has just been said, however, it follows that the considerations given below are only applicable to a limited extent. They should thus be read with many reservations which it would hardly be possible, and of little use, to state in detail and at the appropriate places. This is all the more true as some of these considerations are of a nature so abstract that reservations will have to be made as a matter of course.

5. In Section 2 above the structure of the production process in a contemporary community was outlined. It was said that an increased input of a factor of production would increase the output, but at a decreasing rate. As factors of production must be included not only *Labour,* in the widest sense, durable real *Capital* in the form of machinery, buildings, means of transport, etc., *natural resources* in the form of earth, minerals, water etc., and the production techniques, the general attitude to production, etc. (i.e. *Culture*) of any given period, but also the raw materials that are produced and pass through the productive apparatus. It should always be kept in mind, however, that in the present context the production process in a given community is considered as a whole. As the raw materials that are used in one sector are the output of another, such intermediary forms will cancel out in an aggregation. When considering a community as a whole we may, therefore, reason as though there were only the basic factors of production: *Labour, Capital, Nature* and *Culture,* each of which has been defined and described in Chapter II, as well as in Chapters III–VI. Strictly speaking this implies that the community considered must be one which conducts no foreign trade, i.e. a closed community. In fact, this assumption is made in the following paragraphs, though it will be modified later.

6. In which ways can the interplay of these factors of production lead to an increase in production when it is remembered that the principal feature of a process of growth is that it is self-sustained? There are several answers to this question. One of these is:

With given quantities of utilized factors of production a given output, that is a given quantity of goods and services, can be achieved. To this quantity of goods produced a certain income, however, will correspond, and

will be of precisely the same value as the value of total output. (See Introduction, page 15). This is because what is paid for the total output
must accrue to the owners of the production factors by way of payment for
their having made the factors available to production. The payment, which
is made by purchasing the output, is thus a payment to the owners of the
factors of production: a wage bill to the wage (and salary) earners, interest
and profit to the owners of *Capital* and a rent to the owners of resources.
With regard to the factor of *Culture,* it appears that the level of the payments made will be influenced by the cultural level. Certain patterns of
Culture form a better basis for material production than others and will consequently yield a larger output and thus lead to a higher income level. What
is essential in this connection is that the total value of output corresponds
to the flow of income [4] which accrues to the inhabitants (or institutions) of
the area in question.

Thus, a given input of factors of production and the resulting output
gives an income to the inhabitants of the area. This income will then be
consumed or saved [5].

It will be seen that, in as far as the income is consumed, the inhabitants
will engage factors of production according to their own input of them in
production. On the other hand, the inhabitants will not use factors of production in proportion to the income saved. From the point of view of the
community the essential fact of saving is thus that the individuals have a
possibility of engaging factors of production for the making of consumer
goods, but omit to utilize this possibility.

From this it follows that the factors of production which, due to saving,
are not applied to the production of consumer goods may be used to produce such goods as represent an increase in the amount of real capital [6].

[4] If it is assumed that part of the output is used in the maintenance and renewal of
the existing capital, the income stated here will be the net income in the sense that
corrections have already been made for depreciation of the existing capital.

[5] The payment of taxes seems to be a third, rather obvious possibility. To prevent the
analysis getting more abstract than is strictly necessary, it may be said that the public,
which receives the taxes, may be assumed to use the yield for the payment of transferred
incomes (as social outlays and interest on national debt) whereby the income is returned
to the citizens, or helps to meet public consumption. Finally, part of the tax yield may be
saved. Consequently, the public sector only means that the consumption stated in the
text may, to a certain extent, be public. Or part of the saving achieved may be public
saving.

[6] This, it should be noted, does not imply that the factors of production made idle by

(*Footnote continued on page 232*)

If the income which, in a given area, corresponds to the production of goods and services is high, that is, if there is a large production, the saving which can be achieved may be relatively large also. From this it follows, however, that in such an area, on the given assumptions, a relatively large amount of factors of production will be available for the production of investment goods or, in other words, for increasing real capital. A rapid increase of real capital will enable production, also, to grow rapidly and this will be accompanied by a similar increase in income, to which will correspond a still greater saving, i.e. a still greater increase in real capital and income. As soon as *Capital* increases, that is as soon as net investment is positive, total production will (or may) increase. The amount of net investment, however, is of course decisive in determining how fast *Capital* will grow. It should be emphasized that here no account is taken of whether the increase in production, i.e. the growth, is offset by (or itself offsets) a simultaneous increase in population. It is, it should be remembered, the particular effect of an increase in the factor of *Capital* only which is being considered.

It is apparent that the process just described may by its nature be self-sustained. This, in fact, is typical of all theories of growth, which aim to include the phenomenon so apparent to-day, viz. that the rich areas tend to become still richer.

It will also be noticed, however, that the process just described will not necessarily result in unlimited growth. For it was mentioned above that

(Footnote continued from page 231)

saving will actually be used to increase the real capital through the production of investment goods. Perhaps those factors of production will remain completely idle, that is without employment at all. The latter contingency, however, will be disregarded in the present context.

It should be emphasized that this assumption is decisive in more ways than one. The first implication of it is that the very considerable difficulties involved in the transfer of production factors from one sector to another are disregarded. The second implication, connected with the first, is that variations in the savings quota may easily, and soon, be accompanied by variations in production of investment goods as opposed to production of consumer goods. Thirdly, however, the assumption implies that full, or at least, constant, employment of available *Labour* is reckoned with. This all-important assumption means not only certain demands on economic policy, but a disregard of the connection which is thought, by many writers on the subject of growth (e.g. Joseph Schumpeter, in his fundamental work, 1934), to exist between business cycles and economic growth. It should be added that although the assumption mentioned here is that generally made in the literature on growth, it may prove a very grave limitation.

although an increased input of a factor of production, such as real *Capital*, will bring about an increase in output, this increase, on the other hand, will fall if the factor in question continues to grow. From this it should follow that the growth process described may well result in a continuous rise in the income level, but not necessarily an unlimited rise[7].

[7] If it were assumed, however, that the increase in production resulting from a given increase in the input of real capital would be constant, there would, it appears, be a continuous and unlimited rise in income. This is the assumption underlying the Harrod-Domar model of growth. (See Domar (1957)). If P stands for the net domestic product (in constant prices), C for real capital, and I for net investment $\left(=\dfrac{dC}{dt}\right)$, we get

$$\frac{dP}{dt} = \frac{dP}{dC}\frac{dC}{dt} = \frac{dP}{dC}I$$

This is the (potential) production resulting from a given investment. We may say that the relationship shown here expresses the supply resulting from a given investment.

The investment during a given period, however, has also an influence on demand as it will create a flow of income (which will increase total income when net investment goes up). This flow of income will depend partly on the amount of the investment, and partly on the prevailing propensity to save. Assuming that out of an extra income of one dollar the amount λ ($0 < \lambda < 1$) is saved, an investment increase of ΔI will result in a flow of income which may be described as follows:

During the first period income grows by the investment increase, ΔI. During the following period part of the income thus created will be consumed. $\lambda \Delta I$ being saved, consumption will amount to $(1-\lambda) \Delta I$. This increase in consumption, however, will give rise to an increase in income of the same size: $(1-\lambda) \Delta I$. This new increase in income will, during the subsequent period, partly be saved and partly consumed. The part saved will be $\lambda (1-\lambda) \Delta I$, while consumption will be $(1-\lambda)^2 \Delta I$. This results in new income of the same magnitude: $(1-\lambda)^2 \Delta I$. It will be seen that this may be continued. The total increase in income appears to be:

$$\Delta P = \Delta I + (1-\lambda) \Delta I + (1-\lambda)^2 \Delta I + \ldots + (1-\lambda)^n \Delta I + \ldots$$
$$= \Delta I \left(1 + (1-\lambda) + (1-\lambda)^2 + \ldots + (1-\lambda)^n + \ldots\right)$$
$$\to \Delta I \frac{1}{\lambda},$$

it being assumed that the propensity to save (λ) is between 0 and 1. We then get

$$\frac{dP}{dt} = \frac{1}{\lambda}\frac{dI}{dt}$$

This formula expresses the effect on demand of a given increase in investment. A necessary condition of continued growth is that from a given investment there should be a similar effect on supply and on demand. This will presuppose that investment moves in such a way that

$$\frac{dP}{dC}I = \frac{1}{\lambda}\frac{dI}{dt}$$

that is to say

$$\frac{dI}{dt}\bigg/ I = \lambda \frac{dP}{dC}$$

(*Footnote continued on page 234*)

7. The account given above of the effects of a change in production and income consequent on a change in *Capital*, and the ensuing theory of a self-sustained growth, have been subject to the limitation that the other factors of production have been given in constant "amounts". A change in the factor of *Capital*, solely, has been considered. The self-sustained process resulting thus appears in this form: larger output $=$ larger income $\rightarrow$ larger saving $=$ larger increase in *Capital* $\rightarrow$ still larger output etc.

A similar analysis could now be carried out for *Labour*. To a certain extent this analysis would be analogous as, in this case too, an increase in input may be assumed to result in increased output. In this case, also, the increase in production must be assumed to diminish with a continued increase in the input.

It is significant that the considerations put forward here about real *Capital* might lead directly to a theory of growth as a self-sustained process. A similar process might in fact take place in the field of manpower if it could be assumed that an increase in production would lead to an increase in population. We could then formulate the following relationship: larger output $\rightarrow$ larger population $\rightarrow$ larger man-power $\rightarrow$ larger output etc.

Some major reservations, however, will have to be made with regard to this process. Firstly, the relationship between an increase in production and the related increase in income, on the one hand, and the increase in popula-

---

(Footnote continued from page 233)

If $\dfrac{dP}{dC}$ is constant an exponential development of investment, and consequently of income, will take place. If $\dfrac{dP}{dC}$ however, falls when C rises another development is possible. Thus, if, as in Chapter II, we assume that

$$P = \beta \, L^{\alpha_1} \, C^{\alpha_2} \, (1 + \gamma)^t$$

and if, in this case the last factor is disregarded (i.e. γ *equals* o) and that it is further assumed that L is constant it appears, as demonstrated earlier, that

$$\frac{dP}{dC} = \beta \, \alpha_2 \, L^{\alpha_1} \, C^{(\alpha_2 - 1)}$$

As $o < \alpha_2 < 1$ it follows that

$$\frac{dI}{dt} \bigg/ I = \lambda \, \frac{dP}{dC} = \lambda \, \beta \, \alpha_2 \, L^{\alpha_1} \, C^{(\alpha_2 - 1)}$$

which tends towards zero as C increases. A similar development may be demonstrated for output, P.

It will also be seen that if it were assumed that the propensity to save (λ) increased with increasing income, this would counteract the tendency demonstrated.

tion on the other is very uncertain. At least no complete theory is available in this field[8].

Secondly, it will be seen that if a steady, unilateral increase in population and man-power is followed by a diminishing increase in production the result will be that *the marginal productivity* (i.e. the production increase resulting from the input of one more man into production) will be less than *the average productivity* (i.e. production per man). It is apparent, however, that at least from this point the new arrivals will depress the income average and thus the standard of living. This must be assumed to weaken the connection between increase of production and increase of population.

8. It follows from what has been said that an increase in man-power, only, can result, at the most, in a growth that will gradually level off. The same may apply to an increase in real *Capital*. It is possible, however, that the tendency of the marginal productivity of real *Capital* to decline will be counteracted by a steady increase in the rate of growth of real *Capital*[9].

What has been said about the effects of an isolated change in the input of one, and only one, factor of production, however, will have to be modified considerably if we study the more likely contingency of simultaneous increases in the input of several factors of production. Thus, if we assume that a process of production involves only two factors of production so that the input of them may be considered to have been fully described in reviewing the input of real *Capital* and *Labour,* the result will be that a simultaneous *pari passu* increase of the two factors will cause a *pari passu* increase in output. A 10 per cent increase in the input of each of the two factors of production will thus achieve a 10 per cent growth of output[10].

---

[8] The most notable attempt to form a model of population is probably T. R. Malthus's famous *Essay on the Principle of Population* published in 1798.

[9] This, in other words, will mean, on the given assumption, a continuous increase in the saving quota accompanying increasing income.

[10] In this case the so-called Law of "Pari-passu Increase" applies. The situation described apparently implies that the production function will be homogeneous to the first degree. It should, incidentally, be amphasized, as in fact has been done previously, that the analysis is "total", or in other words, it deals with the community as a whole. Apparently the Cobb-Douglas production function applied earlier will fulfil the condition stated if $\alpha_1 + \alpha_2 = 1$. In this case the production function implies, so to speak, that all factors of production have been taken into account. (See Chapter II). If, on the other hand, there are several factors, e.g. an unspecified third factor which is kept constant it will follow from the considerations quoted above that a pari passu increase in input of the two specified factors will not result in a corresponding increase in production.

(*Footnote continued on page 236*)

A production function thus specified, in which simultaneous variations of similar magnitude in both factors of production is considered, may indicate a theory of growth which allows for development in production (and in come) following a simultaneous increase in the input of factors of production and which does not necessarily impose a ceiling on development. (We must, it seems, assume a connection between the propensity to save and the increase in population in so far as it is assumed that saving and increase in population do, in fact, correspond to each other so that real *Capital* and population are growing at the same rate). It will be seen, however, that in this growth process there need not be any increase in per capita production and income. The latter will be brought about only through sustained increases in saving relative to income without similar increases in population. It also appears that even if *Capital* should grow more rapidly for a period, whereby a per capita increase in production and income would be possible, such a process of growth, in which the factors of production do not grow *pari passu,* will put a ceiling to the self-sustained movement. This is in accordance with what was said above concerning an isolated increase in the input of real *Capital.*

9. Now, it is in fact characteristic of the industrialized areas that per capita production and income are increasing steadily. As has been shown, a per capita increase may take place in consequence of special increases in the input of real *Capital.* This effect, however, seems to be subject to a limitation—as was suggested above—which will come into effect quickly or slowly as the speed with which the rate of increase in production, following an isolated increase in real *Capital,* will decline. Added to this is the fact that there have been cases of sustained increase in per capita production in spite of the fact that investment has not represented an increasing proportion of total production.

The present considerations, however, have hitherto in this analysis been strictly limited. Not only the influence of natural resources, but also the effects of changes in production techniques, in the widest sense, have so far

---

(*Footnote continued from page 235*)

A 10 per cent increase in the specified factors will cause a production increase of less than 10 per cent.

If α_1 and α_2 are estimated, on the basis of empirical material, it may be found that $\alpha_1 + \alpha_2 < 1$. This may be taken as a sign that the production function used is incomplete. That is to say, there are factors of production which are not included in the production function used.

been disregarded. Changes in production techniques are, however, among the most characteristic features of a growing community.

Natural resources have previously been defined as those means of production that are not produced. Farm land, mines, water, and air are cases in point; it being understood that by resources is meant not only the natural factors of production that are actually exploited, but also those that may (theoretically) be exploited.

It is obvious that these factors of production occupy a position, in the production process, which may, to a large extent, be considered to be similar to that of real *Capital*. This is clearly the case when real *Capital* replaces natural resources as when we compare the cost of extracting coal from a British mine deep underground to the cost of open cast mining in the United States, or if we compare saltpetre production in Chile, where saltpetre is obtained from mines, with synthetic saltpetre production in Norway.

There will, however, be obvious difficulties in making analogies between the factor *Nature* on the one hand and the factors *Capital* and *Labour* on the other. There is good reason to inquire how much total production will grow in the event of a 5 per cent increase of *Capital*, it being assumed, for example, that the principle of equalizing cost has been realized so that this increase in output is distributed among the most productive sectors of society. It is also reasonable to enquire, by way of an analogy, into the effects of a 5 per cent increase in the labour force. But what will be the significance of a 5 per cent increase in natural resources generally? In simple cases this question may be answered, for example through an examination of the effects of a 5 per cent increase in the agricultural area. But what would a 5 per cent increase in the oil resources of the *Middle East* imply? It seems that the difficulties of comparing natural resources and *Capital* and *Labour* are caused mainly by the fact that *Nature* supplies a given stock of resources and this stock cannot be changed as such. In the case of *Capital* and *Labour* a stock is available at a given instant, but a change in size and composition is possible.

It appears that the problem of the effect of a change in the amount of factors applied can hardly be posed or answered, in a general way, in relation to natural resources, as it can with real *Capital* and man-power. It would seem, in other words, that we can hardly deal with natural resources as a whole, as we can with real *Capital* and man-power, but only with particular resources. This is because a change in the stock of *Capital* or *Labour* can be visualizad while this is much more difficult, if not impossible, as far as natural resources are concerned.

One of the difficulties encountered in dealing with natural resources, as a variable factor of production, as compared to real *Capital* and man-power, is that the adjustment of factors of production to one another, which makes production possible, is largely effected unilaterally in the sense that the composition of real *Capital* is primarily adapted to the basis given by *Nature* (and with corresponding adaptations in the labour force), whereas resources are not adapted in the same way to *Capital* and *Labour*.

A further difficulty with the "concept of resources" is, that if production is considered as a whole the value of natural resources will depend on the actual economic situation, or more particularly on relative prices. A shift in demand may cause a certain resource to lose value[11]. The same applies to existing items of *Capital* or a given supply of skilled *Labour,* for example, although here transfers to other applications are, perhaps, often easier. Above all, such losses in relation to real *Capital* and *Labour* will, however, be limited in time in so far as the size and composition of *Capital* and *Labour* can be changed in the course of time.

One consequence of these facts will be that in describing the process of production, i.e. the relationship between the various factors of production, special attention will be given to the effects of alternative combinations of real *Capital* and man-power. Even so it seems clear that the more abundant the resources—*ceteris paribus*—the larger the output. The more farm land, the larger the yield; the larger the iron content in iron ore, the larger the output of raw iron per ton of iron ore, etc.

10. In view of the rapidly growing consumption of raw materials provided by *Nature,* exhaustion in certain important fields cannot be regarded as unlikely.

It should be pointed out, however, that there are many indications that the rate of exhaustion of natural resources, incidental to growth, will increase more slowly than will the actual rate of production. It thus appears from Table VII. 1 that the big increase in production achieved in the industrialized countries since the Second World War has not resulted in a similar rise in the consumption of raw materials, although there have been considerable increases. The fact that the consumption of raw materials has not

---

[11] A consequence of this will be that fluctuations in demand need not be growth-promoting.

increased at quite the same rate as industrial production is due to raw material savings, and further due to production increases that are to a certain extent attributable to further processing of the products. If production is considered as a whole it may be seen, even more clearly, that the consumption of raw materials increases at a lower rate than does production. The growing share of services in total production should be emphasized here.

TABLE VII.1

The Use of Raw Materials in Industrial Areas.
(Thousand Million Dollars at 1950 Prices)

	1938	1954
Industrial input		
of natural raw materials and fuels	25.4	33.7
of manufactured raw materials	0.8	5.5
Gross value of manufacturing output	101.6	188.1
Ratio of "natural" input to output	0.250	0.179
Ratio of total input to output	0.268	0.208

Note : The "industrial areas" are defined as *North America, Western Europe,* and Japan. Source : GATT (1958, p. 43).

Although it may quite incontestably be demonstrated that raw material consumption grows at a lower rate than production, and although, perhaps, as shown in Chapter V, we need not expect, within the next twenty years or so, a serious shortage of the principal raw materials, we cannot conclude that the problems referred to here may be dismissed lightly. The crux of the matter is not that raw material consumption is decreasing in relation to production, but that, in relation to known resources, it is rapidly increasing —which will undoubtedly give rise to problems, indeed to serious problems, in the long run. It may be added that the problem considered here is not merely whether there will be tin, copper, and oil in sufficient quantities in future. The problem is of a much wider scope and includes e.g. the question whether there will be adequate space for mankind. Thus the problems of nuisance from noise in modern urban communities, as well as traffic and parking problems, may be regarded as part of the present problem.

11. Among the four factors of production which were mentioned in Chapter II and described in more detail in Chapters III–VI, *Culture* has

not yet been dealt with in the present context. This factor, as has already been mentioned, should be considered in a very broad sense, namely, as the way in which people live. In many respects this factor is similar to natural resources in the production process, as will be apparent if it is considered as a quality of the factor *Labour*. For then it appears as a factor of production which adjusts itself passively so to speak, to variations in the input of labour in given situations.

This does not, of course, exclude considerations concerning the importance of *Culture* to production. An obvious example is the significance of the level of education of the labour force. A larger output due to a higher level of education must, generally, be expected but it must also be emphasized that the use of real *Capital* as a factor of production often presupposes a suitable adjustment in the education of the labour force.

Another aspect of the cultural pattern should be dealt with here, viz. the general attitude towards life. Whether the general attitude of the people of capitalist countries that are in the middle of a process of growth is taken to be a cause of the growth or a result of it, the significance of the attitude is indisputable and is, indeed, given special attention by such writers as *Karl Marx, Max Weber,* and *Joseph Schumpeter.*

Though it is scarcely possible, within the framework of the present book, to provide a just and fairly comprehensive survey of this problem its implications will nevertheless have to be elucidated. This is done, by way of illustration, on the basis of the three writers just referred to.

Karl Marx argues, in a great many different ways, that the prevailing cultural pattern is an integral part of the existing economic-political system. To Karl Marx the essential thing is that production takes place under capitalist conditions, i.e. by the use of real *Capital* owned by the capitalists, but carried out by the wage earners. Quite apart from the fact that to Marx the main problem was to discern trends and to determine the fate that awaits the capitalist system, it should be noted that he attaches great importance to the capitalists having set themselves one sole aim : accumulation, i.e. the increase of real *Capital*. Although Marx, as is well-known, does not conclude that the capitalist system will be characterized, in the long run, by a sustained accumulation of real *Capital*—and by the consequent continuous growth envisaged by modern theory of growth—the interesting thing is that the general attitude to life of the capitalists becomes an all-important condition for continued accumulation, no matter whether this attitude is assumed, as by Marx, to lead through a series of crises to a final collapse, or is expected to bring continued growth (possibly with interruptions in the form of crises).

Max Weber bases himself, in his analysis of the turning-point in the development of capitalism, on that very attitude of the owners of capital referred to above. Weber's thesis is briefly, and roughly, this: the triumph of Protestantism, and especially of Calvinism, signifies, on the one hand, a religious commandment for material activity and production, and a prohibition—or at least a religious warning—against the enjoyment of the goods produced on the other. This duality must imply, to use the modern terminology, a marked propensity for thrift and investment which promotes capitalist development. The cultural pattern thus becomes growth-promoting. It is a fact of little importance in this context that in Weber's description of cause and effect a distinct contrast appeared to Marxist analysis. Nor does it really matter very much whether or not the theory is "tenable"—a number of writers have argued strongly against it. What concerns us here is the fact that Weber's theory is a good illustration of the importance to the growth and development of production of the cultural pattern.

A further example may be mentioned, viz. *Schumpeter*'s combined growth and trade cycle model[12], which will be dealt with in more detail below in connection with the treatment of the effects of changes in production techniques.

12. In the text above such differences in production as may be attributed to different inputs of factors of production such as *Labour,* real *Capital,* and *natural resources* have been considered. Further, the general attitude towards life has been dealt with in order to show the significance of the factor *Culture*—which, however, deserves a more detailed study.

If we consider the development of production in a given industrialized area with a certain amount of natural resources, the significant fact emerges that a very considerable part of the production increases that are observed can neither be explained on the score of increase in the labour force, nor by reference to the larger amounts of real *Capital* that are employed. A third, and separate phenomenon makes itself very strongly felt, viz. repeated improvements of production techniques, including improvements in the quality

---

[12] See Schumpeter (1934) (a translation of his *Theorie der wirtschaftlichen Entwicklung,* from 1912).

of the real *Capital* applied[13]. This is a very characteristic aspect of the cultural pattern of the industrialized areas.

It should be noted that the changes in production techniques referred to here include not only the actual utilization of previous technical inventions in the narrow sense, but any new combination of the factors of production. The essential thing is that a change in the ratio of input to output is achieved[14].

The importance of this particular part of *Culture*, viz. innovations, is obvious. It represents improved efficiency in the process of production and will consequently counteract the tendencies, referred to above, whereby isolated (or at least relative) increases in the input of one factor of production result in gradually diminishing increases in production. If innovations occur, the result may at the same time be not only a lessening of the tendencies towards a gradually diminishing return, but the result may perhaps even be an increase in production beyond the increased input of factors. Indeed, if these innovations have a sufficiently powerful effect it will be possible, in the course of time, to detect a continuous acceleration in the rate of growth in production.

Little discussion will be required to prove that innovations in industrialized areas have, in fact, had the described effect. It will probably be sufficient here to refer to the fact that the real output per man has shown sustained, if varying, increases in *Western Europe* and *North America*. It seems

[13] Merely by way of illustration it might be mentioned that in a study relating to Norway (Aukrust and Bjerke, 1958) it is stated that out of an annual average increase, from 1900 to 1956, in the net domestic product of 3.39 per cent, 0.46 per cent is accounted for by increased employment, 1.12 per cent by increased *Capital*, and 1.81 by improved "techniques" including the increases in output due to improvements of the cultural level in general.

Using slightly different methods, Solow (1957) has calculated that out of an increase in private non-farm gross national income per man-hour in the United States from $0.623 to $1.275 (1939-dollars) in the period 1909 to 1949, $0.570, or as much as 80–90 per cent, may be attributed to increased productivity. The same, very large share is stated by Fabricant (1959).

It goes without saying that not only the underlying theory, but also the empirical material (especially with regard to *Capital*) is too slender to permit a rigid application of the figures. There may be reason to draw attention to the fact, actually quite evident, that the assumed nature of the relationship between production and factors of production, which constitutes the starting point, that is the initial hypothesis, will influence the figures arrived at.

[14] In the words of Schumpeter this means that what matters is *innovations* versus *inventions*, cf. Schumpeter (1934, Chapter II, and 1939, Chapter III).

more than doubtful, however, when we keep the foregoing considerations in mind, if we shall be able to explain these movements merely by referring to the increase in real *Capital* per man.

13. With regard to innovations two questions arise. Firstly, whether there is reason to expect that they will be carried out in a more or less continuous succession as time passes and secondly why they appear to be closely associated with the industrialized communities.

If innovations are introduced at a fairly constant rate there will be systematic, continued shifts in the ratio of input to output[15]. This, however, need not be the case. Although inventions might be made at a uniform rate, innovations may proceed at a non-uniform rate. This is precisely where we see one of the connections with the trade cycles disregarded by the theory of growth. Trade cycles are a coherent part of the process of growth because, *inter alia,* innovations increase during a boom. Some writers go so far as to say that trade cycles are little but the ebb and flow of the process of innovation. The series of changes observed during the trade cycle may consequently be regarded as the repercussions of these cycles of innovations[16].

On this point however, opinions are divided. Another, or at least a supplementary hypothesis, is current, according to which innovations are effected more regularly in modern industrialized communities in *Western Europe, Oceania* and *North America,* and more or less independently of short trade cycles. There should thus be a considerable difference between growth processes in the nineteenth century and those of more recent date. At any rate the opinion seems to be becoming more and more common that radical changes have taken place in the industrialized, capitalist communi-

---

[15] In the Cobb-Douglas Function previously used

$$P = \beta \, L^{\alpha_1} \, C^{\alpha_2} \, (1 + \gamma)^t$$

the factor $(1 + \gamma)^t$ has been added in order to include this fact. Strictly speaking it might be argued, starting from the relationship between P, L, and C without innovations, that is

$$P = \beta \, L^{\alpha_1} \, C^{\alpha_2},$$

that innovations will have the effect of α_1 and α_2 gradually changing as the innovations take place. It might thus be assumed that α_1 and α_2 were functions of time. It has here been attempted, by means of the factor $(1 + \gamma)^t$, to take account of these variations. It may then be hoped that α_1 and α_2 can be considered as true parameters during relatively shorter periods.

[16] Apparently it would suffice to consider the average movement. It will be seen, however, that according to the viewpoint expressed business cycles and the process of growth will be inseparable.

ties during the present century and that decisive structural changes in the economies may be said to have occurred[17]. Whether these changes signify a weakening of the process of innovation can scarcely be decided as yet.

A further question has been posed, viz. why is the process of innovation so intimately associated with the industrialized communities? This question may be considered to be—in the present context—a minor one relating to cause and effect. In any event, and to all appearances, it is a matter of an intimate and complex interaction between the way of life and the attitude to life. A certain attitude to life is inherent in and sustains the industrialized communities[18].

What is referred to is, above all, the "creed of industrialized society", understood here as the rational endeavour to make *Nature* a servant and achieve the "maximization of income" and the "minimization of effort and cost involved". Three points, however, should here be emphasized.

Firstly, this attitude has developed in the industrialized countries since the Middle Ages—and especially since the Industrial Revolution. It will probably be difficult, and indeed of little interest, to decide what is cause and what is effect. It should further be noted that this creed is just as dominant in the socialist countries of *Eastern Europe* and the *USSR* as in *Western Europe* and *North America*. The leaders at least in the communist world, as well as in the underdeveloped countries, are under the influence of this creed.

Secondly, the importance to production and to the organization of economic life of such an attitude should be stressed. So long as inherited ideas, rituals, and religiously motivated actions dominate men's lives, a growth that will lead to larger per capita production will scarcely be feasible. If, by contrast, the experimental attitude comes to prevail, that is an attitude marked by doubt and a critical attitude and an empirical re-examination of previous actions, then an increase in per capita production will be possible[19].

Thirdly, attention should be drawn to the fact that the intimate inter-rela-

---

[17] Not only Schumpeter, but also various books by Galbraith may be quoted to illustrate this.

[18] There is probably good reason to refer here to the sociological problems which were formulated in Germany (F. Tönnies) and in France (E. Durkheim and Levy Bruhl) at the beginning of this century on the basis of the contrast between "Gemeinschaft" and "Gesellschaft". The following paragraphs show much of the influence of Schumpeter (1950). (See especially Chapter XI, "The Civilization of Capitalism").

[19] The following quotation from Schumpeter (1950, p. 123) may clarify these some-

(*Footnote continued on page 245*)

tion between *Culture* and production becomes more than obvious when reference is made to the importance of the "creed".

14. It will be seen that by enlarging the theory of growth to take due account of innovations, a theory of self-sustained growth can be achieved. Thus growth and the increase in wealth incident to it will make possible further innovations, one reason being that an ever stronger effort can be made to intensify education and research. This means that by reference to the production function used above, we may achieve and maintain a high value for the paramter γ, the level of which will, in fact, be determined by the amount of innovation. This is thus a third example of the self-sustained elements in the process of growth.

The essential part of the process is, as mentioned, the improved ratio of output to input. Here it should be noted that precisely the same result is achieved when the distribution of the factors of production is changed—without necessarily changing production techniques—in such a way that employment in more productive sectors increases. Seen from the point of view of society as a whole these changes may also be regarded as innovations through which new production patterns are created, with the corresponding new consumption patterns. The fact is that no community is in perfect equilibrium in the sense that the marginal productivity for the separate factors is everywhere the same. In every community, however, there is probably such a tendency, more or less pronounced, in the direction of equlibrium. Precisely because of the innovations referred to, however, and also on account of fluctuations in demand, disturbances will always occur. The consequence of this will be that by relative movements of the factors of production advantages will be obtained through migrations of real capital and labour between the sectors.

(Footnote continued from page 244)

what sweeping statements: "Suppose that some "primitive" man uses that most elementary of all machines, already appreciated by our gorilla cousins, a stick, and that this stick breaks in his hand. If he tries to remedy the damage by reciting a magic formula—he might for instance murmur Supply and Demand or Planning and Control in the expectation that if he repeats this exactly nine times the two fragments will unite again—then he is within the precincts of pre-rational thought. If he gropes for the best way to join the fragments or to procure another stick, he is rational . . .".

It follows from what has been said that if the underdeveloped countries succeed in achieving growth, which roughly means industrialization in the very widest sense, the cultural pattern will change. Western civilization will dominate not only in a technical sense but in the widest sense of the word "civilization".

A well-known example of this is the shift, described in previous chapters, from primary industries (such as agriculture) to secondary (such as manufacturing industry) and to tertiary (such as services). These migrations, so typical of a developing community, may be regarded as an indication that the marginal productivity varies according to the various applications. From this it follows that total production will grow with these shifts.

It should further be noted that these shifts in production are accompanied by and correspond to shifts in demand—with a more rapidly accelerating increase in demand as regards, for example, industrial products as compared to agricultural products.

It may be difficult to give a quantitative evaluation of the importance of this fact[20]. It is indisputable, however, that the growth process is closely connected with these changes in the distribution of factors according to industries and the related appearance of new products. More generally it may be argued that total production is driven upwards through new goods being introduced into the market in a continuous chain, the newcomers preventing the rate of growth from slackening[21].

It should, however, be noted that the connection between the growth processes described earlier and the one mentioned here—viz. the migration in the direction of the more productive sectors which are also characterized by a more rapid improvement of the input-output ratio—is very intimate. Anyhow, it can hardly be a matter of a simple chain of cause and effect.

It follows that the question of growth cannot be reduced simply to one of enforcing a development in manufacturing industry and other urban activities. Though this must be assumed to be the long term result of growth, experience shows—in accordance with a priori considerations—that a necessary prerequisite of growth is a development in agriculture concurrent with industrialization. For industrialization will result in an increase in the flow of income and a subsequent increase in demand. In pre-industrialized areas, this increase in demand will perhaps principally be in the direction of food. If the increase in demand is not met by an increase in supplies, difficulties are bound to arise. Such difficulties may be, for example, shifts in relative prices which are unfavourable to growth. On account,

[20] A very accurate description of these relations was given by the 17th century writer William Petty, "The Petty Effect" has, therefore, been suggested as an appropriate term. In Colin Clark's book (1957) a more detailed account of the phenomenon may be found.
[21] See Stigler (1947).

however, of the hidden unemployment which is generally thought to exist in agriculture it is often possible to provide urban trades with labour but, at the same time, effect increases in production in agriculture. In order that the process of growth may continue smoothly it is thus necessary that there should be a balanced growth in the various trades.

15. The interaction of the various trades during the process of growth was mentioned above from which it should be noted that it follows that growth has a tendency to spread and to stimulate further growth in industry as a whole.

Exactly the same arguments, however, may be adduced with regard to the various areas of a country in which the process of growth has started. The continuous increase in economic activity and consequently in demand, which are characteristic features of growth, will tend to spread to other areas. This tendency on the national level has, of course, its counterpart on the international level, as will be shown below.

Contrary, however, to this "Spread Effect"— to use the phrase of *Gunnar Myrdal*[22]—there is a "Backwash Effect". The developing areas attract "active" money capital and skilled labour, including "entrepreneurship" from other areas which are, and will continue to be, stagnating.

The question, then, is whether the "Spread Effect" will overcome the "Backwash Effect". Here, Myrdal argues strongly that the "Backwash Effects" will be strong in relation to the "Spread Effects" particularly in the backward countries. This is, *inter alia,* due to the absence more or less of a national policy in the backward countries. The development thus tends to be concentrated in a few areas and does not spread to other areas. It should be emphasized that if the present argument holds true it implies a special self-sustained factor which in itself will tend to accelerate growth in wealthy countries rather than promote growth in the underdeveloped areas.

16. These considerations, which refer to areas within a given country, can easily be applied to the interaction of growth in different countries, and if they have any truth in them the result will be that within the group of relatively highly developed areas[23] there will be a tendency for the growth of one area to promote growth in other areas as well. This applies, at any rate, in so far as there will be opportunities for a more or less free trade to develop

[22] Myrdal (1957).
[23] The regions of *North America, Western Europe, Oceania,* the *USSR* and *Eastern Europe.*

and to make itself felt. On the other hand the "Backwash Effects" from the developed areas will tend to affect the underdeveloped areas adversely so that the advantages they gain from trade with the developed areas will be comparatively slight.

This, however, leads to the question as to whether the processes dealt with above will be affected at all by trade with other countries taking place. It is a generally acknowledged fact and one that requires no further comment, that the very existence of foreign trade implies that the real income of the countries engaged in trade is higher than it would have been had there been no trade. This, however, is of little interest in the present context, inasmuch as the question dealt with here is how a possible increase in real income is affected by the fact that foreign trade is taking place. This question can hardly be treated satisfactorily within the framework of the present study. It will be seen, nevertheless, in the first place that the very fact that the level of real income is higher as a result of trade will, for the reasons given above, promote growth. Secondly, it appears that practically all the factors that propagate growth in a country will also affect the relations between the countries. In other words, here too there is a "Spread Effect". Among such effects may be mentioned: the contact between the various countries makes it possible for inventions made in one country to be used in other countries as well. In other words, a spread of *Culture* takes place which promotes growth. Further, growth in one area will tend to start growth in areas which produce goods to which demand is directed during the growth. Finally, international trade also renders possible capital transfers between the various areas, by means of which more rapid growth may be achieved in the world as a whole, as real *Capital* may then, theoretically, come into use precisely where the greatest benefits may be derived from it.

On the other hand it should also be recalled that the "Backwash Effect" which has been given such prominence by Myrdal, works, as was mentioned above, in the opposite direction. It is, *inter alia,* due to this effect that the underdeveloped areas have remained, in spite of the growth in the industrial areas of the world, at such a very low technical and economic level.

17. Considering how complicated the relations involved in a process of growth must necessarily be, there is good reason to call into question some of the major contentions of the present study which are based upon a specific function of production, viz. the *Cobb-Douglas* Function (including

a trend factor which enables us to describe a development marked by innovation). In the following text also a number of arguments will be based on this function.

It should, however, be noted first of all that the *Cobb-Douglas* Function at any rate on essential points provides a description which is in agreement with what is actually observed. Secondly, it should be noted that here the Function is only applied for the purpose of obtaining rough, though essential guidance about future development [24].

B. *Comparative Models of Growth*

1. The main purpose of this book is to compare the possibilities of economic growth in the various regions of the world. The aim of the foregoing chapters has, therefore, been to collect material which can be used in making such comparisons.

The starting point must necessarily be an evaluation of the situation at the beginning of the period and the development which has led up to that situation. This was the subject of Chapter I. The rates of growth given there might now be applied to the years 1955 to 1980 with such modifications as a general survey of the possibilities of the regions might suggest. To go no further than this, however, would be unsatisfactory. An attempt has, therefore, been made to collect information and make estimates regarding the factors that may be assumed to determine the development of production within the period. These factors have been grouped in four categories, as has been described in detail in Chapter II. In Chapters III–VI each of these categories has been dealt with separately. Finally, the first part of this Chapter has attempted to describe the nature of the functional relationships which may be assumed to exist between the various factors, the interaction of which constitutes the process of growth.

All considerations regarding the future must be based on knowledge or assumptions about previous development, about the factors contributing to the process of growth, and about the nature of the relationships which prevail among these factors during the process.

[24] Compare also the use made of the Cobb-Douglas Function in "Growth Models for Illustrating the Effects of Alternative Employment and Investment Policies" in UN (1958, g).

TABLE VII.2

Economic Growth 1955-80.

	Population			Total Net Domestic Product				
	1955 (Million)	1980 (Million)	Annual Rate of Growth 1955-80 (Per cent)	1955 (Billion)	1980 Min. (Billion)	1980 Max. (Billion)	Annual Rate of Crowth, 1955-80 Min. (Per cent)	Annual Rate of Crowth, 1955-80 Max. (Per cent)
North America	182	280	1.7	342	716	1,028	3.00	4.50
Western Europe	297	343	0.6	244	376	543	1.75	3.25
Oceania	13	20	1.7	12	28	36	3.50	4.50
USSR	197	286	1.5	109	291	416	4.00	5.50
Eastern Europe	112	143	1.0	51	95	136	2.50	4.00
Latin America	183	365	2.8	48	120	153	3.75	4.75
Middle East	95	169	2.3	15	33	42	3.25	4.25
Asia	1,418	2,326	2.0	107	165	211	1.75	2.75
Africa	193	289	1.6	20	37	47	2.50	3.50
Total	2,690	4,221	1.8	948	1,861	2,612	2.73	4.14

	Per Capita Net Domestic Product				
	1955 (Dollars)	1980 Min. (Dollars)	1980 Max. (Dollars)	Annual Rate of Growth, 1955-80 Min. (Per cent)	Annual Rate of Growth, 1955-80 Max. (Per cent)
North America	1,875	2,550	3,670	1.2	2.7
Western Europe	820	1,100	1,580	1.2	2.7
Oceania	955	1,400	1,800	1.5	2.6
USSR	550	1,020	1,450	2.5	3.9
Eastern Europe	455	665	950	1.5	3.0
Latin America	265	330	420	0.9	1.9
Middle East	160	195	250	0.8	1.8
Asia	75	70	90	—0.3	0.7
Africa	105	130	165	0.9	1.8
Total	350	440	620	0.9	2.3

Note: The figures in the Table relating to the year 1955 have been taken from Chapter I (Table I. 1, cf. p. 27). The figures for population in 1980 have been taken from Chapter III (Table III.10). The remaining figures have been obtained by giving, for each region, a hypothetical maximum and minimum annual rate of growth for total net domestic product (columns 7-8 in the Table), and by calculating, total as well as per capita, production in 1980 on this basis.

Although an attempt has been made to collect empirical material in all these three fields, each forecast will, nevertheless, be a shot in the dark, at least to a certain extent, as the information that may be acquired in the three fields is subject to varying degrees of uncertainty. It is not possible, therefore, to say how large will be the economic growth of each of the nine regions in the period 1955–80. Nor is it possible to fix maximum and minimum limits within which the growth will be confined. Nevertheless it will probably be useful to start by making certain assumptions about maximum and minimum rates of growth for each region, as in Table VII. 2, and, subsequently, to use these figures as a starting point in an analysis as this may otherwise become too vague.

It appears from what has been said, that these rates of growth cannot be considered as real prognoses. They have been established in accordance with the empirical material and observations contained in the earlier parts of this book as well as those presented in the Appendix. The position is perhaps best described if we say that, on the basis of an over-all estimate, supported by this material, there is more likelihood that the rates of growth will be within these limits rather than outside them. Current knowledge of these matters, however, is very imperfect and it is conceivable that the development might lead to rates of growth, in some regions, which are either below the minimum or above the maximum given in the Table. On account of this the rates have been given in round figures (divisible by 0. 25).

It should be frankly stated that these projections, from a scientific point of view, have a rather poor basis. This is indicated by the fact that the explicit arguments underlying the projections are somewhat scanty. The present state of our knowledge, however, seems to exclude a more satisfactory, explicit reasoning.

2. A more coherent impression of the process of economic growth is obtained when the figures in Table VII. 2 are compared with some of the most important figures given in Chapters III and IV (regarding the direct factors of growth) and certain other figures estimated on the basis of our knowledge of some significant relationships in the growth process. This has been done in Table VII. 3, where figures, some based on facts and others on estimates that have been used in the approach of this book to the problems under consideration, have been arranged in such a way as to illustrate the possible relationships that may exist between them. Thus a numerical

counterpart is obtained to the theoretical considerations regarding models
of growth contained in the first part of this chapter. The Table may therefore serve to illustrate these theoretical considerations. At the same time it
provides an opportunity of throwing some light on the relationship between
the rates of growth shown in Table VII. 2 and the projections, shown in
previous chapters, regarding *Labour* and *Capital*. The figures α_1 and α_2
(columns 14 and 15) should indicate the effects of certain changes in
Labour and *Capital* as mentioned below.

Any comparison of this kind must be based, of course, on some assumptions and these can only be hypothetical, especially at the present stage of
the theory of growth. The model in Table VII. 3 has been constructed on
the assumption that the connection between the factors and the net domestic
product during the process of growth may be described by a *Cobb-Douglas*
function of the type mentioned in Chapters II and VII A [25]. This does not,
of course, imply that the connection is considered to be of precisely the
nature suggested by this function. Other formulas might be applied. It is
clear, furthermore, that no short formula can give an exhaustive description
of the immensely complicated workings of the process of growth. A function
of this type, however, has the advantage that it combines the factors in a
way which is analogous, in some important respects, to the way in which
these seem to be associated in the process of growth.

The figures for *L*, *C*, and *P* correspond to those given in Tables III. 10,
IV. 9, and VII. 2 respectively. For *L*, however, only one value has been
applied for each region in 1980 (see column 2), whereas in Table III. 10
a minimum and a maximum was shown. It is hard to say whether, during
the period under review, working hours will be shortened most at maximum
or at minimum economic growth. Rapid growth will result in increased
wealth and will make shorter working hours possible. Conversely, a considerable reduction of working hours will tend to retard the increase in production. In Table VII. 3 the averages of the maximum and minimum
figures for the number of man-hours in 1980 have therefore been used and
these averages have been applied both at maximum and minimum growth.
For *Western Europe*, however, a slightly larger figure than the average has
been included. Otherwise a larger annual decline in the number of man-
hours than it seems reasonable to assume would result.

---

[25] See pages 36, 226, 235 f and 243.

For *Labour* (*L*) and *Capital* (*C*) annual rates of growth are shown in columns 3, 7, and 8 corresponding to those for *P* (the net domestic product) which are shown, on the basis of Table VII. 2, in columns 12 and 13 in Table VII. 3.

With regard to the parameters, an attempt has been made to produce some sort of an estimate for α_1 and α_2 for the nine regions. Often such attempts have been concerned with separate sectors of the economy, but in some cases also with the economy of a country as a whole. The available material, however, is far too scanty and too much disputed to give any safe principles as to what values may be assigned α_1 and α_2 in certain conditions [26]. Even so, the results of enquiries made, and certain theoretical considerations, would seem to justify two general arguments which are partly based on available studies and partly on our general knowledge of the nature of production. They are as follows:

a. Normally *the sum* of α_1 and α_2 will be *approximately* equal to 1. If $\alpha_1 + \alpha_2 = 1$, a one per cent increase in both *Labour* and *Capital* will result in a one per cent increase in production, and this often seems fairly reasonable. If the natural factors, however, are already fairly extensively exploited it seems likely that a further supply of *Labour* and *Capital* will not lead to a proportional result. This is the reason why $\alpha_1 + \alpha_2$ has been put at less than unity in the three densely populated regions: *Western Europe, Eastern Europe,* and *Asia* as opposed to unity in the other regions. In *Asia,* where the shortage of natural factors will probably prove to be a particularly intractable problem, $\alpha_1 + \alpha_2$ has been put as low as 0.85 [27].

b. The available data as well as *a priori* considerations seem to indicate that *α_1 is highest in the developed regions,* whereas α_2 is highest in the underdeveloped regions. When *Capital* per worker is high a little additional *Capital* has no very significant influence on output. An increase in *Labour,* and especially in skilled labour, however, is a very important change. The reverse is the case in the underdeveloped regions with their redundant *Labour* and lack of *Capital.* On the whole a diminishing series of figures has therefore been inserted in column 14 of Table VII. 3, while an increasing one has been inserted in column 15.

The values for α_1 and α_2 given in the Table may thus be regarded as hypothetical quantities, determined in accordance with these two arguments.

[26] Cf. the first part (A) of the present Chapter, especially the footnotes, p. 235 and 243.
[27] See Chapter V B, page 168–70.

TABLE VII.3

Analysis of Growth.

	L			C					P				
	1955 (Billion Hours)	1980 (Billion Hours)	Annual Rate of Growth (Per cent)	1955 (Billion Dollars)	1980 Min. (Billion Dollars)	1980 Max. (Billion Dollars)	Annual Rate of Growth Min. (Per cent)	Annual Rate of Growth Max. (Per cent)	1955 (Billion Dollars)	1980 Min. (Billion Dollars)	1980 Max. (Billion Dollars)	Annual Rate of Growth Min. (Per cent)	Annual Rate of Growth Max. (Per cent)
	1	2	3	4	5	6	7	8	9	10	11	12	13
N. A.	143.2	169.4	0.67	1,015	2,260	3,148	3.25	4.63	342	716	1,028	3.00	4.50
W. E. ..	304.6	280.0	—0.33	850	1,528	2,046	2.38	3.57	244	376	543	1.75	3.25
Oceania	11.3	13.0	0.56	40	95	125	3.52	4.66	12	28	36	3.50	4.50
USSR .	232.2	247.6	0.25	325	1,008	1,442	4.63	6.14	109	291	416	4.00	5.50
E. E. ...	136.9	155.1	0.49	175	369	494	3.03	4.24	51	95	136	2.50	4.00
L. A. ...	165.8	298.5	2.38	140	332	450	3.51	4.78	48	120	153	3.75	4.75
M. E. ..	99.7	160.5	1.92	35	85	111	3.61	4.72	15	33	42	3.25	4.25
Asia	1,478.1	2,238.5	1.67	270	469	686	2.23	3.80	107	165	211	1.75	2.75
Africa .	228.1	318.1	1.34	50	104	143	2.98	4.29	20	37	47	2.50	3.50
Total ..	2,799.9	3,880.7	1.31	2,900	6,250	8,645	3.12	4.46	948	1,861	2,612	2.73	4.14

TABLE VII.3 (continued)

		Partial Rates of Growth (Per cent)						Net Domestic Product per Man-hour				
		Min.			Max.			1955 (Dollars)	1980		Annual Rate of Growth	
α_1	α_2	r_L	r_C	γ	r_L	r_C	γ		Min. (Dollars)	Max. (Dollars)	Min. (Per cent)	Max. (Per cent)
14	15	16	17	18	19	20	21	22	23	24	25	26
N. America	0.80	0.20	0.54	0.65	1.81	0.54	0.93	3.03	2.39	4.23	6.07	2.31	3.80
W. Europe	0.75	0.20	—0.25	0.48	1.52	—0.25	0.71	2.79	0.80	1.34	1.94	2.09	3.60
Oceania	0.75	0.25	0.42	0.88	2.20	0.42	1.16	2.92	1.06	2.15	2.77	2.88	3.91
USSR	0.70	0.30	0.18	1.39	2.43	0.18	1.84	3.48	0.47	1.18	1.68	3.74	5.24
E. Europe	0.65	0.30	0.32	0.91	1.27	0.32	1.27	2.41	0.37	0.61	0.88	1.93	3.48
L. America	0.60	0.40	1.43	1.40	0.92	1.43	1.91	1.41	0.29	0.40	0.51	1.31	2.31
Middle East ...	0.50	0.50	0.96	1.80	0.49	0.96	2.36	0.93	0.15	0.21	0.26	1.26	2.26
Asia	0.35	0.50	0.58	1.12	0.05	0.58	1.90	0.27	0.07	0.07	0.09	0.11	1.07
Africa	0.50	0.50	0.67	1.49	0.34	0.67	2.14	0.69	0.09	0.12	0.15	1.11	2.10
Total	...	...	...	...	...	...	...	...	0.34	0.48	0.67	1.39	2.77

Note : The symbols are explained in the text, p. 36, 253 and 256.
Source : Tables III. 10, IV. 9, and VII. 2 cf. pp. 252–53.

With a view to a further analysis of the rates of growth shown for the net domestic product these rates have been subdivided into three parts (in columns 16–21 of Table VII. 3), of which r_L is meant to represent the growth which, through the application of the version of the *Cobb-Douglas* function here used, will be, as it were, attributed to the increase in L, whilst r_C represents the part which is attributed to the increase in C, and γ the part which is attributed to other changes [28].

If we assume that the relationship between factors and output can be described by this function it follows, if the year 1955 is chosen as the base point, that:

$$P_{1980} = \beta \, L_{1980}{}^{\alpha_1} \, C_{1980}{}^{\alpha_2} \, (1 + \gamma)^{25}, \tag{1}$$

P_{1980} being the net domestic product in 1980, and L_{1980} and C_{1980} the corresponding figures for *Labour* and *Capital*.

It also follows that

$$P_{1955} = \beta \, L_{1955}{}^{\alpha_1} \, C_{1955}{}^{\alpha_2} \, (1 + \gamma)^0. \tag{2}$$

Thus dividing (1) by (2), we get

$$\frac{P_{1980}}{P_{1955}} = \left(\frac{L_{1980}}{L_{1955}}\right)^{\alpha_1} \left(\frac{C_{1980}}{C_{1955}}\right)^{\alpha_2} (1 + \gamma)^{25}. \tag{3}$$

All the values of P, L, C, α_1 and α_2 in this formula may be read directly in Table VII. 3 for each region separately. The corresponding values of γ may then be found by solving the equation.

Now, if L in a certain region is increased by 1 per cent, P will rise by α_1 per cent. Similarly P will rise by α_2 per cent if C is increased by 1 per cent. The partial rates of growth r_L and r_C (columns 16, 17, 19, and 20) have therefore been calculated by multiplying the rates of growth for L by α_1 and the rates of growth for C by α_2. It appears that r_L has the same values at minimum as at maximum growth because, as mentioned, the same numbers of man-hours have been assumed.

The calculations may be checked by means of the formula

$$r_L + r_C + \gamma = r,$$

r being the total rate of growth for P.

---

[28] See the prefatory remarks in Chapter II and the more detailed description in Chapter VII A., pp. 226 ff.

In evaluating these figures it should be borne in mind that r_L and r_C are based on assumed values (though confirmed by certain investigations) of α_1 and α_2, which thus have an indirect influence also on the values arrived at for γ. The probability of the assumed values may, perhaps, to a certain extent be judged by the apparent likelihood of the other values arrived at.

The figures for r_L are of course large in the regions that have a large increase of population. *Latin America* is thus highest, whereas *Western Europe* with its negative increase in L is lowest. *Asia* also is relatively low in spite of a large estimated population increase because α_1 has been given a low value. In this region there is, as is well- known, considerable under-employment in agriculture and the production increase resulting from larger supplies of labour is therefore often slight.

The quantity r_C must of course be highest in the underdeveloped regions because α_2 has been given a high value there[29]. In the *USSR*, however, it is high too because there a particularly large increase in invested *Capital* is expected.

With regard, finally, to γ it has already been emphasized above (on p. 242), that in certain cases it is of very considerable size, as is suggested by a number of investigations. Even though such calculations are based on many assumptions this should, nevertheless, indicate that occasionally a very substantial part of total growth cannot be directly attributed to increases in the amounts of *Labour* and *Capital* but must be explained as deriving from natural and cultural factors that have promoted growth in the period in question.

The figures in Table VII. 3 seem, on the whole, to support this point of view. As far as the developed regions are concerned more than half of the total increase is due to the influence of γ. The same was the case, to a certain extent, in the enquiries concerning past developments which were mentioned in the first part (A) of this chapter. In fact the rates of growth shown here, and especially the maximum rates, presuppose a rapid technical and scientific development which will improve the general conditions in which the direct factors operate—and thus increase γ.

The very low figures for *Asia* must presumably be interpreted as indicating that the natural basis is not, as a whole, rich in relation to the requirements of the period under review and that in large parts of the region it will

---

[29] Cf. the argument on p. 253 above.

take some time before modern techiques and other factors promoting growth can spread sufficiently to offset the limited natural resources.

For the other three underdeveloped regions, γ is rather larger than for *Asia*. This is due especially to *Nature* which may be expected to gain in importance in these areas because they possess resources which may be exploited to an increasing extent to provide exports of raw materials, including oil and (mainly for *Latin America*) food, to *North America* and *Western Europe* and also for food to *Asia* as well. These exports will probably be quite considerable, especially at maximum growth (just as maximum growth may perhaps also make the prices of primary products most favourable). It, therefore, seems quite natural that there should be such a large difference between the minimum and maximum values of γ for *Latin America,* the *Middle East,* and *Africa.*

Nevertheless γ is a good deal lower for all the underdeveloped regions than for the developed. This seems to accord with the fact that the cultural factors of large parts of the underdeveloped regions will probably, as shown in Chapter VI [30], continue to have a retarding influence on economic growth for a long time to come. Much has still to be done in the spheres of enlightenment and education before these areas, with their isolated village communities, will be able to partake effectively in economic growth of the type experienced by the industrial countries.

In the previous paragraphs an attempt has been made to relate the rates of growth shown in Table VII. 2 to projections regarding the factors of growth and to certain, practical and theoretical observations. There may be differences of opinion as to how much help this will be in gauging the intrinsic probability of the estimates. It is certain, however, that it would require far more extensive material and a far greater knowledge of the nature of growth processes to prepare real prognoses. The figures may therefore, as emphasized in the first part of this Chapter (A) (page 230), only be regarded as projections which may serve as the basis of certain comparisons between various regions and groups of regions.

3. Such comparisons, however, may also be made without definite estimates of the actual rates of growth. In comparative studies of this kind it is rather the *relationships* between the rates that concern us. In the following section some reflections are made on this point. First, however, it will be

---

[30] See *inter alia* pp. 213–14 and 221.

necessary to deal with a problem which is of considerable practical consequence in this context.

Even if it is assumed that the rates of growth will remain within the maximum and minimum limits indicated, it is clear that there is ample scope for variations. Some of the rates might approximate to the minimum, others to the maximum, or they might all be close to the maximum or minimum, and so on. It is obvious, however, that all these combinations are not equally likely to occur. To a certain extent there is a correlation between the rates of growth of the various regions.

Certain theoretical reflections on the nature of this correlation have been made in Chapter VII A, 16 (p. 247–48). Here the task is to make more direct estimates of the possibilities of such connections existing between the regions through which the rate of growth in one region may be influenced by the development in one or more of the other regions.

The principal type of connection is, of course, *foreign trade*. When a country experiences economic growth it will normally increase its purchases from other countries. Thus production and income in the export industries of these countries will be increased, the foreign exchange position will be consolidated, and a greater economic development, in other industries also, may begin.

It should be emphasized, however, that the centrally planned economies of the *USSR* and *Eastern Europe* have traded very little with the rest of the world. There is therefore little relation between the rates of growth in these two regions on the one hand and those of the remaining regions on the other. The rates of growth in the centrally planned economies themselves, however, are probably fairly intimately connected. Mainland China also is presumably connected particularly in this way with the *USSR*, but only little with the countries outside the Communist Bloc.

The economies of the *USSR* and *Eastern Europe* are subject, to a certain extent, to co-ordinated planning which may possibly cause certain parts of the economy of the *USSR* to grow at the expense of the economies of some parts of *Eastern Europe*—or vice versa. This would thus be a kind of planned backwash effect (see page 247). It may probably be assumed, however, that a large growth in the *USSR* will generally lead to a relatively large growth in *Eastern Europe*. A favourable development in *Eastern Europe* should also promote growth in the *USSR*, though the effect will hardly be quite as pronounced there.

Similarly it must be assumed that the rates of growth in the remaining seven regions are mainly positively correlated as a spread effect makes itself felt through the regions' imports from one another.

Generally speaking, there is probably a general tendency for countries and regions with large domestic products to play a leading role in these relationships, whether the large domestic product is due to large human numbers or to a high income level or to both. The spread effect which penetrates from a region with a large domestic product into a region with a smaller one will normally be stronger than that which works in the opposite direction.

In practice this implies, especially, that a spread effect issues from the two large industrialized regions, *North America* and *Western Europe,* partly into *Oceania* and partly into the four underdeveloped regions.

The situation may be illustrated by means of the available statistics of GATT and the United Nations[31]. A distinction is made there between the industrialized countries (*North America, Western Europe,* and Japan) on the one hand and the non-industrialized or primary exporting countries (the rest of the world except the *USSR, Eastern Europe,* and China) on the other. The former of these groups achieved a net domestic product, around 1955, of approximately $ 600 billion, whereas in the latter group it amounted to only about $ 130 billion. The annual imports of the industrialized countries from the non-industrialized countries were valued at a little more than $ 20 billion. Imports in the opposite direction were roughly the same in value.

Trade between the two groups thus amounted to only a little over 3 per cent of the net domestic product of the industrialized countries, but to about 15 per cent of the net domestic product of the other group.

Now, if an autonomous expansion of 10 per cent were assumed in the industrialized countries, the total of their income would rise by about $ 60 billion. If the marginal import quota in the trade here considered were, for example, 10 per cent, this would result in an increase in exports from the non-industrialized countries of about $ 6 billion, or about 4.6 per cent of their total annual income.

An autonomous 10 per cent expansion in the non-industrialized group, on the other hand, would only increase their income by about $ 13 billion.

---

[31] GATT (1957) and United Nations (1958, d).

If the marginal import quota were, say, 20 per cent in this case, the exports of the industrialized countries would thus increase by $ 2.6 billion, or by about 0.63 per cent only of the total annual income.

Consequently, the rate of growth in the industrialized countries will have a quite considerable influence on the economic growth of the countries exporting raw materials. The spread effect thus emanating from *North America* mainly affects *Latin America,* whereas that emanating from *Western Europe* is directed, rather, towards *Oceania* (through the import of food and wool), the *Middle East* (oil), and *Africa* (various raw materials). From the latter three regions some of the spread effect may "return" to *Western Europe*; little of it "returns" to *North America.* The reason for this is that about two-thirds of the imports, mentioned above, from the industrialized countries to the primary producing countries came from *Western Europe* and only one-third from *North America.* A certain spread effect also moves directly from *North America* to *Western Europe*; but less in the opposite direction because in this relationship *North America* is dominant.

Directly and indirectly, therefore, a high (or low) rate of growth in *North America* will tend to cause a high (or low) rate in *Western Europe, Oceania, Latin America,* the *Middle East* and *Africa.* Possible spread effect tendencies in the opposite direction will be less pronounced.

These considerations may be summed up by saying that if the rate of growth in *North America* should be high (e.g. close to the maximum fixed in Table VII. 2), there will be a tendency for the other five regions mentioned here to have relatively high rates of growth also. The reverse would be the case if *North America*'s rate of growth approximated the minimum fixed in the Table.

The spread effect issuing from foreign trade, on the other hand, will probably affect *Asia* substantially less. In the case of Mainland China the reason for this is given on page 259. Most of the other countries in that region export to the industrialized countries little of the primary products which are particularly involved in rapid expansions, viz. oil and minerals. There is thus no reason to expect that growth in *Asia* will depend on growth in *North America* or in the other more or less industrialized regions to the same extent as would be the case with the other underdeveloped regions.

Inter-regional influences, however, are exerted also through *capital movements.* In the nineteenth century the capital export of the United Kingdom was a factor which promoted growth in many countries of the world[32]. Since the Second World War the United States has been the principal exporter of capital. Capital export, however, falls into two categories which may in some, but certainly not all, respects have the same effects.

One category is the traditional *private* capital export for business reasons. In this much store is set by security, which depends, among other things, on political stability in the area in question. Furthermore *Capital* will tend to be attracted to countries which offer possibilities of expansion as markets and sources of raw materials. This latter consideration has been decisive for American concerns which have invested in oil extraction or other types of mining in the *Middle East* and *Latin America*.

It is therefore likely that the export of American private capital will be mainly to the regions that have a comparatively extensive trade with *North America*, that is, to those which are also affected through foreign trade by the North American rate of growth.

Capital has at the outset the effect of stimulating growth in the region that imports it and is thus able to increase its investment. On the other hand, the possibilities of growth are temporarily diminished in the region exporting capital which is compelled to restrict its internal investment. In the years following capital export the contrary holds true, however, as interest and proceeds from the direct investment as well as indemnities are transferred. Part of the earnings, however, will often be spent on new investment in the capital-importing country. If these processes take place over a long period of time the total effect will mainly be that the two regions stimulate one another's economic growth to a certain extent. Private capital movements should, therefore, tend to have the effect, in the event of a large growth in *North America*, of stimulating economic growth in *Western Europe, Oceania, Latin America*, the *Middle East*, and *Africa*, to a limited degree in *Asia*, but for the time being scarcely at all in the *USSR* and *Eastern Europe*.

The second category of capital movement since the Second World War is the *public export of capital*. It may take place through national organizations such as *The Export-Import Bank*, or through international bodies such as *The World Bank (I.B.R.D.)* and others. The purpose will often be to directly promote economic growth, especially in the underdeveloped countries.

---

[32] Cf. pp. 119 ff.

Public capital export is mainly from *North America* although part of it comes from European countries such as the United Kingdom and France through the *Colombo Plan* and the programmes for the French Union. On the other hand *Western Europe* receives public capital imports from *North America* to a large extent, as mentioned below.

When these public capital movements are in the form of loans the effects will be largely the same as those of private capital exports. There is the difference, however, that here the element of risk may be disregarded. Also, the loans may be granted according to requirement or from political motives. It is likely, therefore, that *Asia* will receive a large share of this sort of capital export, especially in the long run.

The possibility that the *USSR* may also become a capital exporter of considerable importance in the course of the period at present under review (1955–80) may also have to be taken into account. This would obviously be a public capital export, and it is likely that a relatively large part of it would go to *Asia* including Mainland China. The *Middle East, Africa,* and *Eastern Europe* may be taken into consideration too. This development, however, is of too recent a date to allow of any evaluation.

Only part of public capital export, however, is in the form of loans. In recent years quite a large part of it has consisted of *grants,* particularly in the case of the great *foreign aid programmes* of the United States. Here there is no question of interest or repayment. The effects will, therefore, be unilateral. Growth will be stimulated in the capital-receiving country, but potential growth will, at least, be restrained in the capital-exporting country. An indirect stimulation of growth, however, may take place in the capital-exporting country if the grant is made subject to its being used partly for purchases in that country. By way of such grants, the United States has, from political and humanitarian motives, surrendered part of its own possibilities of growth to *Western Europe* and, to an increasing extent, to *Asia* and certain other regions.

Often foreign aid is in the form of *military assistance* in the common interests of defence, but such aid may generally have the same effects as the economic aid referred to above. The receiving country earns foreign currency through the stationing of foreign troops and the building of military installations on its soil and the construction of warships in its shipyards, etc. Of course it is also a form of economic aid in a wider sense when *North America* thus partly solves the defence problems of some Western European and Asiatic countries so that the public finances of those countries are relieved [33].

That is in reality what happens also when *North America,* and especially the United States, spends 10 per cent of its net domestic product on defence, including strategic bombers and missiles with nuclear warheads which constitute an essential but very costly part of total Western defence. The large Soviet defence budget is of similar importance to *Eastern Europe.*

Finally it should be mentioned that *the technical assistance* which has in recent years been given to underdeveloped countries is also, in fact, a form of capital export which is not meant to yield interest or to be repaid. It is merely an increase in the investment of the underdeveloped countries in knowledge of various kinds, as mentioned in Chapter II, page 51. Those industrialized countries that place experts etc. at the disposal of such technical aid programmes thus renounce the use of this intangible capital for the promotion of their own growth. In the long run they may perhaps derive some advantage from trade connections etc., which may result, but the primary motive is not usually of an economic nature.

The foregoing reflections may perhaps with some justification be summed up as follows. The economic connections between the regions generally tend to make the rates of growth of most regions positively correlated. A large (or small) growth in *North America* especially will tend to be followed by a large (or small) growth in the other regions with the exception of the *USSR* and *Eastern Europe,* which are, however, mutually correlated in the same manner. As far as *Asia* is concerned the links with the other regions are relatively weak and may depend to a large extent on whether that region can reap the benefit of public capital exports from *North America,* and to a certain extent from the *USSR* also.

4. When the possibilities of growth in the various areas are compared on this basis it will be necessary to confine the comparison to a few of the many possibilities that are in fact conceivable. The following reflections will be based on the figures in Table VII. 2, and are therefore hypothetical in the same sense as the Table itself is. The figures will, as a rule, be calculated in such a way that either the minimum rate or the maximum rate of growth in the Table is used for all regions. This would seem to be the procedure most in conformity with the conclusions made above about

---

[33] Concerning the US grants and loans, cf. page 121 f.

the correlation between the rates of growth. However, this may have to be modified in certain cases as can be seen from what was said above.

By reference to Table VII. 2 the regions may be compared, either one with another, or one group of regions with another group or with a single region. Many combinations, of course, are possible. The following account has been confined to the five combinations which seem at present to afford the greatest interest from an economic, political, or human viewpoint.

a. *Developed and Underdeveloped Regions*

In the present book the regions *North America, Western Europe, Oceania,* the *USSR* and *Eastern Europe* have been termed *developed* for the sake of brevity. In Table VII. 4 these five have been grouped together. The remaining four regions have been included in another group, which thus comprises *Latin America,* the *Middle East, Asia* and *Africa.*

In consequence of the rapid increase in population, the *underdeveloped* regions are expected to have a larger proportion of the world's total population in 1980 than they had in 1955. On the other hand, whether maximum or minimum rates of growth are assumed, they will account for a slightly smaller proportion of the total income than at the beginning of the period. This is true particularly on the maximum assumption, and is due to the fact that the relative difference between the maximum and the minimum rate has been put higher for the developed regions than for the *underdeveloped.* The reason for this is threefold.

Firstly, the uncertainty prevailing about the United States' trade cycles and the retarding factors mentioned in Chapter II[34] make it difficult to say to what extent the possibilities af growth in *North America* will be utilized. The same applies in some degree to the other *developed* regions, whereas the non-industrialized countries are less influenced by trade cycles proper— disregarding the sectors that experience spread effects from the industrialized countries.

Secondly, it is difficult, on the basis of available information to make estimates of growth in the *USSR* and *Eastern Europe.* It is even more difficult to judge whether, in the near future, the demand for higher consump-

[34] See page 58 f.

TABLE VII.4

Developed and Underdeveloped Regions.

	Population				Net Domestic Product						Net Domestic Product (Dollars Per capita)		
	1955		1980		1955		1980 Min.		1980 Max.		1955	1980 Min.	1980 Max.
	Million	Per cent	Million	Per cent	Billion Dollars	Per cent	Billion Dollars	Per cent	Billion Dollars	Per cent			
1. Developed regions	801	29.8	1,072	25.4	758	80.0	1,506	80.9	2,159	82.7	945	1,405	2,015
2. Underdeveloped regions	1,889	70.2	3,149	74.6	190	20.0	355	19.1	453	17.3	100	115	145
	2,690	100.0	4,221	100.0	948	100.0	1,861	100.0	2,612	100.0	350	440	620
Underdeveloped regions as percentage of developed regions											10.7	8.0	7.1

Source: Table VII. 2.

tion will lead to a decline in the very high investment quotas that have hitherto been maintained in the *USSR*.

Finally though changes in rates of growth in the *developed* regions lead to similar changes in the *underdeveloped* regions through spread effects, the latter changes will presumably be less pronounced than the former.

The last three columns of Table VII. 4 are the most interesting, from a human point of view. They show production and income levels. It should be strongly emphasized, however, that a purely numerical comparison of income and production between the two groups of regions is beset with difficulties. The difference in way of life between a citizen of New York and a peasant in an Asian or African village is so great that it cannot really be expressed numerically. Nevertheless the figures may give some impression of development during the period, and it is significant that both the minimum and the maximum rates of growth imply a widening of the gap in wealth. Only if the developed regions should have the minimum, and the underdeveloped regions the maximum rate of growth, would the relation between the two levels remain almost unchanged. This, however, would imply assumptions which do not seem to be supported by our present knowledge of conditions of growth.

The conclusion which appears most likely, then, is that the *underdeveloped* regions, which are, for the most part, beset by the difficulties of a tropical climate, and whose techniques and cultural patterns are very different from those of the industrialized countries, must undergo very great changes before they can embark on a process of economic growth of the modern type. It will be particularly difficult to bring about these changes so long as these four regions experience the very large increase in population which is in prospect just now.

b. *The West and the East*

While the present dividing lines persist in international politics much interest attaches to the respective possibilities of growth in the *West* and the *East* in the narrower sense of the words, i.e. *North America* and *Western Europe* on the one hand, and the *USSR* and *Eastern Europe* on the other. The two blocs are compared in Table VII. 5.

About 1955 the *West* preponderated considerably with regard to human

TABLE VII.5
The West and the East.

| | Population | | | | Net Domestic Product | | | | | | Net Domestic Product (Dollars Per capita) | | |
| | 1955 | | 1980 | | 1955 | | 1980 Min. | | 1980 Max. | | 1955 | 1980 Min. | 1980 Max. |
	Million	Per cent	Million	Per cent	Billion Dollars	Per cent	Billion Dollars	Per cent	Billion Dollars	Per cent			
1. The West	479	60.8	623	59.2	586	78.6	1,092	73.9	1,571	74.0	1,225	1,750	2,520
2. The East	309	39.2	429	40.8	160	21.4	386	26.1	552	26.0	520	900	1,290
	788	100.0	1,052	100.0	746	100.0	1,478	100.0	2,123	100.0	950	1,405	2,020
The East as percentage of the West											42.4	51.3	51.0

Source : Table VII.2.

numbers, and even more so as far as production was concerned. In both fields the figures suggest a certain relative progress for the *East* in the course of the period. The relative change in population, however, is slight; in production it is a good deal greater, whether minimum or maximum rates of growth are assumed. On both assumptions the *East* would thus seem to be in for the most rapid growth, so that at the end of the period it should have achieved a per capita income equalling about one-half of that of the *West* compared with a little over 42 per cent of it in 1955. It would be a significant change but by no means revolutionary. It should be emphasized, however, that in making this politically important comparison particular care must be taken in making direct use of both maximum and minimum rates of growth.

Thus, *inter alia*, it should be stressed that economic balance is quite different from *military balance*. According to the Table total net domestic product in 1955 was between three and four times as large in the *West* as in the *East*. The military balance is perhaps more difficult to appraise but it can hardly be believed that the *West* has a military superiority of the same magnitude. Certainly production is one of the factors on which military strength depends, but other factors, also, are of vital importance. Among these are the depth, geographical formation and situation of the land areas of the countries in question and their defence efforts in relation to their economic capacity. According to available information the *East* spends a larger quota of its net domestic product on defence than is the case in the *West*. Added to this is the important fact that on account of the lower income level a larger number of man-hours is obtained for the same outlay of money in the *East* than in the *West*. The *USSR*, especially, can keep many more soldiers for a billion dollars than can the United States. This fact, however, may lose some of its importance as defence becomes mechanized and the numerical strength of the forces thus becomes less significant.

If the purely economic balance, only, is considered, it will be necessary to keep in mind what was said in Section *a* (p. 265 f) about the very great uncertainty that prevails—for various reasons—with regard to estimates of the situation in the United States and the *USSR*, these countries being the dominant pair of the two groups. Even more importance perhaps attaches to the fact that the correlation mentioned in 3 (p. 258 f) between the rates of growth of the regions exists only in a very slight degree between *East* and

West—if at all[35]. If growth in *North America* becomes comparatively slight and perhaps approaches the minimum rate, this will result in a similar tendency in *Western Europe*. It will have scarcely any influence on the *USSR* or *Eastern Europe,* however.

The *West* may thus conceivably be nearer to the minimum than to the maximum, whilst at the same time the *East* is nearer to the maximum than to the minimum. The reverse may also be the case, though from what is at present known of the matter, the former contingency appears to be the more likely. In this connection it may be mentioned that the rates of growth shown for the *USSR* have been estimated with some caution in relation to the current plans of the Government of the *USSR*.

A really safe estimate is, of course, out of the question. Judging, however, from the relative improvement of the *East's* position, shown in the Table, it appears more likely at present that the actual improvement will be greater rather than smaller.

A question which has been much debated in recent years is whether the *USSR* will reach the production level of the *West,* and if so, when this will occur. If what has just been said about the relative growth of the *West* and the *East* is related to Table VII. 2 the projections shown may perhaps best be summarized by saying that the *USSR's* production per capita stands a fair chance of being largely on a level with that of *Western Europe* about the year 1980, but it will still be far below that of *North America*. It should be remembered that, here, production as a whole is being discussed, whereas public discussion often deals with industrial production, steel production, or some other part of the whole. It takes longer, of course, to develop the economy over a broad front than to promote growth in separate sectors. Here, again, reference should be made to what has been said about the military balance which, also, in 1980 will be determined to a great extent by other factors than the level of total production.

In comparing the *West* and the *East* it would, of course, be particularly interesting to look a little beyond 1980. It is clear, however, that the uncertain factors already mentioned would be rapidly increased by any considerable lengthening of the period. Nevertheless, it may be possible to throw some light on the question by considering the factors which have lead to

---

[35] The fact that a more extensive correlation may be possible in the future will be referred to in Chapter VIII, page 280.

the high rate of growth which has been achieved by the *USSR* for some years. Three facts may be mentioned.

The best known of these is the policy pursued, which has deliberately given investment (including "investment" in technical knowledge) and thus growth a higher priority than consumption. Also, in deciding the nature of the investment attention has been given to the long-term promotion of growth. This policy will probably be modified gradually. If the present political system is preserved, however, it will presumably be possible to maintain, for a long time, a high investment quota in comparison with most other countries.

Another important fact is that the *USSR* is still a relatively young industrial power. The Western countries also grew very fast during the early stages of industrialism, and in spite of the difference in political system the *USSR* seems to pass—though more rapidly—through more or less the same stages of development as once did Britain and later some other countries.

The third fact is connected with the second. The natural resources of the *USSR* are not yet so extensively utilized as those of the Western countries, especially of *Western Europe*. The knowledge available suggests that there are very considerable natural resources in the *USSR*, not only in relation to current production, but also in relation to population.

There are thus many indications that the *East*, and especially the *USSR*, will fulfil, even for a number of years beyond 1980, some of the most necessary conditions of growth and thus bring its level of development still nearer to that of the *West*.

Finally, it should be stressed that the possibilities of making a really effective comparison between these two important parts of the world are limited by our imperfect knowledge of economic conditions in the *USSR* and *Eastern Europe*. This state of affairs should gradually change as more information becomes available. It should be remembered, however, when trying to look far into the future, that there may occur technical and political changes of very great consequence to the matters under consideration here.

c. *North America and Western Europe*

For many decades *North America* has experienced a faster economic growth than the European countries from which most of the United States' and Canada's immigrants came. The two World Wars have, furthermore, adversely affected *Western Europe* much more than *North America,* and the reconstruction of *Western Europe* after the Second World War would have been extremely difficult without American aid. *Western Europe* still receives considerable military aid from the United States and Canada, and this is, in reality, as mentioned in Section 3 (p. 263), a form of capital import. It is therefore difficult to calculate how much importance should be attached to the fact that in recent years *Western Europe* has achieved a quite substantial growth, both absolutely and in relation to *North America*. Can anything be said with regard to the prospects?

In Table VII. 2 both the minimum and the maximum rates of growth have been put rather higher for *North America* than for *Western Europe*. This applies to the absolute rates of growth and also to that of per capita production, although the difference here is very slight because a large part of *North America*'s increase in production is offset by the very considerable increase in population.

There can indeed be no doubt that the purely physical conditions of *North America* will continue to be more favourable, in the coming decades, to economic growth than those of *Western Europe*. Larger capital investment and more plentiful natural resources—per capita—are the reasons for this. Investment in knowledge is also very large, as noted in Chapter VI.

As already mentioned, however, some uncertainty prevails concerning growth in the United States, partly on account of trade cycles, which seem to be more marked there than in *Western Europe,* and partly on account of the uncertainty as to retarding factors such as shorter working hours and reduced saving quotas. It may be useful here to remember that whereas *Western Europe* will, by 1980, have hardly reached the present income level of *North America,* even at the maximum rate of growth assumed for *Western Europe, North America* itself will by then have reached a level considerably higher than any at present known. It is difficult to judge how people will react under such circumstances.

It should be added, however, that uncertainty exists in both directions. As mentioned earlier, *North America* voluntarily relinquishes a not insignificant part of its sources of growth by spending large amounts on defence and foreign aid, and *Western Europe* profits to a great extent from this. If part of this expenditure can be released, *North America*'s possibilities of growth will expand.

One thing seems certain, however, namely that *North America*'s level of income and production in 1980 will still greatly surpass that of *Western Europe* but it is uncertain how the great possibilities which this implies will be utilized. Needless to say, it is of great importance whether *North America,* which also at that time will have the highest level of income, will use its abundance for military purposes, for the promotion of internal growth, or as capital aid for other regions.

d. *The USSR and Eastern Europe*

The *USSR*'s total net domestic product in 1955 was estimated to be a little more than double that of *Eastern Europe.* This gap between the two regions is expected to widen a good deal during the period under consideration. Both the minimum and the maximum rate of growth have been put at a considerably higher value for the *USSR* than for the *Eastern European countries* partly because of what has been experienced in recent years and partly on account of the great natural resources to be found in the *USSR,* a country which covers a larger area than any other single country.

Both population and per capita production may be assumed to increase at a higher rate in the *USSR* than in *Eastern Europe* and the former is, therefore, likely to increase its economic superiority within the Communist Bloc. This implies that the economic centre of gravity of the group will have moved towards the East, and a further move in that direction may be expected in view of the fact that it is in the eastern parts of the *USSR* especially that the large reserves of natural resources are to be found.

The development of the *USSR* has in practice removed the traditional boundary line between *Europe* and *Asia.* A continuation of this development may, perhaps, gradually, but at an increasing rate, cause the connections and problems of the *USSR* to be extended partly in new directions. In the preceding paragraphs the focus of interest has been the relationship of the *USSR* and *Eastern Europe* with Western countries, but perhaps there will gradually be a change in this state of affairs so that the relationship with *Asia* and with *North America*—across the Pacific and the Polar Sea— will come to be of increasing importance.

e. *Two Groups of Underdeveloped Countries*

It was apparent from what was said in Section *a* (p. 265–67) that most of the underdeveloped countries faced great difficulties compared with the in-

TABLE VII.6

Two Groups of Underdeveloped Countries.

	Population				Net Domestic Product						Net Domestic Product (Dollars Per capita)		
	1955		1980		1955		1980 Min.		1980 Max.		1955	1980 Min.	1980 Max.
	Million	Per cent	Million	Per cent	Billion Dollars	Per cent	Billion Dollars	Per cent	Billion Dollars	Per cent			
1. Latin America, the Middle East and Africa	471	24.9	823	26.1	83	43.7	190	53.5	242	53.4	175	230	295
2. Asia	1,418	75.1	2,326	73.9	107	56.3	165	46.5	211	46.6	75	70	90
	1,889	100.0	3,149	100.0	190	100.0	355	100.0	453	100.0	100	115	145
Asia as percentage of the three other regions											42.6	30.3	30.3

Source : Table VII. 2.

dustrialized countries. There is a considerable difference, however, between the various regions in this respect. It has already been emphasized (in Section 3, p. 259 f) that the spread effect from the industrialized countries is felt, especially, by the primary exporting countries which can supply oil and minerals. There is a dividing line here which does not always follow the regional boundaries. On the whole, however, this effect should put *Latin America,* the *Middle East,* and *Africa* in a more favourable position than *Asia.* A comparison between the three former regions on the one hand and *Asia* on the other is made in Table VII. 6.

Already in 1955 the three sparsely populated regions had an average level of production which was estimated at more than double that of *Asia,* as measured in per capita output. This difference of level will be further increased, at minimum as well as at maximum rates of growth, in the course of the period. Only in the event of the three sparsely populated regions, on the one hand, approaching the minimum rate of growth, while *Asia* on the other, achieves the maximum rate will the relation between the two levels remain fairly constant. This, however, does not appear very likely.

A rapid increase of population is expected in all of the four regions. It is, however, more easy for the sparsely populated regions to sustain such an increase because they possess larger natural resources per capita and their exports are of the kind which would profit from the growth of the industrial countries, consisting mainly of oil and minerals as they do.

The first group of countries in the Table occupies, therefore, we may say, an intermediate position between the developed regions on the one hand and *Asia* on the other. As far as the latter region is concerned any substantial increase in the income level would seem to depend partly on a slower increase in population and partly on public capital export and technical assistance from the developed regions. This support from the wealthier regions of the world depends, in its turn, on political considerations.

Incidentally, a subdivision of the region of *Asia* would be desirable for the purposes of this study. Japan and Mainland China between them account for about one-half of the population of that region and they are both largely situated in the temperate zone, whereas the greater part of the remainder of the region has a tropical or sub-tropical climate. The two northern countries also have cultural traditions which differ from those of the southern countries, which incidentally vary greatly. Japan long ago carried out a considerable industrialization and is not regarded as an underdeveloped country. Mainland China now seems to be making a great effort to achieve a similar development. Unfortunately little information is obtainable concerning it and at present, therefore, it is not possible to judge the situation. It may be mentioned, however, that in Table IV. 3 the investment quotas for Japan and Mainland China have been put much higher than those for the rest of *Asia*. It is also apparent from Chapter VI that there is much less illiteracy in China and in Japan than in most of the southern countries of *Asia*. In Japan there is hardly any illiteracy at all. One reason for these facts may be that a certain industrial development has long been taking place not only in Japan, but also in northern China (especially Manchuria). The information available about developments in Mainland China is, however, so scarce and uncertain that it is impossible to make reliable forecasts.

It seems fairly certain, however, that the southern parts of the region display the features that were mentioned above as being characteristic of the region as a whole. It is conceivable, though, that the two northern countries may achieve a more rapid growth. As far as Mainland China is concerned a reduction in the expected increase in population will be of great importance in raising its income level.

For practical reasons it has been necessary to base the comparisons, that have been made, on the figures in the Tables. This may prove a temptation to forget some of the reservations and conditions to which these projections are subject. It is therefore desirable that this account should conclude with some general reflections on certain features of the patterns of development that are conceivable in certain conditions.

Such reflections are contained in Chapter VIII, which serves to emphasize the fact that development is, largely, the same as change, which can only be expressed in figures partially and uncertainly.

Reference should also be made to the Appendix where an attempt has been made to give some very brief accounts of the patterns of development that might be expected in the individual regions.

Conclusion

——

Whether the rate of economic growth proves to be large or small, one thing seems certain, namely that over the next few decades big changes will take place in the economic and social structure of all the nine regions of the world. This can be seen from the sections dealing with the various regions in the Appendix. The purpose of this chapter is to draw attention to certain conditions and problems of a more general nature, and particularly those that are likely to play an important rôle in the relationships between the regions.

The relative increase in industrial production and services that has been a characteristic feature of all modern economic development[1] may be expected to continue. In many of the highly developed countries only a small part of the population will be employed directly in agriculture as time goes on. Again, this structural change will possibly be much more marked in the underdeveloped regions, where, on the whole, a very high percentage of the population is still employed on the land. In many of these areas there is considerable under-employment in agriculture, but as pointed out in Chapter V B some profound cultural changes will have to take place before agriculture can be modernised and industry expanded.

The trend towards urbanization will presumably be greatest in countries where there is a simultaneous switch-over to large-scale collective farming on the lines of the development that has taken place in the USSR and which is now being gradually introduced in Mainland China. Similarly, a relative decline in agricultural employment may also be expected in many tropical areas, to the extent to which they succeed in introducing more rational methods of agricultural cultivation and in providing alternative employment in the towns.

As a natural corollary to this development various changes will take place

---

[1] See pp. 70–71.

in the traditional *patterns of Culture* that, in agricultural communities in all countries, have persisted without any essential changes over long periods until the process of industrialization began to make itself felt. People who leave the countryside and take up employment in industry and trade in the towns find themselves in a quite different milieu—a milieu where continuous change forms an essential part of the cultural pattern. In such circumstances they can hardly be expected to remain uninfluenced by the many innovations which—as pointed out in Chapter VII A [2]—are so important to economic growth.

Thus the new features of the cultural patterns that develop will usually either be influenced by the industrial countries or be directly imported from them. As, at the same time, there will be an increasing exchange of specialists, technicians and trade representatives, and as illiteracy will gradually decline, each of the nine regions will acquire an increasing knowledge of conditions in the remainder. Radio, films and television will also contribute to this.

This will mean that the poorer peoples of the world will get to know more about the big gap in economic levels between their own countries and those that are wealthier, and this may possibly prove to be a source of international tension. On the other hand, if peace is preserved, generally speaking, these circumstances may lead to increased international trade and communication between the various regions. This again will mean a more rapid spread of modern scientific knowledge and technology. Broadly speaking it may be assumed that the spread effects mentioned in Chapter VII will grow in intensity, which in turn will increase the tendency to a closer correlation between the rates of growth in the individual regions. It is important to note, however, that this must not be taken to mean that the rate of growth in the various regions will tend to be the same. What is implied is that if the dominant regions (such as *North America*) succeed in attaining a high utilization of their possibilities of growth, this will have the effect of allowing the other regions to achieve a high rate of growth in relation to *their* possibilities, but these again may be vastly different from the inherent possibilities in *North America*.

A wider knowledge, throughout the world, of the ways of life in the more highly developed countries may however lead to other effects in the underdeveloped regions, especially in cases where newly independent states are

[2] See p. 242.

founded on a political and administrative pattern similar to that of the industrial countries. The desire to copy the consumer habits of the wealthier countries may make it more difficult than it would otherwise have been to accumulate the necessary amount of *Capital* in the poorer countries, the result being that economic growth will be retarded in the long run.

Some internal tensions may also arise when the population concentrated around the industrial centres in a poor country is thus drawn into new cultural patterns, whilst the larger part of the agricultural population, for all practical purposes, remains outside this influence.

The development of industry in the under-developed countries may also lead to other consequences. As the standard of living is low, the workers in the new industry will only receive very *low wages* compared with those paid in the older industrial countries. For instance it is kell-known that Japan has achieved big exports of manufactured goods on the basis of low wages. More recently there has been a tendency towards a similar export trade from India. It is reasonable to assume that this kind of development will become quite common in the next few decades, as and when the necessary conditions are created for building up industry in any of the countries where there is a large population that is insufficiently and not very productively employed in subsistence farming.

These countries often have relatively modest natural resources. In any case they suffer from a lack of capital resources, including intangible capital in the form of science and technical know-how. They do, however, have a surplus of *Labour*. It would, therefore, be only natural to try to combine the *Capital* and knowledge available in the wealthy countries with the *Labour* force available in the poorer countries. The Japanese-Chinese immigration into the USA is in fact an example of this, but for political reasons it is unlikely that mass migrations of this kind will take place within the next few decades. It is more likely that *Capital* and technical knowledge will migrate in the opposite direction. If this should occur some of the under-developed regions will perhaps be able to develop a considerable export trade based on their own cheap *Labour* combined with *Capital* and technical know-how partly drawn from the developed regions. This is a possibility, the consequence of which is that the future prospects of some of the under-developed countries may look rather brighter than the general arguments contained in this book would seem to indicate. In that case these countries would also be in a position to buy more machinery and other industrial

280

CONCLUSION

goods from the more highly developed countries, thus also indirectly bene-
fiting the latter.

This is one way in which the pattern of *inter-regional* trade may alter.
It is generally accepted that the industrial countries trade with each other
on a large scale because they specialise in different products. On the other
hand, countries that limit their production to certain raw materials have
not much to offer each other. About 1955 the industrial countries bought
twice as much from each other as they did from the primary exporting
countries. On the other hand, the primary exporting countries did not buy
even half as much from each other as they did from the industrial countries[3]. As and when more and more countries become partly industrialized
the patterns of trade will become more varied.

The conditions described will quite possibly be of special significance in
the case of *Asia*. It was pointed out in Chapter VII that this region has only
a very restricted surplus of primary products that may be in greater demand
in the future on account of expansion in the industrial countries. On the
other hand *Asia* has a far greater population employed in subsistence farming than any other region, and this may provide a potential source of cheap
labour for future industrial development. It must be remembered, though,
that the development of its export industry can only take place over a long
period of years.

Another change in the pattern of trade that may conceivably take place,
particularly if political relations develop favourably, is that there may be
increased trade contacts between the centrally planned economies and the
rest of the world. The continued industrialization of the *USSR, Eastern
Europe* and Mainland China may normally be expected to have this effect
—because, as stated above, industrialization usually increases trade. In this
case it may be expected that the extent and character of the trade will depend on political decisions which will be influenced by the demands of the
centrally planned economies as their standard of living rises and their people
learn more about the ways of life of the western peoples. If inter-regional
trade is expanded it will mean that the rate of development in the regions
concerned will become more correlated with that of the other regions.

There is yet another direction in which the trade pattern may conceivably
change. The trade in *primary products* has often been characterized by big

[3] UN (1958, d, Chapter IV, Table 1).

fluctuations both in prices and in quantities, and this has often prevented the under-developed countries from being able to carry out long-term programmes of development. When their incomes from export trade decrease seriously, they also have to reduce their imports of machinery and other investment goods. In recent years various experiments have been made to keep a more effective control of the trade in certain commodities by means of buffer stocks and/or agreements between the importing and exporting countries. If this kind of arrangement can be made more systematically there can be little doubt that the under-developed regions which export these commodities will for the most part benefit by it. This applies especially to *Latin America*, the *Middle East* and *Africa*.

It is possible, however, that efforts to stabilize the raw materials' market may encounter considerable difficulties—partly because there may be conflicting interests between the buying and selling countries. For some time to come, therefore, these markets will presumably represent an uncertain element in the relations between the regions.

Apart from these possible changes in the trade patterns there are grounds for believing that the *volume* of trade between the regions will increase considerably, and it is quite likely that it will increase by a bigger percentage than production itself. As previously mentioned, the industrialization of the various countries has the effect of promoting trade relations, and on the basis of the arguments in Chapter V it is probable that there will be a big increase in inter-regional trade in food and primary products.

Development along these lines will have the effect of uniting the regions more closely in the economic sense, and the spread effects described in Chapter VII will thereby be increased. It seems then to be increasingly likely that when the economically strong regions exploit their possibilities of development to a high (or low) degree, the other regions will be influenced in the same direction. This tendency will be all the more marked if the high rate of growth forces the prices of food and primary products to rise compared with other prices. In those of the under-developed countries that have rich resources an expansion will then follow as a result of the development in the industrial countries.

Some of the problems connected with the *movement of capital* between the regions have been dealt with in Chapter IV and Chapter VII B. Here it may be added that these movements will presumably mean that development of the more backward regions during the period under review will to a considerable extent depend on the import of *Capital* from the more developed countries. In certain cases the technical assistance given by the latter countries may perhaps be of even greater importance.

This was, in fact, the kind of thing that happened in the relationship between the colonies and the metropolitan countries in former days, though conditions in other respects were of course quite different. Former colonies are, however, now rapidly becoming independent and new forms of relationship between the regions may arise. There are two sets of circumstances in which it is possible that this would create a kind of dependence between certain factors in the regions supplying the *Capital* and those being developed with the help of this *Capital*. If the investment is made by private firms the control of production will remain in the investing country, and profits and interest from it will also go to that country. Again, there is another sense in which a form of dependence may be created when *Capital* is exported under public auspices in such a way that in practice—even though it may not be formally recognized—it is bound up with political conditions or in some way influences the receiving country's position in the two main political groups of the world.

In this connection it should be emphasized that the maximum rates of growth mentioned here will require investment in the under-developed countries on a scale that cannot conceivably be realized without considerable capital imports. As we have mentioned previously, it is possible that in those of the under-developed regions that are in a position to export oil and other minerals on a large scale the price relationships may shift in favour of the exporting countries concerned. It is true that some of the profits will still go to the various American and European mining companies, but on the other hand these areas will presumably have no difficulty in attracting capital imports on a commercial basis. This applies especially to *Latin America*, the oil producing countries of the *Middle East* and certain areas in *Africa*.

The problem appears to be far more difficult in *Asia*, partly because the region will probably have to import large quantities of food (cf. Chapter V B). It seems probable that the maximum rate of growth in this region will require considerable imports of *Capital*, and these will presumably largely be in the form of public capital transfers dependent on political decisions.

Even if these capital transfers can be obtained it should be borne in mind that the difference between the economic levels of the developed and the under-developed regions will in fact become still greater (cf. Table VII. 4). As will be seen from Table VII. 6, this applies especially to *Asia,* and means a step away from the goal of levelling out of the differences between the rich and poor countries which is often expressed.

The question has often been raised as to whether it is possible to stop the present tendency towards a widening gap by providing more *Capital* from the developed countries. The purpose of this book does not allow of a discussion of the political considerations, but a study of the various Tables appended should serve to indicate the size of the problem.

It might be asked how much *further Capital* would be needed in order to increase *Asia's* minimum rate of growth by one per cent—i.e. from 1.75 to 2.75—provided that the other conditions for such an increased rate of development were present. Such an increase would mean that by 1980 the net domestic product would be 211 billion dollars instead of 165 billions, i.e. an increase of 46 billion dollars. If, as in Table IV. 8, an estimate is made on the basis of a marginal capital/output ratio of 4.00, further capital supply amounting to 4 × 46 would be needed, i.e. 184 billion dollars or an average of about 7.4 billion dollars a year in the 25 years covered by the Table. On the same basis an increase of one per cent in the maximum rate of growth from 2.75 to 3.75 would require extra *Capital* amounting to 228 billion dollars in the period under review, or an average of about 9 billion dollars a year.

Again, one might inquire how much extra *Capital* would be needed to bring *Asia's per capita* annual rate of growth up to the same level as the average for the rest of the world (cf. Table VII. 2) so as to ensure that the standard of living in *Asia* does not decline relatively during the course of this period. This would mean that by 1980 *Asia's* net domestic product per capita should be 95 instead of 70 dollars allowing for a minimum rate of growth, and 134 dollars instead of 90 if it achieved a maximum rate of growth. The extra *Capital* required would, on the same basis as the previous estimates, be 232 billion dollars for the minimum rate of growth, or 9.3 billion dollars a year. The maximum rate of growth would require extra *Capital* amounting to 409 billion dollars, or about 16.4 billion dollars a year.

It should be remembered that these amounts are additional to the considerable capital imports that will presumably be necessary for the rates of growth previously mentioned in this book. For purposes of comparison it may be mentioned that the total sum of public grants and loans allocated by the United States to other countries in the years 1945–57 amounted to an average of about 5 billion dollars a year (cf. Table IV. 5). If the developed regions were to export a further 7–16 billion dollars of *Capital* a year this is likely to affect their own general rate of growth. Apart from this it is important to keep in mind that the development of a region not only depends on *Capital* but equally on other factors, including that of *Culture*.

This leads, therefore, to a few final remarks regarding the *conditions* on which the arguments put forward in this book are based.

Generally speaking it is true to say that all long-term projections require a certain continuity of development so that past experiences can be used as a basis for estimating possible future trends of development. For the purposes of this book, therefore, it has been assumed that there will not be any revolutionary changes in technical developments or revolutionary political changes during the period under review. It may now be asked whether it is at all possible to foresee developments in these fields.

It has often been said that we are going through the second technical or industrial revolution, and it is a fact that the use of nuclear energy, automation and other modern techniques are beginning to play an increasing rôle. However, there is little likelihood of nuclear energy rapidly replacing coal, oil and hydro-electric power for all purposes. The kind of development expected is a continuous process whereby the new form of energy will gradually be used increasingly side by side with the traditional forms—in the same way as coal was introduced two centuries ago. Similarly, automation is a further development of mechanization, which has been in the process of development over a number of years.

It has also been taken for granted that there will not be any sudden improvement in the technique of food production. In this field experiments are now being made in the mass cultivation of algae and in the direct exploitation of sea plankton. Besides experiments are being made in developing laboratory methods, the purpose of which is to replace or supplement the processes whereby sunshine promotes the creation of green matter in plants.

In each of these cases the same applies as with all other inventions in the history of technology, namely that detailed and therefore often very protracted studies are necessary in order to discover the underlying principles. Secondly, it requires large investment, the training of many scientists and technicians, the accumulation of practical experience and a struggle against tradition, as well as clashes of interest between producers, before production can be started on a really large scale. In other words, even if it is quite likely that one or more of these factors will come to play an important rôle in the future world economy this will not necessarily disturb the picture of a continuous process of development—a picture which is still today, as it always has been, the most realistic way of judging the progress of technology.

In this connection it will be important to note what success attends the efforts to overcome the *disadvantages of tropical climate*. There is good reason to believe that the big increase in the consumption of foodstuffs that will presumably take place will draw increasing attention to the cultivation reserves which exist in tropical areas. If these are to be properly exploited, however, it will no doubt be necessary to make a special drive to exploit more fully the technical knowledge and scientific achievements of the industrial countries, including those of medicine and hygiene. This is perhaps one of the main fields in which the industrial countries in the temperate zones can contribute towards increasing the possibilities of economic growth in the tropical countries. In addition, however, far-reaching changes will have to be introduced to overcome the difficulties caused by climatic conditions, and as these will take time there is all the more reason to assume that there will be a continuous process of development.

It is more likely that an interruption in the process of development—if any—will be *political*. We have already pointed out that this book is written on the assumption that no large-scale war will break out during the period covered—although in retrospect the two world wars seem to have had astonishingly small influence on the total development of the world's economy. Naturally, precisely because a big war in many ways disturbs the economic balance, powerful forces follow it to restore the balance so that a more harmonious development can take place. An example of this is the support given by *North America* to the reconstruction of *Western Europe* after the Second World War.

An even more widespread third world war, including the use of nuclear weapons, would, however, cause such destruction and such a big reduction in world population that for a long time after it had ended the economic conditions would be such that it would be useless to try and make a prognosis of them at the present time. This being so, the arguments in this book have been based on the assumption that no such war will break out in the period up to 1980.

At the same time—although this is not such an important condition as the first—it has been presumed that the *present political groupings of countries* will not be essentially altered in the period under review. Any major alterations in this direction would probably mean, *inter alia,* that the present division into world regions would no longer be relevant.

In this connection the question is often posed as to whether any of the so-called un-committed countries in *Asia* and *Africa* may possibly alter their attitude towards the existing power blocs. In so far as this question can be assumed to have any connection at all with the problems dealt with in this book, the only thing that can be said is that the un-committed countries will presumably make their own comparisons between the economic growth taking place in areas with different political systems and be influenced accordingly. These may include general comparisons between the *West* and the *East,* but there is more likelihood of their comparing countries where the economic level—and hence also the economic problems—are most similar to those in the majority of the un-committed countries themselves, such as Mainland China and India (see the section on *Asia* in the Appendix and, more generally, the final remarks about *Asia* in Chapter VII B). It should be pointed out that the differences between the two big Asiatic countries are not only caused by their different economic systems. There are also big differences in climate, natural resources and cultural traditions. The results of their efforts to develop economically will, therefore, depend on much more than the difference in their methods of economic policy. This is, *inter alia,* a single consequence of the fact that *Nature* is a factor of production. Nevertheless, when these matters are discussed very often more importance is attached to the difference between the political systems than is justified.

Even if the political groupings remain largely unchanged in the period under review there is another aspect of the world political situation that may be a decisive factor for economic growth and consequently also for the economic balance.

At the present time the *world expenses for national defence* are in the neigbourhood of 100 billion dollars a year, which is somewhat less than its total net investment. It is therefore important whether this factor will show a relative decline in the period under consideration or even be further increased. It is chiefly *North America* and the *USSR* and to a somewhat lesser degree *Western* and *Eastern Europe,* that maintain this large defence apparatus. If this burden could be reduced it would benefit the development of these regions. In addition it might also increase their capacity to export *Capital* to the underdeveloped regions, but the extent and direction of these exports would largely depend on political considerations.

More generally speaking it might be said that if any of the developed regions were to export a greater amount of *Capital* to any of the under-developed regions—possibly as a part of a competition for political influence —this might to some extent upset the basis for the arguments we have put forward, irrespective of whether the *Capital* is made available because of a reduction in the defence budget of the country concerned.

Finally there is a further problem in connection with the assumptions on which the arguments in this book are based. Briefly, the question is whether a new attitude towards *family planning*, including new and easier methods of practicing it, can be so popularized that towards the end of the period under review the world population increase can be reduced essentially. Even if this should happen it is unlikely that it would have any discernable effect on the man-power situation before 1980; but a reduction in the birth-rate figures might in some regions—and particularly in *Asia*—have the effect of increasing the chances of a higher standard of living, although this again would presumably also be most noticeable after 1980.

This book has been in preparation for just over three years. During the course of the necessarily lengthy studies of the whole complex of problems dealt with here it has been apparent how much easier it would have been if more satisfactory information had been available. No doubt this applies to all research work. Any such work reveals certain other aspects that might usefully be further elucidated on more or less related subjects. We shall therefore conclude this book with some *suggestions for further research work* in the field of economic growth and the balance of world economy.

The science of economics as it exists today bears the stamp of having been almost exclusively developed in *Western Europe* and *North America* in the age of industrialism. More often than not, therefore, its approach to a problem is determined by the conditions in a community of this particular type. The same also applies to various other branches of science, or at least to those sectors of them that relate to social conditions. From a practical point of view it is most essential nowadays that we should also study other types of communities in the world, and there is no doubt that such studies would also be of great value in themselves.

One of the most important fields of study should be the *centrally planned economies,* particularly as exemplified by the *USSR, Eastern Europe* and Mainland China. The material that has so far been available concerning these countries has been rather sparse and difficult to compare with similar material from other countries. In future, however, it is probable that these countries will themselves be increasingly interested in having their own particular problems and conditions examined in empirical and theoretical studies. It would also be useful to make a study of the economies of these countries in so far as they are related to the geographical and historical background and to get a clearer idea of the various similarities and differences between them and other types of community in the way they function.

Similarly it is essential that a detailed and unprejudiced study should be made of the economy in those regions which for purposes of reference have been called "under-developed". Existing literature concerning these countries is sparse both in comparison with literature about *Western Europe* and *North America* and in proportion to the size of the problems with which these regions are faced. It is not only a question of collecting more information about actual conditions in the countries concerned. One may take for granted that the very way in which the economic systems work differs in many respects from that of the developed regions; in other words, certain measures may often have quite a different effect from the same type of measures in the wealthier industrial countries. This means that it will be necessary to revise the theoretical models that are used in the science of economics before they can be applied to conditions in the under-developed countries.

There are some more general problems which in the light of the experiences of this book it seems desirable to deal with in greater detail.

The population theory as it stands today is very difficult to fit into an economic model. There is, in fact, no real population theory that can be used in describing changes in population. It would for example be very useful to investigate how population develops in a tropical agricultural community, particularly after it has been affected by western methods of hygiene; this should make it possible to get a more general picture of what might be called the dynamics of population development and their connection with other factors.

Like the population theory the *science of the progress of technology* is only in its infancy. Seen superficially it would look as if new inventions are often made quite accidentally. In reality they are usually the product of systematic research and effort, and in future this will increasingly be so. To put it briefly one might say that knowledge is something that is produced and then distributed. This process is dependent not only on the use of both labour and capital but also on the cultural milieu and on the demand for factual knowledge created by economic development. In this respect the various regions will have differing demands over the next few decades, and it would be useful to make a separate study of the conditions of growth of technology from the regional point of view.

Further, it would be useful to have a more detailed knowledge of the *natural resources* in the various regions—or rather, more generally, of the factor *Nature*[4] in relation to the character of demand and of technique existing over the next few decades. It would also be possible to take these things into consideration in elaborating the methods of dealing with economic problems and economic science generally. In this work an attempt is made in this direction, but the results show that more research is needed. At this point attention should be drawn to the remarks in Chapter V B (pp. 138 ff) regarding the lack of information concerning the conditions for the production of food.

The above remarks regarding *Nature* also apply to *Culture*. A systematic study is also needed of the connection between economic development and the relative position of, and changes in, cultural elements.

In these as in all fields of research the principle applies that knowledge is something that is produced, and that production takes time. For every year that passes the sum of knowledge grows, both in the sense of concrete information about present economic developments and as regards theoretical work.

This being so it is essential that the projections set out in this book should be *constantly revised*. In another five years' time it will be somewhat easier to foresee how things will develop up to about 1980. In ten years' time it will be still easier. But both in five and in ten years' time it will be possible to make a more accurate prognosis if a previous attempt has been made—even on the basis of a broad and incomplete mosaic—which can then gradu-

[4] See Chap. II, p. 43 ff.

ally be improved, revised and expanded as and when new facts emerge and the situation changes[5]. This has in fact been one of the aims of this present work—viz. to make a contribution to a continuous process by which our picture of the conditions surrounding us is gradually expanded, refined and adapted to the demand of the varying periods of time.

[5] Cf. Haavelmo (1954, Part VI).

Regional Surveys and Prospects
—

1. *North America*

A. Survey

The North-American region is here taken to mean the United States, Canada and Greenland. These areas comprise a total of about 21.5 million sq. km. In 1955 they had a population of 182 millions. The region's land area is about sixteen per cent of the total land area of the world, but its population is less than seven per cent of the total world population. It is, therefore, a relatively thinly populated region. Within the area, however, there are wide differences in the density of population, as practically the whole of the population lives in the United States (excluding Alaska) and the southern parts of Canada.

The way in which the population is distributed indicates the suitability of the various areas of the region for exploitation, and this, again, is dependent on the natural conditions. Roughly one-third of the area may be termed productive, i.e. it consists of cultivated agricultural land, grassland or forest. In proportion to population the productive area is somewhat more than twice as big in *North America* as it is in the world as a whole. Furthermore, there are considerable reserves of land, particularly in Canada, that could be cultivated, just as there are considerable areas of forestland that could be exploited. This does not exhaust at the present time the possibilities of increasing vegetal agricultural production, as extensive cultivation is the usual practice, which means that it is still technically possible to increase the yield by more intensive cultivation.

Generally there are good supplies of metals and natural sources of energy in *North America*. As these resources have already been heavily exploited in the United States, however, the costs of extracting some raw materials are steadily and rapidly increasing. This applies in particular to two such important raw materials as oil and iron ore, and it is possible, therefore, that an increasing proportion of the United States' consumption of these raw materials will in the future have to be covered by imports. In that case Canada may become one of the iron-ore exporting countries, and in such an event this trade will remain within the North-American region. In addition, *Latin America* will presumably be one of the regions that will contribute towards satisfying the North-American demand for these raw materials.

Practically the whole of the population of *North America* is descended from many different races from other parts of the world, and this is, no doubt, one of the main reasons for the extremely rapid rate of economic growth that has taken place in this region. On the whole the type of people who emigrated to this region were people of initiative and resolve, and their original spirit of energy and drive has presumably been further strengthened by the great possibilities offered by the natural resources. Again, the great majority of these emigrants came from *Europe* and were therefore already at an advanced stage of development in relation to the times in which they lived. Moreover, it is quite likely that such a mixed population has contributed to the breaking down of many of the old prejudices and differences that existed in the home countries of these emigrants or between their countries of origin, and which stood in the way of economic development. In this connection, however, it should be mentioned that in Canada, where most of the population is English-speaking there is still a large element of the population that only speaks French. This is one example of differences that have not been eradicated in spite of emigration.

Although the majority of the present population of *North America* was born there, their inheritance from their emigrant ancestors still appears to be one of their dominant features; for the fact is that the North-American population still has the spirit of enterprise which is so important for economic growth. This particular quality is largely dictated by the desire for ever-increasing material wealth. Since the end of the Second World War, however, the population has been—and still is—increasing, considerably. It is possible that this may be taken as a sign of a less material attitude to life, as a big increase in the number of children will—anyhow in the short term—usually have the effect of slowing down the process of improving the standard of living. On the other hand, the increase in the population as a whole means a greater demand for consumer goods, and this again may turn out to be an inducement to increasing production by intensifying the exploitation of the production factors, and in the long term, when the population "bulge" reaches the productive age, it should be possible to increase the labour force considerably and hence, in a region like *North America,* to create a basis for a big production rise.

North America's favourable position as regards the quantity and quality of the production factors has resulted in a present-day per capita production that is nearly twice as big as that in *Oceania* and *Western Europe,* which are the two regions that most nearly resemble *North America.* The distribution according to the main branches of industry of production, income, etc. is typical of a highly developed region. Agriculture comprises only about 5 per cent of the total production, whilst the services are responsible for more than half the total, the remainder coming under the heading of manufacturing, mining and construction.

Net investment in *North America* comprises approximately 11 per cent of total net domestic product. Compared with the other economically highly developed regions this is a rather low percentage, but as the region has a very high total production it nevertheless represents about 30 per cent of the world's total net investment. Furthermore, it should be remembered that a considerable part of the annual production goes into the renewal of *North America's* huge capital equipment, and this part of investment is not included in the figures for net investment. Furthermore, the region's expenditure on defence is very large and absorbs a part of the total production roughly corresponding to the net investment. Finally it may be mentioned that the region's gifts to other regions reduces that part of the total production that is at the disposal of the region itself, and, in the short term, its loans have a similar effect.

Thanks to *North America's* wealth of natural resources its trade with other regions is of relatively little importance to the region as a whole. On the other hand this trade is of considerable importance to the other regions. *North America* has granted credit and gifts that have provided the basis for a larger export of goods and services to these regions than would presumably otherwise have been possible, and in addition these credits and gifts have built up dollar reserves in other regions. This has facilitated international payments and thereby also paved the way for increased international trade.

North America's exports of goods to other regions amounts to the equivalent of about 5 per cent of its net domestic product, whilst its imports of goods is even less. Among the most important imports are coffee, tea, sugar, rubber, oil, copper and tin, whilst machinery and articles of transport are the principal articles of export in addition to such items as grain, timber, paper, coal, iron and steel products. *North America*'s most important trading partners are *Latin America* and *Western Europe*; these two regions account for about two-thirds of *North America*'s foreign trade, which is about evenly distributed between the two.

Since the end of the Second World War the United States has granted considerable loans and gifts to other countries. Initially the main purpose was to help reconstruction, but in recent years the money has been allocated with rather a different aim, viz. largely for the purpose of building up the defences of the free world. During the period July 1945 to December 1957 the United States made grants totalling 62 billion dollars, the greater part of which was in the forms of gifts.

Apart from the fact that this has resulted in a flow of dollars to the other regions, the expansion in the United States' direct private investment in foreign countries during the post-war period has resulted in an important export of *Capital*. In the ten-year period from December 1946 to December 1956 these exports have been to the tune of about 10 billion dollars to countries outside the North-American region. A little less than half of this was invested in *Latin America,* and especially in the oil industry.

As the result of these and other forms of capital investment abroad, the United States—and thus *North America*—today stands as a net creditor in relation to the other regions. At the end of 1957 the United States assets abroad amounted to 54 billion dollars and its liabilities to 31 billion dollars, which means that it has net assets of 23 billion dollars in other regions.

B. Prospects

The possibility of significant economic growth in *North America* in the period up to 1980 appears at the present time to be good. The region has excellent resources of land and raw materials, both of which should be sufficient in the period under review. On the other hand, however, it might be profitable for *North America* to meet some of its demands for raw materials by increased imports from other regions; such an increase in imports would not present any problem for the region from the point of view of foreign currency.

The bulge in the birth-rate in the post-war years will mean that there will be a big increase in the productive age groups in the period up to 1980.

The extent to which this increase will be reflected in the availability of labour will, however, depend on whether any changes take place in the period of apprenticeship, whether the hours of work are altered, and whether there is an increase or decrease in the number of persons—particularly women—joining the ranks of the labour force.

Developments in the *Capital* stock will depend on the extent of annual investment. This is difficult to estimate in view of the fact that the large production and the high standard of living in *North America* allow for a wide margin within which investment can develop. If need be, *North America* could well afford a large expansion of its investment activities. But even if one of the conditions assumed in this book is that a serious decline in the economy should be avoided—if necessary with the help of public measures —it is nevertheless not anticipated that these will take the place of private saving and investment initiative which will still be the most important factor in the development of investment activities.

On this assumption it would presumably be unrealistic to imagine that there will be any alterations of major importance in the part of production that goes into investment. However, both in judging this situation and in estimating the future labour situation, hours of work, etc., we are on more uncertain ground in the case of *North America* than in the case of the other regions. *North America* has a vast superiority over the other regions as far as its production level and its standard of living are concerned. Whilst it is possible, for instance, in forming an estimate of the way in which developments will take place in *Western Europe* and *Oceania* to take account of the pattern of past developments in *North America,* there is no corresponding basis of experience for forming an opinion as to the future economic behaviour of the population of *North America.*

The problems referred to can be summarized by the question as to whether the spirit of enterprise, which is a feature of *North America,* will persist to the same degree as hitherto or whether the population will gradually develop a less material attitude to life and will be more inclined to be satisfied with the standard of living that it has already achieved. If a change of this nature should take place it would influence the rate of economic growth, by slowing down the process of increasing productivity, by creating a demand for more leisure time, etc., etc.

Even if there are grounds for believing that at some stage or other in the development of its economic life a community will naturally slacken its efforts, it may be assumed that this will be a slow process and that the effects of such a change in mentality on production some 20 or 25 years hence would, in any case, be of only a limited nature.

In addition, there are certain special conditions which would seem to indicate that there will not in fact be any slackening in the efforts to achieve a high degree of economic growth. Although it is true that the North-American region is superior to the other regions both as regards its production in general and its standard of living, it is nevertheless subject to severe competition particularly from the *USSR* and to a certain extent also from *Western Europe* in certain more specialized but extremely important sectors of its economy. The Second World War and the political situation in the post-war years have resulted in intensive research being undertaken in the field of military science. This research work has had some very striking results which have opened up a wide perspective for developments in civil life. Even if there should be a slackening in the military field—which is incidentally one of the unknown factors in estimating future economic growth—it may be assumed that the importance of taking part in the race for supremacy in the exploitation of atomic energy for civil purposes and for the conquest of space will play such a rôle in the future that a great effort will be made to develop these sciences. Even if research in these fields is primarily a public matter, it may be assumed that the general spirit of competition will counteract any tendency there might be to slacken in the production race in general; and furthermore as time goes on technical progress will gradually create new demands which will serve to maintain public interest in earning ever larger incomes.

In estimating *North America*'s future economic growth it has therefore been assumed that there will not be any essential changes in the factors governing economic growth.

The number of persons in the productive age groups (15–64 years)— which can partly be estimated on the basis of the size and composition of the population in 1955—is expected to rise by about 1.5 per cent a year. However, owing to the shortening of hours of work which will probably take place, and the increase in the period of apprenticeship or training—though in the case of women this will probably be counterbalanced by the increase in the number taking jobs outside their homes—the increase in the number of man-hours is only estimated to be an average of two-thirds per cent a year for the period 1955–80.

The annual investment quota, which was approximately 11 per cent about the year 1955, is estimated to keep within margins of about 10–14 per cent in the period up to 1980.

Under these conditions the annual growth in the net domestic product from 1955 to 1980 is estimated to be a minimum of 3 per cent and a maximum of 4.5 per cent. Per man-hour this means that the minimum growth in the net domestic product will be about 2.25 per cent, whilst the maximum growth in the net domestic product per man-hour will be 3.75 per cent. For purposes of comparison it may be mentioned that in the United States the average annual growth in the gross national product per man-hour in the period 1900–57 was 2.3 per cent and in the post-war period 1947–57 3.2 per cent[1]. The ratio between the increase in *Capital* and the increase in the net domestic product—i.e. the marginal capital/output ratio—will be somewhat more than 3 for the period 1955–80 in the case of both the minimum and the maximum rate of growth, whilst the average capital/output ratio at the beginning of the period was approximately 3.

Apart from the fact that *North America*'s economic development will obviously be of importance to the region itself, it will also have some influence on the rate at which development will take place in most of the other regions, i.e. partly through the normal channels of trade and commerce and partly on account of economic aid which it may be assumed that the United States will continue to provide. On the other hand one can only make a tentative prognosis of the importance that *North America*'s economic growth will have in these ways. As regards trade with other regions, it may be assumed that this will increase with economic growth in *North America*; possibly at a greater rate than that of net domestic product. The growing demand for raw materials that would result from a period of continued economic growth in *North America* may be presumed to be sufficient grounds for this assumption. As mentioned previously, *Latin America* will presumably be one of the regions that will benefit most from a development along these lines.

The assumption that continued economic aid will be available to the other regions is purely guess-work. It is not unreasonable to suppose, however, that there will be a certain element of competition in relation to the *USSR* in the matter of providing economic aid to under-developed areas. Apart

[1] National Planning Association (1959).

from this *North America* will presumably also continue in the future, and most likely to an increasing degree, to feel that it has some responsibility for the way in which things develop in the other regions, and this in itself will mean that a considerable amount of *Capital* will be transferred to under-developed areas.

2. *Western Europe*

A. SURVEY

For the purposes of this book *Western Europe* is regarded as consisting of 18 countries with a total area of 3.6 million sq. km. and a total population of 297 millions (1955). It is a densely populated region having 82 inhabitants per square kilometre. In comparison with the other regiions, *Western Europe* has the next to smallest area and the next to largest population.

On the whole the climate is temperate, although the Mediterranean countries have a sub-tropical climate and the northernmost parts of the region an arctic climate. The temperatures vary considerably, not only in the North-South direction but also East-West, as the part of the region that is furthest to the West has a specifically maritime climate with warmer temperatures—thanks to the Gulf Stream—than at similar latitudes elsewhere. In the temperate parts of the region there is a fairly abundant rainfall practically everywhere, and there are no large arid areas. The sub-tropical part of the region (Portugal, Spain, Greece and the larger part of Italy) is in the area of winter rains, and the climate is semi-arid.

The Alpine ranges of fold-mountains—the Pyrenees and the Alps—divide the region sharply into a southern and a northern section, but in spite of this natural obstacle to communications there are many railways and roads connecting the two sections. At present a road tunnel is in the process of construction under Mont Blanc, and this will further facilitate traffic between France and Italy.

Conditions are particularly favourable for transport by water, on account of the many lakes, fiords, bays and inlets and the short and mild winters. In connection with many of the larger rivers there is a well-developed system of canals; more particularly the Rhine and its tributaries with interconnecting canals which are of great importance to the industries located in this area. The chief deposits of heavy raw materials are favourably placed from the point of view of transport, partly because there are no long distances to cover and partly because transport is mostly by ship.

Western Europe has a productive area of about 2.7 million sq. km. (corresponding to three quarters of the total area). Of this, one million sq. km. is arable land, 0.8 sq. km. grassland and the remaining 0.9 sq. km. forestland. There are wide variations in the yields per unit of area, largely due to the differences in climate and relief. The yield per unit of area is restricted in the North by the cold climate and in the South by the lack of rain. As a rule the land being farmed in the mountain districts is small and dispersed over large areas and is therefore difficult and uneconomical to cultivate.

On the whole the yields per unit of area are higher in *Western Europe* than anywhere else in the world. Nevertheless it may be assumed that productivity can be increased even further in the future. As there is little possibility of extending the area under cultivation any increase in agricultural production will have to be based on still more intensive cultivation.

Western Europe is in a fairly good position as regards *natural sources* of power and valuable minerals. The largest coal deposits are located in Great Britain and Western Germany. There are also deposits in Belgium, France and Holland. The total reserves are estimated at about 350–400 thousand million tons. On the other hand there is very little *oil,* and the "proved reserves" are less than the present annual consumption. Hydroelectric power is used more particularly in the Alps and in Scandinavia. In addition, measures are now being taken to make use of some of the wide rivers which have a fall less than has hitherto been considered necessary.

The region has considerable resources of iron ore and is in fact almost self-sufficient in this respect. The largest deposits are to be found in France, Sweden and Great Britain. Other mineral deposits only exist on a smaller scale, and as production is insufficient to meet demand they have to be imported both in the form of ore and of crude metals.

As regards fertilizers or raw materials for these, there are large deposits of potash but only small and quite inadequate deposits of natural phosphates.

As far as its population is concerned, *Western Europe* is an almost homogeneous region. The differences between the various countries are no longer of particular significance in comparison with the variations in languages and cultures in other regions. There are two main language groups (the Teutonic and the Romance) in the region; each of these is divided into several national languages. In more recent times, however, these language differences have not been a serious hindrance to cultural exchanges either at the intellectual or the technical level. As far as education is concerned, the southern European countries are rather backward. In the Mediterranean countries between one quarter and one half of the population is illiterate, whilst in the remainder of *Western Europe* only a very small percentage of the population is illiterate.

From the point of view of politics most West-European countries enjoy democratic rule, only two countries (Spain and Portugal) having dictatorships. The German and Italian dictatorships of the period between the wars have been succeeded by what seem to be well-founded democratic institutions, but a similar development has not taken place in the Iberian Peninsula.

As far as economic conditions are concerned this region is midway among the five developed regions. For a long time industry has been the principal occupation in the central parts of *Western Europe,* whilst agriculture predominates in certain parts of the periphery in the South and North. There is a tendency everywhere, however, towards a still higher degree of industrialization and a relative reduction in agriculture.

Western Europe has a considerable international trade with other regions. Its imports mainly consist of industrial raw materials, oil and foodstuffs, and its exports almost exclusively consist of industrial products and a few specialized items of food. In recent years the region's exports have been increasing significantly, largely as a result of the expansion of Western Germany's foreign trade. Furthermore, the United Kingdom carries on a large trade with the Commonwealth. In contrast to several of the other regions, internal trading takes place on a large scale within *Western Europe.* Several highly specialized industrial products, including transport equipment and chemicals are exchanged in considerable quantities, as also are some raw materials (including iron ore) and certain agricultural products (fruit and livestock products).

Although it is true that as a unit *Western Europe* must be regarded as belonging to the developed regions, the southern parts of this region (Portugal, Spain, Southern Italy and Greece) are typically under-developed areas. Most of the characteristics common to under-developed areas outside of *Europe* can be found in Southern Europe, for example the per capita national income, the distribution of occupations, the standard of literacy and the general cultural milieu.

B. Prospects[1]

During the period under review there will probably be only a small increase in the population of *Western Europe*. As will be seen from Table VII. 2 the annual increase has been estimated at about 0.5 per cent, which is lower than that of any other region. As the distribution of age groups in *Western Europe* will tend towards a relatively larger proportion of the population being in the older age groups—as a natural corollary of the falling death-rate and the low birth-rate—and as the hours of work will probably be reduced and holidays extended, there will be a small negative rate of growth of man-hours (as seen in Table VII. 3). In other words, the total supply of man-hours is estimated to be 5–10 per cent lower in 1980 than it was in 1955.

In view of this situation it is obvious that it will only be possible to achieve an increase in the net domestic product in total as well as per capita in *Western Europe* by increasing productivity—partly by increasing real capital and partly by improving capital equipment. This will be all the more important as the available resources have already been fairly exhaustively exploited. In fact it may be expected that in *Western Europe, Nature* will have a rather retarding influence in so far as the exploitation of natural resources may be assumed not to increase *pari passu* with the increase in *Capital*. (This accounts for the assumption that the sum of α_1 and α_2 is slightly lesst han unity in Table VII. 3).

A scarcity of natural resources may, however, be partly overcome by a more abundant supply of *Capital* and an increase in the factor *Culture* (including innovations) and also partly by foreign trade. As to the latter, *Western Europe* seems to be more dependent than any other region but *Oceania* on a steady expansion of world trade. As a considerable proportion of *Western Europe*'s economic activities are based on imports of raw materials and as the principal part of *Western Europe*'s exports consists of manufactured goods, it is plain that the way in which the major raw materials producing countries develop will be important for the development of *Western Europe*.

---

[1] It is attempted in this book to indicate certain lines of development for the world as a whole. It follows that within the given framework the treatment of the individual regions will appear rather scanty. This is particularly so in the case of *Western Europe* (and *North America*) for which a wealth of data and studies are available. It is not, however, possible to include this abundance of material in the present context.

In fact, there can be little doubt that future developments in *Western Europe* will largely depend on the trend not only in *North America* but also in *Latin America, Africa* and *Asia*, i.e. in the countries which produce raw materials, and are more important trading partners for *Western Europe* than is *North America*. As industrialization is progressing in these countries and their imports of manufactured goods are, therefore, gradually increasing, *Western Europe* has found an outlet which may prove to be of vital importance to its future economic growth. It will readily be understood that *Western Europe* is, therefore, anxious that the under-developed countries should find some other solution to their payments problems than that of restricting trade. Even if exports of *Capital* from *Western Europe* to these countries has a restrictive effect on the region's own development, they will no doubt prove to be valuable for its long-term economic development.

In Chapter VII B it has been assumed that the renewal and expansion of capital equipment will enable the net domestic product per capita to increase between 1.75 and 3.25 per cent. It will also be seen from Table VII. 3 that the net domestic product per man-hour has been estimated to increase between 2 and rather more than 3.5 per cent. From past experience it looks as if even the maximum estimate does not necessarily presuppose that there will be a permanent boom in the period up to 1980. As to whether there is more likelihood of the maximum rate being achieved rather than the minimum, will depend *inter alia* on the extent to which shorter trade cycles become a serious retarding factor. This, again, will to a certain extent depend on the trend of developments in *North America,* although it appears that *Western Europe* is less dependent to-day on the shorter cycles in *North America* than it was in the past.

As will be seen from Table VII. 3 the greater part of the increase in the real product per capita can be attributed to the factor *Culture*. In other words, if the maximum rate of growth of at least 3.5 per cent per man-hour is achieved, 2.75 per cent will be due to *Culture* (cf. Table VII. 3 indicating a value of γ equal to 2.79 per cent). This high percentage must—as in the case of the other developed regions—assume a high rate of gross and net investment which implies a high rate of innovations.

Apart from these considerations it may be added that if the plans of *Western Europe* for a common market are carried out, and if the transition can be smooth and combined with a high rate of growth, the individual Western European countries will be able to specialize more, and the resulting increase in productivity will increase this region's chances of attaining the maximum rate of growth estimated. However, there are so many reservations attached to this that it would be unwise to jump to any hasty conclusions.

Among the conditions that influence the rate of economic growth in this region are the terms of trade. As far as *Western Europe* is concerned, these conditions will deteriorate *pari passu* with the extent to which the present considerable—and in the future still further intensified—exploitation of natural resources may cause increases in the prices of raw materials. Although a deterioration in the terms of trade will only be of minor importance in relation to the absolute level of real income in the region, nevertheless in view of the problems connected with the balance of payments that will result from this development, it may be of some significance to the region's future economic growth by forcing some of the West European countries to adopt a more restrained policy.

In *Western Europe* as a whole an annual increase in the per capita income of 1–3 per cent will mean an increase over the period under review of between one-third and just over double the present level. If the maximum rate of growth is achieved, this will mean a standard per capita by 1980 more or less corresponding to the present level in *North America* (cf. Table I. 1). Taking into account the differences in the various parts of the region —i.e. particularly the difference between the northern and southern parts —it will be seen that, if the maximum rate of growth is achieved, the northern parts of *Western Europe* will by about 1980 have attained a standard that is well above the present standard in *North America*.

3. *Oceania*

A. SURVEY

Oceania comprises Australia and New Zealand plus groups of smaller islands in the Pacific Ocean. With its total land area of approximately 8 million sq. km. *Oceania* is one of the smaller regions, though it is more than twice as big as *Western Europe*. From the point of view of population— about 13 millions in 1955—*Oceania* is lowest on the list of regions, and with only 1–2 persons per sq. km. it is the least densely populated.

From a superficial study of the area and its present population it might perhaps be thought that there ought to be vast possibilities for expansion here, but this first impression becomes somewhat modified after a more detailed study of the soil conditions and the climate. Approximately 40 per cent of *Oceania* is in the tropical zone, and the remaining 60 per cent is in the sub-tropical and temperate zones. The possibilities of development in this region are, however, not so much conditioned by temperature as by the varying degrees of rainfall. In the northern parts of Australia the year is divided into a rainy season and a dry season; the rainfall being in the summer period (November–May). In the southern parts the rain comes with the antarctic winds, particularly in the winter period. The intermediate belt —apart from the eastern area which is influenced by the Pacific Ocean— has practically no rainfall at all and largely consists of unproductive desert. In addition there are areas where the rainfall can vary so much from one year to another that a period of favourable conditions for agriculture and cattle-breeding may be followed by a period of drought when the grass withers and cattle and sheep stocks have to be reduced. Furthermore, as evaporation generally takes place at a high rate this only leaves a relatively small part of Australia—i.e. in the south—where the conditions are really favourable for agricultural cultivation.

New Zealand is in the warm, temperate zone. On the whole it has an ample rainfall, but the topographical conditions are not too favourable for agriculture.

In fact only about 3 per cent of *Oceania* is under cultivation, but per head of population the area cultivated is nevertheless large in comparison with other regions. The possibilities of bringing more land under cultivation depend *inter alia* on the expansion of the artificial irrigation systems which already exist on a large scale. In 1956 about 0.7 million hectares (or 3–4 per cent of the cultivated area of Australia) were artificially irrigated. There are huge areas of natural grassland in *Oceania* but only a relatively small area of forest land.

The main crop in *Oceania* is wheat. Extensive cultivation is the normal method in Australia—but not in New Zealand—and apparently there has been a good deal of soil exhaustion which means that there is a danger of some cultivated areas becoming desert.

The great expanses of grassland provide the necessary basis for *Oceania*'s large stocks of cattle and sheep. The latter is the basis of a wool production that is almost half of the total of the world, whilst the former is responsible for a considerable production of butter, cheese and meat.

Among its other natural resources *Oceania* has supplies of iron, copper, lead, zinc and uranium as well as many other metals. Furthermore, there are good resources of coal and a considerable production of phosphates.

The main part of *Oceania*'s population is of European origin, with the result that the cultural pattern is similar to that of *Western Europe*. Throughout most of its recent history immigration has played an important rôle in *Oceania* and has contributed towards the considerable increase in population. So far in this century there has been an average increase of about 1.7 per cent per year. The population increase has been particularly marked since the end of the Second World War, partly on account of the high birth rate and partly because of the high level of immigration.

Compared with the total world production (measured in terms of the net domestic product) *Oceania*'s net domestic product is only small, i.e. a little more than 1 per cent. Per capita, however, the net domestic product in *Oceania* is a little more than that in *Western Europe,* though only about half that in *North America*. Although it is true that in a certain sense *Oceania* may be characterized as an agricultural region, it is in fact also highly industrialized and indeed the greater part of the population is employed in manufacturing industry and in services. Its manufacturing industries are, however, mainly based on home consumption.

In the post-war years a considerable portion of production went into investment. As far as can be seen[1] this has not, however, been reflected in any particularly noticeable increase in the net domestic product, but in view of the fact that investments in housing schemes and public works make up a large proportion of the total investment it is possible that the results of much of this investment will only become apparent after the lapse of a period of years.

Foreign trade is an essential factor in *Oceania*'s economy. In recent years exports and imports of goods and services have each accounted for 20–25 per cent of the region's net domestic product. *Exports* are mainly restricted to a few specialized products. Wool is the most important of these and accounts for more than 40 per cent of the total visible export trade. Food exports are on a similar level and among the main items are exports of grain, dairy products, meat, sugar and fruit. *Oceania*'s *imports* cover a much larger range of products. Apart from mineral oils it is chiefly manufactured

[1] In their official publications neither Australia nor New Zealand estimate the domestic product in terms of constant prices, which makes it difficult to estimate the rate of growth.

goods that are imported, including various kinds of machinery. *Oceania*'s exports are mainly directed to *Western Europe*—particularly the United Kingdom—and similarly the greater part of its imports come from *Western Europe*. In addition, *Oceania* does some trade with *North America* and *Asia*.

B. PROSPECTS

Although, as we have previously indicated, the possibilities of development in *Oceania* are not quite as great as one might at first be inclined to think from its total area compared with its present population, there is no doubt that the region has sufficient natural resources to be able to absorb the estimated population increase in the period up to 1980.

In view of the important part played by immigration in the growth of *Oceania*'s population, there is an added element of uncertainty in making a prognosis of the likely future trend of development in population. It is estimated that the average annual growth of the population will be 1.7 per cent in the period up to 1980. This corresponds to the average annual increase in *Oceania*'s population since the turn of the century, but the rate of growth is less than that during more recent years. In spite of this increase in population it is not considered likely that there will be any great increase in the available labour force. As in the other highly developed regions, it may be assumed that hours of work will be much reduced and that the period of apprenticeship and training will be increased. On the basis of assumptions which take these factors into account (cf. Chapter III) it is estimated that the average annual increase in the number of man-hours in the period up to 1980 will only be about 0.5 per cent.

As far as investment is concerned, it is not considered likely that the high investment quota of recent years will continue in the future. Although it is true that the saving quota has also been high it has on the whole been somewhat lower than the investment quota, which means that it is possible that the investment level will fall in the long run. Furthermore, the proportion of the net domestic product devoted to investment is a good deal lower in *Western Europe* and *North America* than in *Oceania*, and in view of the many similarities between these three regions both from the economic and the institutional point of view this comparison may possibly also indicate a somewhat lower investment level in *Oceania* in the years to come. It is thought, however, that in the period up to 1980 the investment quota in *Oceania* will be somewhat higher than in *Western Europe* and *North America*, i.e. on the assumption that the proportion of net investment to net domestic product will be something like 12–16 per cent.

Assuming that these will be the conditions for the development of the factors of production, it is estimated that the future rate of growth of *Oceania*'s net domestic product will be between 3.5 and 4.5 per cent annually. In forming an estimate as to whether the actual rate of growth will be more likely to approach the minimum or the maximum just quoted, undoubtedly one of the important factors to be borne in mind is the relationship between the prices of exports and of imports of the region. Owing to the fact that foreign trade plays such an important rôle in *Oceania*'s economy, it will be seen that a favourable development of export prices as compared with import prices will mean that the region will be in a position to develop its import trade, thereby achieving a noticeable increase in the sum of goods and services available for consumption and investment, and *vice versa* the effect will be the opposite if export prices develop unfavourably. *Oceania*'s exports are largely concentrated on agricultural products, and as mentioned in Chapter V it is most likely that on the whole demand for food products will rise more than that of other goods, which again should work in favour of *Oceania*.

4. *The USSR*

A. SURVEY

This region differs from the others in that it consists of one single State or Union made up of 15 separate and widely differing republics.

With an area of 22 million sq. km. (one-sixth of the world's land area) the *USSR* is the largest State in the world consisting of one continuous stretch of land. As a region it is equal in size to *North America*. Its population of 197 million inhabitants (1955) is equal in size to that of *North America*, *Latin America* or *Africa*. With about 9 inhabitants per sq. km. the *USSR*, like the two *Americas*, is a thinly populated region.

The distribution of the population is very uneven, with 80 inhabitants per sq. km. in the Ukraine on the one hand and completely uninhabited areas in North-East Siberia on the other. The central western areas are the main centre of the densely populated parts. The population becomes more sparse towards the North, the East and the South. This distribution results from the climate, the location of natural resources and the history of the various parts of the region.

Being a thinly populated region, the *USSR* is in a relatively favourable position as regards the number of its inhabitants compared with its agricultural resources. The area under cultivation—about 10 per cent of the total land area—could be expanded to some extent, but not as much as might perhaps be thought. This is due to the unfavourable climatic conditions in large areas of the *USSR*. In northern Russia and in North and East Siberia there is a short growing season because of the long and severe winters. In the southern parts of Russia and Kazakhstan the more favourable temperatures are often offset by drought which reduces large areas of land to semi-desert and desert.

The best conditions for agricultural cultivation are to be found in the "black earth" region which stretches from the western borders of Russia to the central parts of Siberia. It is in this belt that there are good possibilities for increasing agricultural production by more intensive cultivation.

The *USSR* has ample resources of timber, and this, no doubt, is one of the reasons why the area, as measured in Standard Farm Land, as shown in Table III. 2 is so much bigger than the productive agricultural area.

The *USSR* is also believed to have excellent mineral resources. Although large parts of the region have not yet been fully surveyed it is evident from the work done so far that it is rich in such resources.

Formerly it seemed as if the full exploitation of these resources would be hindered by the fact that they were largely to be found at great distances from the existing centres of population and industry. For instance, more than half of the *USSR*'s potential supply of hydro-electric power and of its total reserves of coal are situated in the thinly populated plains of Siberia. Transport by sea, which is the cheapest method of transport, can only be used to a limited extent and most of the rivers run in the wrong direction, i.e. North-South or South-North, whereas the need for transport is East-West and *vice versa*. The result of this is that 85 per cent of all the transport of the *USSR* is by railway, and about 1955 one-fourth of the *USSR*'s total coal production was still being used for this purpose. There is a growing tendency, however, in the direction of creating new industrial centres nearer to the sources of raw materials which will, no doubt, play an increasing rôle in the more economic exploitation of the natural resources.

It is estimated that the region has about one-fifth of the total energy resources of the world, including great resources of gas and oil. At the present time oil production is increasing rapidly (at an annual rate of 9–10 per cent), and in recent years the region has not only been able to meet its increasing domestic demand but has been able to export. The oil centres that have so far been developed are for the most part in the central and southern parts of the region, and a pipeline system is at present under construction to facilitate distribution and export. The coal deposits are more dispersed, and it is estimated that about 20 per cent of the world's coal reserves are in this region. Production is increasing at a rate of about 3 per cent per annum.

There is no reliable information as to the extent of the *USSR*'s deposits of uranium, but it appears that *Eastern Europe* and the *USSR* together have sufficient supplies to meet their needs.

Deposits of iron ore in the *USSR* seem to be ample, as also do the reserves of coking coal. This region also has the largest deposits of manganese in the world. It would thus appear to have the basis of raw materials that it needs for its planned steel production. Other metal deposits exist in varying quantities, among the most important of which are copper, bauxite, lead, zinc and tin. In addition, it appears that the region has deposits of several of the so-called rare metals which will, no doubt, play an increasing rôle in future metallurgy. Finally it may be mentioned that the *USSR* has considerable deposits of apatite, pyrites and potash, which should provide the chemical industry with a solid foundation of raw materials.

Finally, as regards resources in general it may be said that judging from developments so far it seems that only climatic conditions may stand in the way of the exploitation of the *USSR*'s deposits of valuable minerals. The Government of the *USSR* seem to aim at making the region as independent as possible, even if it is not always economically advantageous to do so.

As regards population, quite large-scale internal migrations sometimes take place, mainly as a result of State economic planning. Since 1939 the population of Siberia has increased by more than one-fourth, whilst the population of the Soviet Far East has increased by nearly three quarters[1]. At the same time there has been a strong trend towards urbanisation following in the wake of industrialization. In 1922 18 per cent of the population

[1] *Izvestia,* 1st May 1959.

lived in the towns (USA 56 per cent) and in 1955 the figure had gone up to 43 per cent (USA 64 per cent). As regards *Labour,* however, there are still large resources in rural areas, which will prove significant in the future when the children of the low birth-rate years of the Second World War reach the age when they will join the labour force. The war affected the population in other ways too, namely as regards the distribution of the sexes (there are at present 20 million more women than men) and the distribution of age groups, and these factors, too, will influence future figures for births and deaths.

Roughly three-quarters of the Soviet population belongs to the Slavonic language group. The remainder consisted, and partly still consists, of people with other languages, religions and forms of economic life. The forty years of communist rule have, however, contributed towards a levelling of cultural differences, and improved the educational standard of the population in the region as a whole. In 1926 practically half the population below 50 years of age was illiterate, but by 1959 the figure had been reduced to 0.5 per cent. The greater part of those who are still illiterate are over 50 years of age. Christianity still exists and the principal church is the Orthodox, but this is separated from the State and has its main adherents among the older generation. Russian is the official language, and school attendance is compulsory for all children between the ages of 7 and 16.

Among the various institutional factors that have influenced the economic growth of this region the most important is that for more than 40 years it has been politically, economically and culturally administered on lines laid down by a centrally directed socialist régime. After the revolution in 1917 the new régime immediately set about constructing an economic system which was to prepare the way for the spread of socialism and lay the foundations of a new society. To a certain extent this deliberately excluded the possibility of the original cultural factors being able to influence the economic growth of the region. It is sufficient to point out, that a plan of industrialization and urbanization was carried out to create a working class that was to be the basis of a socialist economic system. Simultaneously a politically reliable civil service was established to direct and control the execution of the plans for agriculture and industry. The support of the intellectuals such as scientists, civil engineers, managers and other officials was guaranteed, by making sure of their political reliability before granting them permission to study for their profession. By these means the régime tried to protect itself against institutional elements that might perhaps have had a restraining effect on the region's economic growth. At the same time the educational system was extended in such a way as to promote those cultural factors that encourage economic growth. Thus there was a very strong emphasis on education in technical and scientific subjects—an investment from which the *USSR* has clearly greatly benefited in recent years. In 1955 the number of students completing their higher education in the *USSR* was 179,000, as against 393,000 in the United States. On the other hand, for technical and industrial courses only, the figures were 66,000 against 23,000 in the United States. It is apparent that the leaders of the *USSR* have to a greater extent than those in any other region made use of the cultural factors in their society to promote economic growth.

As regards its present stage of economic development—as considered in this book—the *USSR* has been placed next to *Oceania*. This stage of development has only been reached during the last 25 years.

As far as employment is concerned, however, agriculture is still the principal occupation. In 1955, for example, 43 per cent of the population was engaged in primary occupations, 31 per cent in secondary and 26 per cent in tertiary occupations. It is characteristic of the rapid rate of development in this region, however, that the corresponding figures for 1928 were 80, 8 and 12 per cent respectively. Nevertheless the *USSR* can rightly be described as a developed industrial society, on the grounds, *inter alia*, that in 1955 40 per cent of its domestic product came from industry, mining and building, whereas agriculture, forestry and fishery only accounted for 28 per cent. These figures, viewed in conjunction with the previous figures, also illustrate the relatively low rate of productivity in agriculture, forestry and fishery and the reserve of labour that exists in these occupations.

For political reasons both agricultural and industrial production are directed towards maintaining a completely self-sufficient national economy. Indeed, there is hardly any other region that could be so confident of its own self-sufficiency. It is therefore only natural that there should be an all round development of industry, with the main emphasis on heavy industry as the basis for a rapid rate of economic growth. If the present aims of the *USSR* for a balanced economy are pursued the industrial sector will retain its peculiar structure, which is different from that of the other regions. At the same time there is a movement to disperse industry. Traditionally the greater part of it has been concentrated in the western part of the Soviet

Union, but since the Second World War great efforts have been made to develop industries in the eastern parts of the region which are rich in resources.

The whole of this economic development is taking place within a framework of carefully prepared long-term programmes. Thus in 1955 the *USSR* was in the middle of its Fifth Five-Year Plan, and to-day—after a short period of the Sixth Five-Year Plan, which was later abandoned—it is in its First Seven-Year Plan.

The estimates of national product in the centrally planned economies differ from those made in the western countries, primarily because they do not take into account the product of some of the tertiary occupations which do not directly contribute to material production. In Table I. 1 it will be seen that the *USSR*'s net domestic product in 1955 was 109 billion dollars. This is a very uncertain estimate. In order to make a comparison with other regions, the official estimate has been adjusted to take into account differences between the official rate of exchanges and a purchasing power rate (cf. Chapter I, p. 24 f) as well as differences in definitions, differences in the system of relative prices, etc. It goes without saying that these adjustments are very uncertain and the interpretation of the figure should thus be made with due regard to all the uncertainties.—In Table I. 4 the annual increase in the net domestic product for 1950–55 is given as 11.1 per cent; this is the official figure issued by the *USSR*. Whether the differences in the conceptions of national income in the East and the West mean that this rate should be reduced for purposes of comparison with western figures it is difficult to say. It may be added, however, that most western students of the Soviet economy are inclined to think that it should be reduced. Nevertheless the fact remains that the *USSR* has a high rate of economic growth—indeed one of the highest in the world.

The creation of CMEA[2] has resulted in co-ordination within the economy of the Eastern Bloc countries (excluding Mainland China); this co-ordination has, increasingly, taken the form of a division of labour, thus paving the way for an extension of intra-bloc trading. As a parallel movement to the activities of CMEA the *USSR* has made considerable loans to its member states. It is estimated that during the period 1945–55 loans totalling about 2 billion dollars were granted in this way.—The other member countries at present account for about three quarters of the *USSR*'s foreign trade.

---

[2] CMEA: Council for Mutual Economic Aid, also called Komekon.

An extensive programme of aid and grants to under-developed countries has been carried out since 1954. This programme, which has mainly political motives, includes trade agreements, technical and military assistance as well as gifts and loans, and is primarily directed to a few countries in *Asia,* the *Middle East* and *Africa.* By the middle of 1959 loans totalling 3 billion dollars had been made, 1 billion of which were allocated in 1958. One-third of the total loans has already been used, and 60 per cent of this, again, has gone towards military assistance. At the same time the trade of the *USSR* with the areas concerned has been doubled.

Since 1956 the region has considerably increased its trade with the developed countries in the West. In fact 25–30 per cent of the foreign trade of the *USSR* today is with non-centrally directed countries. Soviet exports are primarily raw materials such as oil, aluminium, gold, coal and grain, but they also include semi-manufactured and manufactured goods. This development is presumably due partly to the wish to market surplus production arising from the abandonment of the Sixth Five-Year Plan, and partly to the desire to import western equipment, which is needed for the implementation of the Seven-Year Plan 1959–65, particularly for the expansion of the chemical industry.

In 1957 the *USSR* exported goods to the value of 4,380 million dollars, which represents about 3.5 per cent of the total world trade. A little more than half of this went to *Eastern Europe,* one-fifth to Mainland China and one-fifth to *Western Europe* and *North America* together. The *USSR* has a net import of machinery, technical equipment and consumer goods and a net export of raw materials, semi-manufactured goods and grain.

As a whole, the *USSR* presents a picture of a developed region that is experiencing a process of rapid economic growth under a political system that appears to have made this development its principal aim. At the beginning of the period under review the *USSR* stood on the threshold of a new period of development in which its principle objectives were intensification of agricultural production, modernisation of the transport system, reconstruction of the power system, the creation of a large scale chemical industry and the development of the most neglected areas of the region. As a region it was self-contained to an exceptional degree, but politically it has been active vis-à-vis other regions. It had very little direct co-operation with the developed regions of the West, but at the same time it had an increasing political interest in economic co-operation with the West as well as, more particularly, with the under-developed areas. Finally, it maintained close contact with neighbouring countries under Soviet political domination, viz. *Eastern Europe* and parts of *Asia*.

B. PROSPECTS

The fact that the *USSR* plans its economic development for a period of several years at a time—at the moment for the seven-year period 1959–65 —should make it possible to form a more reliable prognosis of economic development for this region than for the others. As regards developments after that, however, any forecast must necessarily be made with the same reservations as with the other regions.

The relatively high birth-rate in the *USSR* (25 per thousand in 1958) together with the very low death rate (7 per thousand) means that at the present time a considerable natural increase in the population is taking place in this region. Nevertheless it is possible that the following factors may change this:

1) The birth-rate may possibly continue to decrease with the increasing degree of industrialization.
2) From 1960 onwards the groups from the low birth-rate years will reach the age when they can reproduce themselves.
3) The very low death rate will inevitably increase sooner or later as the age distribution of the population changes.

The effect of these factors will not, however, be fully felt until after 1980. The man-power necessary to meet the increase in production can be found by further reducing the reserve of *Labour* still existing in rural areas. This demand for *Labour* will be limited by the increasing use of mechanization and automation, but at the same time the available number of man-hours will be reduced on account of the reduction in the working week that is planned to take place over the period 1960–80 (about 25 per cent).

In the period under review it is estimated that the population will increase by 45 per cent, and this larger population will have to be supplied with food at a time when the standard of living will presumably be rising. This means that there will be an increased demand for food in this period. The little that is said on this subject in the Seven-Year Plan seems to indicate that the *USSR* intends to increase its agricultural production primarily by means of more intensive cultivation in the areas already under cultivation, and also that the necessary means to achieve this will be at the disposal of the agricultural producers. One of the principal aims will be to expand the production of fertilizers and increase mechanization and specialization. The biggest expansion will take place in industrial crops and livestock production. The target will be to more than double agricultural productivity.

Whether the *USSR* will be able to increase its production of agricultural products by at least 8 per cent per annum during the years 1959–65, will largely depend on the outcome of the various organizational changes in agriculture that are now being made. Generally it would seem that food production will be able to keep pace with the growing demand in the period up to 1980, and it is possible that the *USSR* will be able to increase its exports of grain to neighbouring regions.

As already mentioned, the region is one of the most favourably situated as regards resources of raw materials. The long-term plans emphasize geological surveying, and, in view of unfortunate experiences in the past, the planned rate of production of many raw materials is very high. Plans for a more effective exploitation of resources include the modernization of the transport system (pipelines, electrification, dieselization) and the creation of a unified national electricity grid. The relative importance of coal will be reduced by half by 1972, whilst the production of gas and oil will be increased by more than 100 per cent; a switch over that appears to be based on economic considerations, which will, in fact, reorganize power production on the same lines as in United States. Big increases in production are also being planned for many other raw materials. Thus the production of iron and steel is to be doubled within the next fifteen years. At the same time the aim is to employ both natural resources and capital equipment more economically. Also, the present process of decentralising the administrative machinery into economic regions appears to be based on the same motives.

The Seven-Year Plan envisages an annual increase in industrial production of 8.6 per cent. This is a lower rate of increase than in the previous periods, but judging by the results obtained in 1957 and 1958 it seems likely that this rate can be achieved. After 1965, however, when the Seven-Year Plan comes to an end, the rate of growth will presumably decline further. The capital goods industry is still the most important, with an annual growth rate of 9.3 per cent, as against 7.3 per cent in the consumer goods industry[3]. In the consumer sector one of the items that will undergo a big expansion during the first part of the period under review is that of housing construction. The great obstacle in the way of carrying out this part of the Plan appears to be the lack of skilled labour.

It is plain that great investment will be necessary to carry out such a large-scale plan of development for the exploitation of raw materials, for transport and agricultural and industrial production. It is perhaps not surprising, therefore, that the *USSR*'s estimates for gross investment assume an annual rate of growth of capital investment of 8.8 per cent.

At this point it should perhaps be mentioned that the *USSR* has now expanded its capital equipment to such an extent, and has for a long time maintained such a high rate of economic growth, that it is likely that it will result in an increased production of consumer goods which will not in itself, necessarily, prevent the high rate of investment. In other words the *USSR* can now afford to do more for the consumer, including making a bigger investment in agriculture. Roughly half of investment is estimated to go into industry, whilst the other half is divided between agriculture, housing construction (both with increasing shares of the total), transport, education and public health.

Within the industrial sector, the great emphasis laid on the production of gas and oil is clearly reflected in the target figures of the Seven-Year Plan. The same applies to the expansion of the chemical industry and to the production of steel and electric power. Forty per cent of investment is to be concentrated in the eastern parts of the region. It should be added, however, that developments in 1957–58 indicate that there may possibly be some difficulty in maintaining the planned investment rate.

The annual increase in the domestic product in the Seven-Year Plan is set at 7.3 per cent, which is 3 per cent lower than in the previous Five-Year Plan. This is, of course, only to be expected when one considers that the rate of increase in industrial production is less than it has been previously and that although agricultural production is still increasing it is doing so at a rate a good deal lower than that of industrial production. After 1965 the rate of growth will decline still further. Taking this into account, as well as the differences of approach to these concepts in the East and West mentioned earlier, it is assumed that in the 25-year period under review the

[3] As previously mentioned, these percentages may be taken to be higher than if they had been estimated according to western methods.

annual rate of growth (cf. Table VII. 2) will be between 4 and 5.5 per
cent (i.e. 2.5–4 per cent per inhabitant). In other words, the *USSR* will
have the highest estimated rate of growth of any region in the period 1955–
80. This growth will bring the net domestic product to between 291 and
416 billion dollars (or between 1,020 and 1,450 dollars per inhabitant).
This means that the region will gain ground in relation to the other developed regions, and indeed if the *USSR* can achieve a maximum rate of
growth and *Western Europe* and *Oceania* only achieve a minimum rate it
will surpass these regions. Nevertheless the *USSR* cannot achieve a per
capita net domestic product of more than about half that in *North America*,
even assuming a minimum rate of growth in the latter. However, it must
be remembered that this kind of comparison is at best purely theoretical, i.e.
taking into account the differences in the relative prices, the definitions of
concepts, the types of economic structure and the problems of the rates of
exchange. The fact that they are included is because the main purpose of
the *USSR*'s economic plans for the period under review is precisely to
ensure that the region's per capita production should "catch up with and
surpass" production in Western Europe and the United States. Even if we
view the matter in the most favourable light for the *USSR* it does not seem
that this goal can be achieved for production as a whole[4].

As previously mentioned, there has in recent years been a tendency for
the *USSR* to increase its trade with other countries, particularly with the
other Eastern-Bloc countries. Trade within this area is planned to increase
by 50 per cent in the period of the Seven-Year Plan. Apart from this, however, very little is known regarding future plans for foreign trade, save that
trade with the "capitalist" countries and the under-developed regions is to
be further expanded in the seven-year period.

Thus, although there does not appear to be any official plan for a large-
scale increase in the *USSR*'s foreign trade, there is reason to suppose that
apart from increased inter-bloc trade there will be an increase in trading
contacts with the other regions—and more particularly in the fairly modest
but highly political offensive towards the under-developed countries (including credit and loan programmes). In addition there are certain aspects
of the Seven-Year Plan that will presumably have to depend on supplies
from the West. In exchange the *USSR* will doubtless export raw materials

---

[4] Cf. also the discussion in Chap. VII (p. 267–271) "The West and the East".

—particularly grain and oil—as well as an increasing quantity of semi-manufactured and manufactured goods. The share of the total national product devoted to foreign trade is unlikely to increase significantly beyond the proportion that it occupies to-day, however. It is improbable that the *USSR* will become dependent on the other regions—even *Eastern Europe*—as far as the main lines of development are concerned.

5. *Eastern Europe*

A. SURVEY

Eastern Europe is here taken to mean East Germany, Czechoslovakia, Poland, Hungary, Yugoslavia, Roumania, Bulgaria and Albania. It is characteristic of these countries that, in contrast to the West European countries, they have a centrally planned economic system. With the exception of Yugoslavia, all the East European states have co-operated closely in the economic field since 1949 and more particularly in recent years.

With its 1.3 million square km. this region is one of the smallest of the nine regions. On the other hand, with its 112 million inhabitants (1955) it is the most densely populated (88 inhabitants per sq. km., cf. Table III.2). Only *Western Europe* and *Asia* have anything like the same density of population.

The region consists of several medium-sized countries with a relatively uniform average density of population, though East Germany is an exception with its very high density of 168 inhabitants per sq. km.

About 60 per cent of the total area of *Eastern Europe* is agricultural land. The greater part of the region has a temperate continental climate. There is a fairly heavy rainfall in the north-western part, which on the other hand has a relatively short growing season. Towards the South-East there is inclined to be a shortage of water in the summer and autumn months. An appreciable proportion of the agricultural area consists of cropland. There is little likelihood of the area under crops being extended to any appreciable degree, as the only potential reserve of land is forestland and this, again, is practically confined to the mountainous regions. The average yield per hectare is between one-half and two-thirds of that in *Western Europe* and has in fact hardly yet reached the same level as before the war. *Eastern Europe* is a net importer of food.

The region has rich resources of timber, 30 per cent of it being covered by forests.

As regards power supply, *Eastern Europe* is quite well off, though the natural resources are unevenly distributed. Poland, Czechoslovakia and East Germany have coal and lignite deposits that provide the basis for a well developed industry as well as affording a considerable reserve. Roumania, Hungary, Czechoslovakia and Poland have certain oil reserves; these are not sufficient, however, to meet the East European demand in the long run unless new sources of supply are found, but this may not be impossible. On the other hand, Yugoslavia, Bulgaria and Roumania are the only countries with resources of water power.

Most of the East European countries seem to have deposits of uranium, although this has only been explored on a large scale in East Germany and Czechoslovakia.

There are several deposits of iron ore, but the content of iron is low and with the extraction technique at present employed it is impossible to exploit them on an economic basis. Iron is therefore imported (from the *USSR*). Bauxite is found in large quantities in certain parts of the region, as also are several non-ferrous metals. East Germany has large deposits of potash and is at present the world's largest producer (25 per cent of the total world output), whilst Poland has considerable deposits of sulphur.

The greater part of the population lives in the north-western part of the region. The number of inhabitants is approximately the same as before the Second World War, due to war losses, compulsory transfers and emigration. On the whole *Eastern Europe* still has a low population increase (1.1 per cent, cf. Table III. 1), but in this case too the figures vary considerably from one country to another.

Urbanization has reached a high degree in the industrial areas in the north-western part of the region, whilst village communities predominate in the south-east. Whereas in East Germany and Czechoslovakia the greater part of the population is employed in secondary and tertiary production and there is a certain lack of *Labour* in primary production, the situation is the reverse in Yugoslavia, Roumania and Bulgaria, where a considerable reserve of *Labour* seems to be concealed among the agricultural population (cf. Table III. 5).

In the whole region the political system is built on the Soviet model. Even so there are significant cultural divergencies. The political situation is probably less stable in *Eastern Europe* than in the *USSR* as the centrally directed régime has been in power for over 40 years in the *USSR* and for only up to

15 years in *Eastern Europe*. The effects of the régime on milieu, culture and mental outlook in general may thus be assumed to be less marked in *Eastern Europe* than in the *USSR*.

From the point of view of its present economic standard (cf. Table I. 1), *Eastern Europe* has been placed immediately after the *USSR* as the least developed of the "developed" regions in the world.

Both as regards population and the net domestic product (51 billion dollars in 1955) it is a small region. *Eastern Europe* has 4 per cent of the total world population and 6 per cent of the total world income (i.e. somewhat above the world average). Within the region, however, the per capita production varies appreciably. East Germany, Czechoslovakia and Poland together account for more than 60 per cent of the region's total net domestic product.

Table I. 4 shows that the annual rate of growth for the period 1950–55 was 9 per cent. This is the official figure given for these countries, but it may be assumed that it is higher than the figure which would be arrived at by western methods of calculation[1]. Nevertheless the rate of growth was fairly high and there was also a high investment quota. In recent years there has been a decline in the investment quota, while at the same time the standard of living has been steadily increasing.

The various plans for economic development are co-ordinated by the Council for Mutual Economic Aid (CMEA)[2], comprising all of the countries with the exception of Yugoslavia.

Each of the member states is to concentrate on the production of the particular type of goods for which it has the necessary natural resources (or other economic advantages), and this again means increasing inter-bloc trading. Simultaneously, trading with the outside world is encouraged to the extent to which it will aid the principle of the division of labour.

A characteristic point in CMEA's planning—which is pretty detailed— is that the *USSR* now co-operates very much more than previously as supplier of important raw materials such as coal, coke, iron ore and rolling-mill products,—it should not be forgotten, either, that this co-operation has its political aspects.

Before the Second World War the region's economic connections with the outer world were characterized by the fact that it mainly exported

---

[1] Cf. the remarks on this subject in the section on the *USSR* (page 312).

[2] Synonymous with Komekon.

agricultural products whilst having to import corresponding quantities of industrial products. About two-thirds of the region's foreign trade went to *Western Europe* while intra-regional trade and trade with overseas countries accounted for the rest; the trade with the *USSR* being insignificant. Since the war, however, the region's ideological, political and economic relations with the *USSR* have, as already mentioned, necessitated a complete revolution in its economic structure and therefore also in foreign trade. Less than one third of its foreign trade now goes to the West, whilst the *USSR* absorbs 60 per cent of its exports. The region's total exports comprise 5 per cent of the total world trade. *Eastern Europe* and the *USSR* are therefore on the same level as regards total exports. Per capita, however, trade is considerably bigger in *Eastern Europe* than in the *USSR*.

Eastern Europe has provided certain loans for other countries. On the other hand, partly as a compensation for that, the *USSR* has extended considerable credits to East European countries.

In quite recent years there has been an increase in trade with *Western Europe* and *North America* and several of the East European countries—more particularly Poland—have acquired credits in the West. *Eastern Europe*'s inter-regional trade now appears to be consolidating, with the main emphasis being laid on trade with the *USSR,* with approximately 20 per cent of the export trade with *Western Europe,* a small but steadily growing trade with the *Middle East* and a small amount with *Asia, Africa* and *Latin America.*

From being a net exporter of foodstuffs—particularly grain—the region has become a food importer, whilst its exports consist largely of industrial products.

As mentioned earlier, Yugoslavia is not a member of the CMEA, and the above remarks concerning co-operation and foreign trade do not therefore apply to it.

All things considered, *Eastern Europe* would appear to be a region that is in a process of rapid economic growth, this development being encouraged by a political system that has presumably made this development one of its main aims. At the same time *Eastern Europe* is going through a period of transition, both as regards the co-ordination of economic planning between the various countries and as regards the levelling out of the big differences in the standard of development in the northern and southern parts of the region.

B. Prospects

The economic plans of the East European countries are, in themselves, a natural starting point for a study of the possible future trend of developments in the economic sphere. Several of the countries in this region are at present preparing Fifteen-Year Plans; Poland is, however, the only country that has published its total targets for the period up to 1972. The Fifteen-Year Plans are to provide a general framework within which the shorter and more detailed plans may be fitted to conform with the long-term objectives.

The relatively low rate of population increase in *Eastern Europe* (1.1 per cent, cf. Table III. 1) will probably decline still further in the period up to 1980 (Table III. 8), though with considerable variations from one country to another. The degree of uncertainty in the forecast is particularly high here, however. Thus, for instance, it is questionable whether the emigration from East Germany which gives this country a negative increase in population will continue on the same scale as hitherto.

It is estimated that by 1980 the population will have increased by about 30 per cent. As the standard of living continues to go up this population will have to be supplied with a relatively larger quantity of food than at present. This can be procured partly by purchases abroad and partly by increasing the region's own agricultural production. Both of these solutions are considered. The increase could be brought about by stepping up the yield per hectare and in most of the East European countries it is therefore also estimated that the annual agricultural production could be increased by not less than 3–4 per cent. In all of the countries a relatively bigger increase is foreseen in livestock production than in crops, and at the same time the increase in livestock production will be greater than hitherto. On the other hand the increase in food production cannot be expected to take place at the same rate throughout the whole of the period up to 1980, and neither is it likely that *Eastern Europe* will be completely self-supporting within the near future, as far as food is concerned (cf. Table V. 16). The results of the CMEA plans will first become apparent in some degree of specialization among the countries concerned.

As mentioned above, the region is relatively better off with regard to mineral resources than, for example, *Western Europe*. The long-term projects hitherto published provide for very substantial increases in the output of these primary commodities in order to eliminate the bottlenecks which in several countries had in the past been a limiting factor of their economic growth.

This is to be done, for example, by a further exploitation of lower grade deposits. At the same time the *USSR* will come to play a more prominent rôle as supplier of raw materials. This is one of the reasons why the countries of *Eastern Europe* now seek to co-ordinate their economic plans with the Seven-Year Plan of the *USSR*. It is especially iron ore and oil which the *USSR* is to supply in the years to come. A re-arrangement of energy production, which corresponds to the development in the *USSR* is planned. A project of very intimate East European cooperation in the field of power production (including unification of the electric power systems) has also been agreed upon.

Old antagonisms based on national traditions cannot be regarded as having been wiped out; it is not impossible that if conditions should become unfavourable to the régime some of these deep-seated antagonisms between the peoples of *Eastern Europe* could suddenly flare up again. One sensitive point, in particular, is that of the problems resulting from the division of Germany. In the same way the relations between the people and the régime in some of the states are to a certain extent unstable; this may occasionally manifest itself in conflicts, which in their turn will have an adverse effect on economic life. In this connection one can call to mind not only the rising in Hungary in 1956 but also the constant state of antagonism between the Catholic Church and its adherents on the one hand and the régime on the other. It is, however, quite clear that the creation of the people's democracies has been the signal for the introduction of many political, social and economic reforms which in the long run should have a positive influence on the possibilities of economic growth in this region.

In Table VII. 2 the annual increase in the net domestic product in *Eastern Europe* is estimated to be 2.5–4 per cent (per capita 1.5–3 per cent) in the period 1955–80. This is a lower figure than that observed for the period 1950–55. It must, however, be taken into account that the plans themselves assume a lower rate of increase than previous plans.

All the East European countries are at present going through a period of rapidly increasing investment, which is a necessary condition for, and a natural consequence of, the reorganization of production now taking place (cf. above). The lack of information on planned rates of increase in total fixed investment, changes in stocks and government expenditure, and in some countries on changes in personal consumption, make it difficult to assess the planned changes in the net domestic product. One thing is clear, however, namely that the rate of growth in consumption is planned to decline substantially in all countries (except Bulgaria). Nevertheless consumption itself is steadily increasing, and the margin between rates of increase planned for domestic product and consumption is everywhere smaller than in the past, which means that the standard of living must still be regarded as being on the increase.

It should be remembered that although there may be many economic arguments pointing to a stronger or weaker growth in *Eastern Europe* it is the political developments in this region as well as those in the *USSR* that are the deciding factor. The decisions as to the investment and production targets are political in character. It goes without saying that in the final issue it is economic laws that determine to what extent growth will be fostered, but within this framework it is the political aspect that will guide the actual turn of events. *Eastern Europe* has both sufficient resources, labour and investment possibilities to enable the present considerable rate of growth to be maintained. The fact that we are going through a transitional period does not, however, make it any the easier to estimate the future rate of growth, and it does not seem to be possible to get nearer to the heart of the problem than to forecast a 2.5–4 per cent growth, as mentioned earlier.

The trade with the *USSR* and *Western Europe* will presumably be stabilized at the same relative level as at the present time, though in the case of the latter region, the future problems of trade will largely depend on how the various European market plans develop. The relatively small trade with the underdeveloped countries may increase during the period under review. It may also be assumed that the present policy of credits and loans to these areas will be continued although it is doubtful whether there will be any question of giving net credits (cf. the loan policy previously pursued by the *USSR* in regard to *Eastern Europe*, page 321). Again it must be emphasized that the trend of developments in trade and commerce will also depend on decisions made at the political level, although it appears that in recent years economic arguments have carried more weight in internal discussions.

Yugoslavia has not been included in the forecast of the future outlined above. As far as the planned economic development of this country in general is concerned, this is not essentially different from the CMEA countries. On the other hand attention should be drawn to the fact that the trend in Yugoslavia's trading relations will continue to be more in the direction of the West than holds true for the rest of *Eastern Europe*.

6. *Latin America*

A. SURVEY

Latin America comprises an area of about 20 million sq.km., and in 1955 it had a population of close to 185 millions, corresponding to about nine inhabitants per square kilometre. In other words it is a thinly populated region. Both in area and density of population it can roughly be compared with *North America*.

The climate is mainly tropical and sub-tropical; only the narrow strip of land in the south stretches into the temperate zone. A particular feature of this region is that the area that cannot be used for agriculture, i.e. the mountainous or desert area, is relatively smaller than in the world as a whole. The area suitable for agriculture, forestry or grassland is, in terms of Standard Farm Land[1], large in comparison with the total area of the region, and the number of square kilometres of SFL is greater than in any other region. *Latin America* has about 3.5 times as great an area of SFL per inhabitant as the average for the world as a whole.

The actual area under cultivation is, however, not as large as might be expected in such favourable conditions. This is largely due to the fact that considerable parts of the region are extremely thinly populated and, related to this, lack adequate means of transport. Even so, the region is estimated to have greater possibilities for expanding its agricultural and forestry areas than any other region—with the possible exception of the *USSR*. Any such expansion will, however, depend partly on large-scale investment being made in means of transport, and also on a successful campaign to enlighten the population about methods of tackling the problems of a tropical climate —in particular those of soil erosion, tropical diseases, and the reduced working capacity of both human beings and domestic animals, especially in the vast lowland area around the river Amazon and its tributaries.

Latin America has considerable mineral deposits. Venezuela produces oil on a large scale and is in fact the second largest producer in the world. Oil is also found elsewhere in *Latin America*. On the whole, however, the region has not yet been systematically explored for oil and other minerals.

[1] Cf. Table III. 2.

There are very large deposits of iron ore, especially in Brazil, and also in Venezuela and other countries. Other metallic ores such as copper, lead, tin, and zinc are mined in considerable quantities, particularly in Mexico and in the countries of the Andes area. In addition there are deposits of antimony, apatite, bauxite, manganese, and sulphur, etc.

A weakness in Latin-American mineral resources, however, is that there appear to be only minor reserves of coal. This is a disadvantage both for the exploitation of the large reserves of iron ore and also for the general development of industry. It means that other methods will have to be used than those traditionally employed and that other sources of power will have to be exploited, such as oil, natural gas and water-falls. Presumably there are plenty of the latter, but to some extent they are to be found in areas that are still relatively isolated, such as among the many tributaries of the Amazon.

The population of *Latin America* is far more mixed than that of any other region of the world. Before the Europeans discovered America the population was Indian (Mongoliform). During the period when Spain and Portugal divided the sovereignty of South America between them, it was naturally Spaniards and Portugese who colonized the region. Later, many emigrants came from Italy, whilst only relatively few came from Northern Europe and elsewhere.

A new element was added to the population by the large influx of slaves from Africa, who were mainly used for work on the plantations in the tropical areas on the Caribbean islands and the countries surrounding the Caribbean Sea.

No measures have been taken to separate the races in *Latin America,* with the result that in the present population the three main racial elements have become mixed in a variety of combinations. In the temperate area in the South, however, the European element still predominates, whilst the African element is particularly concentrated around the Caribbean archipelago. Finally, the original Indian racial characteristics become more and more dominant towards the relatively isolated areas in the interior of South-America.

The period of European colonisation has clearly left its mark on Latin-American *Culture*. The immigrants from the Iberian peninsular became the dominant class, and they introduced their language, their religion—and the feudal system. At the present time Portugese is spoken in Brazil, but apart from this Spanish is the universal language of the region, with the exception of the little island republic of Haiti, where the language is French. The Catholic Church is firmly established throughout the region, and the feudal system of land ownership has persisted to the present day—often with huge areas of land belonging to a single owner. At the same time there are many smaller properties, some of them run on the system of subsistence farming.

Nowadays there are only a few, small colonies in European hands. The remainder of the region long ago shook off colonial rule and now consists of twenty independent republics—apart from the island of Puerto Rico, which is a commonwealth associated with the United States.

Originally the various Latin-American countries drafted their constitutions on the same lines as that of their great North American neighbour. In practice, however, they have frequently been subjected to dictatorships, and coups d'état—often organized by army officers—have been a prominent feature of their history. Nevertheless, such revolutions have not made very much difference to the daily lives of the inhabitants.

There is at present a considerable degree of illiteracy in large parts of the region, often as much as about 50 per cent and in some countries up to 70 and 80 per cent of the population. In the temperate zone in the South, however, the majority of the population can read and write, and in most of the countries the standard of education is improving.

The *economic conditions* in *Latin America* can best be summarized by stating that among the four regions characterized as under-developed *Latin America* is the most advanced. The greater part of the population is still engaged in farming—though on the whole a somewhat smaller proportion than in *Asia* and *Africa*—and to a certain extent agriculture is run on a large-scale commercial basis with the export trade particularly in view. Industrialization has progressed rapidly in recent years, and in some countries it is feared that it is being forced too much at the expense of agriculture. It should be remembered that the rapid increase in the population results in a corresponding increase in the demand for food, but on the whole agricultural production has increased too slowly. This is reflected in the fact that, in spite of its considerable reserves of arable land, Latin American exports of grain and meat to other regions have declined compared with the pre-war period.

It is in fact in the central, tropical areas of this region that we find the characteristics of economic life peculiar to the underdeveloped countries.

Civilization has made greater strides in the North and in the South—particularly in the sub-tropical and temperate zones of the South—and indeed one can hardly call Argentina, and certainly not Uruguay, under-developed countries. In Mexico a rapid development has also taken place, and the same applies to Venezuela, particularly on account of the enormous income derived from oil.

The region has a considerable export trade with the rest of the world, particularly in primary products. *Latin America* can certainly be said to belong to the category of primary exporting countries and this is reflected in its national economy. In 1956 the region's total exports of primary products amounted to 6.5 billion dollars (at 1950 prices). Half of this was tropical agricultural products while the exports of mined products amounted to 2.5 billion dollars.

Oil constituted the largest of the individual items (1.9 billion dollars), with coffee as the next largest (1.7 billion). Other important export commodities are sugar, cotton, wool, meat and metals, of which copper is the most important.

This means that the region is very sensitive to fluctuations in the demand for primary products from the industrialized countries, and in particular from the United States and *Western Europe*.

An increasing world-demand for these products is usually reflected in higher prices and larger quantities of goods exported. The relatively stagnant state of the industrial countries in the years between the two world wars thus had an adverse effect on the Latin American economy. From about 1935 to 1957, however, there was an improvement in the export terms of the region, resulting in a considerable economic growth; the net national product (measured in terms of fixed prices) went up by nearly 5 per cent a year.

The greatest amount of foreign trade is with the United States, both as regards exports and imports. Indeed the United States—where the demand for imports of raw materials is steadily increasing—regards *Latin America* as one of its principal sources of supply. There has also been a growing political interst in the United States in conducting a "good neighbour" policy and in helping the other American republics. Thus a considerable amount of capital has been imported from the United States, partly in the form of direct investment by American firms and partly through public channels such as, for example, the Point Four Programme. At the same time a reverse movement has been taking place in so far as some wealthy Latin Americans have placed some of their capital in the United States.

Generally speaking, *Latin America* presents a picture of a region that is, at present, under-developed, but where considerable economic growth has taken place over a long period of years. Quite a large part of the more developed forms of economic life is controlled by United States firms or capital. This may account for such feelings of distrust and suspicion as may exist in *Latin America* of "The Colossus in the North". As a whole, however, it seems that this situation is gradually improving. This is of some significance in view of the fact that the United States would seem to be destined to play a significant rôle in the development of the Latin American economy over the next few decades.

B. PROSPECTS

The population is increasing at a tremendous rate in *Latin America*— at a greater rate than in any other region—and if it continues at this rate throughout the period under review it will be doubled by 1980. It is, therefore, essential that production should be increased rapidly if the standard of living is to be improved simultaneously. There would appear to be a good natural background for such an increase in production, and as the labour force will also be steadily increasing it should not be necessary to find extra capital in a very high proportion to the increase that takes place in production.

The marginal capital/output ratio has indeed been rather low, viz. 2.5–3 in the period 1951–56. If we estimate on the basis of 2.75 for the period 1955–80, an annual increase in the net domestic product of well above 4 per cent (close to 1.5 per cent per capita) would require a net investment of 11–12 per cent of the net domestic product.

The actual investment quota for the period 1951–56 was approximately 11, which is high for what is largely an under-developed region. The chances of maintaining such a high quota, and if possible even increasing it, will depend, more specifically, on the conditions for Latin American exports and on the amount of *Capital* that can be imported.

The region's export trade is dominated by primary products, which mostly go to the industrialized regions. *Latin America's* exports of raw materials to *North America* and *Western Europe*, i.e. its two most important buyers, have been estimated by the ECE[2], assuming an annual rate of growth in *North America* of about 2.80 per cent and in *Western Europe* of 2.38 per cent, to increase from 3.5 billion dollars in 1954–56 to 6.5 billion in 1975 in the case of *North America,* and from 2 to 2.5 billion in the case of *Western Europe.*

The rate of growth in *North America* assumed by ECE is lower than the average of the figures given in Chapter VII, and since the import of raw materials in the industrial countries increases in relation to the rate of growth—as they are obliged to import an increasing proportion of their consumption of raw materials—the figure for 1975 would seem to have been estimated very conservatively.

A significant factor will be how the price relationships between primary products and manufactured articles develop in the future. If the rate of economic growth in *North America* approaches the figure of 4.5 per cent, mentioned as the maximum in Chapter VII B, which would also mean a considerable increase in the imports of raw materials, it would be a reasonable conclusion—as *Henry G. Aubrey*[3] puts it—to assume that price relationships will develop in favour of primary commodities, and in that case it is not impossible that the export to *North America* and *Western Europe* will be in the neighbourhood of eleven billion dollars in 1975. This would correspond to an annual increase of 3.25–3.50 per cent in the period 1955–75 for this part of the Latin American export trade, and presumably this progress would continue in the years up to 1980, especially if the assumed rate of growth in *North America* comes into effect.

Thus it is anticipated that the income from the export trade will be increasingly from *North America,* and Aubrey also assumes that the increase in United States' imports of important primary products will largely come from *Latin America.* This again means that industry in the United States will presumably be interested in investing in mining and the exploitation of other natural resources in *Latin America.*

On the whole there seem to be fairly good prospects of finding *Capital* for the necessary investment. Provided the price relationships develop favourably it looks as if it might be possible for the region to finance an increasing proportion of the necessary investment out of its own saving, and in this way it should be possible to restrict increases in capital imports from

[2] UN (1958, d, Chap. V, p. 12).
[3] Aubrey (1957, p. 169).

the United States and thereby also limit Latin American dependency on that country. A high rate of economic growth in the United States is, therefore, of primary importance for *Latin America,* as it means an increased revenue from exports.

Presumably the increasing exports will be provided by mining and tropical agriculture, in particular. It will, therefore, be necessary for future development for a further exploration of the tropical areas to be made and for the conditions for the maintenance of health and of the productivity of the soil to be studied. At the same time it is possible that there may be a quite considerable export of non-tropical agricultural goods (cf. Chapter V B).

However, a rate of growth of, say, 4 to 4.5 per cent would mean a big expansion of the Latin American home market. The total income will probably rise 150–200 per cent during the course of the period, and if the per capita income is increased, an increasing proportion of the total income will be used for industrial goods and services. The process of industrialization may, therefore, be assumed to continue.

On the other hand it may be assumed that more importance will be attached, relatively, to the development of agriculture than has been the case in the past 20 years, when the production of non-tropical farm products has not kept pace with the population increase. This is partly due to the fact that in the naturally fertile area of the pampas, in the temperate zone in the south, the farmers have employed methods of cultivation that have seriously reduced the productive capacity of the soil[4].

Nevertheless it is to be expected that the drift away from agriculture to secondary and tertiary forms of production will continue, *inter alia,* because agriculture is being increasingly mechanized—more particularly in the temperate grain-producing areas. This in its turn will mean that urbanization will presumably advance at a rapid pace. However, a marked degree of economic growth—for which it would appear there are favourable natural and financial conditions—will not be achieved unless a very much larger proportion of the population is given training and instruction in those subjects which a modern industrialized community requires to a far greater degree than do more primitive economies.

On the basis of the estimates made in Chapter VII it may be possible, under favourable conditions, for *Latin America* to achieve a net domestic

---

[4] UN (1959, b, p. 175).

product per capita by 1980 that is not much lower than that for *Eastern Europe* in 1955. If this can be done it may truly be said that in the course of the period under review this region will have succeeded in breaking the vicious circle of poverty, and the expression "under-developed" will generally speaking, no longer apply to it.

However, even if the external conditions for this—and in particular the development of the North American market—are present it will be necessary for the region to make a great effort to improve its general cultural level and especially to raise the standard of education of the masses.

7. *The Middle East*

A. SURVEY

The *Middle East* is here taken to include the countries where *Europe, Asia* and *Africa* meet. Turkey, Cyprus and Egypt are included in this region. It has an area of 6.5 million sq. km. and a population of nearly 100 million corresponding to an average density of 15 persons per sq. km. over the whole area[1]. The density of the population is twice as great as that of *North America* or *Latin America*. In terms of Standard Farm Land the density is 50 per sq. km.

These average figures do not illustrate very well the actual natural conditions, however, as the greater part of the area consists of uninhabitable mountain regions or deserts. Thus, the density of the population varies enormously within the region, with the cultivated areas in Egypt—where there are 600–700 persons per sq. km.—at the one extreme and at the other the huge areas on the Arabian peninsular, where scattered desert tribes live in almost complete isolation.

Generally speaking the standard of living of the inhabitants in this area is very low—in some cases being at just about the same level as in the poorest parts of the world. The region has very little trade with the surrounding world. It is true that its share in world trade has increased noticeably, but it still only amounts to 4 per cent of the total; this corresponds to a foreign trade per inhabitant equal to that of the world average, but this level has only been reached on account of the dominating importance of oil.

For centuries this region has served as an important link and transit

[1] Cf. Table III. 2.

area between *Europe* and *Asia,* and since the Second World War it has also become extremely important because of the increasing oil consumption in the world. In addition, it is of considerable political and strategic importance on account of its position near to three continents.

Only a small proportion of the total area of 6–7 million square kilometres is cultivated land—certainly less than 10 per cent. In view of its climate— a long, hot and dry summer and a mild winter with very little rain—the chances of increasing the area under cultivation would mainly seem to lie in expanding the system of irrigation which is at present the basis of a major part of the agriculture of the region, e.g. in the area between the Tigris and the Euphrates and along the banks of the Nile. This would seem to be possible both from the technical and the economic point of view. In addition it should be possible to expand agricultural production by reducing the area lying fallow and by a general improvement in the methods of cultivation.

The *Middle East* has on the whole very little forest land. It is only in the north that there are any large forests, and these are no longer of any great economic importance. The consumption of wood is lower than in any other region.

With the exception of oil there are no mineral resources of any importance either, though it should be remembered that the region has not yet been completely surveyed geologically. There are some deposits of chromium, copper, lead, silver, etc., but these are scattered and give only a low percentage yield.

On the other hand the oil deposits seem to be the richest in the world. Almost two-thirds of the world's known reserves are to be found in Iraq, Iran, Kuwait and Saudi Arabia (cf. Table V. 19). Moreover, the oil is of a very high quality and the production costs are low partly because the oil does not have to be pumped up and partly because all the wells produce unusually large quantities. Taking into account these very large energy resources, we get a very significant picture of the economic state of the region if we consider that the consumption of energy is only the equivalent of about 250 kgs of coal per capita per year (1955), i.e. lower than all the remaining regions but *Asia*.

From the racial point of view the region is rather mixed, though the population mainly consists of Caucasiforms. Culturally, however, the region may be regarded as homogeneous, inasmuch as a series of features point in the direction of a common cultural background. Thus, there is a common language over a large part of the area, and similarly the religious differences are relatively small. Furthermore, for centuries large parts of the region belonged to the Ottoman Empire and have thus acquired similar systems of law and administration. Finally the production methods show a large measure of similarity, the greater part of the population living as small farmers with the same primitive forms of cultivation and conditions of property ownership.

One of the countries, however, is essentially different from all the others in this region, namely Israel. With its own language and religion, a relatively highly developed economy, and with strong ties with many of the Western forms of Culture, it is in a category of its own.

As regards the standard of education the *Middle East* is not really essentially different from other under-developed areas. As will be seen from Table VI. 1 three quarters of the population may be assumed to be illiterate. In recent years, though, extensive plans for the development of the educational system have been made.

As regards the political situation events in recent years have clearly shown that conditions are far from being stable. Constitutionally the countries vary from monarchies to republics, but it is evident that the practical application of the terms of a constitution may be totally different from its formal wording. In most of the countries, parties, in the Western European sense, are not of any great importance, whilst individuals and groups of persons are the dominating factor.

As will be seen from Chapter I (cf. Table I. 1) it is estimated that the net value of the production of goods and services as measured by the net domestic product at factor costs was something like 15 billion dollars in the *Middle East* in 1955. In terms of per capita income this places the region lower than *Latin America* but higher than *Asia* and *Africa*.

At the same time it should be mentioned that conditions vary a good deal within the region. For one thing the economic level measured in terms of the net domestic product per capita is considerably higher in Turkey than in Syria and Saudi Arabia—quite apart from Israel, where income and production are at a totally different level than in the rest of the *Middle East* and are in fact more in line with some West European countries. Secondly it should be borne in mind that the distribution of income in the region— just as in most of the under-developed areas—is evidently more uneven than for instance in *Western Europe* and *North America*. This must be taken into account when using the average figures for the whole region as a basis for conclusions regarding the standard of living of the mass of the population.

Over the whole of the region—with the exception of Israel—one finds an economic structure typical of those found in the under-developed areas. The greater part of the population live an isolated life as small farmers; they cultivate the land by primitive and not very productive methods, often on the basis of a neglected irrigation system; they have extremely little contact with those parts of the community where a monetary economy exists; their relations with the State are limited to the payment of taxes and conscription to the armed forces; a considerable portion of production—it is said not to be unusual for it to be up to one half—has to be handed over to a landowner living in the town, various forms of share-cropping being common.

In the northern parts of the region the crops consist of rye, barley and wheat. In the south the crops consist of maize and rice as well as some millet. In addition dates are grown, particularly in Iraq. Cotton is important, especially in Egypt which is responsible for 5 per cent of world production. In fact, cotton accounts for three quarters of the total exports from Egypt.

The urban population of the region, for the most part, make their living by running small shops or workshops. In cases where they have achieved a high degree of skill in the handicrafts this is the result of encouragement from the consumer habits of the upper classes and of a specialized export trade. Similarly trading is run on a small scale and is adapted to local requirements.

Some estimates put the part of the population working in manufacturing industry as being between 10 and 15 per cent, but by far the majority of these undoubtedly consist of handicraftsmen.

It is a characteristic feature that apart from such manufacturing industries as are usually found locally—for instance the cement industry—the existing industry is for consumer goods—such as textiles.

There is a remarkable contrast between the general technical and industrial level and the oil industry, which has reached a level of technical perfection which is comparable to, say, the best in *Western Europe*. In actual numbers the employment of local labour in the oil industry is insignificant. Nevertheless experience in this industry shows that the local population can be trained to fulfil the demands of highly developed industrial production satisfactorily.

About 1955 the region produced as much as 20 per cent of the total world production of oil. The various foreign companies operating the oil wells have, by agreement, to pay royalties to the individual countries. Since the early nineteen fifties the general rule has been that the profit on production should be divided "fifty-fifty". In addition, the region benefits from the oil industry by the fact that both current production and large-scale investment [2] stimulate local economic activity. Finally the oil countries have agreements whereby they get preferential treatment in buying oil for their own consumption.

The importance of oil to the region is illustrated by the fact that oil makes up two-thirds of total exports. In exports as well as imports *Western Europe* is the main trading partner of the region, with 40–50 per cent of the trade. Characteristically, exports consist of a few raw materials. Apart from oil these are grain, cotton and various kinds of fruit. In the same way as many other under-developed countries, this region will therefore be very sensitive to changes in the prices of raw materials.

B. PROSPECTS

Whereas in area as well as in population the *Middle East* is among the smallest of the regions dealt with here, its rate of population increase has in recent years been among the biggest in the world (cf. Table III. 1). It is probable that this population increase will continue in the future. Thus, it is estimated, that the population will be doubled in the next 25 years. This estimate is based on the assumption that production, especially agricultural production, will rise considerably in large parts of the region. It should be remembered that the general level of income is still very low so that it can hardly be expected that the fall in the birth-rate that normally follows industrialization and urbanization will manifest itself very quickly here.

The region seems to have a fair chance of enjoying a significant increase in production during the years to come. Improvements in agricultural methods will make a large-scale expansion possible, and the foreign currency earnings

---

[2] During the first ten post-war years foreign investments in the region totalled 1.5 billion dollars. Of this amount 90 per cent constituted oil investments, the remainder being invested in Israel.

and transactions connected with oil production seem to provide a suitable background for the initial steps towards industrialization. It is well known that most of the under-developed countries encounter difficulties over their balances of payments and that these are naturally aggravated by an attempt to industrialize. This, however, is not the case in certain parts of the *Middle East*. In recent years this area has received more than one billion dollars a year in royalties, and there does not seem to be any danger of the oil reserves being seriously depleted within the period under review. Furthermore the enormous increase in world consumption of oil together with the prospects of oil reserves in other parts of the world running out will increase the importance of *Middle East* oil assets. This is, *inter alia,* the background for the assumed rate of increase of per capita income, cf. Table VII. 2.

For the purpose of this study we may perhaps divide the region into three groups of countries. The first group includes the countries with only small oil reserves but where there are the beginnings of economic growth. This obviously applies to Israel and presumably also to Cyprus as well as to Turkey, where industrialization began in the years between the two world wars. This process has accelerated considerably in the post-war years, when industrialization has been forced up to an even higher level due to the investment of foreign *Capital*. In 1948 industrial production in Turkey had already reached a level that was 30 per cent higher than the pre-war level. One important indication of the stage of industrialization in Turkey is that heavy industry is fairly well developed. On the other hand Turkey's constant balance of payments difficulties has forced it to restrict its expansion.

In Egypt there are some signs of the beginning of true industrialization. At the same time agricultural reforms are being planned in the matter of parcelling out land and regulating the relations between fellah and landowner. Here again currency difficulties are a major stumbling block to the development now beginning. The other major difficulty is the pressure of the constant increase in population which has so far largely outweighed the increase in production.

For centuries Lebanon has had a production level that would appear to exceed that of the average of the region. It has a tradition of considerable foreign trade, partly based on transit traffic. In the post-war years agricultural production has been significantly increased by means of irrigation schemes. The country appears to be laying the foundations for industrialization, but this has hardly started yet and is unlikely to do so at any great speed for the next 10 or 20 years.

It is questionable whether Syria should be included in this group at all. The justification for including it would be the agricultural reforms—improved irrigation schemes and parcelling out of land that have been introduced in recent years. It is doubtful, however, whether a true industrialization will be got under way during the next twenty years. In any case any developments in this direction will depend to a large extent on foreign capital investment.

The second group covers the oil countries. Apart from oil, the production in these countries is on the whole very small. In Iran and Iraq, however, some development has taken place both in agriculture (irrigation and land reforms) and in publicly subsidized industry. The background for these developments is the influx of foreign exchange obtained from the sale of oil. In the sheikdoms around the Persian Gulf there are barely sufficient possibilities of domestic production to employ the whole of the revenue from oil. Provided conditions remain more or less stable, however, these countries would seem to have a very good chance of being rapidly industrialized.

There is little hope of a similar development in Saudi Arabia, however, which not only has practically no natural resources—apart from oil—but where the royalties on oil on the whole seem to go into (conspicuous) consumption.

The third group includes countries that are historically known as the poorest in the region: Jordan, Aden, Yemen and certain sheikdoms on the Persian Gulf. With their very meagre resources these countries presumably have very few possibilities themselves of initiating economic growth within the foreseeable future.

From these remarks it may be concluded that the differences in the standard of living within the region will become greater as time goes on. Other factors must, however, also be taken into account in judging the future possibilities of the region. One important factor is the political instability that prevails in large parts of the region. Not only will this stand in the way of the conscious planning of economic policy but it may delay the process of development by discouraging foreign capital investment and foreign technical assistance. Characteristically enough, it seems as if an element of instability appears simultaneously with a slight improvement in the standard of living. The question is, then, whether it is possible to stimulate economic growth at such a rate that the troublesome elements are kept satisfied. At the same time it seems that a more or less profound social revolution is essential in certain areas if the process of economic growth is to be started or encouraged at the rate desirable.

In addition it should be mentioned that with the possible exception of Lebanon, and also obviously of Israel, one of the serious handicaps to development is the lack of industrially-minded groups. Industrialization, whether it is carried out by semi-public enterprises or by private enterprise, cannot be accelerated unless there are groups willing to accept the responsibility and risk and have the ideals and the attitude towards life that have been the force behind the process of growth in other countries. Even so no economic growth is possible at all without a conscious national policy. One of the first serious obstacle to be overcome, therefore, is the lack of public officials with sufficient vision and initiative.

8. *Asia*

A. SURVEY

Asia has by far the largest population of the nine regions, viz. about 1,400 millions, which is more than half of the total world population. *Asia* has an area of 21.7 million sq. km., which is only about 16 per cent of the total area of the world; in other words *Asia* is approximately the same size as either *North America, Latin America* or the *USSR,* but somewhat smaller than *Africa.* Furthermore, a part of the total area consists of desert and inaccessible mountain areas, thus leaving only some 9 million sq. km. that can be regarded as productive, i.e. arable land, pasture and forest. Even allowing for the fact that there are favourable conditions of climate and soil in a large part of the productive area of the region, it is obvious that *Asia* has the greatest pressure of population of all the regions in relation to its production possibilities. It is true that two of the smaller regions, viz. *Western Europe* and *Eastern Europe,* have an equally dense population, but these relatively highly developed regions can better afford to invest sufficient capital in agriculture for an intensive exploitation of their farming resources. Both *Western Europe* and *Eastern Europe* are, also, relatively rich as regards other resources so that they have been able to build up their industrial production on a large scale, and at the same time to exchange their surplus industrial goods for agricultural products.

22*

As regards supplies of other natural resources *Asia* is also, on a per capita basis, in the least favourable position. It appears to have only limited oil reserves; among the "proved reserves" the most important are those in Indonesia and British Borneo, but in recent years some new oilfields have been discovered in Mainland China. The region has fairly large deposits of coal, but Manchuria is the only place where their quality and location are suitable for large-scale exploitation. The same kind of restrictions also apply in the case of iron ore deposits.

Moreover, *Asia*'s resources both of arable land and mineral deposits are unevenly distributed over the various countries of the region, and as both from the geographical and from the economic and political points of view *Asia* is divided into "sub-regions" certain countries are far worse off for natural resources than might be expected.

Taking the region as a whole, however, it may be said that its huge population and its relatively modest resources are already an obstacle to efforts to raise production and the standard of living. The problems caused by this population pressure will presumably become intensified as time goes on.

Asia's population seems to be increasing at least at the same rate as the world population. Since the end of the Second World War the death-rate has gone down appreciably almost everywhere in the region, but only in Japan has there been a marked decline in the birth-rate. Whereas in the period 1930–40 the annual population increase for the whole of the region was about 12 per thousand, it was about 17 per thousand in the five-year period 1950–55.

As the fall in the death-rate has especially affected the infant mortality, the big population increase will manifest itself particularly in a big increase in the number of children. The increase in the productive age groups will not make itself felt until later.

The governments of some countries in *Asia*, recognising the population problem, have recommended measures for restricting the number of births; so far, however, these measures have only been effective in the case of Japan, where the number of births per year have been halved since 1945. India is still at the experimental stage; Mainland China, after a great intensification of family planning propaganda during the period 1956–58, seems now to have suspended it again[1].

[1] See for instance the Report of an Indian delegation to China in 1959, (Chandrasekhar, 1959).

The population of *Asia* is largely Mongoliform, particularly in China, Japan, Korea (chiefly the "younger" racial groups), Burma, Thailand, Indo-China and Indonesia (chiefly the "older" racial groups). The 500 million or so inhabitants living in India, Pakistan and Ceylon, however, are Caucasiforms, as also are the relatively small population groups of European origin.

Asia's cultural pattern is very varied and there are important differences between the "sub-regions".

The population of *Asia* is concentrated in the big river valleys and on the larger groups of islands, and each of these population centres has bred its own form of *Culture*. Such "sub-regions", with their own specific types of *Culture,* are to be found for instance in the Ganges-Brahmaputra area (India) and along the East Chinese rivers of the Hwang-Ho and Yang-tse-Kiang (China), as well as to a lesser degree in the Mekong valley (Burma, Thailand). The two most important island cultures are Japan and Indonesia.

These racial and cultural differences will have to be taken into account in making a prognosis of the possibilities of future economic growth in this region, but it is difficult to try to assess how much importance should be given to cultural elements in such a prognosis (cf. Chap. VI), and care will, therefore, have to be taken in drawing any definite conclusions from the cultural pattern. For example it would no doubt be wrong to assume—as is often done—that Japan's cultural milieu is the only one of the main Asiatic cultures that is favourable to economic growth, on the grounds that Japan has hitherto been the only country where industrial development has taken place on European-American lines. It is true that the economic developments in Japan are witnesses to the fact that the Japanese cultural pattern has so far been favourable for economic growth, but it is questionable what conclusions may safely be drawn concerning the relationship between the other cultures and economic growth from the fact that no similar economic developments have taken place elsewhere.

From the political point of view Mainland China (including North Korea and Vietminh) differs essentially from the other Asiatic countries. Since the revolution in 1949 it has been more and more influenced by the economic, social and cultural changes that have been taking place under the communist régime which culminated in the creation of the People's Communes in 1958–59. Since Mao-Tse-Tung assumed power the rate of economic growth in Mainland China has—judging from the evidence available[2]—been considerably more marked than in any other Asiatic country. This will undoubtedly raise serious economic and political problems for the rest of the countries of *Asia* if they cannot achieve a similar rate of growth. In this connection it is presumably of minor importance if it should be proved that China is more favoured than the rest of *Asia* as regards natural resources.

The level of education is low throughout the region; apart from Japan illiteracy is common, varying from about 50–60 per cent in China to about 80 per cent in India and even higher in the other sub-regions (cf. Table VI. 2). Education plays an important part in the current Five-Year Plans of the various Asiatic countries, but even if mass-communication methods such as radio and films are used extensively it will be some time before the effects will be felt. It is not only a question of teaching the people to read and write but also—and this is equally important—of allowing them to adjust themselves to new working methods and living habits. It is not yet possible to say to what extent a profound social revolution such as that now in progress in Mainland China can help this process of cultural readjustment.

With the exception of Japan and China all the bigger countries of *Asia* are in a process of transition from a colonial administration to national independence—which in most cases coincides with internal political emancipation. This aspect of *Asia*'s political development is undoubtedly of great importance for the economy of the region. The transition to national independence is often accompanied by a breaking down of traditional trade patterns as well as by a change of direction in internal economic policy. From being a supplier of raw materials to a mother country and a market for the latter's finished products, the tendency now is for the Asiatic countries to sever their connection, economically, with the mother country partly by building up a home industry of manufactured goods—supported by subsidies and import restrictions— and partly by spreading their foreign trade over a greater variety of products and more countries. This sometimes means that in the transition period there is a flight of *Capital* from the colonies to the mother country which impedes the development of new industry. At the same time the process of internal political emancipation will tend to

[2] Although the higher rate of growth in China is, to a certain extent, due to the extraordinarily low level of production after the civil war which ended in 1949, it seems that the growth rate continued at a high level even after 1952, when production reached pre-war standards.

strengthen the desire of the peoples for a higher standard of living, and this will further aggravate the problem of accumulating *Capital*.

All these symptoms of transitional difficulties have been found in several of the Asiatic countries since the end of the war. These problems, and the increased pressure of population, have made it extremely difficult for the new rulers to promote economic growth.

In this critical situation most of the Asiatic countries have, however, been favoured with relatively stable political conditions—and this incidentally also applies to Japan and the communist régime in Mainland China. The governments concerned have been strong enough to restrain the people's desire to increase consumption, and as a result the price levels have remained relatively stable in most of the countries during the period since 1955, and not inconsiderable resources have been available for investment (though this applies more especially to Japan and China).

The greater part of the population (approximately 65 per cent in the region as a whole) is employed in subsistence farming. The yield per person is so low that only small consumption is possible. Only in Japan and also in recent years in Mainland China, and to a certain extent in India, has industry been of importance[3].

The low income level—lower than in any other region—means that both consumption and the accumulation of *Capital* are necessarily greatly restricted. Hence industrialization and increased agricultural productivity through greater mechanization can only be realized slowly.

In dealing with economic conditions in *Asia* it should be borne in mind that Japan is unique. It has a good deal higher average income per capita than *Asia* as a whole—approximately 200 dollars as against approximately 60 dollars—and it has already completed the first stages of industrialization and has at present more than 50 per cent of its population employed in secondary and tertiary occupations.

Until the end of the Second World War the bulk of the countries of *Asia* were, as already mentioned, colonies and largely dependent on their mother countries. Their foreign trade consisted, as far as exports were concerned, chiefly of a small number of raw materials, whilst imports were mainly industrial consumer goods from the parent country.

Since the end of the War, however, this pattern has gradually changed.

[3] A Survey of the post-war industrialization in *Asia* is published in UN (1959, f) pp. 66–159.

The export trade still consists of relatively few primary products (rubber, tea, rice, vegetable oil, tin, sugar, jute and cotton together make up more than half of the total), but the markets for them are becoming gradually more wide-spread, whilst the former parent countries now buy less than previously. At the same time the sum of exports has declined from about 15 per cent of total world trade to only about 10 per cent. The changes in the import trade have been even more marked. Imports of consumer goods have decreased, whilst the proportion of investment goods has increased; and at the same time suppliers have changed, with the United States gradually increasing its proportion of the trade whilst the European share has declined. As far as Mainland China is concerned, the *USSR* is its chief trading partner.

The declining export trade and the changes that have taken place in the import trade have resulted in the balance of trade which was favourable before the War now being adverse. This has been remedied by large-scale imports of *Capital*—primarily from the United States, but also to a certain extent from the *USSR* and some of the countries of *Western Europe* (mainly the United Kingdom and Western Germany).

It should, however, be emphasized that *Asia* (excluding Mainland China) is still very dependent on other regions. The nature of its export trade is such that the income from it is very sensitive to fluctuations in the prices of raw materials. At the same time long-term economic plans are dependent on imported investment goods which has resulted in *Asia*'s economy now being even more sensitive to import fluctuations arising from changes in export earnings.

B. Prospects

The main problem which *Asia*'s economy will have to face during the period under review will be lack of resources—primarily arable land—in relation to the big, and still rapidly increasing, population. Even if other resources are discovered in the future, such as deposits of oil, coal, iron ore, uranium, etc.,—and this is not impossible, as large areas of the region have yet to be explored—this will only partly make up for the lack of arable land. Even without an increase in the present very low per capita food consumption the estimated population increase (approximately 900 millions) over the 25-year period up to 1980 will demand such a big expansion in agricultural production that a large proportion of the small investment means available will have to be allocated to agriculture in order to satisfy the demand for food.

The shortage of arable land relative to the rapidly increasing population and the lack of investment resources have been the principal reasons for the low estimated rate of growth in per capita income in the period under review, viz. *minus 0.3 per cent* per annum under minimum conditions, corresponding to a decline from about 75 dollars per capita at present to approximately 70 dollars per capita in 1980, and *plus 0.7 per cent* per annum under maximum conditions, which would imply an increase in income to 90 dollars per capita in 1980.

Whether the maximum or the minimum estimate for per capita net domestic product will be achieved or not will be decided by the increase in population and agricultural production, and the availability of local and foreign capital.

In Chapter III it is estimated that Asia's population will increase by rather more than 2 per cent per annum during the period under review. This figure is based on the assumption that the death-rate will continue to decline and the birth-rate will continue at the present level. Of course, a major decline in the birth-rate from the beginning of the period would alter this prognosis, but it is improbable that there will be any decline until the latter part of this period. Even if a satisfactory method of family planning were to be discovered in the near future—i.e. a method that could be used with little trouble and at small cost—it would be many years before the method became known and popularised throughout *Asia*. As mentioned previously it is only in Japan, which is relatively highly developed, that the birth-rate has so far been reduced. There is little chance of similar reductions in India and Mainland China within the first decade or so.

In Chapter V the opinion is expressed that *Asia* has only limited possibilities of increasing its agricultural production. The only countries with relatively favourable conditions as regards agricultural resources are Burma, Thailand and Indo-China. The maximum increase in agricultural production for the whole region is estimated to be approximately 60 per cent for the period under review, i.e. an annual rate of growth of 1.88 per cent, compared with a population increase—as previously mentioned—of rather more than 2 per cent. In other words, even under the maximum estimate for the development of agriculture, there will be a steadily increasing demand for imports of foodstuffs if the consumption per inhabitant is not to decline. In Table V. 16 an estimate of the extent of this import demand is given at about 1,000 million crop units by the year 1980, corresponding in value, in 1955 dollars, to more than 6 billion dollars. Obviously such large-scale imports of foodstuffs will make it more difficult for the Asiatic countries to find the necessary *Capital* to import machinery and tools for their industrial investment projects. To-day, *Asia*'s trade balance with other regions already shows a deficit, partly because its pre-war net food exports have been replaced by net imports—on a modest scale—of food.

If production and per capita income are to be increased, or even to be maintained at the present level, it will be necessary to invest considerable sums in agriculture and other forms of industry as well as in schools, roads, harbours, etc. It is doubtful whether the countries of *Asia* will be able to save enough to finance these investments themselves, and it is probable that considerable capital imports will be necessary from the other regions if the standard of living—which is already lower than in any other region—is to be raised or even maintained at its present level.

The possibilities for future economic development, however, vary considerably in the individual "sub-regions" of *Asia*. Japan is unique among the countries of *Asia* in that in spite of its lack of natural resources it has reached a stage of economic development where growth is to some extent self-sustaining. The country has considerable real *Capital* both in agriculture and also, more particularly, in industry, and the level of education is a good deal higher than in any other country of *Asia*. Furthermore, the changes in the trade patterns that are now taking place in the other countries of *Asia*, whereby the main emphasis in imports is for investment goods such as machinery and tools, are working in Japan's favour by creating new markets for its industrial products.

In the other "sub-regions" Indonesia has a significant population pressure, whilst at the same time both internal and external political difficulties tend to slow down the process of economic growth. Burma and Indo-China also have political disturbances that hinder the Government in carrying out a policy to increase economic growth, but on the other hand this part of Asia is relatively rich in natural resources, especially arable land and forests.

In the region as a whole, however, it is the conditions prevailing in Mainland China and India that will be decisive as far as economic development is concerned. It may be useful, therefore, to examine some of the various problems that will be of importance for the economic development of these two countries during the period under review. These problems are of particular interest as China and India represent two completely different types of community as regards the manner in which they are trying to promote the development of production and improve the standard of living. China, on the one hand, is centrally planned to a high degree and has close connections with the *USSR* and *Eastern Europe*. India, on the other hand, has an economic policy designed on the lines of western political traditions.

These two countries, together, have more than two-thirds of the total population of *Asia,* and the way in which their national economies are developing will decide whether *Asia* can overcome poverty or whether it will succumb to a Malthusian cycle in which the shortage of food will limit the increase in population.

In the post-war period both those countries have taken vigorous measures to promote economic development, and in both cases some progress has been made in agriculture and more particularly in industry during the course of the First Five-Year Plans. The greatest progress seems to have been achieved in Mainland China, where the authorities keep a detailed control over every stage of production and where the so-called Peoples' Communes have mobilized all available *Labour* to help in the national production drive. In India, on the other hand, it has been necessary to reduce the targets several times during the course of the present Five-Year Plan. One of the causes of this has been that the unfavourable prices that exports have realized in recent years have aggravated the shortage of investment capital.

In both countries a good deal of emphasis is laid on industrialization— in China particularly in the heavy industries—and the official plans for the distribution of investment show that the greater part of it is for the development of new industries and the expansion of those already existing. However, to discern the trend of economic developments over a longer period of time it is necessary to take due account of the importance of agriculture. Even under the most favourable conditions it will only be possible to raise the standard of living very slowly. In other words in 1980 the greater part of the population's total consumption will still be food, as it was in 1955. In both countries the increase in population will presumably continue at the present rate for at least the next decade or so, and this means that there will be a rapidly increasing demand for agricultural products[4]. If, therefore, Mainland China and India cannot satisfy this demand out of their own domestic agricultural production there will, as previously mentioned, be such an increased demand for food imports that it will be difficult to satisfy the need for imports of industrial goods (including machinery and tools for investment).

It would seem that the governments of both countries in their First Five-Year Plans invested too little in agriculture—presumably because they thought that the necessary production increase could be achieved without such investment. In recent years, however, following poor harvest years in both countries, the picture has changed. Agriculture has been given more consideration in the general economic policy, and in both China and India it appears that certain changes have been made in the distribution of *Capital* and *Labour* in favour of agriculture.

The creation of the Peoples' Communes in China in 1958–59 had as one of its main purposes an increase in agricultural production, although this step was ostensibly taken in order to mobilize all available man-power.

The fact that more *Capital* and *Labour* are being directed to agriculture, however, will mean that in both countries the plans for industrialization will be dependent on help from the outside to a greater extent than was previously recognized. On the other hand, as the two governments represent two different political systems there is an increasing likelihood that they, and the other countries in *Asia*, will find the governments of the more developed countries willing to increase their loans and grants to them.

The fact that there is such a big difference between the estimated rate of investment for the period 1955–80 under the minimum and maximum conditions (i.e. 6 per cent and 11 per cent respectively, cf. Chapter VII B) is because of the uncertainty in making a prognosis of India's and China's ability to find sufficient investment capital.

As regards the question of the extent to which cultural factors may influence economic developments in *Asia*, there is, of course, a continual interplay between these factors and the prevailing economic conditions. If agricultural production and consumption do not expand adequately the retarding effect of the cultural factors will be more noticeable (i.e. in political and social disturbances), and *vice versa* if the economic difficulties can be suc-

---

[4] In addition, a large part of the new industry is based on raw materials such as cotton, tobacco, etc.

cessfully overcome at this critical stage it will be easier to solve the various problems of cultural adjustment.

9. *Africa*

A. SURVEY

In the present context *Africa* includes the whole of the African continent with the exception of Egypt. This region has therefore a total area of approximately 29 million square kilometres and a total population of approximately 200 millions (1955). *Africa* is bigger in area than any of the other eight regions. Its population, however, may be compared with those of the *USSR, North America* and *Latin America*. Hence it has a low population density; in 1955 there were about 7 persons per sq. km., and within the region there are only a few areas with more than 10–20 persons per sq. km.

Africa is primarily a tropical region. Its tropical belt covers more than three-quarters of its total area and contains a similar proportion of its population. A considerable part of tropical Africa is covered with forests. In the area nearest to the equator these are predominantly rainforests; but further to the North and South the landscape takes on the character of savanna, the countryside being more open and the precipitation less abundant. The borders of the tropical areas are largely semi-arid or arid, and consequently there are extensive desert areas both in the northern and southern parts of the region.

The northernmost and southernmost parts of *Africa* have a sub-tropical climate—with winter rains and mediterranean vegetation in some places—but even here there are large areas that are subject to drought.

Owing to dry climate and inaccessibility, large parts of the region cannot be exploited. According to Table III. 2 only about one-third of the total area is productive, i.e. farmland, pasture and forest.

If we estimate the region's agricultural resources in terms of Standard Farm Land (SFL) there are, however, only two regions, *Oceania* and *Latin America*, that are more favourably placed as regards the number of persons per square kilometre SFL. In 1955 there were 14 persons per sq. km. SFL in *Africa,* and at the same time *Latin America* had 10 persons per sq. km., while—at the other extreme—*Asia* had almost 100 persons.

Africa is, therefore, among those regions where there is a favourable relationship between agricultural resources and density of population. It is doubtful, however, whether these resources can be exploited under the pre-

vailing social and economic conditions in the region. It should be emphasized that most of the agricultural resources are to be found in the tropical
area—where both man and animals face serious difficulties from the environment. If these resources are to be exploited the difficulties thus arising from a hot and humid climate must be overcome, at least partly, and
that again requires an advanced agricultural technique and modern tropical
hygiene. But very few farming societies of the region have, in fact, reached
a stage in their economic and social development that permits them to apply
these methods in an attempt to utilize the resources.

The same applies to the exploitation of the mineral resources and water
power. It is well-known that *Africa* has a wealth of ferrous and non-ferrous
metals. South Africa, in addition, has rich coal deposits and North Africa
has been proved to have considerable reserves of oil. Tropical Africa seems
to be rich in water power, while it has only limited resources of coal and oil.

However, there are only relatively few areas where this mineral wealth
is being exploited for the benefit of local industry. An exception to this is
the Union of South Africa, which has already developed its industry to the
point where it can utilize its natural resources. A similar development seems
to have been initiated in North Africa.

In tropical Africa only a few isolated areas, where European immigration
and residence have left their influence, have achieved a similar level of
development. The mineral wealth that is exploited in these "island communities", however, mostly supplies the industries of other regions as the
ores and metals are mainly exported to *Western Europe* and *North America*.

The majority of *Africa*'s 200 million inhabitants are Negriforms; especially in tropical Africa, where both young and old Negriform types are to
be found. The older racial groups are rather to be found in the central parts
of *Africa* in the rain forest belt, whilst the younger racial groups live in the
more accessible areas outside this belt.

Although *Africa*'s Negriform population seems to have similar racial
characteristics it is by no means uniform; language, religion, economic and
social life vary from one tribe to another, and the tribes themselves vary in
size. As a whole, however, the peoples of Central Africa have remained in
small isolated communities almost uninfluenced by the currents of civilization that have gradually influenced the cultural patterns and economic life
of their neighbours.

The peoples of North Africa, at the other extreme, have had the closest contacts with other nations and have always been influenced by migrations and civilizations from the rest of the Mediterranean area.

In the history of Central Africa there has been little organization of states, although there have been examples in the surrounding areas, such as the Mali Kingdom and Ethiopia as well as the kingdoms along the Mediterranean coast.

When European countries colonized *Africa* the indigenous peoples became subject to European countries and the region was divided into colonies, protectorates and other forms of dependent area.

The moves towards independence that are at present taking place in former colonial territories are characteristic of *Africa*'s present political life. The process of political and national emancipation in *Africa* has, however, created difficulties, partly because of the immigrants from the parent European countries settled in the dependent areas—mainly of South, North and East Africa. The number of such settlers is small compared with the indigenous population of *Africa*, but this immigration has been important for the development of economic and political life in the region.

The clash between these immigrants and the indigenous populations of *Africa* has, *inter alia,* paved the way for a number of serious race conflicts, the root of which lies in the fact that the "European" population fears losing its economic and political supremacy over the non-European majority. The European minority is trying to retain its power by means of segregation and other coercive measures. Part of the price of these is a growing spirit of resistance among the other racial groups.

The unrest and the disturbances resulting from the struggle for independence have also brought into conflict the traditional ways of life, still observed by the old tribal communities, and the new attitude to life of those groups of the population working for political freedom. On the one hand this struggle may bring about changes in the cultural patterns of these peoples which, anyhow, seems to be a condition for economic growth. On the other hand, there is a danger of internal difficulties arising in the newly founded States, such as the disorders that have already been witnessed in West and Central Africa.

It will be seen, therefore, that the rulers of the newly independent States are faced with many problems, which are aggravated by the primitive economies and the low cultural level—as considered from the point of view of growth—of the majority of *Africa*'s population.

There is widespread illiteracy in this region—between 75 per cent and 80 per cent of the population in 1955—but education is increasing, particularly in tropical West Africa. The numerous languages hinder the development of these educational programmes, however. In tropical Africa there is the further difficulty that there are few languages that can be written.

The economic conditions in the region are largely determined by the fact that agriculture is the most important occupation. Some three-quarters of the population lives directly from the land, but the production per capita is low and is usually little more than enough to satisfy the needs of the family. In some instances subsistence farming produces occasional crops for the market, and in some districts agriculture is now being gradually changed to market production.

It is obvious, however, that under these conditions income, consumption and saving are at a low level, and the formation of *Capital* is very limited in most of the African communities.

These particular economic conditions would appear to prevail especially in tropical Africa, where economic growth is not only restricted by illiteracy and primitive social conditions but also by the tropical milieu itself. Owing to the danger of cattle diseases, caused by the tse-tse fly, it is impossible to keep cattle in the greater part of Central Africa, and in these parts human beings are also exposed to the danger of constant illness due to the unhealthy environment.

Nevertheless there are more favourably situated parts of the region, where Europeans have settled and have a share in the agriculture, plantations, mining and industry, and where economic life has reached a higher stage of development.

As already mentioned, the descendants of the Dutch and British immigrants have created a modern society in the sub-tropical parts of South Africa. For this they were favoured with good natural resources in the form of easily accessible farmland and a wealth of useful minerals. This has resulted in the level of income in the Union of South Africa being higher than in the region as a whole. In sub-tropical North Africa (Tunisia, Morocco and Algeria) there are signs of a similar development under the auspices of the French colonial settlers and with the help of French Capital, although in recent years this has been greatly hindered by political unrest which has resulted in foreign Capital being withheld or even withdrawn.

There are, however, also some prosperous "islands" in tropical Africa.

On the East African plateaux and around the rich mineral belt in Central Africa European settlers have, with the help of funds from their parent countries, created communities with a highly developed economy, but these communities have only affected the economic life of a few of the neighbouring tribes. In tropical West Africa European initiative has also resulted in the foundation of similar centres which might conceivably be used as bases for further economic growth; in this case, however, a larger proportion of the African population has been affected by the economic activities of the Europeans, than is the case in East Africa.

These prosperous "islands", which are mainly under European administration, are a growth-promoting element in *Africa*'s economy. However, current political unrest is in many cases a potential threat to the prospects of continued economic development in large parts of the region.

Since the war most of the "parent countries" have invested considerable sums in their former colonies and dependencies in *Africa*. A large part of this investment has been made in social overhead *Capital* such as communications, education, etc. Investment, however, has also been made in agriculture and power supplies. This is especially so in the former British and French colonies.

In spite of this investment, however, the public services available are still poor; throughout the greater part of the region the transport network is extremely primitive.

Economic relations between Africa and the rest of the world have developed along the lines of the African dependent areas exporting raw materials to their respective parent countries and the latter supplying manufactured goods in return.

This pattern of trade can still be discerned in spite of the change in status of the former colonies. Indeed, in some cases, their economic dependence on the rest of the world is as great as ever because they have to rely on foreign financial and technical assistance in order to carry out their economic development plans.

Africa is, thus, predominantly an exporter of vegetable and mineral raw materials. In 1955 the exports of ten raw materials, only, earned more than two-thirds of its total income from foreign trade. The main items were tropical plantation products such as cocoa, coffee, sugar, fibres and various metals such as copper, chromium, cobalt, iron and uranium. *Africa*'s imports on the other hand consist mainly of manufactured goods.

The direction of this international trade was in 1955 still determined by the close economic ties between the individual dependencies—or former dependencies—and their parent countries. In most cases the latter were responsible for about two-thirds of the trade of the colonies concerned.

Africa's trade balance with the rest of the world is on the whole adverse, its deficit being accounted for by capital imports, mainly from *Western Europe*. In this connection it should be mentioned that the export earnings of most of the countries in *Africa*—like those of other countries producing raw materials—are very sensitive to price fluctuations of raw materials. This is a factor of great importance for investment in *Africa* as export earnings make a valuable contribution to industrial investment.

In fact, however, there seems to be a growing demand for *Africa*'s export products, and this has perhaps contributed towards increasing the desire to invest in the region's economic development. Large sums of foreign *Capital,* both public and private, have gone to *Africa* in the post-war years, and as a result *Africa*'s long-term economic plans rest on a rather solid foundation.

B. Prospects

As indicated at the beginning of this survey, it is unlikely that *Africa* will have the same kind of problems as regards the relation between its population and its resources that *Asia* will have in the years to come. In this particular respect (i.e. resources compared with population) *Africa* resembles *Latin America,* which is more favourably placed than the other underdeveloped regions.

A considerable extension of the area under cultivation is still possible in many parts of the region, and as much of the area already under cultivation is exploited extensively it is likely that the increase in food production will keep up with the increase in population. This is all the more so as it is generally assumed that the growth of the population will only be moderate in the period under review.

As may be seen from Table III. 8 it is estimated that the population will grow at the rate of 1.6 per cent per year, or a little less than the world average, and by 1980 *Africa*'s population will therefore have increased by 50 per cent to 290 millions. This low rate of increase is based on the assumption that the death-rate will continue to be high throughout the greater part of the period. That is to say, it will not be until towards the end of the period considered, that *Africa* will reach the rate of population increase of *Asia* and the other under-developed regions.

The natural conditions for a process of economic growth would therefore appear to be relatively favourable. Nevertheless it is probable that the region's economic development will be fairly limited during the period under review, because it will be difficult to mobilize the other factors of growth that are essential if the natural resources are to be fully exploited.

A point to which particular attention should be drawn in this connection is that there are in *Africa* certain political, cultural and purely human difficulties which may possibly prove to be more of a hindrance to its economic development than these normally encountered by under-developed communities in trying to break the vicious circle of poverty.

There is, of course, no way of judging the extent to which these factors may influence the trend of *Africa*'s economic development, but they cannot be ignored.

One complex of problems already seems to have arisen in connection with the achievement of political independence which—as mentioned above —is now being realized in this region. It is not only a question of possible clashes between former dependent areas, which are either already independent or are in the process of achieving independence, and their respective parent countries, but also of conflicts between the settlers from the parent country (who thus loose the protection of their parent country) and the African population. Clashes of this kind will—especially if they lead to open conflict—naturally have a retarding influence on the process of economic growth already set in motion by the parent country and the settlers. Political events in the past in North, East and South Africa show that conflicts of this kind are likely to arise.

Other political problems also seem to occur in and between the African States during the process of their formation and also after independence from their parent countries is achieved. If these problems should lead to disputes on territorial or internal political matters this will also tend to retard the process of economic growth.

In other words, the political conditions appear to contain certain unstable elements that may prove to have a retarding effect on the economic growth of the region.

However, even if the political conditions remain stable and generally favourable to economic growth other conditions may not be so in parts of

Africa. This is partly because it takes time to alter the old cultural patterns in the primitive agricultural communities (cf. Chapter VI) where the greater part of the population of tropical Africa still lives. This may be done relatively easily in the areas around the coastal towns and the various other prosperous "islands", for it is here that the new attitude to life will be cradled (i.e. an attitude adjusted to a modern economy) because of the frequent contacts of their peoples with this type of community. In the hinterland of Central Africa, however, the process will presumably take very much longer owing to the poor means of communication and the big language difficulties.

These examples of possible retarding elements in the growth factor *Culture* illustrate the scepticism with which many research workers view a too optimistic belief in rapid economic growth in *Africa*. This scepticism seems justified, and is reflected in Table VII. 2 where it is estimated that the per capita income will increase by 0.9 per cent per year under minimum conditions and by twice that amount under maximum conditions of growth. Under these conditions the per capita income will be 130 and 166 dollars respectively by 1980, which means that *Africa* will have reached the same income level as the enjoyed by the *Middle East* in 1955.

Whether the minimum or maximum conditions will prevail will largely depend on how *Africa*'s economic contacts with the rest of the world develop. The region's export earnings will, no doubt, continue to be based on the production and export of tropical products and raw materials of mineral origin. These earnings will partly decide the possibilities of investment during the period under review.

The question as to whether the region will be able to meet its demand for *Capital* by its export earnings will depend, *inter alia,* on the consumption of raw materials in *Western Europe* and *North America*—the two regions to which it is expected that *Africa*'s exports will continue to go.

It must, finally, be recalled that for growth to be started huge sums are needed for investment in social improvements (including education), and in fact, it is most likely that *Africa* will continue to be a capital importing region. On the other hand, *Africa* seems to be a relatively profitable place for the investment of foreign *Capital*—due to its having good resources of certain raw materials that are becoming scarce in Europe and the United States. But political developments will of course greatly influence the extent and direction of such capital imports.

It would appear probable that public funds will continue to be sent to *Africa* from *Europe* and the United States in the form of loans and grants. In addition the *USSR* may offer the newly independent countries Capital. In this way they may become the object of a political struggle between the West and the East to gain or maintain influence in the under-developed regions.

Another source of progress may be sought in the further development of the prosperous "islands" that are to be found both in North Africa and in tropical Africa. In these areas, however, the part of the population that would appear to have the ability to direct such a process of economic development are now at enmity with the remainder of the African population, which is at present struggling to gain political power in the areas concerned. The outcome of this struggle will have a great effect on several important factors in the structure of *Africa*'s economy.

Bibliography

Ashton, E. H.

"The Endocranial Capacities of the Australopitheci-
nae", *Proceedings Zool. Society.* London 1950.

Ashton, E. H. and Spence, T. F.

"Age Changes in the Cranial Capacity and Foramen
Magnum of Hominoids", *Proceedings Zool. Society,*
London 1958.

Aubrey, Henry G.

United States Imports and World Trade, Oxford
1957.

Aukrust, Odd and Bjerke, Juul

"Realkapital og Økonomisk Vekst 1900–1956", *Ar-
tikler, 4, Statistisk Sentralbyrå,* Oslo 1958.

Bagby, Philip

Culture and History, Prolegomena to the Comparative Study of Civilizations, London 1958.

Banco Central de Reserva del Peru

Renta Nacional del Peru 1942–1956, 1958.

Baranski, N. N.

Die ökonomische Geographie der USSR, Berlin
1957.

Barnett, A.

The Human Species, a Biology of Man, London
1957.

Barnett, A. Doak

The Rise of Mainland China, National Planning
Association, Washington 1959.

Belshaw, Horace

Population Growths and Levels of Consumption,
London 1956.

Benedict, Ruth

Patterns of Culture, New York 1934.

Bergson, Abram

Soviet Economic Growth, Evanston (Ill.) 1953.

Bjerke, Juul

see Aukrust, Odd

Brown, Harrison

The Challenge of Man's Future, New York 1954.

Brown, Watson

*Discussion (A). Symposium on Man and Animals in
the Tropics,* Australian Academy of Science, Brisbane 1957.

Cassirer, Ernst

An Essay on Man, An Introduction to a Philosophy
of Human Culture, New York 1944.

Chandrasekhar, S.

"China's Population Problems", *Population Review
No. 2,* Madras, June 1959.

Chasteland, Jean-Claude — "La population des démocraties populaires d'Europe", *Population*, no. 1, Paris 1958.

Childe, Gordon — *What Happened in History,* London 1954 (rev. ed.).

Choh, Ming Li — *Economic Development of Communist China,* Berkeley 1959.

Clark, Colin — *The Conditions of Economic Progress,* London 1957 (3rd ed.).

Cooper, A. G. S. — *Skin cancer. Symposium on Man and Animals in the Tropics.* Brisbane 1957.

Darlington, P. J. — *Zoogeography. The Geographical Distribution of Animals,* New York 1957.

Darwin, Charles Galton — *The Next Million Years,* London 1953.

Dolci, Danilo — *Inchiesta a Palermo,* Turin 1956.

— *Una politica per la piena occupazione,* Turin 1958.

Domar, Evsey D. — *Essays in the Theory of Economic Growth,* New York 1957.

East, Gordon and Moodie, A. E. — *The Changing World,* London 1956.

Eckstein, Alexander with the assistance of Y. C. Yin and Helen Yin — "Communist China's National Product in 1952", *The Review of Economics and Statistics,* Vol. XL, No. 2, Cambridge (Mass.) May 1958.

Economic Commission for Asia and the Far East (ECAFE) — see United Nations

Economic Commission for Europe (ECE) — see United Nations

Economic Commission for Latin America (ECLA) — see United Nations

Fabricant, Solomon — "Economic Progress and Economic Change", *34th Annual Report of the National Bureau of Economic Research,* New York 1945.

— "The Study of Economic Growth", *National Bureau of Economic Research, 39th Annual Report,* New York 1959.

Food and Agricultural Organization (FAO) — *Food Composition Tables for International Use,* Rome 1949.

— *Possibilities of Increasing the Supply of Food and Agricultural Products by Exploitation of New Areas and Increasing Yields,* Rome 1954.

— *Problems of Animal Feeding in Europe,* Rome 1955.

— *Calorie Requirements,* Rome 1957.

(FAO)   *Food Balance Sheets, 1954–56*, Rome 1959.

–   *Fisheries Statistical Yearbook*, Rome (yearly).

–   *The State of Food and Agriculture*, Rome (yearly).

–   *Yearbook of Agricultural Statistics (Production)*, Rome (yearly).

–   *Yearbook of Agricultural Statistics (Trade)*, Rome (yearly).

Ford, E. B.   "Polymorphism in Plants, Animals and Man", *Nature*, 180, London 1957.

Franzsen, D. G. and Willers, J. J. D.   "Capital Accumulation and Economic Growth in South Africa", *International Association for Research in Income and Wealth*, Series VIII, London 1959.

Garland, J. M. and Goldsmith, R. W.   "The National Wealth of Australia", *International Association for Research in Income and Wealth*, Series VIII, London 1959.

GATT   *International Trade 1956*, Geneva 1957.

–   *International Trade 1957*, Geneva 1958.

Gilbert, Milton and associates   *Comparative National Products and Price Levels*, Paris 1958.

Goldsmith, R. W.   see Garland, J. M.

Gopalaswami, R. A.   *Census of India*, Vol. I, New Delhi 1953.

Grünig, Ferdinand   "An Estimate of the National Capital Account of the Federal German Republic", *International Association for Research in Income and Wealth*, Series VIII, London 1959.

Guerrin, André   *Humanité et subsistances*, Neuchâtel 1957.

Haavelmo, Trygve   *A Study in the Theory of Economic Evolution*, Amsterdam 1954.

Hagen, W.   *Vorkommen von Kohle, Eisen, Erdöl, Gold und Uran auf der Welt*, Essen 1954.

Hoyle, Fred   *A Decade of Decision*, London 1953.

The International Bank for Reconstruction and Development   *Annual Reports 1954/55–1957/58*, Washington.

International Institute of Agriculture   *International Yearbook of Agricultural Statistics*, Rome 1931.

International Labour Organization   *Yearbook of Labour Statistics 1958*, Geneva 1958.

International Monetary Fund   *International Financial Statistics 1957*, Washington 1957.

Jackson, E. F.   "Social Accounting in Eastern Europe", *International Association for Research in Income and Wealth*, Series IV, London 1955.

The Joint Committee on Atomic Energy	*Background Material for the Report of the Panel on the Impact of the Peaceful Uses of Atomic Energy*, Washington 1956.
Joint Economic Committee, Subcommittee on Foreign Economic Policy	*Soviet Economic Growth*, Washington 1957.
–	*Trends in Economic Growth*, A Comparison of the Western Powers and the Soviet Bloc, Washington 1955.
Kristensen, Thorkil	"Kundskabsinvesteringen", *Økonomi, Politik, Samhälle* (Essays in Honour of Bertil Ohlin), Stockholm 1959.
Kuznets, Simon	*Economic Change*, London 1954.
–	*Towards a Theory of Economic Growth* (Paper given at Columbia University's bicentennial conference on "National Policy for Economic Welfare at Home and Abroad" in May 1954, Reproduced in February 1956).
Ladell, W. W. S.	"The Influence of Environment in Arid Zones on the Biology of Man" in UNESCO (1957, a).
Landøkonomisk Driftsbureau	*Undersøgelse over landbrugets driftsforhold*, København 1958.
Lee, Douglas H. K.	*Climate and Economic Development in the Tropics*, New York 1957.
Lewis, Cleona	*Debtor and Creditor Countries 1938, 1944*, Washington 1945.
McDougall, D.	*The World Dollar Problem*, London 1957.
McNeill, William H.	*Past and Future*, Chicago 1954.
Malthus, T. R.	*An Essay on the Principle of Population*, 1798.
Marzewski, Jan	*Planification et croissance économique des démocraties populaires*, tome I & II, Paris 1956.
–	*Le rôle des comptes nationaux dans les économies planifiées de type sovietique*, London 1955.
Michailov, N. M.	*Sovietunionens Geografi*, Stockholm 1945.
Moodie, A. E.	see East, Gordon
Morant, G. M.	"The Significance of Racial Differences" in UNESCO (1956, b).
Mukherjee, M. and Sastry, N. S. R.	"An Estimate of the Tangible Wealth of India", *International Association for Research in Income and Wealth*, Series VIII, London 1959.
Myrdal, Gunnar	*Economic Theory and Underdeveloped Regions*, London 1957.

National Planning Association — *National Economic Projections 1962–65, 1970,* Washington 1959.

Oakley, K. P. — *Man the Tool Maker,* London 1958.

Organization for European Economic Co-operation (OEEC) — *Statistics of National Product and Expenditure, 1938, 1947 to 1952,* Paris 1954.

— *Europe's Growing Needs of Energy,* Paris 1956.

— *Statistics of National Product and Expenditure, 1938, 1947 to 1955,* Paris 1957.

— *Economic Development of Overseas Countries and Territories Associated with OEEC Member Countries,* Paris 1958.

— *Towards New Energy in Europe,* Paris 1960.

Osborn, Fairfield — *The Limits of the Earth,* Boston 1953.

Petroleum Press Service — "Evolving Oil Prices", London July 1959.

The President's Materials Policy Commission — *Resources for Freedom, The Paley Report,* Vol. III, New York 1952.

Pressat, Roland — "La population de la Chine et son économie", *Population,* no. 1, Paris 1958.

Putnam, Palmer — *Energy in the Future,* New York 1953.

Ranek, Leo — "Hovedtrækkene i markedsudviklingen i Sovjetunionen og i de østeuropæiske lande", *Landbrugsraadets Meddelelser,* København, juni 1959.

Redfern, Philip — "Net Investment in Fixed Assets in the United Kingdom 1938–1953", *Journal of the Royal Statistical Society,* Part II, London 1955.

Rensch, B. — "Die Abhängigkeit der Struktur und der Leistungen tierischer Gehirne von ihrer Grösse", *Die Naturwissenschaften,* 45. Jahrgang, Berlin, Göttingen, Heidelberg 1958.

Rostow, W. W. — "The Take-off into Self-sustained Growth", *Economic Journal,* London 1956.

Sastry, N. S. R. — see Mukherjee, M.

Saushkin, Y. G. — *Economic Geography of the Soviet Union,* Oslo 1956.

Sauvy, Alfred — "La population de la Chine", *Population,* no. 4, Paris 1957.

— "La population de l'Union Soviétique – Situation, croissance et problèmes actuels", *Population,* no. 3, Paris 1956.

Schenke, Wolf — *Neue Weltmacht China,* Hamburg 1957.

Scholander, P. F. — "Evolution of Climatic Adaptation in Homeotherms", *Evolution*, No. 9, U.S.A., 1955.

Scholander, P. F., Hammel, H. T., Hart, J. S., LeMessurier, D. H. and Steen, J. — "Cold Adaptation in Australian Aborigines", *Journal of Applied Physiology*, Vol. 13, No. 2, U.S.A., September 1958.

Schumpeter, Joseph — *The Theory of Economic Development*, Cambridge (Mass.) 1934.

– *Business Cycles*, New York 1939.

– *Capitalism, Socialism and Democracy*, London 1950 (3rd ed.).

Schwartz, Harry — *Russia's Soviet Economy*, London 1954.

Scott, Anthony — "Canada's Reproducible Wealth", *International Association for Research in Income and Wealth*, Series VIII, London 1959.

Shimkin, D. B. — *Minerals. A Key to Soviet Power*, Cambridge (Mass.) 1953.

Solow, Robert M. — "Technical Change and the Aggregate Production Function", *Review of Economics and Statistics*, August 1957.

Spence, T. F. — see Ashton, E. H.

Statistiske Departement, Det — *Statistiske Efterretninger 1957*, København 1957.

Steemann Nielsen, E. — "Primary Oceanic Production", *Galathea Report*, Vol. I, Copenhagen 1959.

Stigler, George J. — *Trends in Output and Employment*, New York 1947.

Swedborg, E. — "Den animaliska produktionen i Sovjetunionen", *Jordbruksekonomiska Meddelanden*, No. 5, Stockholm 1959.

Thomson, George — *The Foreseeable Future*, London 1955.

United Nations Educational, Scientific and Cultural Organization (UNESCO) — *Progress of Literacy in Various Countries*, Paris 1953.

– *Basic Facts and Figures*, Paris 1956. (a)

– *The Race Question in Modern Science*, Paris 1956. (b)

– *Arid Zone Research VIII*, Paris 1957. (a)

– *World Illiteracy at Mid-Century*, Paris 1957. (b)

United Nations, ECE — *European Steel Trends*, Geneva 1949. (a)

– *International Capital Movements During the Inter-War Period*, New York 1949. (b)

– "Nations and Per Capita Incomes—Seventy Countries—1949", *Statistical Papers*, Series E, No. 1, New York 1950. (a)

United Nations   *World Iron Ore Resources and Their Utilization,* New York 1950. (b)

–, ECAFE   *Economic Survey of Asia and the Far East 1950,* New York 1951.

–, ECE   *A Study of Trade Between Asia and Europe,* Geneva 1953. (a)

–   *Determinants and Consequences of Population Trends,* New York 1953. (b)

–   *Survey of World Iron Ore Resources,* New York 1955.

–, ECAFE   *Economic Survey of Asia and the Far East 1955,* Bangkok 1956. (a)

–, ECLA   *Economic Survey of Latin America 1955,* New York 1956. (b)

–   *Peaceful Uses of Atomic Energy,* New York 1956. (c)

–   "Statistics of National Income and Expenditure", *Statistical Papers,* Series H, No. 9, New York 1956. (d)

–   "Statistics of National Income and Expenditure", *Statistical Papers,* Series H, No. 10, New York 1957. (a)

–, ECE   *Economic Survey of Europe in 1956,* Geneva 1957. (b)

–   "Per Capita National Product of Fifty-five Countries, 1952–1954", *Statistical Papers,* Series E, No. 4, New York 1957. (c)

–   *Report on The World Social Situation,* New York 1957. (d)

–   *Yearbook of International Trade Statistics 1956,* New York 1957. (e)

–   *Yearbook of National Accounts Statistics 1957,* New York 1958. (a)

–   *Peaceful Uses of Atomic Energy* (Proceedings of the Second United Nations International Conference on the Peaceful Uses of Atomic Energy), Vol. I–II, Geneva 1958. (b)

–   *The Future Growth of World Population,* New York 1958. (c)

–, ECE   *Economic Survey of Europe in 1957,* Geneva 1958. (d)

–, ECLA   *Economic Survey of Latin America 1956,* New York 1958. (e)

United Nations, ECAFE	*Economic Survey of Asia and the Far East 1957,* Bangkok 1958. (f)
–, ECAFE	"Growth Models for Illustrating the Effects of Alternative Employment and Investment Policies", *Economic Bulletin for Asia and the Far East,* Vol. IX, No. 1, Bangkok 1958. (g)
–, ECE	*Economic Survey of Europe in 1958,* Geneva 1959. (a)
–, ECLA	*Economic Survey of Latin America 1957,* New York 1959. (b)
–, ECAFE	*Population Trends and Related Problems in The ECAFE Region,* Bangkok 1959. (c)
–	*World Economic Survey,* New York 1959. (d)
–	*Yearbook of National Accounts Statistics 1958,* New York 1959. (e)
–, ECAFE	*Economic Survey of Asia and the Far East 1958,* Bangkok 1959. (f)
–	*Demographic Yearbook,* New York (yearly).
–	*Statistical Yearbook,* New York (yearly).
US, Department of Commerce	*Current Population Report,* Series P-25, No. 187.
–	*Statistical Abstract of the United States,* Washington (yearly).
USSR, Council of Ministers, Central Statistical Administration	*The USSR Economy,* London 1957.
Voskuil, W. H.	*Minerals in World Industry,* New York 1955.
Weber, Max	"Die protestantische Ethik und der Geist des Kapitalismus", *Gesammelte Aufsätze zur Religionssoziologie,* Tübingen 1920–21.
Whyle jr., William H.	*The Organization Man,* New York 1956.
Willers, J. J. D.	see Franzsen, D. G.
Witt, Nicholas de	*Soviet Professional Manpower, Its Education, Training and Supply,* Washington 1955.
Wittern, K.	*Berichte über Landwirtschaft,* Sonderheft, Neue Folge 159, Hamburg 1954.
World Petroleum Report	*World Petroleum Report,* volume 5, New York February 1959.
Yates, P. Lamartine	*Forty Years of Foreign Trade,* London 1959.

Index

(The index does not contain references to the bibliography)

––––